Digital Twin-Driven Lifelong Learning Systems

Zornitsa Yordanova
https://orcid.org/0000-0002-6056-8445
University of National and World Economy, Bulgaria

Hamed Nozari
https://orcid.org/0000-0002-6500-6708
University of National and World Economy, Bulgaria

IGI Global
Scientific Publishing
Publishing Tomorrow's Research Today

Vice President of Editorial	Melissa Wagner
Director of Acquisitions	Mikaela Felty
Director of Book Development	Jocelynn Hessler
Production Manager	Mike Brehm
Cover Design	Jose Rosado

Published in the United States of America by
IGI Global Scientific Publishing
701 East Chocolate Avenue
Hershey, PA, 17033, USA
Tel: 717-533-8845 | Fax: 717-533-7115
Website: https://www.igi-global.com E-mail: cust@igi-global.com

Library of Congress Cataloging-in-Publication Data

LCCN: 2026024583 (CIP Data Pending)
ISBN13: 9798260016749
Isbn13Softcover: 9798260016756
EISBN13: 9798260016763

British Cataloguing in Publication Data
A Cataloguing in Publication record for this book is available from the British Library.

Table of Contents

Detailed Table of Contents

Artificial intelligence is reshaping higher education by enabling personalized, adaptive learning environments. This chapter examines how AI-driven personalization, combined with digital twin technologies, creates dynamic ecosystems that simulate and enhance individual learning journeys. Drawing on contemporary literature, it explores key mechanisms such as intelligent tutoring systems, adaptive content delivery, open learner models, and large language model applications. It highlights digital twins as persistent learner representations supporting continuous simulation and feedback. The chapter also addresses ethical concerns, including data privacy, algorithmic bias, and equitable access, while proposing a framework for sustainable, lifelong AI-powered learning. Practical implications for educators, policymakers, and technology developers are outlined, along with key directions for future research in this evolving interdisciplinary field.

This chapter takes a conceptual approach to explore the role of the digital twin in shaping a new generation of self-adaptive learning systems. Unlike traditional adaptive learning systems that rely primarily on past data and limited settings, the proposed framework considers the learner as a dynamic entity with cognitive, behavioral, affective, and contextual dimensions. In this regard, the digital twin is upgraded from a simple representational tool to a cognitive mirror that enables real-time monitoring, analysis, prediction, and adjustment of the learning trajectory. This chapter provides a theoretical foundation for the development of intelligent, human, and self-evolving learning ecosystems.

Digital twins are reshaping corporate learning by transforming training from static and episodic instruction into continuous, adaptive, and data-driven learning processes. Through the integration of real-time analytics, simulation, artificial intelligence, and feedback mechanisms, organizations can develop immersive and personalized learning environments aligned with workforce and organizational needs. This chapter examines the conceptual foundations of digital twins in learning, including their relationship with experiential learning, situated learning, and human capital theory, while distinguishing them from conventional simulations and VR/AR technologies. It also explores applications in workforce upskilling, leadership development, competency-based learning, and real-time decision-making. Drawing from recent studies and case-based applications, the chapter highlights how digital twins enhance engagement, knowledge retention, continuous performance feedback, predictive skill development, and scalable workforce training within intelligent corporate learning ecosystems.

This chapter examines the regulatory, legal, and governance challenges associated with AI-driven and digital twin–enabled intelligent learning systems. It highlights how adaptive AI technologies and real-time digital twin simulations are transforming education into personalized, data-driven ecosystems. However, the rapid adoption of these technologies has outpaced legal and policy frameworks, creating concerns related to data privacy, algorithmic bias, accountability, and ethical governance. The chapter develops an integrated governance framework combining AI governance theory, data governance principles, and policy design strategies. It further explores global and national regulatory landscapes, stakeholder roles, and implementation challenges. The study concludes that effective governance requires transparency, inclusivity, and adaptive regulatory mechanisms to ensure responsible, equitable, and sustainable deployment of intelligent learning systems.

The convergence of artificial intelligence, the Internet of Things, and digital twin technology is creating the conditions for a new paradigm in education: hypersituated learning. This chapter argues that the learner's digital twin is the infrastructural condition through which hypersituated learning becomes pedagogically coherent at scale. By integrating cognitive profiles, behavioural patterns, and real-time contextual data, the learner's digital twin enables continuous, situated, and proactive personalisation across lifelong learning pathways. However, this convergence carries a structural tension: the same architecture that enables personalisation simultaneously enables continuous observation, algorithmic inference, and control. Drawing on surveillance capitalism, algorithmic governmentality, and the philosophy of technology, the chapter examines the conditions under which this paradigm serves cognitive emancipation rather than heteronomy, proposing a governance framework built on pedagogical intentionality, algorithmic transparency, and democratic oversight.

Preface

In the era of digital transformation, learning and education systems are undergoing more fundamental changes than ever before. The emergence of technologies such as artificial intelligence, the Internet of Things, big data analytics, cloud computing, and especially digital twins have opened up new horizons for redefining the concept of lifelong learning, smart education, and adaptive ecosystems. The book Digital Twin-Driven Lifelong Learning Systems is an attempt to explore this profound transformation and to map a future in which learning will no longer be a static, limited, and linear process, but will become a dynamic, intelligent, personalized, and continuous system.

This book is the result of a collection of scientific, conceptual, and technological perspectives on the field of digital twin-driven smart learning; an interdisciplinary field that lies at the border between educational sciences, artificial intelligence, data science, systems engineering, and digital policymaking. The chapters cover a wide range of topics, from the conceptual foundations of self-adaptive learning systems and cognitive and behavioral modeling, to the design of multi-agent learning ecosystems, data governance, ethical considerations, legal frameworks, and applications of the Internet of Things and fuzzy optimization in the analysis of learning processes.

In this work, the digital twin is introduced not only as a virtual model of the learner or educational environment, but also as a transformative infrastructure for creating intelligent, adaptive, and real-time interactive learning. Such an approach can enable continuous analysis of learner behavior, predict educational needs, design personalized learning paths, and develop educational decision-support systems. On the other hand, the integration of explainable AI capabilities, multi-agent architectures, and fuzzy models in these ecosystems provides a platform for creating flexible, transparent, and uncertainty-resistant learning environments.

One of the main goals of this book is to present a comprehensive picture of the future of education in the era of Education 5.0; an era in which humans, artificial intelligence, and cyber-physical systems are in continuous interaction. In this vision, learning is defined beyond the classroom and traditional educational courses and becomes a continuous, personal, and data-driven experience. Therefore, this book attempts to create a bridge between theory and technology and chart new paths for researchers, policymakers, educational system developers, and digital learning activists.

Chapter 1 introduces the transformative role of artificial intelligence in shaping personalized and adaptive learning environments within higher education. The chapter positions AI-driven personalization and digital twin technologies as foundational to the creation of dynamic educational ecosystems capable of continuously responding to individual learner needs. Through its discussion of intelligent tutoring systems, adaptive content delivery, open learner models, and large language model applications, the chapter establishes how persistent learner representations can support simulation, feedback, and lifelong educational development. At the same time, it foregrounds critical ethical concerns surrounding privacy, algorithmic bias, and equitable access, while proposing a sustainable framework for responsible AI-powered learning. By integrating theoretical perspectives with practical implications, the chapter sets the stage for understanding how intelligent systems are redefining learner engagement and institutional practice.

Chapter 2 provides the conceptual foundations for self-adaptive learning systems enhanced through digital twin integration. Moving beyond traditional adaptive systems that rely on static or historical data, the chapter reimagines the learner as a multidimensional and evolving entity shaped by cognitive, behavioral, emotional, and contextual factors. The digital twin is presented not merely as a representation of the learner, but as a "cognitive mirror" capable of real-time monitoring, prediction, and adaptation of learning trajectories. Through this conceptual lens, the chapter establishes a theoretical basis for intelligent educational ecosystems that are human-centered, continuously evolving, and capable of supporting more responsive forms of personalized learning.

Chapter 3 examines the transformative impact of digital twins within corporate learning ecosystems, highlighting their ability to shift organizational training from static instruction toward continuous, adaptive, and data-driven development. The chapter explores how real-time analytics, artificial intelligence, simulation technologies, and feedback systems can create immersive learning experiences aligned with workforce demands and strategic organizational goals. By connecting digital twins to experiential learning, situated learning, and human capital theory, the chapter distinguishes these systems from conventional simulations and virtual environments. Its discussion of workforce upskilling, leadership development, competency-based training, and predictive skill enhancement demonstrates the growing importance of intelligent learning infrastructures in supporting agile and future-ready organizations.

Chapter 4 expands the discussion of digital twins into the broader context of higher education transformation. It presents digital twins as convergent infrastructures capable of integrating pedagogy, governance, institutional operations, and intelligent systems within interconnected educational ecosystems. Drawing on constructivist, experiential, socio-technical, and systems theories, the chapter examines applications ranging from smart campus management and virtual laboratories to personalized learning analytics and institutional planning. Through case-based analysis, the chapter illustrates how digital twins enable anticipatory governance, enhanced learner engagement, and data-informed decision-making. Importantly, it also addresses institutional readiness, ethical governance, equity, and data integration challenges, positioning digital twins as critical infrastructures for the future of adaptive and intelligent higher education.

Chapter 5 presents a dynamic digital twin framework designed to model, analyze, and predict learning processes over time. The chapter conceptualizes the learner as a time-dependent system characterized by variables such as knowledge acquisition, engagement, and retention. Through interpretable mathematical relationships and scenario-based analysis, the proposed framework demonstrates how digital twins can provide adaptive feedback and optimize learning outcomes. By emphasizing predictive capabilities and longitudinal modeling, the chapter contributes a quantitative perspective to intelligent learning systems and highlights the potential of digital twins to sustain engagement and improve knowledge retention in evolving educational contexts.

Chapter 6 explores the integration of cognitive and behavioral modeling within digital learning systems through the proposed Digital Twin–Cognitive-Behavioral Modeling (DT-CBM) framework. The chapter emphasizes the evolution of digital learning from static content delivery to dynamic, context-aware environments capable of modeling the learner holistically. By integrating multimodal data sources such as clickstreams, physiological signals, facial expressions, and assessment data, the framework constructs a living computational representation of learner cognition and behavior. The discussion of knowledge tracing, affective state recognition, self-regulated learning detection, reinforcement-based optimization, and explainable AI demonstrates how intelligent systems can generate transparent, actionable insights for both learners and educators. The chapter ultimately advances a vision for lifelong adaptive learning grounded in explainability, responsiveness, and human-centered design.

Chapter 7 investigates the convergence of explainable artificial intelligence and digital twins as a foundation for adaptive learning design. The chapter presents the learner's digital twin as a continuously evolving virtual representation capable of integrating academic, behavioral, and contextual data to personalize educational pathways. Machine learning and multi-objective optimization methods are employed to balance learning efficiency, conceptual understanding, and student motivation. Central to the chapter is the emphasis on explainability, where transparent AI mechanisms clarify algorithmic decisions for learners and educators in accessible language. This focus on trust, interpretability, and user engagement positions explainable AI-driven digital twins as essential components of future smart education systems.

Chapter 8 addresses the social and ethical dimensions of Education 5.0 within AI-driven digital twin ecosystems. Drawing on bibliometric analysis, the chapter examines how artificial intelligence and data-driven technologies are reshaping higher education institutions through personalized and adaptive learning environments. While recognizing the efficiency and predictive capabilities of digital twins, the chapter critically interrogates concerns related to privacy, surveillance, algorithmic bias, and the reduction of learners to data points. It further highlights the declining role of human interaction, empathy, and mentorship within increasingly automated educational systems, alongside the risks of digital inequality in developing contexts. The chapter ultimately advocates for a balanced and human-centered approach that preserves inclusivity, ethics, and meaningful educational relationships within technologically advanced learning environments.

Chapter 9 explores the emergence of collaborative lifelong learning ecosystems built upon multi-agent architectures and digital twin technologies. The chapter proposes a conceptual framework in which cognitive digital twins model learners' cognitive, behavioral, and skill-related states, while intelligent agents dynamically optimize learning pathways, assessment processes, and collaborative interactions. In addition to examining adaptive and self-evolving educational systems, the chapter highlights the transformative potential of emerging technologies such as federated learning, edge computing, the metaverse, and neuromorphic computing. By integrating these innovations, the chapter envisions intelligent ecosystems capable of supporting scalable, collaborative, and continuously adaptive lifelong learning experiences.

Chapter 10 examines the legal, regulatory, and governance challenges arising from AI-driven and digital twin-enabled intelligent learning systems. As education becomes increasingly personalized and data-driven, the chapter emphasizes the growing gap between technological advancement and existing legal frameworks. Issues of data privacy, algorithmic bias, accountability, transparency, and ethical governance are critically analyzed through the lens of integrated governance theory. By exploring international regulatory landscapes, stakeholder responsibilities, and implementation barriers, the chapter provides a comprehensive policy-oriented perspective on responsible educational innovation. Its proposed governance framework underscores the necessity of adaptive, inclusive, and transparent regulatory mechanisms to ensure equitable and sustainable deployment of intelligent learning technologies.

Chapter 11 introduces the concept of the "hypersituated learner" and examines how digital twins, artificial intelligence, and the Internet of Things are enabling a new paradigm of highly contextualized and continuously personalized learning.

The chapter argues that learner digital twins provide the infrastructural foundation necessary for hypersituated learning at scale by integrating behavioral, cognitive, and contextual data into adaptive educational pathways. At the same time, the chapter critically addresses the structural tensions between personalization and surveillance, highlighting the risks of algorithmic control and continuous observation. Drawing on critical theories of surveillance capitalism, governmentality, and philosophy of technology, the chapter proposes a governance framework grounded in pedagogical intentionality, algorithmic transparency, and democratic oversight to ensure that technological advancement supports learner autonomy rather than technological domination.

Chapter 12 presents an integrated framework that combines digital twin technology with fuzzy multi-objective optimization to design adaptive learning pathways under conditions of uncertainty. In this framework, the digital twin serves as the predictive core, while optimization techniques guide decision-making by balancing learning performance, cognitive load, and time constraints. Through scenario analysis and Pareto optimization, the chapter demonstrates the effectiveness and stability of the proposed model across varying conditions. The findings underscore the capacity of digital twins to significantly improve predictive accuracy and optimize educational decision-making, contributing valuable insights into adaptive lifelong learning systems capable of operating under complex and uncertain conditions.

Chapter 13 examines the integration of Internet of Things technologies with digital twin systems for real-time monitoring and interpretation of learner behaviors. The chapter proposes a conceptual framework that reconceptualizes the learner as a dynamic and evolving system rather than a collection of isolated indicators such as grades or attendance. Through the transformation of multi-source data into behavioral signals and time-based learning trajectories, the framework enables deeper personalization and adaptive educational interventions. The chapter highlights the potential of IoT-integrated digital twins to support more responsive, intelligent, and ethically designed smart learning environments capable of continuously adapting to learner needs and behaviors.

Chapter 14 concludes the volume by presenting a comprehensive conceptual framework for digital twin-driven lifelong learning ecosystems. Responding to the accelerating disruption of workforce skills and the limitations of traditional educational models, the chapter introduces the Digital Twin-Driven Lifelong Learning System (DT-LLS), a five-layer architecture spanning learner data acquisition, digital twin modeling, adaptive intelligence, learning delivery, and continuous evolution. Grounded in an extensive literature synthesis, the framework addresses critical challenges related to lifelong continuity, ethical governance, scalability, affective modeling, and interoperability across learning contexts. The chapter further outlines guiding principles centered on learner sovereignty, transparency, equitable design, and human-AI complementarity, while proposing an ambitious research agenda for the future of personalized and adaptive lifelong learning ecosystems.

We believe that the development of lifelong learning systems based on digital twins can play a key role in improving the quality of education, reducing learning gaps, improving educational decision-making, and increasing the resilience of education systems in the face of global changes. We also hope that the topics raised in this book will inspire future research and the development of a new generation of smart learning ecosystems; Ecosystems in which learning is not only adaptive and data-driven, but also humane, ethical, and forward-looking.

Finally, we would like to express our sincere gratitude to all the researchers, writers, and experts who contributed their knowledge and efforts to the creation of this book. We hope that this work can take an effective step towards the development of interdisciplinary knowledge in the field of digital twins and lifelong learning, and can be used as a valuable reference for future research and applications.

Zornitsa Yordanova
University of National and World Economy, Bulgaria

Hamed Nozari
University of National and World Economy, Bulgaria

Chapter 1

AI-Driven Personalization and Adaptive Learning Environments

Deepak Gupta
http://orcid.org/0000-0003-3929-1362
Institute of Technology and Management, Gwalior, India

Ilkhomjon Ibrokhimov
http://orcid.org/0009-0003-0559-6552
Kimyo International University in Tashkent, Uzbekistan

Feruza Jumaeva
Bukhara State Pedagogical Institute, Uzbekistan

Timur Abdullaev
Mamun University, Uzbekistan

Abdinazarova Nilufar
Karshi State University, Uzbekistan

Pardaev Jamshid
Termez University of Economics and Service, Uzbekistan

Jurayev Baxrom
Shakhrisabz State Pedagogical Institute, Uzbekistan

Kurbonbekova Mohichekhra
Tashkent State University of Economics, Uzbekistan

ABSTRACT

Artificial intelligence is reshaping higher education by enabling personalized, adaptive learning environments. This chapter examines how AI-driven personalization, combined with digital twin technologies, creates dynamic ecosystems that simulate and enhance individual learning journeys. Drawing on contemporary literature, it explores key mechanisms such as intelligent tutoring systems, adaptive content delivery, open learner models, and large language model applications. It highlights digital twins as persistent learner representations supporting continuous simulation and feedback. The chapter also addresses ethical concerns, including data privacy, algorithmic bias, and equitable access, while proposing a framework for sustainable,

DOI: 10.4018/979-8-2600-1674-9.ch001

lifelong AI-powered learning. Practical implications for educators, policymakers, and technology developers are outlined, along with key directions for future research in this evolving interdisciplinary field.

INTRODUCTION

The proliferation of artificial intelligence (AI) technologies across sectors has found particularly fertile ground in education, where the promise of individualized, responsive, and continuously improving learning experiences aligns with longstanding pedagogical aspirations. Personalized learning—broadly defined as tailoring educational content, pace, and pathways to individual learner characteristics—has evolved from teacher-led differentiation to sophisticated computational systems capable of processing vast learner data in real time (Bernacki et al., 2021). Within this evolving landscape, AI-driven personalization represents not merely an incremental improvement but a fundamental reconfiguration of the learner–content–educator relationship, one that redistributes instructional agency, reshapes pedagogical roles, and opens new possibilities for democratizing high-quality learning experiences.

Contemporary higher education institutions face mounting pressure to serve increasingly diverse student populations with varied prior knowledge, learning styles, motivational orientations, and life circumstances. Traditional one-size-fits-all curricula, even when digitally delivered, remain inadequate in addressing these heterogeneities. Adaptive learning environments powered by AI offer a compelling alternative: systems that dynamically adjust instructional variables in response to ongoing learner interaction, effectively creating what Tapalova and Zhiyenbayeva (2022) describe as "personalized learning pathways" driven by AI in education (AIEd) capabilities. These pathways are not fixed sequences but fluid, responsive structures that evolve in real time as learners engage, struggle, succeed, and develop.

The emergence of digital twin technology adds a further transformative dimension to this landscape. Originally developed in industrial and engineering contexts, digital twins—virtual replicas of physical entities enabling simulation, monitoring, and predictive analysis—are increasingly applied to educational settings. In the context of lifelong learning systems, a learner's digital twin can serve as a persistent, evolving model that aggregates competencies, behaviors, preferences, and outcomes, allowing AI systems to make informed instructional decisions at any point in a learner's educational journey (Jankovskis et al., 2024; She et al., 2023). Unlike conventional learner profiles that capture static snapshots, the digital twin is a living computational entity that grows in fidelity and predictive power as it accumulates interaction data over time.

This chapter situates itself at the intersection of these two powerful trends: AI-driven personalization and digital twin-enabled learning systems. It examines the theoretical foundations, technological mechanisms, empirical evidence, ethical considerations, and future directions of this convergence. The chapter is intended to serve as both a comprehensive scholarly review and a practical guide for educational researchers, institutional policymakers, learning technology developers, and practicing educators seeking a rigorous synthesis of the current state of the field.

The discussion proceeds through an examination of conceptual frameworks, core technological enablers, empirical evidence on impacts, ethical and implementation challenges, a proposed integrative framework, future research directions, and a concluding synthesis. Throughout, the chapter draws on a broad corpus of peer-reviewed literature to provide an evidence-based analysis of both the opportunities and the significant challenges characterizing this rapidly evolving field.

BACKGROUND

Defining Personalized Learning in the AI Era

Personalized learning is a concept with diverse and sometimes contested interpretations across educational research, policy, and practice. Bernacki et al. (2021) systematically categorized personalization along four dimensions: who personalizes (learner, educator, or system), what is personalized (content, pacing, feedback, goals), how personalization occurs (algorithmically, collaboratively, or through self-direction), and for what purpose (efficiency, engagement, equity, or mastery). This multidimensional framework is essential when evaluating AI-driven systems, as different technologies emphasize different dimensions, and conflating them risks producing misleading assessments of any particular system's capabilities or limitations.

Shemshack et al. (2021) further identified core components of personalized learning—including learner profiles, adaptive pathways, flexible content, and feedback mechanisms—arguing that genuine personalization requires all components to be systematically integrated. The introduction of AI enables this integration at scale, allowing systems to simultaneously address multiple personalization dimensions across thousands of learners without proportional increases in educator workload. Arantes (2024) cautions, however, that the term "personalization" in educational policy discourse often conflates distinct technological and pedagogical phenomena, frequently serving as a rhetorical vehicle for EdTech market expansion rather than a precise descriptor of measurable educational practice.

The convergence of AI personalization with digital twin technology represents a qualitative advancement over earlier adaptive systems by enabling continuous, longitudinal personalization rather than episodic adaptation. Where conventional adaptive systems adjust to learner behavior within discrete learning sessions, digital twin-enabled systems maintain persistent learner representations that inform personalization decisions across extended learning journeys, making them particularly well-suited to lifelong learning contexts where educational needs evolve over years and decades (Bayly-Castaneda et al., 2024).

Digital Twins as Learner Representations

The digital twin concept, originally developed for physical systems such as aerospace components and manufacturing processes, involves the creation of a dynamic virtual counterpart that mirrors the state, behavior, and evolution of its physical equivalent in real time. Applied to education, a learner's digital twin functions as a persistent, multidimensional computational representation that integrates cognitive, affective, behavioral, and contextual data to enable simulation and prediction (She et al., 2023). The twin exists in continuous correspondence with the learner it represents, updating its model as new behavioral data, performance records, and contextual information become available.

Jankovskis et al. (2024) identify several defining characteristics of educational digital twins: real-time data synchronization between the learner and the digital model, bidirectional communication enabling both system-to-learner and learner-to-system feedback, predictive simulation allowing anticipation of learning trajectories, and scalable deployment across institutional or national learning ecosystems. These characteristics make digital twins particularly valuable in lifelong learning contexts, where learner needs, goals, and contexts evolve continuously over extended timeframes that exceed the operational scope of any single educational institution.

The integration of digital twins with AI personalization creates a synergistic architecture in which the twin provides the persistent learner model while AI algorithms interpret this model to generate adaptive instructional interventions. This architecture transcends episodic interactions to support coherent, long-term educational journeys—a critical requirement for lifelong learning systems as envisioned by Bayly-Castaneda et al. (2024).

Lifelong Learning and the Role of AI

Lifelong learning—the continuous, voluntary pursuit of knowledge and skills throughout an individual's life—has gained renewed urgency in the context of rapid technological change, evolving labor markets, and aging populations. Traditional educational institutions, designed primarily for initial formation phases and operating on cohort-based, time-limited models, are increasingly ill-equipped to support the agility and continuity that lifelong learning demands. AI-enabled adaptive systems offer significant potential to bridge this gap by providing personalized learning experiences that are available on demand, context-sensitive, and responsive to real-time learner needs (Bayly-Castaneda et al., 2024).

Gašević et al. (2023) argue that empowering learners for the age of AI requires not only technological provision but also the development of learner agency, self-regulation, and metacognitive competencies that allow individuals to navigate increasingly complex and AI-mediated educational environments. AI systems that function as collaborative partners—rather than directive instructional systems—align more closely with the autonomous, goal-directed nature of lifelong learning.

The role of AI in lifelong learning extends beyond content delivery to encompass credential recognition, competency mapping, career pathway modeling, and community-of-practice facilitation. Digital twin architectures that capture and synthesize learning across diverse contexts provide the integrated learner representation necessary for AI systems to function effectively across the full complexity of a lifelong learning career.

CORE TECHNOLOGICAL ENABLERS

Intelligent Tutoring Systems

Intelligent Tutoring Systems (ITS) represent one of the most mature technological implementations of AI-driven personalization in education, with roots in educational computing research dating to the 1970s and a robust empirical literature accumulated over four decades of development and evaluation. These systems employ computational models of domain knowledge, learner cognition, and pedagogical strategy to provide individualized instruction and feedback without continuous human intervention. Lin et al. (2023) conducted a systematic review demonstrating that ITS implementations across diverse educational contexts consistently produce positive outcomes in learning achievement, time-on-task, and learner engagement when compared to traditional instructional approaches. The authors identified mastery-based pacing and immediate corrective feedback as the most consistently effective personalization mechanisms, noting that the benefit of these mechanisms is particularly pronounced for learners who enter courses with incomplete prerequisite knowledge.

Wang et al. (2023) examined ITS applications in real educational contexts from a social experiment perspective, identifying key success factors including alignment with curriculum standards, instructor involvement in system configuration, and iterative refinement based on learner performance data. Their review highlighted that the most effective ITS implementations are those in which the system operates as a complement to, rather than replacement for, human educators, with teachers retaining meaningful oversight of the instructional process. This finding—that human–AI collaboration consistently outperforms either human-only or AI-only instruction—is one of the most consistent and consequential in the ITS literature.

Contemporary ITS architectures increasingly incorporate deep learning and reinforcement learning capabilities that allow the system to improve its pedagogical models over time based on accumulated interaction data. This learning-while-teaching paradigm positions ITS as dynamic educational partners capable of evolving their instructional strategies in response to the changing needs of individual learners (Gligorea et al., 2023). The integration of ITS with digital twin architectures further enhances their capabilities by providing access to longitudinal learner data that extends beyond individual course interactions.

Large Language Models in Education

The emergence of large language models (LLMs), exemplified by systems such as GPT-4 and related transformer-based architectures, has introduced qualitatively new possibilities for conversational, context-sensitive educational support. LLMs are trained on vast corpora of human-generated text and develop rich representational capacities that enable nuanced language understanding, multi-step reasoning, and contextually appropriate text generation across virtually unlimited topic domains. Kasneci et al. (2023) conducted a comprehensive analysis of ChatGPT's educational applications, identifying opportunities including on-demand tutoring, essay feedback, question generation, language practice, and accessibility support for learners with diverse needs.

Tlili et al. (2023) investigated chatbot applications in educational settings using ChatGPT as a case study, finding that while AI chatbots effectively support information retrieval and immediate feedback, they also introduce risks of over-reliance, academic integrity concerns, and potential propagation of misinformation. These risks reflect design, implementation, and governance choices rather than inherent technological limitations—findings that underscore the importance of thoughtful pedagogical integration. Ghaleb and Sattarov (2025) further found that quality of educational outcomes using ChatGPT is significantly modulated by student course engagement and the presence of institutional regulatory support, reinforcing the view that effective AI integration requires both learner-side engagement and institutional governance frameworks. Sajja et al. (2024) proposed an AI-enabled intelligent assistant framework for personalized and adaptive learning in higher education, integrating LLM capabilities with learner profile modeling to provide contextually relevant, personalized guidance.

Lodge et al. (2023) introduced the concept of co-regulation in AI-assisted learning, arguing that generative AI functions most effectively when it supports collaborative self-regulation—helping learners monitor their understanding, identify knowledge gaps, and strategically direct their own learning processes. This perspective positions LLMs not as autonomous instructors but as responsive cognitive scaffolds within broader adaptive learning architectures, a framing that aligns with the learner empowerment orientation emphasized by Gašević et al. (2023).

Learning Analytics and Open Learner Models

Learning analytics—the measurement, collection, analysis, and reporting of data about learners and their contexts for the purpose of understanding and optimizing learning—provides the empirical foundation for AI-driven personalization. Ouyang et al. (2023) demonstrated that the integration of AI performance prediction with learning analytics significantly improved student outcomes in online engineering courses, enabling timely identification of at-risk learners and targeted interventions that reduced course failure rates. Their findings highlight the value of predictive analytics as a complement to reactive adaptation, enabling proactive support that reaches learners before failure occurs.

Open Learner Models (OLMs) represent a specific approach to learner modeling in which the system's representation of the learner is made transparent and directly accessible to the learner themselves. Hooshyar et al. (2021) conducted a systematic literature review of OLMs in higher education, finding that access to one's own learner model supports self-regulated learning by enabling metacognitive reflection, goal-setting, and strategic planning. When integrated with digital twin architectures, OLMs provide the transparency layer that allows learners to understand and actively shape their own educational trajectories.

Figure 1 illustrates the AI-Driven Personalization Framework in Digital Twin Learning Systems. The central node integrates learner profiling, adaptive content delivery, digital twin simulation, learning analytics, and continuous feedback loops to support holistic personalized learning (Authors' synthesis from reviewed literature).

Figure 1. AI-driven personalization framework in digital twin learning systems

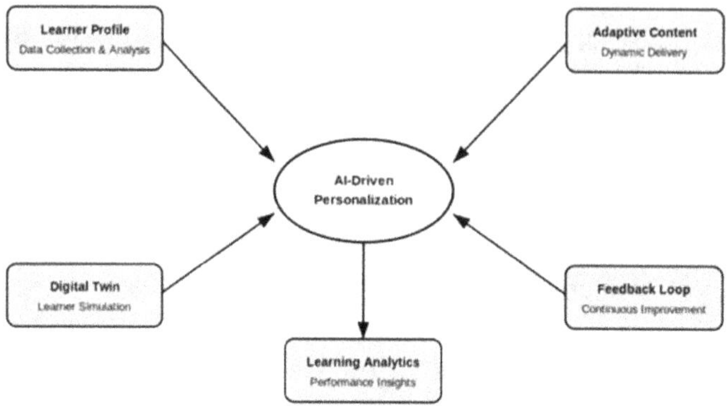

Figure 1 illustrates the central node integrates learner profiling, adaptive content delivery, digital twin simulation, learning analytics, and continuous feedback loops to support holistic personalized learning. Source: Authors' synthesis from reviewed literature.

EMPIRICAL EVIDENCE ON IMPACTS

Academic Performance and Engagement

The empirical literature on AI-driven personalization presents a broadly optimistic picture, though with important nuances regarding the conditions, populations, and timeframes in which benefits are most consistently realized. Du Plooy et al. (2024) conducted a scoping review of personalized adaptive learning in higher education, identifying consistent positive associations between adaptive learning system use and academic performance outcomes, particularly for students entering courses with significant knowledge gaps. The adaptive scaffolding provided by these systems appears most beneficial for learners who would otherwise struggle with undifferentiated instructional approaches, suggesting that AI personalization may function as an equity-enhancing intervention capable of partially compensating for prior educational disadvantage.

Liu and Wan (2024) developed and empirically tested innovative models for enhanced student adaptability and performance, finding that AI-driven environmental adaptations—encompassing both content presentation and social-collaborative features—produced statistically significant improvements in student engagement and academic outcomes across multiple disciplinary contexts. Muthuswamy and

Absamatov (2025) similarly identified key determinants of student engagement in higher education, finding that elevated engagement levels are directly associated with improved academic performance—a relationship that AI-driven personalization systems are particularly well positioned to leverage by dynamically calibrating the challenge, relevance, and social dimensions of learning experiences.

Crompton and Burke (2023) surveyed the state of AI in higher education across a broad corpus of recent research, noting that while enthusiasm for AI-powered learning tools is substantial, rigorous empirical evidence of long-term learning gains remains limited. Many published studies rely on short-duration interventions, convenience samples, and outcome measures that capture immediate post-instruction performance rather than durable learning or transfer. They call for longitudinal studies that track learner outcomes across full degree programs or career trajectories, and for mixed-methods research designs that combine quantitative outcome measurement with qualitative investigation of the mechanisms through which AI personalization produces its effects.

Self-Regulated Learning and Learner Autonomy

Self-regulated learning (SRL)—the capacity to plan, monitor, and evaluate one's own learning processes—is widely recognized as a critical competency for lifelong learning. Zimmerman's influential model of SRL identifies forethought, performance, and self-reflection as the three recursive phases of self-regulation, all of which can be supported by well-designed AI personalization systems. Ghaleb and Pardaev (2025b) demonstrated that literature reading self-efficacy is a significant positive predictor of academic achievement, underscoring the broader principle that learners' confidence in their own competencies mediates the relationship between instructional conditions and learning outcomes. Hooshyar et al. (2021) found that open learner models and AI-driven feedback systems can effectively scaffold SRL development, particularly when they provide actionable, specific, and timely information about learning progress.

Lodge et al. (2023) extended this finding to generative AI contexts, demonstrating that co-regulatory interactions with AI tutors can enhance metacognitive awareness and strategic learning behaviors when interactions are structured to promote learner reflection rather than passive information receipt. Their research highlights the importance of interaction design in determining whether AI systems develop or atrophy self-regulatory capacities.

Gašević et al. (2023) argued that AI systems that prioritize learner empowerment over computational efficiency maximize their long-term educational value by developing the self-regulatory capacities that sustain lifelong learning. This perspective challenges prevalent paradigms that optimize AI-driven systems primarily for short-term performance metrics, advocating instead for evaluation frameworks that include learner autonomy, metacognitive development, and transfer of learning as core outcome categories.

Equity and Access Considerations

The potential of AI-driven personalization to advance educational equity is substantial but contingent on deliberate design choices, inclusive governance processes, and ongoing equity monitoring. Adaptive systems that accurately identify and address individual learning needs can mitigate some of the effects of prior educational disadvantage, providing additional support to learners who have historically been underserved by standardized instruction. However, Holmes and Tuomi (2022) caution that AI systems trained on biased datasets risk perpetuating and amplifying existing educational inequities, encoding historical patterns of advantage and disadvantage into algorithmic recommendation structures that appear objective but embed deeply subjective values and assumptions.

Nguyen et al. (2023) proposed a comprehensive framework of ethical principles for AI in education, emphasizing fairness, transparency, accountability, and privacy as foundational requirements for ethical AI deployment. They argue that equitable AI personalization requires not only technically unbiased algorithms but also participatory design processes that center the perspectives of historically marginalized learner communities. Bhatti and Pardaev (2025) further demonstrated that institutional accreditation plays a meaningful role in fostering inclusive education through its effects on educational equity and technology integration. Kuleto et al. (2021) similarly highlighted that equitable access to AI-enhanced learning environments requires addressing infrastructure disparities, digital literacy gaps, and affordability barriers that disproportionately affect learners from low-resource contexts.

Table 1 presents a comparative analysis of AI-driven personalization approaches currently deployed in educational settings, summarizing each approach's underlying AI technique, depth of personalization, degree of digital twin integration, and primary implementation limitation.

Table 1. Comparative analysis of AI-driven personalization approaches in educational settings

Approach / System	AI Technique	Personalization Depth	Digital Twin Support	Key Limitation
Intelligent Tutoring Systems	Rule-based & ML	Content & pacing	Partial	Scalability constraints
Adaptive Learning Platforms	Recommendation algorithms	Learning paths	Limited	Data privacy concerns
Large Language Models	Transformer-based NLP	Dialogue & feedback	Emerging integration	Hallucination risk
Digital Twin + AI Systems	Simulation & deep learning	Full learner modelling	Full	High implementation cost
Open Learner Models	Bayesian networks	Self-regulated pathways	Moderate	Learner cognitive load

ETHICAL AND IMPLEMENTATION CHALLENGES

Data Privacy and Security

AI-driven personalization is inherently data-intensive, requiring the collection, storage, and analysis of granular learner behavioral data to function effectively. This data dependency creates significant privacy implications, particularly in educational contexts where learners may be unaware of the extent and granularity of data collection or the ways in which their data is processed, shared, and monetized. Nguyen et al. (2023) identified data privacy as a primary ethical concern in AIEd, noting that the granularity of behavioral data captured by adaptive systems—including response times, error patterns, navigation behavior, and emotional indicators derived from webcam or biometric analysis—far exceeds what is typically collected in traditional educational settings. Research in adjacent domains illuminates the stakes of this trust relationship: Ghaleb and Pardaev (2025a) found that information source credibility and transparent communication style are critical mediators of trust formation, with implications for how educational AI systems should communicate their data practices to learners.

Institutional responses to these privacy challenges vary considerably across national and sectoral contexts, creating a fragmented landscape that complicates compliance for multi-institutional or international learning systems. Holmes and Tuomi (2022) documented this regulatory heterogeneity, noting that while instruments such as Europe's General Data Protection Regulation (GDPR) and the United

States' Family Educational Rights and Privacy Act (FERPA) provide important baseline protections, neither was designed with the specific characteristics of AI-driven educational data collection in mind. They advocate for education-specific data governance frameworks that establish clear principles of data minimization, purpose limitation, meaningful learner control over personal learning data, and accountability mechanisms.

The long-term stewardship of learner data represents a particularly underexamined challenge in the context of lifelong learning systems. Digital twin architectures that accumulate learner data over decades create repositories of extraordinary sensitivity—data that may reveal not only academic history but also cognitive development, health conditions, employment trajectories, and personal circumstances. Developing adequate governance frameworks requires close collaboration between educational institutions, technology developers, legal scholars, and learner communities.

Algorithmic Bias and Fairness

Machine learning algorithms that drive personalization systems are trained on historical educational data that necessarily reflects past patterns of educational inequity, social advantage, and institutional bias. When deployed without critical examination, these algorithms risk encoding and perpetuating biased assessments of learner potential, preferences, and likely trajectories. Kasneci et al. (2023) identified algorithmic bias as a significant challenge in LLM-based educational applications, noting that models trained primarily on text produced by privileged, English-speaking populations may perform substantially worse for learners from other linguistic and cultural backgrounds, effectively reproducing linguistic hierarchies within ostensibly neutral AI systems.

The manifestations of algorithmic bias in educational AI are diverse and often subtle. Systems may underestimate the capability of learners whose interaction patterns differ from those of the predominantly Western, university-educated populations on which they were trained, or over-recommend remedial content to learners from groups that have historically underperformed on standardized assessments, creating self-fulfilling prophecies of underachievement. Addressing these manifestations requires both technical interventions—including representative training data curation, fairness-constrained optimization, and adversarial debiasing techniques—and institutional commitments to ongoing equity monitoring and participatory governance. Nguyen et al. (2023) recommend that educational AI developers adopt proactive bias assessment protocols that evaluate system outputs across demographic subgroups before deployment and continuously throughout system operation.

Educator Readiness and AI Literacy

The effectiveness of AI-driven personalization systems depends critically on the readiness of educators to understand, critically evaluate, and appropriately deploy these technologies. Luckin et al. (2022) argued that empowering educators to be "AI-ready" requires comprehensive professional development that goes beyond technical training to encompass understanding of AI capabilities and limitations, critical evaluation of algorithmic outputs, and pedagogical integration strategies that leverage AI capabilities while preserving the educational values and relational dimensions of teaching that AI systems cannot replicate.

Long and Magerko (2020) contributed foundational work on AI literacy competencies, identifying 17 competencies organized around knowing, doing, and understanding AI that provide a basis for curricula designed to develop informed and empowered engagement with AI systems. Ammer and Mamadjanova (2025) found that educational digital literacy and self-directed learning are significant positive predictors of e-learning motivation and effectiveness. Chiu et al. (2023) extended this discussion to higher education contexts, identifying faculty development, infrastructure investment, and institutional strategy as key enabling conditions for effective AIEd implementation, arguing that technology provision without parallel investment in human capacity development represents a predictable pathway to implementation failure.

The development of AI literacy among learners themselves is equally critical. Learners who understand how AI systems work, what data they collect, how recommendations are generated, and what the limitations of algorithmic judgment are, are better positioned to engage critically and productively with AI-enhanced learning environments. Agrawal et al. (2026) identified fundamental barriers and limitations in AI's capacity to decode complex non-human signals, highlighting that even sophisticated AI systems operate within significant interpretive constraints—an insight that supports the case for cultivating learner AI literacy.

Technical and Infrastructure Barriers

The deployment of sophisticated AI-driven personalization systems, particularly those integrated with digital twin architectures, requires substantial technical infrastructure including high-performance computing resources, reliable high-bandwidth internet connectivity, interoperable data standards, robust cybersecurity measures, and institutional data engineering capabilities. Sadiku et al. (2021) documented significant disparities in these infrastructure capabilities across institutional and national contexts, noting that resource-constrained environments—including many institutions in the Global South, rural communities in high-income countries, and under-resourced urban schools—face substantial barriers to AI-powered educational innovation.

Gligorea et al. (2023) identified system interoperability as a particularly challenging technical barrier, noting that adaptive learning systems often operate in proprietary silos that prevent integration with broader institutional learning management systems, student information systems, and learner credential repositories. The development of open standards for learner data interoperability represents a significant technical and governance challenge whose resolution is prerequisite to the realization of digital twin-enabled lifelong learning at scale.

Figure 2 illustrates the Adaptive Learning Cycle in AI-Enhanced Educational Environments. The five-stage cycle—Assess, Personalize, Deliver, Monitor, and Refine—depicts the continuous, iterative nature of AI-driven adaptive instruction within digital twin learning systems (Authors' synthesis from reviewed literature).

Figure 2. Adaptive learning cycle in AI-enhanced educational environments

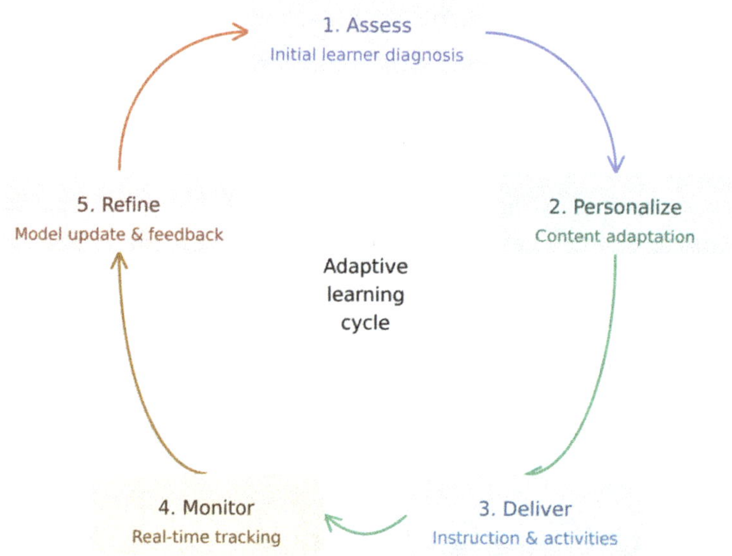

AN INTEGRATIVE FRAMEWORK FOR AI-DRIVEN PERSONALIZATION

Framework Overview

Drawing on the empirical and theoretical literature reviewed in preceding sections, this chapter proposes an integrative framework for AI-driven personalization within digital twin-enabled lifelong learning systems. The framework comprises five interconnected layers: (1) Learner Data Infrastructure, (2) Digital Twin Learner Modeling, (3) AI Personalization Engine, (4) Adaptive Instructional Interface, and (5) Ethical Governance and Evaluation. These layers function as a coherent system in which data flows continuously between components, enabling dynamic, responsive, and ethically accountable personalization across the full temporal span of a learner's educational life.

The framework is designed to be both descriptive of effective current practice and normative in its articulation of design principles that should guide future system development. Each layer embodies both technical specifications and educational values—particularly learner agency, equity, and transparency—that determine whether technical capabilities translate into genuine educational benefits. The Learner Data Infrastructure layer encompasses the collection, storage, and management of multimodal learner data including academic performance records, behavioral interaction logs, self-reported preference data, and competency credentials from diverse educational contexts.

Digital Twin Learner Modeling Layer

The Digital Twin Learner Modeling layer maintains persistent, evolving representations of individual learners that integrate data from the infrastructure layer into coherent, multidimensional models. These models encompass cognitive competency maps structured around domain ontologies, learning style profiles derived from interaction pattern analysis, motivational orientations inferred from engagement data, and historical learning trajectories across all educational contexts the learner has engaged with. She et al. (2023) demonstrated that digital twin approaches to learner modeling offer significant advantages over episodic snapshot models, particularly in their capacity to represent learning as a dynamic, temporally extended process.

Jankovskis et al. (2024) further highlighted the potential of digital twin architectures to enable cross-institutional learner continuity, allowing personalized learning support to persist across educational transitions—between courses, institutions, credential levels, and career phases—that would otherwise fragment the learner's developmental history. This continuity is particularly valuable for mature, nontraditional, and returning learners whose educational trajectories are characteristically non-linear and multi-institutional.

AI Personalization Engine

The AI Personalization Engine applies machine learning and AI reasoning capabilities to the digital twin learner model, generating individualized instructional recommendations, content selections, feedback formulations, and difficulty adjustments calibrated to the current state and trajectory of each learner. This engine integrates multiple AI approaches including collaborative filtering for content recommendation, reinforcement learning for pacing optimization, natural language processing for contextually appropriate feedback generation, and predictive analytics for early identification of learners at risk of disengagement or failure.

Critically, the personalization engine is designed to operate transparently, with explainable AI mechanisms that allow learners, educators, and administrators to understand the basis of personalization decisions and to challenge or override recommendations where appropriate. The engine also incorporates fairness-aware learning algorithms that continuously monitor and mitigate demographic disparities in personalization outcomes, treating equity as an operational rather than merely aspirational commitment embedded in the technical architecture of the system.

Adaptive Instructional Interface and Ethical Governance

The Adaptive Instructional Interface is the learner-facing layer of the framework, presenting personalized content, activities, and feedback through responsive, accessible, and pedagogically coherent interfaces. The interface supports multiple instructional modalities including text-based content, interactive simulations, collaborative learning environments, multimedia presentations, and conversational AI tutors. Sajja et al. (2024) emphasized the importance of designing adaptive interfaces that support, rather than determine, learner choices, preserving learner agency while providing intelligently curated pathways.

The Ethical Governance and Evaluation layer represents the systemic commitment to responsible AI implementation that must permeate all other layers. This layer encompasses ongoing bias monitoring against demographically disaggregated outcome data, regular privacy auditing, learner rights protection mechanisms including the right to explanation and the right to override algorithmic recommendations, educator oversight mechanisms, and comprehensive impact evaluation. Long-term evaluation extends to the development of lifelong learning competencies—including self-regulation, AI literacy, and adaptive expertise—which Gašević et al. (2023)

identify as the ultimate indicators of AI-enhanced education's contribution to individual capability and societal flourishing.

FUTURE RESEARCH DIRECTIONS

Longitudinal and Ecological Studies

The existing empirical literature on AI-driven personalization is dominated by short-term experimental and quasi-experimental studies conducted within bounded course or program contexts, a methodological limitation that constrains the conclusions that can be drawn about sustained educational impacts. Crompton and Burke (2023) explicitly call for longitudinal research designs that track learner outcomes over extended time horizons, capturing the sustained educational impacts that are theoretically central to the lifelong learning mission. Such studies would need to navigate significant methodological challenges including learner attrition over multi-year follow-up periods, rapid technology evolution, and the attribution of educational outcomes to specific AI interventions within complex, multi-factor educational ecologies.

Ecological studies that examine AI-driven personalization as it operates in authentic educational environments would provide valuable insights into implementation fidelity, contextual moderators of effectiveness, and the social dynamics of human–AI co-participation in learning communities. Mixed-methods research designs combining quantitative outcome measurement with ethnographic observation, interview-based inquiry, and participatory research approaches would be particularly valuable in capturing the full complexity of AI-enhanced educational experience.

Human-AI Collaboration and Cross-Cultural Adaptations

Luckin et al. (2022) and Lodge et al. (2023) both highlight the importance of understanding productive human–AI collaboration patterns in educational contexts, yet models of effective collaboration remain undertheorized and empirically underdeveloped relative to their practical importance. Future research should investigate how learners and educators most effectively partner with AI systems across diverse educational contexts, identifying the complementary roles, interaction patterns, trust development processes, and boundary conditions that characterize productive human–AI educational partnerships.

The dominant AI personalization research and development community operates primarily in English-language, Western-educated contexts, creating significant gaps in knowledge about the effectiveness and cultural appropriateness of these systems for the majority of the world's learners. Kasneci et al. (2023) note that LLM-based educational tools exhibit significant performance disparities across linguistic contexts. Bhatti and Sattarov (2025) demonstrated that cultural contact, cultural attachment, and visit motivation are significant determinants of spiritual and identity formation in cross-cultural educational contexts, a finding that underscores the depth and complexity of cultural variables that AI personalization systems must account for if they are to serve learners across the full range of human cultural diversity.

Integration with Emerging Technologies and Policy Frameworks

The trajectory of technological development suggests that AI-driven personalization will increasingly intersect with emerging technologies including extended reality (XR) for immersive learning environments, affective computing for emotion-aware instructional adaptation, neuroimaging-informed cognitive load assessment, and blockchain-based credentialing for portable, learner-controlled competency records. Holmes and Tuomi (2022) advocate for prospective ethical analysis of emerging AIEd technologies—anticipating potential harms before they materialize rather than responding reactively to already-deployed systems.

The policy landscape surrounding AI in education is evolving rapidly but unevenly, with significant variation in regulatory approaches, institutional governance frameworks, and stakeholder engagement processes across national and regional contexts. Future research should examine the educational effectiveness of different policy approaches to AI regulation in education, investigating whether and how specific governance choices affect both the quality of AI-driven personalization and the equity of its outcomes. Developing the evidence base needed to inform these policy choices requires close collaboration between educational researchers, policymakers, technologists, and learner communities.

CONCLUSION

This chapter has examined the convergence of AI-driven personalization and digital twin technologies within the context of lifelong learning systems, offering a comprehensive synthesis of theoretical foundations, technological mechanisms, empirical evidence, ethical challenges, and future directions. The central argument is that AI-driven personalization, when implemented within thoughtfully designed digital twin architectures and governed by robust ethical frameworks, offers transformative potential for advancing equitable, effective, and sustainable lifelong learning that meets the diverse and evolving needs of contemporary learners across all phases of their educational lives.

The review demonstrates that intelligent tutoring systems, large language models, learning analytics, and open learner models each contribute distinct and complementary capabilities to the personalization ecosystem, and that their integration within digital twin architectures amplifies their collective value. The digital twin provides the persistent, longitudinal learner representation that allows personalization to extend across the temporal boundaries constraining individual educational episodes. Empirical evidence consistently supports the positive impact of adaptive AI systems on academic performance, engagement, and self-regulated learning, though methodological limitations—particularly the dominance of short-term, small-scale, controlled studies—call for more rigorous longitudinal and ecological research designs.

The ethical challenges associated with AI-driven personalization—including data privacy, algorithmic bias, educator readiness, learner AI literacy, and infrastructure equity—are substantial and require deliberate, ongoing institutional attention embedded in the design, implementation, and governance of these systems from the outset. The integrative framework proposed in this chapter positions ethical governance not as an external constraint on AI innovation but as a constitutive dimension of responsible system design—a framing that reflects a broader philosophy of human-centered AI development in which technological capability serves pedagogical aspiration.

As AI-driven personalization technologies continue to evolve at a pace that challenges both researchers and practitioners, the educational community faces both an extraordinary opportunity and a profound responsibility. The opportunity lies in harnessing AI's capacity for individualized, responsive, and continuously improving instruction to genuinely democratize access to high-quality lifelong learning. The responsibility lies in ensuring that this capacity is deployed in ways that respect learner dignity, promote educational equity, preserve human agency, build institutional trust, and serve the fundamental social purposes of education. Meeting this dual imperative requires sustained, interdisciplinary scholarly inquiry, participatory institutional practice, principled policy engagement, and ongoing dialogue between researchers, developers, educators, policymakers, and learners whose collective commitment will determine whether AI-driven personalization fulfills its transformative promise.

REFERENCES

Agrawal, A., Nagaraj, S., Imambi, S. S., Borse, K. T., Dhange, P. G., Goud, V. S., & Gupta, D. (2026). Barriers and limitations in artificial intelligence for decoding non-human signals. In Ameur, W., & Arbi, A. (Eds.), *Harnessing AI for human-animal communication* (pp. 85–116). IGI Global Scientific Publishing., DOI: 10.4018/979-8-3373-5483-5.ch004

Ammer, M. A., & Mamadjanova, T. (2025). Effects of educational digital literacy, educational aspirations, self-directed learning on e-learning motivation and effectiveness. *Educational Sciences: Theory & Practice*. Advance online publication. DOI: 10.12738/jestp.2025.1.18

Arantes, J. (2024). Digital twins and the terminology of ‘personalization’ or ‘personalized learning’ in educational policy: A discussion paper. *Policy Futures in Education*, *22*(2), 210–226. DOI: 10.1177/14782103231176357

Bayly-Castaneda, K., Ramirez-Montoya, M.-S., & Morita-Alexander, A. (2024). Crafting personalized learning paths with AI for lifelong learning: A systematic literature review. *Frontiers in Education*, *9*, 1424386. Advance online publication. DOI: 10.3389/feduc.2024.1424386

Bernacki, M. L., Greene, M. J., & Lobczowski, N. G. (2021). A systematic review of research on personalized learning: Personalized by whom, to what, how, and for what purpose(s)? *Educational Psychology Review*, *33*(4), 1675–1715. DOI: 10.1007/s10648-021-09615-8

Bhatti, M. A., & Pardaev, J. (2025). *Exploring accreditation’s role in fostering inclusive education via educational equity and technology*. Revista Electrónica de LEEME., DOI: 10.58262/LEEME.56.05

Bhatti, M. A., & Sattarov, A. (2025). *Impact of religious tourism on spiritual belief: Role of visit motivation, cultural contact, and cultural attachment*. European Journal for Philosophy of Religion., DOI: 10.24204/ejpr.2025.4814

Chiu, T. K. F., Xia, Q., Zhou, X., Chai, C. S., & Cheng, M. (2023). Systematic literature review on opportunities, challenges, and future research recommendations of artificial intelligence in education. *Computers and Education: Artificial Intelligence*, *4*, 100118. Advance online publication. DOI: 10.1016/j.caeai.2022.100118

Crompton, H., & Burke, D. (2023). Artificial intelligence in higher education: The state of the field. *International Journal of Educational Technology in Higher Education*, *20*(1), 22. Advance online publication. DOI: 10.1186/s41239-023-00392-8

Du Plooy, E., Casteleijn, D., & Franzsen, D. (2024). Personalized adaptive learning in higher education: A scoping review of key characteristics and impact on academic performance and engagement. *Heliyon, 10*(22), e39630. Advance online publication. DOI: 10.1016/j.heliyon.2024.e39630 PMID: 39524879

Gašević, D., Siemens, G., & Sadiq, S. (2023). Empowering learners for the age of artificial intelligence. *Computers and Education: Artificial Intelligence, 4*, 100130. Advance online publication. DOI: 10.1016/j.caeai.2023.100130

Ghaleb, M. M. S., & Pardaev, J. (2025a). Effects of advertisement language, communication style, information seeking behavior and information source credibility on customers' intentions towards international products via brand trust. *El Profesional de la Información, 34*(2). Advance online publication. DOI: 10.3145/epi.2025.ene.34203

Ghaleb, M. M. S., & Pardaev, J. (2025b). Literature reading self-efficacy and academic achievement. *Educational Sciences: Theory & Practice, 25*(2), 77–92. DOI: 10.12738/jestp.2025.2.06

Ghaleb, M. M. S., & Sattarov, A. (2025). *Use of ChatGPT in education and quality of education: Role of student course engagement and regulator support.* Revista Electrónica de LEEME., DOI: 10.58262/LEEME.55.0020

Gligorea, I., Cioca, M., Oancea, R., Gorski, A.-T., Gorski, H., & Tudorache, P. (2023). Adaptive learning using artificial intelligence in e-learning: A literature review. *Education Sciences, 13*(12), 1216. Advance online publication. DOI: 10.3390/educsci13121216

Holmes, W., & Tuomi, I. (2022). State of the art and practice in AI in education. *European Journal of Education, 57*(4), 542–570. DOI: 10.1111/ejed.12533

Hooshyar, D., Pedaste, M., Saks, K., Leijen, A., Bardone, E., & Wang, M. (2021). Open learner models in supporting self-regulated learning in higher education: A systematic literature review. *Computers & Education, 154*, 103878. Advance online publication. DOI: 10.1016/j.compedu.2020.103878

Jankovskis, D., Cirule, I., & Carbone, A. (2024). Digital twins and e-learning: Navigating challenges and opportunities. In Casalino, G. (Eds.), *Higher education learning methodologies and technologies online. HELMeTO 2023. Communications in Computer and Information Science* (Vol. 2076). Springer., DOI: 10.1007/978-3-031-67351-1_12

Kasneci, E., Sessler, K., Kuchemann, S., Bannert, M., Dementieva, D., Fischer, F., & Kasneci, G. (2023). ChatGPT for good? On opportunities and challenges of large language models for education. *Learning and Individual Differences*, *103*, 102274. Advance online publication. DOI: 10.1016/j.lindif.2023.102274

Kuleto, V., Ilic, M., Dumangiu, M., Rankovic, M., Martins, O. M. D., Paun, D., & Mihoreanu, L. (2021). Exploring opportunities and challenges of artificial intelligence and machine learning in higher education institutions. *Sustainability (Basel)*, *13*(18), 10424. Advance online publication. DOI: 10.3390/su131810424

Lin, C.-C., Huang, A. Y. Q., & Lu, O. H. T. (2023). Artificial intelligence in intelligent tutoring systems toward sustainable education: A systematic review. *Smart Learning Environments*, *10*(1), 41. Advance online publication. DOI: 10.1186/s40561-023-00260-y

Liu, L., & Wan, L. (2024). Innovative models for enhanced student adaptability and performance in educational environments. *PLoS One*, *19*(9), e0307221. Advance online publication. DOI: 10.1371/journal.pone.0307221 PMID: 39240797

Lodge, J. M., de Barba, P., & Broadbent, J. (2023). Learning with generative artificial intelligence within a network of co-regulation. *Journal of University Teaching & Learning Practice*, *20*(7), 02. Advance online publication. DOI: 10.53761/1.20.7.02

Long, D., & Magerko, B. (2020). What is AI literacy? Competencies and design considerations. In *Proceedings of the 2020 CHI Conference on Human Factors in Computing Systems* (pp. 1–16). ACM. DOI: 10.1145/3313831.3376727

Luckin, R., Cukurova, M., Kent, C., & du Boulay, B. (2022). Empowering educators to be AI-ready. *Computers and Education: Artificial Intelligence*, *3*, 100076. Advance online publication. DOI: 10.1016/j.caeai.2022.100076

Muthuswamy, V. V., & Absamatov, A. (2025). *Determinants of students engagement and their role in boosting students' academic performance among higher education institutions*. Revista Electrónica de LEEME., DOI: 10.58262/LEEME.56.13

Nguyen, A., Ngo, H. N., Hong, Y., Dang, B., & Nguyen, B.-P. T. (2023). Ethical principles for artificial intelligence in education. *Education and Information Technologies*, *28*(4), 4221–4241. DOI: 10.1007/s10639-022-11316-w PMID: 36254344

Ouyang, F., Wu, M., Zheng, L., Zhang, L., & Jiao, P. (2023). Integration of artificial intelligence performance prediction and learning analytics to improve student learning in online engineering course. *International Journal of Educational Technology in Higher Education*, *20*(1), 4. Advance online publication. DOI: 10.1186/s41239-022-00372-4 PMID: 36683653

Sadiku, M. N. O., Musa, S. M., & Ajayi-Majebi, A. (2021). Artificial intelligence in education. *International Journal of Scientific Advances, 2*(1), 5–11. DOI: 10.51542/ijscia.v2i1.2

Sajja, R., Sermet, Y., Cikmaz, M., Cwiertny, D., & Demir, I. (2024). Artificial intelligence-enabled intelligent assistant for personalized and adaptive learning in higher education. *Information (Basel), 15*(10), 596. Advance online publication. DOI: 10.3390/info15100596

She, M., Xiao, M., & Zhao, Y. (2023). Technological implication of the digital twin approach on the intelligent education system. *International Journal of HR; Humanoid Robotics, 20*(2), 2250005. Advance online publication. DOI: 10.1142/S0219843622500050

Shemshack, A., Kinshuk, , & Spector, J. M. (2021). A comprehensive analysis of personalized learning components. *Journal of Computers in Education, 8*(4), 485–503. DOI: 10.1007/s40692-021-00188-7

Tapalova, O., & Zhiyenbayeva, N. (2022). Artificial intelligence in education: AIEd for personalised learning pathways. *Electronic Journal of e-Learning, 20*(5), 639–653. DOI: 10.34190/ejel.20.5.2597

Tlili, A., Shehata, B., Adarkwah, M. A., Bozkurt, A., Hickey, D. T., Huang, R., & Agyemang, B. (2023). What if the devil is my guardian angel: ChatGPT as a case study of using chatbots in education. *Smart Learning Environments, 10*(1), 15. Advance online publication. DOI: 10.1186/s40561-023-00237-x

Wang, H., Tlili, A., Huang, R., Cai, Z., Li, M., Cheng, Z., & Li, Y. (2023). Examining the applications of intelligent tutoring systems in real educational contexts: A systematic literature review from the social experiment perspective. *Education and Information Technologies, 28*(7), 9113–9148. DOI: 10.1007/s10639-022-11555-x PMID: 36643383

KEY TERMS AND DEFINITIONS

Adaptive Learning: An educational methodology that employs data analytics and machine learning algorithms to dynamically adjust instructional content, pacing, and learning pathways based on individual student performance and behavioral patterns, with the goal of optimizing each learner's educational outcomes.

Algorithmic Bias: Systematic and repeatable errors in the outputs of AI systems that result from flawed assumptions or inequities embedded in the training data, design processes, or optimization objectives of machine learning models, often producing discriminatory outcomes for certain learner groups.

Artificial Intelligence in Education (AIEd): The application of AI technologies—including machine learning, natural language processing, and intelligent agent systems—to enhance teaching and learning processes through automated personalization, predictive analytics, intelligent feedback, and adaptive instructional design.

Digital Twin: A persistent, dynamic virtual representation of an individual learner that integrates cognitive, behavioral, affective, and contextual data in real time, enabling AI systems to simulate learning trajectories, predict educational outcomes, and generate personalized instructional interventions across extended timeframes.

Intelligent Tutoring System (ITS): A computer-based instructional system that uses computational models of domain knowledge, learner cognition, and pedagogical strategy to deliver individualized, adaptive instruction and feedback, simulating the benefits of one-on-one human tutoring without requiring continuous educator presence.

Large Language Model (LLM): A transformer-based AI system trained on vast corpora of human-generated text that develops representational capacities for nuanced language understanding, multi-step reasoning, and contextually appropriate text generation, enabling conversational educational support across virtually unlimited subject domains.

Learning Analytics: The systematic measurement, collection, analysis, and reporting of data about learners and their educational contexts, used to understand and optimize learning processes, predict academic outcomes, identify learners at risk, and inform the design of adaptive instructional interventions.

Lifelong Learning: The continuous, voluntary, and self-motivated pursuit of knowledge and skills throughout an individual's life, extending across formal education, workplace learning, and informal self-directed study, requiring educational systems capable of providing flexible, adaptive, and persistent support across diverse contexts and career stages.

Open Learner Model (OLM): A learner modeling approach in which the system's computational representation of a learner's knowledge state, learning trajectory, and competency profile is made transparent and directly accessible to the learner, enabling metacognitive reflection, self-regulated learning, and informed educational decision-making.

Personalized Learning: An instructional paradigm that tailors educational content, pacing, feedback, and learning pathways to the individual characteristics, needs, preferences, and goals of each learner, leveraging data-driven insights and adaptive technologies to provide differentiated educational experiences at scale.

Self-Regulated Learning (SRL): A metacognitive learning process in which learners actively plan, monitor, evaluate, and adjust their own learning strategies and behaviors in pursuit of academic goals, encompassing cyclical phases of forethought, performance, and self-reflection as foundational competencies for lifelong educational engagement.

Chapter 2
Conceptual Foundations of Self-Adaptive Learning Systems With Digital Twin Integration

Hamed Nozari
http://orcid.org/0000-0002-6500-6708
University of National and World Economy, Sofia, Bulgaria

K. Tanya
http://orcid.org/0009-0000-6678-6892
Birla Institute of Technology and Science (BITS), Dubai, UAE

Seema P. Suthar
Birla Institute of Technology and Science (BITS), Dubai, UAE

Jaanavi Bakshi
http://orcid.org/0009-0005-5096-8727
Birla Institute of Technology and Science (BITS), Dubai, UAE

ABSTRACT

This chapter takes a conceptual approach to explore the role of the digital twin in shaping a new generation of self-adaptive learning systems. Unlike traditional adaptive learning systems that rely primarily on past data and limited settings, the proposed framework considers the learner as a dynamic entity with cognitive, behavioral, affective, and contextual dimensions. In this regard, the digital twin is upgraded from a simple representational tool to a cognitive mirror that enables

DOI: 10.4018/979-8-2600-1674-9.ch002

real-time monitoring, analysis, prediction, and adjustment of the learning trajectory. This chapter provides a theoretical foundation for the development of intelligent, human, and self-evolving learning ecosystems.

1- INTRODUCTION

The rapid evolution of digital technologies in recent decades has fundamentally transformed the landscape of educational systems. The emergence of e-learning, web-based learning systems, and then intelligent platforms based on artificial intelligence (AI) have marked a gradual shift from static learning to dynamic and interactive learning environments (Nozari, 2026). However, despite these advances, many existing learning systems still operate at a limited level of adaptability, making decisions based primarily on predefined patterns and historical data. This is despite the fact that the human learning process is inherently dynamic, nonlinear, and context-dependent, requiring approaches that can understand and manage this complexity in real time.

In response to these limitations, the concept of "self-adaptive learning" has been proposed as a step beyond adaptive learning. Unlike traditional adaptive systems that are only adjusted based on certain parameters such as knowledge level or past performance, self-adaptive learning seeks to create systems that can continuously analyze the learner's state, learn from ongoing interactions, and dynamically adjust the learning path (Zhang et al., 2026). Such a system not only responds to surface changes, but is also able to consider deeper cognitive and behavioral patterns and shape educational decisions based on them. However, achieving this level of intelligence requires a conceptual and technological infrastructure that can provide an accurate representation of the learner's state in real time (Kabashkin, 2026).

In the meantime, digital twin technology, as one of the key innovations in industrial and engineering fields, has shown significant capacity to respond to this need. A digital twin is traditionally defined as a virtual, simultaneous representation of a physical system that allows for monitoring, analyzing, and predicting the system's behavior through real-time data (Shamsuddoha et al., 2026). The transfer of this concept to the learning domain has paved the way for a new approach in which each learner has a dynamic digital twin that continuously represents his or her state in various dimensions. This representation can include information beyond educational performance, such as attention level, mental engagement, interaction patterns, and even cognitive states.

Despite this potential, the use of digital twins in learning systems is still in its infancy and has often been used in a limited way and without a unified conceptual framework. Many existing studies have focused on technical aspects or specific applications of this technology, while its theoretical and conceptual dimensions in the field of intelligent learning have received less attention (Yordanova et al., 2026). In other words, a comprehensive understanding of how digital twins can serve as the core of a self-adaptive learning system has not yet been developed.

In this regard, this chapter aims to fill this conceptual gap by providing a unified theoretical framework for integrating digital twins with self-adaptive learning systems. The main focus is on redefining the role of digital twins from a mere representational tool to a "cognitive mirror" that can dynamically reflect the mental and behavioral processes of the learner. This view enables the transition from reactive learning systems to predictive and self-evolving systems, where instructional decisions are made not only based on past data, but also taking into account the current situation and future trends (Zhang et al., 2020).

The main innovation of this chapter is in presenting a new conceptual perspective in which learning is considered as a living and evolving system, and the digital twin acts as a mechanism for continuous synchronization between physical reality and the digital space. This approach paves the way for the formation of a new generation of learning systems that are capable of achieving real-time, deep personalization, intelligent interaction, and continuous evolution within an integrated framework. In the following, this chapter attempts to chart a clear path for the development of future learning systems by examining the evolution of learning systems, explaining the foundations of self-adaptive learning, redefining the concept of the digital twin, and finally presenting an integrated conceptual framework.

2- EVOLUTION OF INTELLIGENT LEARNING SYSTEMS

The section "The Evolution of Intelligent Learning Systems" can be considered as one of the key foundations for understanding the current and future state of educational systems. This evolution has not only resulted from technological advances, but also from a change in the view of the nature of learning, the role of the learner, and the way of interacting with knowledge. In this path, learning systems have moved from static and one-sided structures to dynamic, interactive, and intelligent environments; however, this evolution has not yet reached a point where it can be called "true self-adaption."

In the early stages, e-learning was proposed as the first step in the digitalization of education. These systems mainly focused on providing educational content in digital formats and the role of the learner in them was limited to a passive recipient. The structure of these environments was based on the transfer of predefined knowledge and no effective mechanism was considered to understand individual differences or learning conditions. In such a system, the learning path was the same for all users, and possible changes in the learner's performance or behavior did not have a significant impact on the way content was presented (Naresh et al., 2026).

With the advancement of technology and the increasing availability of learning data, a new generation of systems called "intelligent tutoring systems" or "intelligent tutoring systems" emerged. These systems attempted to create a level of adaptability in the learning process by utilizing knowledge models, learner models, and decision rules. In this approach, learner performance was monitored in a limited manner and based on that, suggestions for continuing the learning path were provided. Although these systems were an important step towards personalizing education, they were still heavily dependent on predefined rules and had limited ability to deal with unexpected changes or cognitive complexities (Nozari, 2026).

In the continuation of this trend, the concept of "adaptive learning" was proposed as a more advanced version of intelligent systems. At this stage, the use of data-driven algorithms and user behavior analysis made it possible to adjust the learning path based on individual characteristics. Adaptive learning systems were able to personalize content based on indicators such as learning speed, test success rate, and interaction patterns. This evolution took education away from a completely uniform state and to some extent responded to individual needs. However, these systems still operated within a relatively limited framework and relied mainly on past data. In fact, adaptability here meant more of "reacting to recorded data" than real-time understanding of the learner's state (Splettstößer et al., 2023).

With the advent of advanced artificial intelligence, especially machine learning and deep learning, a new generation of learning platforms emerged that were capable of analyzing large volumes of data and extracting complex patterns. These systems were able to analyze learner behavior at deeper levels and make predictions about future performance. They also enabled intelligent feedback and suggested diverse learning paths. At this stage, the interaction between humans and systems has become more complex, and the systems have been able to play the role of an intelligent guide to some extent (Kalogeras et al., 2025). However, even these advanced systems face limitations.

One of the most important challenges of AI-based systems is the inability to create a comprehensive and continuous representation of the learner's state. Most of these systems analyze data in a discrete manner and at specific time intervals, and lack an integrated view of the momentary changes in the cognitive, emotional, and behavioral states of the learner. In addition, many of the decisions made in these systems are based on pre-trained models that cannot be easily updated in real time and in direct interaction with the learner (Yordanova & Nozari, 2026).

As a result, although the path of evolution of learning systems from static to intelligent and then to adaptive and data-driven shows significant progress, there is still a fundamental gap. This gap is related to the lack of systems that can continuously, in real time, and with a deep understanding of the learner's situation, re-adjust themselves. In other words, current systems are more "reactive" than "self-evolving." They can respond to changes, but they are unable to independently reinvent their course based on changing circumstances (Horváth et al., 2022).

This limitation highlights the need to move to a new generation of learning systems in which adaptability is considered not as a peripheral feature, but as the core of the system. In such a system, learning is understood as a dynamic and evolving process that requires continuous monitoring, real-time analysis, and intelligent feedback. This is where the concept of self-adaptive learning comes in; a concept that goes beyond predefined settings and seeks to create systems that can independently and continuously evolve with the learner (Dobaj et al., 2023).

In this context, it can be concluded that the evolution of learning systems, although it has come a long way, has not yet reached a point where it can fully cover the real complexities of human learning. This situation paves the way for the introduction of new approaches that can fill this gap and elevate learning to a deeper, more dynamic and intelligent level. One of the most promising of these approaches is the integration of digital twin concepts with learning systems, which can enable accurate, real-time and multidimensional representations of the learner's state and pave the way for the true realization of self-adaptive learning.

3- CONCEPTUAL FOUNDATIONS OF SELF-ADAPTIVE LEARNING

Self-adaptive learning, as an emerging concept in the field of intelligent learning systems, represents a transition from reactive and semi-dynamic approaches to systems that are able to continuously, autonomously, and in interaction with the environment, reorganize and evolve themselves. In this framework, learning is no longer a linear process or based on predefined paths, but is considered as a dynamic, complex, and context-dependent system in which the interaction between the learner, the content, the environment, and the intelligent system is constantly changing.

To understand this concept in depth, it is first necessary to clearly distinguish between "adaptive learning" and "self-adaptive learning." In adaptive learning systems, changes are usually made based on predetermined rules or models that have been trained on past data. These systems can change the level of difficulty of content or the order in which it is presented based on user performance, but these changes often occur within a limited and predictable framework. In contrast, self-adaptive learning seeks to create systems that not only respond to data but also are able to recreate their decision-making structure over time. In other words, here adaptability is promoted from the level of "parameter tuning" to the level of "system evolution."

A key element in self-adaptive learning is the concept of "real-time monitoring." In this approach, the learner's state is continuously and instantaneously assessed. This state can include a variety of indicators, including educational performance, level of engagement, speed of response, and even indirect cues such as behavioral patterns or level of mental engagement. The importance of this monitoring is that the system can detect subtle and gradual changes in the learner's state and respond appropriately before these changes lead to a decline in performance (Rivera et al., 2022).

Another important element is "Context-Awareness". In self-adaptive learning, the system's decisions are not based solely on raw data, but also on the context in which this data was generated. For example, a decline in a learner's performance may be due to the difficulty of the content, mental fatigue, or even environmental conditions. A self-adaptive system must be able to recognize these differences and respond appropriately to each situation. This level of understanding requires models that can analyze the complex relationships between different variables (Uhrmacher et al., 2024).

In addition to these, "dynamic feedback loops" also play a fundamental role in self-adaptive learning. Unlike traditional systems where feedback is provided intermittently, often after the completion of an activity, here feedback is generated continuously throughout the learning process. This feedback is not only provided to the learner, but is also used as input to adjust the system's behavior. In this way, a continuous learning cycle is formed in which the system and the learner are learning and adapting simultaneously.

To better explain these concepts, Figure 1 shows the conceptual framework of self-adaptive learning, in which the main components of the system and how they interact are represented as a dynamic cycle.

Figure 1. Conceptual model of self-adaptive learning system

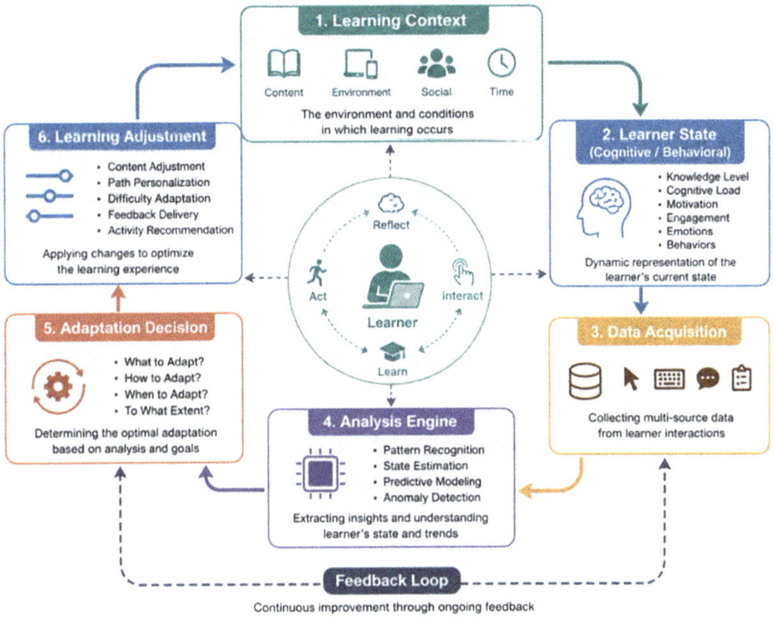

As shown in Figure 1, self-adaptive learning is designed as a closed, dynamic cycle in which each component plays a specific role in the overall process. This cycle begins with the "learning context," which includes all the environmental, content, and contextual factors in which learning occurs. This context provides the initial context in which the learner's state is formed.

In the next step, the "learner state" is introduced as one of the most important elements of the system. This state is a combination of cognitive and behavioral dimensions that are dynamically changing. Unlike traditional approaches that limit the learner to a few simple indicators, here an attempt is made to present a multi-dimensional and detailed picture of his state.

Then, data related to this state are extracted through the "data collection" layer. This data can come from a variety of sources, such as user interactions, activity results, and other measurable indicators. It is then fed into an "analytics engine" that extracts patterns and interprets the learner's current state.

Based on the results of this analysis, "adaptive decisions" are made. These decisions can include changing the difficulty level of the content, suggesting new learning paths, or providing specific feedback. Ultimately, these decisions are implemented in the form of "learning process adjustments" that create changes to the learning experience.

The key to this structure is the existence of a "feedback loop" that feeds the system's output back to its input. This loop allows the system to continuously evaluate its performance and correct it if necessary. In this way, learning becomes a living, evolving process.

In summary, self-adaptive learning is based on three fundamental principles: continuous monitoring, intelligent analytics, and dynamic adaptation. Together, these three elements form a system that is able to optimize the learning path independently and in interaction with the learner. However, the full realization of this concept requires tools and technologies that can provide a more accurate representation of the learner's state, a topic that will be explored in more depth in the next section with the introduction of the digital twin.

4- DIGITAL TWIN IN LEARNING: FROM REPRESENTATION TO COGNITION

The concept of a digital twin was initially introduced in the industrial and engineering fields to create an accurate, dynamic, and synchronized representation of physical systems. In these applications, a digital twin acts as a virtual model that uses real-time data to monitor the state of the system and allows for analysis, prediction, and optimization. By continuously connecting the physical and digital worlds, this technology creates an intelligent feedback loop that leads to more accurate and faster decision-making. The transfer of this concept to the field of learning is not only a new application, but also a paradigm shift in how the learning process is understood (Bellini et al., 2021).

In the context of learning, a digital twin is a digital representation of a learner that dynamically and continuously reflects his or her state in various dimensions. These dimensions can include educational performance, interaction patterns, participation rate, and even more complex indicators such as cognitive load, focus, or motivation. At this level, the digital twin goes beyond a simple user profile and becomes a dynamic entity that is constantly updating. This feature allows for a deeper and more accurate understanding of the learning process.

However, many of the early applications of digital twins in learning remain limited to the "representation" level. At this level, the main goal is to collect and display data about the learner, without actively using this data in the decision-making and adaptation process. In other words, the digital twin in this case plays the role of a passive mirror that only reflects the current state, without playing a role in changing it. This approach, although useful, does not exploit the full potential of this technology (Yitmen et al., 2021).

To overcome this limitation, it is necessary to upgrade the digital twin from the representation level to the "cognition" level. At this level, the digital twin not only stores and displays data, but is also able to interpret it, identify hidden patterns, and make intelligent decisions based on them. This transformation transforms the digital twin into a "Cognitive Twin"; an entity that can model the cognitive state of the learner and act as an intelligent interface between the learner and the system.

In this framework, the cognitive twin is presented as a "cognitive mirror" that reflects not only observable behaviors, but also mental processes. This mirror is able to detect subtle changes in attention, mental engagement, or cognitive fatigue and convert them into usable signals for the system. Such a capability allows for the creation of truly intelligent and self-adaptive learning systems, as instructional decisions are made based on a deeper understanding of the learner's state.

To illustrate this conceptual shift, Figure 2 illustrates the transition structure from representation-based digital twin to cognitive digital twin in Learning Systems.

Figure 2. From representation-based digital twin to cognitive digital twin in learning systems

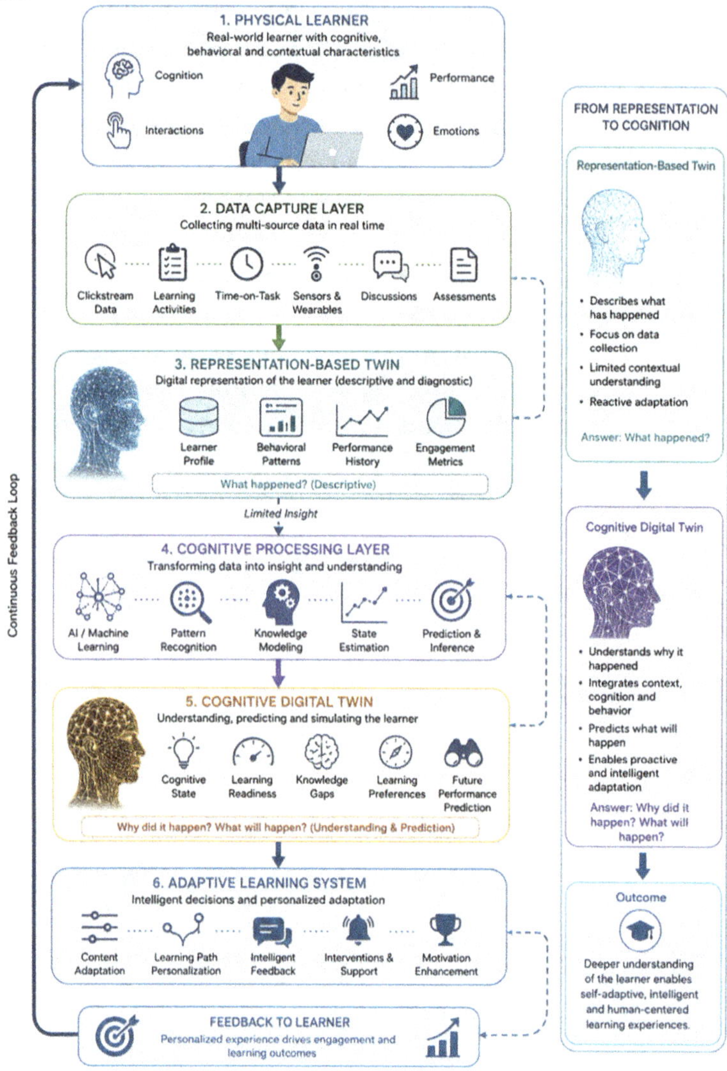

As shown in Figure 2, the process starts with the "physical learner," whose behaviors and interactions are considered the main source of data. This data is extracted through the data collection layer and transferred to the representation-based twin. At this stage, the digital twin acts as a dynamic profile that stores and organizes information about the learner. However, this level of twin lacks the ability to perform deep analysis and data interpretation.

In the next step, the data enters the "cognitive processing layer," where artificial intelligence techniques are used to extract patterns and understand complex relationships between variables. This layer plays a key role in transforming raw data into usable knowledge. The output of this process is the formation of a "cognitive twin" that is able to not only describe, but also interpret and predict the learner's state.

As an intelligent entity, the cognitive twin can help the learning system make more accurate adaptive decisions. For example, if the twin detects that the learner is experiencing cognitive fatigue, the system can automatically reduce the difficulty level of the content or suggest an appropriate break. This type of decision-making is only possible if the system has a deep understanding of the learner's state, an understanding that is provided by the cognitive twin.

Another important point in this structure is the existence of a feedback loop that returns the system's output back to the learner. This loop allows the learning process to be continuously and dynamically adjusted. In effect, the cognitive twin acts as an intermediary that receives information from the learner, analyzes it, and then returns the results to him in the form of adaptive decisions.

In summary, the transition from representational to cognitive twins is a fundamental step towards the realization of self-adaptive learning systems. This evolution allows for a deeper understanding of the learning process and paves the way for systems that not only respond to the learner's behavior, but are also able to "think along" with him and intelligently guide the learning path.

5- A CONCEPTUAL FRAMEWORK FOR DIGITAL TWIN-DRIVEN SELF-ADAPTIVE LEARNING

The conceptual framework of self-adaptive learning based on the digital twin is the connection point between three main areas: the human learner, intelligent technologies and cognitive-behavioral representation in the digital space. In this framework, the digital twin is not simply a virtual version of the learner, but acts as a cognitive and analytical core that can continuously monitor, interpret, predict and translate the learner's state into educational decisions. The main goal of such a framework is to move from reactive learning systems to systems that can dynamically adjust themselves to the cognitive, behavioral, emotional and contextual changes of the learner (Rojek et al., 2025).

In traditional or even adaptive learning systems, the personalization process is usually based on a limited set of data such as grades, responses, duration of presence on the platform or the rate of completion of activities. Although this approach is more advanced than uniform training, it is not able to provide a complete picture of the learner's real state (Nozari et al., 2025). A learner may be successful in terms of apparent performance, but may suffer from high cognitive load, reduced motivation, or a loss of concentration. It is also possible that his low score is not the result of a knowledge deficit, but rather an inappropriate learning path, content difficulty level, or contextual conditions. Therefore, the future learning system must be able to go beyond surface data and build a multidimensional, vivid, and interpretable picture of the learner. This is exactly the role that the digital twin plays in the proposed framework (Walmsley et al., 2024).

The proposed framework in this chapter is based on the idea that each learner can have a "learning twin"; a digital entity that is continuously updated with real-world data and represents the learner's state at multiple levels. This twin not only records performance information, but can also reflect behavior, interaction, cognitive patterns, emotional cues, learning preferences, and mental readiness. In this sense, the digital twin becomes a "Cognitive Learning Twin"; That is, an intelligent representation that is able to understand the current state of the learner, predict the possible future path, and help the adaptation engine make decisions.

Figure 3. Conceptual framework for digital twin-driven self-adaptive learning

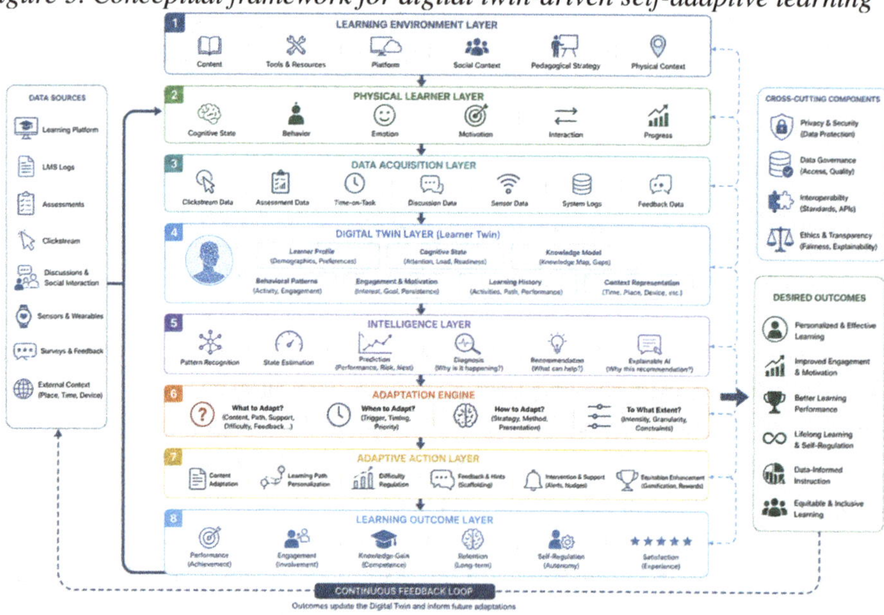

Figure 3 shows the proposed conceptual framework. This framework consists of several interconnected layers, each of which plays a specific role in transforming raw learning data into self-adaptive decisions. The first layer is the "learning environment." This environment includes the learning platform, learning content, interaction tools, learning management system, contextual conditions, and educational resources. At this level, learning is considered not as an isolated activity, but as a process within a digital and social ecosystem. The content that the learner studies, the type of activities he or she does, the level of his or her interaction with peers, and the way in which the platform is used all play a role in shaping the learning experience.

The second layer is the "physical learner layer." In this framework, the learner is not just a user, but a dynamic human system with cognitive, behavioral, emotional, and motivational dimensions. His or her cognitive state includes the level of knowledge, attention, cognitive load, conceptual understanding, and mental readiness for learning. The behavioral dimension includes clicks, participation, response patterns, time spent on activities, and how to interact with the content. The emotional and motivational dimension also includes interest, fatigue, self-confidence, learning anxiety, and the level of mental engagement. The importance of this layer is that all self-adaptive decisions should ultimately lead to the improvement of the learner.

The third layer is the "data collection layer." This layer is responsible for receiving multi-source data from the learner's interactions with the educational environment. This data can include click data, time spent on activities, test results, descriptive responses, participation in discussions, content navigation paths, data from sensors, or even direct feedback from the learner. The important point is that data should not be viewed only in quantitative and raw form, but should be interpreted in relation to the context in which it was produced. For example, a long time on a piece of content may indicate deep interest, but in another situation it could indicate confusion or excessive difficulty of the content.

After data collection, the information enters the "digital twin layer". This layer is the heart of the proposed framework. Here, the scattered data is transformed into a unified representation of the learner. The digital twin includes the learner's profile, knowledge map, behavior patterns, learning history, cognitive state, level of engagement, learning preferences and current context. The main difference between this layer and traditional learning profiles is that it is dynamic and alive. Traditional profiles are usually static or invariant, but the digital twin is continuously updated with new interactions of the learner. Therefore, if the learner experiences a drop in concentration, an increase in errors or a decrease in participation over a period of time, these changes are reflected in the digital twin (Vimal et al., 2025).

The next layer is the "intelligence layer". This layer is responsible for transforming the digital representation into understanding, prediction and interpretation. At this level, the system attempts to answer deeper questions: What is the learner's current state? Why has his performance changed? Is he experiencing a knowledge gap or is the problem related to the level of difficulty of the content? Will the current trend lead to a decline in performance? What kind of intervention would have the most impact? This layer can use various methods of analysis, pattern recognition, state estimation, prediction, and interpretability. However, at a conceptual level, the main importance of this layer is that it transforms the digital twin from an information display tool to a cognitive and decision-making mechanism.

After analysis, the results are fed into the "adaptation engine." The adaptation engine is responsible for deciding what to change, when to change it, how to change it, and how much to change it. These four questions form the core of decision-making in self-adaptive learning systems. For example, if the system detects that the learner is weak in a particular concept, it may retrace the learning path and provide reinforcement content. If it detects that the learner is cognitively ready for more complex content, it may increase the level of difficulty. If signs of decreased motivation are observed, the system may suggest motivational feedback, interactive activities, or a more varied learning path. Thus, adaptation here is not limited to changing the content, but also includes adjusting the path, timing, type of feedback, type of activity, level of difficulty, and even the way the system interacts with the learner.

The next layer is the "adaptive action layer." This layer translates the output of the adaptation engine's decisions into an actual learning experience. Adaptive actions can include personalizing the learning path, adjusting the difficulty level, suggesting new resources, providing intelligent feedback, activating educational intervention, changing the type of activity, or motivating support. The importance of this layer is that it turns analytical decisions into a tangible experience for the learner. If this layer is not designed properly, even the most accurate analysis will not have the desired educational effect.

Next is the "learning outcomes layer." This layer shows how the adaptive actions have affected the learner's performance, engagement, retention of learning, self-regulation, competence, and overall progress. In the proposed framework, learning outcomes are not limited to just grades or test scores. A self-adaptive learning system should also be able to consider the quality of the learning experience, the sustainability of learning, the ability to transfer knowledge, increased self-confidence, and the development of self-regulation. This multidimensional view also makes the evaluation of the system deeper and more human.

The most important feature of the framework in Figure 3 is the existence of a "continuous feedback loop." This loop causes the system's outputs to feed back into the digital twin and the learner's state. In other words, each adaptive action becomes a new source of data. If the system provides simpler content, it should check whether this change has actually improved learning. If the learning path is changed, its impact on motivation, performance, and engagement should be analyzed. This feedback loop transforms the system from a linear mechanism into a living, learning system. In such a structure, not only does the learner learn from the system, but the system also learns from the learner.

The proposed framework is also based on the principle that the digital twin should be "descriptive," "diagnostic," "predictive," and "prescriptive." At the descriptive level, the twin shows what happened. At the diagnostic level, it explains why it happened. At the predictive level, it suggests what is likely to happen next. At the prescriptive level, it suggests what action should be taken. These four levels make the digital twin a complete tool to support self-adaptive learning (Gupta et al., 2024).

Conceptually, the main value of this framework is that it does not consider learning as a static and fully programmable process. On the contrary, learning is understood as a living, contextual, and changing process that requires constant monitoring and adaptation. The digital twin acts as a cognitive intermediary; that is, it establishes a link between the learner's actual experience and the system's intelligent decisions. Without such an intermediary, the educational system would only react to scattered data, but with the digital twin, it can achieve a unified and dynamic understanding of the learner.

Ultimately, the conceptual framework for self-adaptive learning based on the digital twin suggests that the future of learning systems lies not in superficial personalization, but in the formation of ecosystems that can understand the learner multidimensionally, predict his or her changes, and continuously redesign the learning experience. This framework transforms the digital twin from a representational technology to a cognitive foundation for the next generation of intelligent learning; a generation in which the educational system not only teaches, but also understands, predicts, adapts, and evolves with the learner.

6- CONCLUSION

This chapter attempts to redefine the path of learning systems evolution from static and reactive structures to dynamic, intelligent, and self-adaptive systems by adopting a conceptual and integrated approach. The starting point of this path was the recognition of the limitations of existing learning systems; systems that, although they have made significant progress by utilizing artificial intelligence and data analytics, still face serious challenges in understanding the deep, real-time, and multidimensional state of the learner. These limitations show that superficial personalization based on past data is not enough to respond to the real complexities of human learning. In response to this challenge, the concept of "self-adaptive learning" was introduced as a new paradigm; a paradigm in which the learning system not only reacts to data, but is also able to continuously, independently, and in interaction with the learner, reorganize and evolve itself. In this framework, learning is considered as a living, dynamic, and context-dependent process that requires continuous monitoring, intelligent analysis, and real-time feedback. Such a view also changes the position of the learner; he is no longer a passive recipient, but an active and evolving entity whose behavior, cognition, and motivation are constantly changing.

In the meantime, the digital twin, as a key technology, plays a pivotal role in realizing this paradigm. As explained in this chapter, the digital twin in the field of learning can go beyond the level of a simple representation of learner data and become a "cognitive twin"; an entity that is able to dynamically model the mental, behavioral, and contextual state of the learner. This transformation from "Representation" to "Cognition" is not only a technical change, but also a profound conceptual change that allows for a better understanding of the learning process and smarter decision-making.

The conceptual framework presented in this chapter, by integrating self-adaptive learning and digital twins, showed how to design a multi-layered and intelligent learning system in which multi-source data from the learner is collected, integrated into a digital twin, then analyzed through layers of intelligence, and finally transformed into adaptive decisions. These decisions are implemented in the form of educational actions such as personalizing the path, adjusting the level of difficulty, providing feedback, and supporting learning, and their consequences are fed back to the system. This feedback loop enables the system to continuously improve its performance and keep pace with the learner's changes. One of the most important achievements of this framework is to provide a multidimensional view of learning. In this view, learning is not limited to educational outcomes, but also cognitive, behavioral, emotional, and contextual dimensions are considered. This approach allows for the design of systems that not only help improve short-term grades or performance, but also lead to the development of deeper skills such as self-regulation, critical thinking, and lifelong learning. In other words, the ultimate goal of such systems is to create a more human, intelligent, and sustainable learning experience.

Conceptually, this chapter has shown that the future of learning systems depends on moving towards ecosystems in which the interaction between humans and artificial intelligence is formed in a synergistic and dynamic way. In these ecosystems, the digital twin acts as an intermediary between the learner's real world and the digital space, enabling continuous synchronization of these two worlds. Such synchronization is the basis for the formation of systems that can act proactively, anticipate the learner's future needs, and provide appropriate interventions before problems arise.

Finally, it can be concluded that the integration of digital twins with self-adaptive learning creates a paradigm shift in the design and implementation of educational systems. This shift is a move from content-based systems and fixed programming to systems that are built on deep understanding, dynamic interaction and continuous evolution. Such a system not only teaches the learner, but also understands him, adapts to him and accompanies him on the path of learning. This vision draws new horizons for the development of the next generation of intelligent learning systems;

a generation in which the boundary between humans and technology becomes less blurred and learning becomes an integrated, personalized and meaningful experience.

REFERENCES

Bellini, E., Bagnoli, F., Caporuscio, M., Damiani, E., Flammini, F., Linkov, I., & Marrone, S. (2021, July). Resilience learning through self adaptation in digital twins of human-cyber-physical systems. In *2021 IEEE International Conference on Cyber Security and Resilience (CSR)* (pp. 168-173). IEEE. DOI: 10.1109/CSR51186.2021.9527913

Dobaj, J., Riel, A., Macher, G., & Egretzberger, M. (2023). Towards devops for cyber-physical systems (cpss): Resilient self-adaptive software for sustainable human-centric smart cps facilitated by digital twins. *Machines (Basel)*, *11*(10), 973. DOI: 10.3390/machines11100973

Gupta, R., Tian, B., Wang, Y., & Nahrstedt, K. (2024). TWIN-ADAPT: Continuous learning for digital twin-enabled online anomaly classification in iot-driven smart labs. *Future Internet*, *16*(7), 239. DOI: 10.3390/fi16070239

Horváth, I., & Tavčar, J. (2022). Designing Cyber-Physical Systems for Runtime Self-Adaptation: Knowing More about What We Miss.... *Journal of Integrated Design & Process Science*, *25*(2), 1–26. DOI: 10.3233/JID210030

Kabashkin, I. (2026). Cognitive Digital Twin Generations: From Foundational Instruments to Meta-Cognitive Ecosystems. *Information (Basel)*, *17*(3), 285. DOI: 10.3390/info17030285

Kalogeras, S., Samadi, S., & Nozari, H. (Eds.). (2025). *AI-Augmented Creativity in Learning Analytics*. IGI Global. DOI: 10.4018/979-8-3373-5117-9

Naresh, P., Sardar, T. H., Ramityal, B., & Almusharraf, A. TR, M., & Jain, V. (2026). A hybrid self-evolving edge-AI framework for scalable digital process twins in enterprise systems. Enterprise Information Systems, 2653241.

Nozari, H. (2026). AI-Augmented Creative Assessment: From Static Tests to Dynamic Insight Generation. In AI-Augmented Creativity in Learning Analytics (pp. 25-42). IGI Global Scientific Publishing.

Nozari, H. (2026). Digital twin-based predictive maintenance in cold chain logistics. *Operations Research*, *60*(1), 481–499. DOI: 10.1051/ro/2025167

Nozari, H., & Samadi, S. (2025). AIoE-Powered Neuromarketing for Decoding the Consumer Brain. In *Artificial Intelligence of Everything and Sustainable Development* (pp. 39–53). Springer Nature Singapore. DOI: 10.1007/978-981-96-7202-8_3

Rivera, L. F., Jiménez, M., Tamura, G., Villegas, N. M., & Müller, H. A. (2022). Designing run-time evolution for dependable and resilient cyber-physical systems using digital twins. *Journal of Integrated Design & Process Science, 25*(2), 48–79. DOI: 10.3233/JID210014

Rojek, I., Mikołajewski, D., Dostatni, E., Cybulski, J., & Kozielski, M. (2025). Personalization of ai-based digital twins to optimize adaptation in industrial design and manufacturing. *Applied Sciences (Basel, Switzerland), 15*(15), 8525. DOI: 10.3390/app15158525

Shamsuddoha, M., Zimmerman, H., Nasir, T., & Sakib, M. N. (2026). Autonomous Supply Chains: Integrating Artificial Intelligence, Digital Twins, and Predictive Analytics for Intelligent Decision Systems. *Information (Basel), 17*(4), 371. DOI: 10.3390/info17040371

Splettstößer, A. K., Ellwein, C., & Wortmann, A. (2023). Self-adaptive digital twin reference architecture to improve process quality. *Procedia CIRP, 119*, 867–872. DOI: 10.1016/j.procir.2023.03.131

Uhrmacher, A. M., Wilsdorf, P., & Kreikemeyer, J. N. (2024). Challenges and promises of self-adaptive simulation models. *Simulation, 100*(12), 1281–1295. DOI: 10.1177/00375497241296878

Vimal, S. P., Suryae, R. R., Rajasimhan, R., Periasamy, V. S., Rajagopal, M., & Ganesan, K. (2025, December). Cognitive Digital Twin Architecture Using Reinforcement-Optimized Deep Learning for Self-Adaptive Industrial Process Control. In *2025 First International Conference of Advances in Engineering and Computing Technologies for Sustainable Development (AECTSD)* (pp. 1-8). IEEE.

Walmsley, T. G., Patros, P., Yu, W., Young, B. R., Burroughs, S., Apperley, M., Carson, J. K., Udugama, I. A., Aeowjaroenlap, H., Atkins, M. J., & Walmsley, M. R. (2024). Adaptive digital twins for energy-intensive industries and their local communities. *Digital Chemical Engineering, 10*, 100139. DOI: 10.1016/j.dche.2024.100139

Yitmen, I., Alizadehsalehi, S., Akıner, İ., & Akıner, M. E. (2021). An adapted model of cognitive digital twins for building lifecycle management. *Applied Sciences (Basel, Switzerland), 11*(9), 4276. DOI: 10.3390/app11094276

Yordanova, Z., & Nozari, H. (2026). Enhancing Innovation and Resilience in Entrepreneurial Ecosystems Using Digital Twins and Fuzzy Optimization. *Digital, 6*(1), 25. DOI: 10.3390/digital6010025

Zhang, H., Bai, T., & Shi, L. (2026). A theoretical method to adaptive design of complex engineering systems based on digital twin. *Digital Twin*, *3*(1), 2537841. DOI: 10.1080/27525783.2025.2537841

Zhang, N., Bahsoon, R., & Theodoropoulos, G. (2020, October). Towards engineering cognitive digital twins with self-awareness. In 2020 IEEE international conference on systems, man, and cybernetics (SMC) (pp. 3891-3891). IEEE.

Chapter 3

Digital Twins and the Transformation of Corporate Learning Ecosystems

Fahad A. Salendab
http://orcid.org/0000-0003-4459-443X
Sultan Kudarat State University, Philippines

ABSTRACT

Digital twins are reshaping corporate learning by transforming training from static and episodic instruction into continuous, adaptive, and data-driven learning processes. Through the integration of real-time analytics, simulation, artificial intelligence, and feedback mechanisms, organizations can develop immersive and personalized learning environments aligned with workforce and organizational needs. This chapter examines the conceptual foundations of digital twins in learning, including their relationship with experiential learning, situated learning, and human capital theory, while distinguishing them from conventional simulations and VR/AR technologies. It also explores applications in workforce upskilling, leadership development, competency-based learning, and real-time decision-making. Drawing from recent studies and case-based applications, the chapter highlights how digital twins enhance engagement, knowledge retention, continuous performance feedback, predictive skill development, and scalable workforce training within intelligent corporate learning ecosystems.

DOI: 10.4018/979-8-2600-1674-9.ch003

INTRODUCTION

The emergence of digital twins in corporate learning marks a significant evolution in the way companies think about their workforce development, organizational intelligence, and professional learning initiatives. Born out of engineering and manufacturing industries as dynamic virtual models able to replicate physical entities through real-time data synchronization, digital twins have matured into flexible cyber-physical platforms incorporating simulation, analysis, prediction, and intelligent decision-making capabilities (García et al., 2024). In terms of corporate learning, this transition does not merely amount to an upgrade of existing educational programs. Instead, it reflects a paradigmatic change from isolated and fragmented learning practices to integrated and adaptive learning environments.

Such transformation is especially important in the context of modern organizational environments characterized by the fast development of technologies, workforce dynamics, digital transformation, and an increasing need for continuous learning and relearning. Traditional corporate learning programs often fail to meet the challenges posed by the changing requirements of competencies, as they are based on generalizing information delivery and assessment activities, and lack flexibility. The use of digital twins provides organizations with the opportunity to design intelligent learning ecosystems, where interactions between performance of the workforce, organizational systems, and learning experiences happen continuously in the form of feedback loops, prediction, and simulation (Thajchayapong et al., 2025). The implementation of digital twins together with AI, LMSs, and workforce analytics tools can provide numerous benefits for learners and organizations.

Even though there is increasing academic attention toward the use of digital twins in engineering, industry, medicine, and education, there is currently a fragmentation of knowledge in the field. The majority of research focuses on the technical aspects of building digital twins, the design of simulations, or their application in isolated cases of employee training, while little attention is devoted to how digital twins operate as socio-technical systems that can facilitate organizational learning and workforce development. Currently, research concerning experiential learning, situated learning, workforce analytics, and human capital development tends to be approached independently rather than as interconnected aspects of a digital learning platform.

This chapter highlights the lack of critical reflection on ethical and organizational dimensions associated with the application of digital twins. While digital twins are heralded for enhancing efficiency, customization, and prediction-based workforce development, their capability for real-time behavioral observation and algorithmic analytics poses questions about organizational surveillance, worker autonomy, privacy, data rights, and the metrication of human potential. Given the abundance of data in corporate contexts, constant behavioral, cognitive, and performance tracking invites interrogation of the ways in which learning is monitored, regulated, and potentially controlled.

The chapter examines digital twins as socio-technical systems that transform corporate learning through real-time coordination, dynamic analytics, predictive workforce development, and immersive experiential learning. The objectives of this chapter are to: (1) explain the conceptual bases of digital twins in organizational learning; (2) differentiate digital twins from simulation tools and virtual/augmented reality technologies; (3) review digital twin applications, strengths, and limitations in predicting workforce development; (4) discuss the ethical, governance, and surveillance implications of data-driven corporate learning; and (5) offer an integrated model for digital twin corporate learning ecosystems. Through an approach that considers theory, technology, organization, and ethics, the chapter discusses digital twins as emergent infrastructures, not mere simulation techniques, that redefine the way knowledge is constructed, skills developed, intelligence managed, and learning governed by organizations.

CONCEPTUAL FOUNDATIONS OF DIGITAL TWINS IN LEARNING

Learning in the context of digital twins originates from engineering applications and refers to a live simulation and virtualization of actual physical systems. However, what differentiates digital twins in learning from conventional learning simulations is that digital twins incorporate continuous interaction in terms of real-time feedback, which leads to predictions and improvements of the learning system. Thus, according to García et al. (2024), digital twins are a decision infrastructure in terms of Industry 4.0, where simulation, data analysis, and control are integrated into one cyber-physical system. This is important since it sheds light on the reasons why the digital twins concept is applicable in education.

When applied to education, digital twins are not only an innovative technical instrument but a tool of fundamental change in terms of learning, transforming the process into a data-rich and continuously adaptive activity. As noted by Zhang et al. (2024), digital twins result in the development of highly interactive and high-fidelity educational systems that minimize the distance between theoretical models and reality thanks to real-time interaction and feedback. When applied to learning factories and engineering education, digital twins merge physical, software, and data-related aspects of the process into one system-oriented environment supporting both education and research processes (Lutters & Damgrave, 2023).

Digital twin technology being applied to modeling learners represents an even deeper epistemological turn. According to Pathak & Upadhyay (2024), digital twins can not only model environments but individuals as well, following their behaviors, skill sets, and learning paths by continuous monitoring. Personalization and adaptive feedback become possible, although there is a danger of algorithmic reductionism and making the learning process dependent upon the measurable indicators. As Ezeoguine, P. E., & Kasumu (2024) point out, benefits include high levels of engagement and immersion, as well as data validation and interpretation issues.

Overall, the use of digital twins in education requires one to consider how learning is defined, quantified, and employed within the framework of such an innovative approach. Thus, the trend described above cannot be regarded merely as a technical development in pedagogy. On the contrary, it represents a deeper shift towards the datafication of educational processes and integration of cyberspace and physical reality in the learning environment. In particular, the key question is no longer whether digital twins improve outcomes but how they affect epistemic authority and distribution of human versus machine agency.

INTEGRATED CONCEPTUAL FRAMEWORK

With the aim of bridging the missing link for a cohesive model, Chapter 4 presents an integrative approach to understanding digital twins, viewing them as multi-layer socio-technical infrastructures within organizational learning ecosystems. Digital twins are more than tools, but represent systemic technologies that connect information technology infrastructure with theories of learning and organizational intelligence.

Digital twins depend on a technological framework in which the physical objects, virtual representations, and real-time data merge together to form a cyber-physical framework. The physical component includes people, workflows, and processes, all of which produce real-time data to support dynamic virtual representations. In addition to replicating physical realities, digital twins provide simulation, prediction, and adaptation capabilities. Continuous integration of real-time data results in a feedback loop where the virtual representations are recalibrated continuously to monitor, predict, and assist in making decisions.

In addition to technology, digital twins rely on a learning theoretical component, which is a combination of experiential learning, situated cognition, and human capital development. Experiential learning applies cycles of action, feedback, and reflection within the context of realistic and simulated experiences to generate results. Situated learning constructs knowledge from authentic activities in order to create the context within which learners can develop competencies. Human capital learning provides an added value from a strategic perspective of aligning skills, performance, and productivity within an organization.

The digital twins are placed in relation to other systems that constitute organizational intelligence. According to this dimension of the conceptual framework, learning is not seen as an isolated activity but as part of an ongoing and data-based process of organizational strategy and decision making. The ability of digital twins to facilitate this process relies on their ability to integrate learning analytics, artificial intelligence, and workforce planning systems to create a coherent system infrastructure capable of producing foresight and enabling action. With the help of performance measurement and data analytics, the organization will be able to detect skill deficiencies, predict future skills needs, and optimize training programs accordingly. However, this ability is also associated with a number of governance, ethical, and data stewardship concerns.

These concepts illustrate that digital twins function within an adaptive learning ecosystem wherein technology, human learning activities, and organizational actions are constantly interconnected. The core assumption of this theoretical framework is that learning, performance, and organizational intelligence are no longer separate concepts because they are evolving together via the constant flow of data, feedback loops, and predictive analytics. Therefore, digital twins change the traditional approach to corporate learning, whereby learning is treated as a set of interventions, to an ever-evolving, integrated process embedded in the organization. This theoretical framework serves as the conceptual basis for further analysis in the chapter.

Key Components of Digital Twins in Learning

1. Physical Entity – It is the actual object represented—an individual learner, a classroom, or more complicated learners' objects of study. Unlike a straightforward starting point for digital twins, the physical entity becomes an epistemic agent influencing the validation, accuracy, and pedagogical utility of the entire modeling procedure. The physical entity not only preconditions the creation of the digital representation but also constantly influences the development of digital twins, their interpretation, and further refinement. According to Liu et al. (2023), the physical entity can be considered the key source of operational truth, providing streaming data necessary to adjust the twin and align its functioning with actuality. As a result, the physical entity becomes a sort of dynamic epistemic controller, which means that any loss of data integrity will negatively affect the predictive and analytical capabilities of the twin. Further, as Wu et al. (2023) state, the success of digital twins is due to mutual interactivity and the fact that the digital twin's output is influenced by the physical entity rather

than copying it. When speaking about education, the physical entity in this case is the evolving system that produces the digital twin's intelligence.

2. Virtual Model – This construct denotes a computational replica whose purpose is to duplicate the state, functioning, and changing characteristics of a particular physical object. Contrary to traditional digital replicas, the virtual model adapts dynamically and becomes an ever-changing computational replica that mirrors the changes in the real world. However, the recent literature challenges the notion that the virtual model serves merely as a "mirror" because the virtual model actually transforms the collected data into a predictive and exploratory simulation space. As such, the virtual model can be viewed as a constantly running engine of simulation in which not only do the system states become duplicated, but the future states are predicted. Specifically, as shown by Zhang et al. (2026), digital twin virtual models develop with regard to deep learning capabilities and data streams, with simulation parameters being updated continuously so that prediction errors are minimized; hence, the model itself evolves. Consequently, one should view the virtual model from an epistemological perspective and understand that the virtual model does not represent reality statically but continually learns about it through the analysis of collected data. Additionally, Tao et al. (2022) consider digital twin modeling as a way to ensure the creation of a "faithful yet evolving portrayal" of the physical object since, by design, virtual models are supposed to contribute to the monitoring, predicting, and optimizing system functioning on all levels of its complexity. From the perspective of education, the virtual model can be considered a cognitive and pedagogical simulator that provides an opportunity for scenario testing and exploratory learning.
3. Real – Time Data Integration – It is an intermediary that links the physical and virtual worlds in digital twin architecture. However, Real-Time Data Integration is transitioning from a mere data integration tool to an engine for real-time continuous data fusion and interpretation, ensuring the ongoing intelligence of the system. Through continuous data flows coming from various sensors, LMS, and other sources, including user interactions, the system constantly re-tunes the virtual model to match the current status of the physical world. It creates a continuous coordination mechanism that transforms heterogeneous data from different places into meaningful information for use. According to Li et al. (2025), multi-source real-time data fusion improves predictive ability and reaction speed. Hence, Real-Time Data Integration is an epistemological activity that affects how accurately the system can make predictions about the real world. Yang et al. (2024) highlight the significance of IoT-supported real-time data integration for adapting decision-making through up-to-date models. Also, Jeddoub et al. (2025) emphasize the importance of interoperability and

comprehensive life cycle data integration. For educational contexts, Real-Time Data Integration provides a cognitive foundation for learning analytics.

Digital Twins' Conceptual Grounding

1. Experiential Learning Theory – It is defined as a four-stage process of experiencing, observing, conceptualizing, and experimenting. Contemporary research goes further to include such technologies as digital twins that transform experiential learning in terms of immersion through interaction with complex simulation models. Such models enable the transition from theoretical concepts to experience-based reflection, decision-making, and system-level observations. According to Speicher et al. (2025), using digital twins within engineering internships allows applying simulated models of manufacturing processes to enhance students' problem-solving skills and improve their understanding of complex systems. It can be assumed that experiential learning is not only possible outside of fieldwork but can also be expanded to a cyber-physical environment. Moreover, Pandey et al. (2025) state that such technology makes it possible for individuals to experience realistic and interactive learning situations with data-driven feedback on actions taken and results obtained.
2. Situated Learning Theory – It complements this paradigm by suggesting that learning is context-driven, emerging as a result of participating in authentic experiences rather than abstract teaching methods. According to this theory, knowledge is built via engagement in real-life or life-like social and material settings where meaning arises from experience, not abstraction (Lave & Wenger, 1991). Modern studies take this idea a step further by highlighting the inherent relationship between cognition and context, thus stating that the process of learning needs a context that reflects the complexity of real-life circumstances. These claims are supported empirically, showing that both immersive and virtual settings, including digital twins, VR, and simulation-based approaches, aid situated cognition by immersing participants in realistic environments that facilitate active interaction and problem-solving. As stated by Wang et al. (2025), immersive virtual environments facilitate situated learning by enabling students to complete authentic tasks that require applying learned information within realistic conditions, rather than being provided in abstract ways. Likewise, Agbo et al. (2023) show how immersive technologies, including VR and digital simulations, aid situated learning by allowing participants to interact with dynamic environments that mimic real-life systems.
3. Human Capital Theory – In the context of education and workforce development, it presents an economic approach to exploring the contribution of digital twins to education and workforce development efforts aimed at improving the quality

of skills and competencies for boosting productivity. As shown by Javed et al. (2026), human capital contributes to better productivity results, and the effect becomes even stronger when complemented with digital capabilities. Namely, digitalization increases efficiency in knowledge use and performance optimization because digital systems provide the possibility of assessing knowledge use and optimizing performance continuously. This conclusion can be connected with the concept of digital twins because these tools create conditions for continuous performance assessment and skill improvement. Likewise, according to Trevisan et al. (2025), digital technologies used in the context of educational and workforce-related systems make it possible to ensure continuous skills development and their adaptation to changing labor market needs. In particular, simulation and digitalization contribute to the development of technical and adaptive skills in an environment characterized by performance tracking and feedback.

Distinction between Simulations, VR/AR, and Digital Twins

It is critical to differentiate digital twins from simulation models and VR/AR technologies based on their functionality and epistemology because these approaches vary in terms of knowledge creation and modification concerning the actual environment. While simulations have found widespread applications in modeling numerous phenomena, modern studies highlight that these systems remain closed and hypothesis-based and are confined to certain boundary conditions. As a result, simulation results are limited by pre-established variables and do not change when responding to dynamic changes in the surrounding world. Simulations, therefore, represent an approximation rather than an evolution of reality. On the other hand, digital twins are an advanced epistemological approach because they provide an opportunity for a continuous two-way data flow between a real entity and its virtual counterpart and allow the system to evolve as a response to the external environment. The approach transforms traditional modeling into a dynamic and self-evolving procedure, which increases its predictive capacity and responsiveness to changing circumstances (Yao et al., 2023).

Concurrently, the utilization of VR and AR technologies, despite their effectiveness as means of immersive visualization and experiential interaction, faces certain theoretical challenges if analyzed from the standpoint of systems integration. The primary significance of VR/AR is that they serve as an augmentation of human perception and interaction capabilities within a simulated or augmented environment, and not as a means of persistent connection to the data collected through the operation of actual systems. This is crucial since, at present, the focus on VR/AR is more related to experience augmentation than decision support systems. However, according to Roullier et al. (2024), the purpose and the role of VR/AR technologies are radically transformed if incorporated into digital twin frameworks.

At a wider view, digital twins excel beyond simulations and VR/AR through their ability to incorporate real-time data from sensors, AI, and feedback mechanisms to create a cohesive adaptive system. The incorporation here does not only pertain to technology, but rather it involves a concept that transforms digital systems into participants rather than representations of reality. Thus, digital twins act as extensions of physical systems, allowing for more than just representation, but rather allowing for visualization, analysis, prediction, intervention, and decision making (Pitzalis et al., 2025). This becomes particularly crucial in complicated systems where modeling fails to provide sufficient information.

Table 1. Distinction between Simulations, VR/AR, and Digital Twins

Feature	Simulation	VR/AR	Digital Twins
Data Source	Predefined	Predefined + sensory	Real-time data
Synchronization	None	Limited	Continuous
Feedback	One-way	Interactive	Bidirectional
System Type	Static	Experiential	Adaptive
Decision Support	Predictive	Experiential	Predictive + Prescriptive

Source: Developed by the author

This table indicates that digital twins differ fundamentally in that they do not merely simulate or visualize reality but continuously co-evolve with it through real-time data integration.

DIGITAL TWINS IN CORPORATE LEARNING ECOSYSTEMS

Extending from the suggested conceptual framework, digital twins may be regarded as holistic systems that integrate technology-based systems, learning activities, and organizational intelligence into comprehensive corporate learning ecosystems.

In their turn, digital twins are transforming corporate learning ecosystems by providing organizations with opportunities to integrate workforce training, business systems, and intelligent analytics within the digital environment. Digital twins are used within companies as ever-evolving virtual models of employees, work-related activities, skills, and organizational processes based on data exchange. Instead of treating workforce training as an isolated learning process, digital twin-based learning ecosystems create conditions where the work process and learning activities continuously interact within the context of digital systems. According to García et al. (2024), such ecosystems contribute to shifting towards intelligent organizational learning where human expertise and artificial intelligence work together to create knowledge and innovate.

One such notable innovation in this context is the incorporation of digital twins into Learning Management Systems (LMS) and Human Resources (HR). Modern companies require interconnected digital frameworks that can link training records, competencies, performance evaluations, and analytics for their workforces in a unified environment. According to Thajchayapong et al. (2025), integrated learning systems improve organizational responsiveness by fostering seamless collaboration between learning portals, analytics tools, and organizational databases.

Digital twins' integration with LMS and HR systems illustrates a wider transformation from static training programs to dynamic competency systems. Corporate learning frameworks often feature generic training courses that fail to reflect the changing dynamics of modern workplaces. Digital twins constantly monitor employee behavior, system interaction, and competency acquisition, allowing corporations to establish immediate feedback loops between their performance and learning interventions. Consequently, companies can identify skill shortages, adjust training programs, and adopt talent development initiatives based on data-driven approaches instead of mere assessments.

Digital twins play an important part in the process of designing personalized and adaptive learning pathways. According to Adhya & Panda (2026), intelligent personalization techniques have the potential to significantly increase the engagement and relevance of training as well as the ability of learners to regulate their own learning through personalized learning trajectories and automated feedback systems. Digital twins make such individualization possible within corporate learning frameworks through constantly updated profiles of each employee that include information about the employee's competencies, behavior at work, learning history, and career goals. Therefore, training will be able to adapt specifically to individual needs instead of providing standardized instruction.

Another aspect of using digital twins is that such technologies allow for the prediction of skills and competencies needed in the future. According to Nayak et al. (2025), digital twins have the ability to diagnose the gap in competency levels that might negatively affect the operations of the company and predict the future needs of the organization to ensure its success in the coming period. Hence, digital twins revolutionize the approach to corporate learning as it becomes not just a reaction but a proactive effort aimed at fostering future competencies.

One of the notable characteristics of digital twin ecosystems is their ability to allow for data-driven learning analytics and performance management. By continuously monitoring metrics such as employee engagement, assessment results, productivity in the work environment, and behavior patterns, organizations are able to gain insights regarding the impact of training programs and their professional development outcomes. According to Ifenthaler et al. (2021), data ecosystems allow companies to significantly improve decision-making based on evidence by allowing them to evaluate the efficacy of their training programs, predict learners' progress, and refine their instructional strategies.

Nevertheless, the increasing use of analytics algorithms poses significant challenges from both an educational and ethical perspective. As noted by Khalifeh et al. (2026), excessive automation can turn professional development into purely quantitative measures of performance while ignoring aspects like emotional intelligence, creative thinking, collaborative skills, and contextual aspects of human learning. Hence, while digital twins could be used to increase efficiency and personalize learning, companies should consider how they will strike a balance between automation and human-led learning strategies.

Digital twins complement competency-based educational approaches and micro-credentialing systems, which are gaining momentum in modern practices of developing corporate workforces. By being focused on competencies rather than qualifications, organizations can take advantage of using digital twins as a way of documenting, verifying, and adjusting employees' competencies amid changing business environments. As stated by Kabashkin (2025), intelligent learner models could help evaluate workforce competencies against industry standards and suggest suitable training courses to assist employees in developing professionally. Thus, competence-based learning becomes more effective through measuring employees' achievements and competencies.

Another trend that makes digital twins highly relevant in the context of corporate learning is micro-credentialing. According to Strielkowski (2025), modular certifications and stacking credentials play an essential role in facilitating lifelong learning and adaptation capabilities of modern employees in digital economies. The use of digital twins helps achieve this purpose through keeping continuously updated profiles of employees' competencies that provide data about learning outcomes and their application at work. In other words, digital twins allow embedding micro-credentials into workforce intelligence systems.

APPLICATIONS AND STRATEGIC BENEFITS OF DIGITAL TWINS

Key Benefits

Digital twins are becoming ever more recognized as disruptive infrastructures within corporate learning ecosystems, where their role is not only about serving as high-end simulations, but rather creating new, data-driven environments through which learning and performing are being shaped. The potential of digital twins includes everything from technical training, development of leaders, and making decisions in real-time. Digital twins thus represent a fundamental change in how organizations approach workforce development through moving from one-off training sessions to more adaptive and integrated learning activities. This is made possible due to the implementation of cyborg learning environments and human-machine learning systems (García et al., 2024).

The other contribution is in the form of increased learner engagement and knowledge retention. Unlike the passive mode of knowledge transfer used in traditional instructional techniques, digital twin technology creates environments in which learning is active because learners engage in interactive systems in which decisions and feedback are intertwined at all times. Such learning scenarios require cognitive engagement as they challenge learners to analyze data, test theories, and modify actions in light of the feedback received. As studies have shown, digital twin-enabled environments increase behavioral, cognitive, and emotional engagement since the learner is forced to interact directly with the dynamic systems rather than passively consume content (Lu & Hu, 2025). Moreover, such an iterative process helps enhance knowledge retention since each cycle of activity and receiving feedback helps consolidate the acquired knowledge. Thus, the benefits of digital twin technology for learning include increased engagement and knowledge retention due to an iterative process involving testing theories and modifying actions based on feedback (Speicher et al., 2025).

In addition to improving engagement, digital twins support workforce development through predicting skill gaps among employees. Since these tools allow continuous observation of the behavior, competency levels, and performance, it is possible to identify emerging skill gaps before they impact work quality. Hence, organizations would be able to create learning programs based on predictive analytics and prepare learners for future scenarios as opposed to creating solutions to current problems. The research on AI-driven digital twins confirms the possibility of developing adaptive training modules and identifying potential skill gaps in advance (Nayak et al., 2025). As a result, workforce development becomes a strategy-driven organizational function that allows anticipating changes and preparing for the future in advance.

There is evidence that digital twins promote significant savings in cost and mitigate risks in the training of organizational personnel. With the help of the development of precise virtual systems based on the modeling of operational processes, firms will have an opportunity to train their staff in executing difficult operations without spending any physical resources and avoiding any dangers in the process. According to the empirical findings on the use of digital twins for training purposes, the introduction of such systems is associated with considerable savings in cost and disruption, as well as improved learning results due to the practice of simulations (Cremonini et al., 2025). Additionally, digital twins may serve as predictive operational systems, allowing testing any decision in a virtual space before putting it into operation and thus ensuring the reduction of risks (Karunaratne et al., 2025).

The other major benefit of digital twins is that they provide scalable training of the workforce irrespective of geographic locations. Unlike training programs that have to take place within physical training facilities, digital twins are not bound by these constraints and can be used to standardize and streamline learning experiences across employees in different locations and time zones. In addition, the use of real-time data makes sure that the process of training adapts to changes and that learners are interacting with dynamically updated models of organizational processes. According to current research, digital twins allow the creation of learning ecosystems wherein workers, systems, and processes can converge and enable two-way information exchange between human and technical elements (García et al., 2024).

Limitations and Implementation Challenges

There are certain difficulties associated with applying the digital twin concept to the learning environment of organizations. First, the development of digital twins is expensive because it includes not only the implementation but also the maintenance of technology that allows collecting, processing, and using big data for analysis, simulation, etc. Also, as mentioned earlier, the technical difficulties related to the use of digital twins include the lack of compatibility among learning management systems, HR platforms, data sources, etc. According to the results of reviews dedicated to digital twin applications in organizations, scalability and system integration represent barriers even in situations where the level of available resources is low (Karanam & Hartman, 2025).

Organizational issues are also relevant to discussing the challenges in implementing digital twins in practice. The introduction of such technology may cause dissatisfaction with the system among employees because their activities would be constantly monitored, and the results obtained could be misused. At the same time, the requirement to have continuous data collection increases the risk of compromising the confidentiality and security of information used to describe employee performance and behavior. Some studies dedicated to personalized learning based on artificial intelligence technologies indicate that such an approach may lead to reducing the learning process to quantitative measures and ignoring other aspects of learning, such as creativity and collaboration (Khalifeh et al., 2026).

Another important limitation refers to the problem associated with the assessment of learning effectiveness in digital twin learning environments. Since learning takes place in complex and dynamic systems, the separation between the effects of particular training activities and the overall performance of the participants is difficult to achieve. This makes existing approaches to assessment ineffective and requires the design of innovative frameworks for assessing learning processes in dynamic contexts. In addition, the emphasis on data-driven analytics might cause an overemphasis on performance metrics that ignore the important qualitative factors of professional development.

The above discussion shows that despite all the advantages of digital twins, their use faces certain limitations, which must be addressed if digital twins are to become effective instruments for learning improvement. In this regard, it is important to recognize that digital twins cannot be considered mere technologies since they comprise more than that.

Case-Based Applications of Digital Twins in Workforce Development

As for the application of DT technology to industrial equipment, there is a case study by Pitzalis et al. (2025), namely, the "Application of Augmented Reality-Based Digital Twin Approaches: A Case Study to Industrial Equipment." This case study offers an essential basis for understanding the way digital twins work, as they represent an integrated system that functions in real time. Using DT and AR in combination, it becomes possible not only to produce dynamic copies of machinery used in a certain factory but also to make use of them for educational purposes. The possibility of detecting a gearbox problem with the help of both virtual and real-time data shows how valuable the idea of digital twin is in terms of predictive maintenance, educational benefits, and decision-making. Finally, the main idea of digital twins lies in their capability of becoming something more than just dynamic copies; they have to be data-driven systems.

Expanding further on this systems-level approach, Lin et al. (2025) apply digital twins not just for industrial equipment, but for learner-centric environments in "Personalized Education with Generative AI and Digital Twins: VR, RAG, and Zero-Shot Sentiment Analysis for Industry 4.0 Workforce Development." While the first example focuses more on optimizing the system and training, the second focuses on personalized learning and adaptive learning. Utilizing the Generative AI-based Personalized Tutor (gAI-PT4I4), digital twins are not just limited to the modeling of systems but are used for dynamic representation and responses based on each individual's behaviors and performances, and their emotional state. The combination of virtual reality, artificial intelligence, and sentiment analysis shows how digital twin ecosystems can aid in instructional adaptation through increased task accuracy and reduced completion times, as well as improved engagement. This is an important development as it goes from a systems-level simulation to a learner-focused approach that shows that the digital twins are not only systems for simulations but infrastructures for personalized learning.

Building upon the previous trend, Karanam & Hartman (2025) have produced an article titled A Systematic Review of Digital Twin (DT) and Virtual Learning Environments (VLE) for Smart Manufacturing Education. It is essentially a comprehensive synthesis of various case studies and places the digital twin model within the wider pedagogical context of innovative learning infrastructure. In contrast to the former case studies that focus specifically on the use of digital twins in industrial maintenance and individualized training, this study attempts to analyze how DT-VLE integration contributes to a higher level of problem-solving skills, enhanced information retention capabilities, and increased self-assurance among learners. On the other hand, it also provides an important critique by identifying some persistent obstacles to implementing digital twins, including scalability issues, complicated technological processes, and economic considerations.

Table 2. Case-Based Applications: A Comparative Analysis

Level of Application	Study	Primary Focus	Key Findings	Design Implications for Corporate Learning Ecosystems
Operational Level	Pitzalis et al. (2025)	Industrial systems and equipment maintenance	Demonstrates how digital twins integrated with augmented reality enable real-time monitoring, predictive maintenance, and interactive training through synchronization of physical and virtual systems	Corporate learning systems should integrate real-time operational data into training environments to align learning with actual system performance and decision-making processes
Individual Level	Lin et al. (2025)	Personalized and adaptive learning environments	Shows that digital twins combined with AI, VR, and sentiment analysis can dynamically adapt instruction based on learner performance, behavior, and emotional states, improving engagement and task efficiency	Organizations should design digital twin systems that model individual learners, enabling personalized learning pathways and adaptive skill development aligned with employee needs
Systemic Level	Karanam & Hartman (2025)	Digital twin–enabled educational ecosystems	Synthesizes evidence showing that digital twin–based virtual learning environments enhance problem-solving, knowledge retention, and learner confidence, while highlighting challenges related to scalability, cost, and technical complexity	Successful implementation requires aligning technological infrastructure, pedagogy, and organizational strategy, with particular attention to scalability and system integration

This table clearly shows that digital twins evolve through three related layers of implementation. At the operational layer, digital twins act primarily as tools for optimizing systems and integrating training by synchronizing data in real time. At the individual layer, digital twins transform into adaptive learning systems that capture and react to individual behaviors and performance. At the systemic layer, digital twins become integrated systems that combine learning, technology, and organizational operations into cohesive ecosystems. This evolution suggests that the true value of digital twins is not in specific implementations but rather in their ability to link operational systems, individual learning, and institutional strategies into a coherent learning infrastructure.

FUTURE DIRECTIONS AND RESEARCH AGENDA

The adoption of digital twins in corporate learning means much more than technological evolution; it represents a paradigm shift in the way learning, performance, and organizational intelligence are created and practiced. Leveraging the main argument of the chapter, namely that digital twins are adaptive, data-intensive, cyber-physical learning infrastructures, future research should focus not on proving the concept but rather on developing a theoretically sound and evidence-based body of knowledge that promotes the widespread application of digital twins.

One of the important directions for future research will be the elaboration of an integrated theoretical framework that strikes a balance between optimizing digital twin operation with respect to data analysis and fostering human-centered learning experiences. Even though research indicates increased motivation, personalization, and skill prediction as some of the positive effects of using digital twins, their impact on epistemic authority, learner autonomy, and knowledge creation remains underexplored.

Multi-level and longitudinal studies should be conducted to investigate the sustainable effects of digital twin ecosystems on workforce development. The current literature mainly employs experimental designs or controlled trials, and thus, sustainability, generalizability, and scalability cannot be guaranteed. Future studies should focus on how digital twins could change the development of skills and teamwork, learning culture, and organizational adaptability through providing continuous feedback and predictive information to decision-making processes and career planning.

With increasing integration among digital twins, learning management systems, and human resources systems, future researchers should pay more attention to interoperability and architectural design of such a system. Future work should not only demonstrate that a coherent architecture is possible but also prove that heterogeneity of systems does not mean that interoperability will suffer at the cost of data consistency and timely feedback.

Not any less important is the need to explore the ethics, governance, and data stewardship of digital twins. The ability of digital twins to depend on ongoing data collection and behavioral analytics raises ethical concerns, such as privacy invasion, surveillance, algorithmic bias, and dehumanization by reducing all aspects of humanness to metrics. It is necessary to conduct future studies on the governance of digital twins in a way that ensures transparency, accountability, and human oversight while still balancing efficiency.

Another significant topic in this domain involves investigating other dimensions of affective, social, and non-cognitive learning in digital twins. As pointed out by the reviewed articles, today most studies focus on the aspect of technical competence and outcomes while forgetting about emotional intelligence, teamworking abilities, creative thinking, and ethical decision-making. Future research should thus investigate the possibilities of incorporating such dimensions within digital twin designs.

Finally, the issues of equity and accessibility as a result of the implementation of digital twins in business and academic environments must be explored. Since the adoption of digital twins requires extensive financial and technical investments as well as a complex information infrastructure, it can increase the inequalities among companies with varying degrees of digital maturity. In this regard, scholars need to study the most affordable ways for implementing digital twins.

DISCUSSION

This chapter helps to support the proposed framework by demonstrating that digital twins are socio-technological entities at the intersection of technological infrastructure, learning theories, and corporate intelligence. They operate in the realm of constant interactions between real-time data, simulation models, and learning processes. Such a view helps emphasize another key argument proposed in the framework – today, learning in corporations tends to be part of highly interactive and data-driven ecosystems in which learning, performance, and strategy are co-evolving.

From a theoretical standpoint, the findings help demonstrate that digital twins facilitate experiential and situated learning through technology. Learners can experience interaction within a system that simulates real-world conditions and helps learners engage in action, reflection, and adaptation. This is consistent with the idea of building knowledge through engagement proposed within the theory of experiential learning. Realistic situations provide the basis for facilitating situated learning and developing skills within an environment that replicates real-life experiences. Research focused on digital twin-enabled learning demonstrates improvements in engagement, problem-solving, and knowledge retention facilitated by integrating cognitive, behavioral, and contextual dimensions of learning (Speicher et al., 2025; Wang et al., 2025).

Organizational perspective reveals the potential to integrate digital twins, analytics, LMS, and workforce planning in order to merge learning and organizational intelligence. Continuous data collection and real-time monitoring will make it possible to detect skills gaps, predict future needs, and create an adaptive learning process in accordance with corporate strategies. Indeed, research shows that data-driven learning solutions provide more effective decision-making based on evidence and predictions, thus meeting the organizational intelligence component of the model.

However, a significant challenge still exists. As these technologies offer enhanced personalized learning, efficiency, and predictive capabilities, they bring into the learning process a data-driven logic that reduces complex phenomena of learning to measurable data. AI learning models indicate that excessive emphasis on analytics can cause neglect of non-measurable components of learning, such as creativity, ethics, and socialization.

Additionally, embedding continuous monitoring and behavioral analytics poses certain ethical issues related to surveillance, autonomy, and data governance. With digital twins generating substantial amounts of employee behavioral, performance, and decision-making data, they have the potential to be used to monitor employees and control their activities, shifting the focus from developing employees to optimizing performance. According to literature focused on human digital twins and behavioral analytics, proper data governance is essential to avoid misuse and ensure that employee autonomy and privacy are respected (Davila-Gonzalez & Martin, 2024).

In particular, the case-based analysis supports the chosen framework in terms of digital twins being implemented at operational, individual, and systemic levels. From an operational perspective, digital twins increase the efficiency of the systems while supporting technical skills. Individual use of digital twins promotes personalized, adaptive learning depending on behavior. As for the systemic approach, digital twins are perceived as an integral infrastructure that connects all elements into a unified ecosystem. Transformation implies integration of various aspects of learning and organizations.

Such results prove that digital twins represent a paradigm shift within the sphere of organizational learning, shifting from static and content-based training towards dynamic and adaptive learning ecosystems. However, their potential depends not only on the technical capabilities of the organization but also on the proper development, implementation, and management of such learning environments. The theoretical model proposed in this chapter provides an important analytical instrument helping to perceive the ongoing paradigm shift. At the same time, it is necessary to keep a critical perspective on the process.

CONCLUSION

Digital twins represent a revolutionary paradigm within business education that involves a change from merely simulation-based learning towards a more socio-technical integration that transforms learning, performance, and organizational intelligence in a comprehensive manner. The convergence of technology architecture, theory of learning, and organizational systems creates an integrated approach in which learning takes place as an ongoing practice within the organizational operation. Such a perspective captures the way in which digital twins combine situated and experiential learning and human resource development.

They go beyond the limits of traditional learning approaches and introduce real-time feedback, skill development prediction, and integration of learning into performance. Numerous examples demonstrate enhanced levels of engagement, adaptive learning experiences, and decision-making in dynamic situations. Coupled with learning analytics and AI, digital twins empower organizations to foresee skill deficiencies and maximize opportunities for development using continuous data analysis.

As pointed out in the chapter, while digital twins have great transformational potential, the issues surrounding them are not limited to technological solutions. Issues such as real-time data collection, algorithmic decision-making, and privacy and autonomy issues can lead to a reduction of the human component in learning to quantifiable parameters. According to research on the impact of artificial intelligence on learning, analytics-heavy AI systems reduce emphasis on the importance of creativity, ethics, and social interaction during the process.

In order for managers to effectively integrate digital twin systems into organizations, they need to go beyond just investing in technology. Managers need to align the digital twin systems to the organization's learning and business strategies, in addition to being prepared technologically and ethically for such integration. Managers should design the systems with a human-centered approach that allows for autonomous learning, reflection, and the development of a broad range of skills rather than performance measures. Managers should consider starting with small pilots and then scaling up depending on the results obtained.

In the end, the future of digital twins in corporate learning is not only about technology but also about how digital twins will be engineered and incorporated into organizational systems. Although digital twins have numerous possibilities that can make the process of learning more efficient, better performance, and even develop a whole workforce strategically, digital twins still have a potential threat that may lead to learning being transformed into an activity of data collection with the ultimate purpose of optimizing and controlling the work of individuals. The most challenging task in this situation is to find ways of using digital twin technology for learning while staying committed to human-based learning.

In such a way, it might be noted that digital twins should be regarded as infrastructures, shaping the future of organizational learning. Ultimately, digital twins' influence depends on whether they can become a tool for empowering human beings, stimulating critical thinking, and enabling effective engagement in meaningful processes, or remain mechanisms of restricting activities to performance parameters.

REFERENCES

Adhya, D. H., & Panda, S. (2026). An integrative systematic review analysis of research on technology-enabled personalized learning and self-regulated learning. *Smart Learning Environments, 13*(1), 3. DOI: 10.1186/s40561-025-00428-8

Agbo, F. J., Olaleye, S. A., Bower, M., & Oyelere, S. S. (2023). Examining the relationships between students' perceptions of technology, pedagogy, and cognition: The case of immersive virtual reality mini games to foster computational thinking in higher education. *Smart Learning Environments, 10*(1), 16. DOI: 10.1186/s40561-023-00233-1

Cremonini, C. E., Capela, C., da Silva, A., Gaspar, M. C., & Vasco, J. C. (2025). Digital twin integration for workforce training: Transforming SMES in the ornamental stone industry. *Systems, 13*(2), 120. DOI: 10.3390/systems13020120

Davila-Gonzalez, S., & Martin, S. (2024). Human digital twin in industry 5.0: A holistic approach to worker safety and well-being through advanced ai and emotional analytics. *Sensors (Basel), 24*(2), 655. DOI: 10.3390/s24020655

Ezeoguine, P. E., & Kasumu, R. Y. (2024). Undergraduate students' perception of digital twins technology in education: Uses and challenges. *Int. J. Educ. Eval, 10*(2), 381–396. DOI: 10.56201/ijee.v10.no2.2024.pg381.396

García, Á., Bregon, A., & Martínez-Prieto, M. A. (2024). Digital twin learning ecosystem: A cyber–physical framework to integrate human-machine knowledge in traditional manufacturing. *Internet of Things : Engineering Cyber Physical Human Systems, 25*, 101094. DOI: 10.1016/j.iot.2024.101094

Ifenthaler, D., Hofhues, S., Egloffstein, M., & Helbig, C. (2021). *Digital transformation of learning organizations*. Springer Cham., DOI: 10.1007/978-3-030-55878-9

Javed, A., Ashraf, J., & Yong, L. (2026). Synergistic effects of digital capability and human capital development on the twin green and digital transition: Evidence from carbon emissions and renewable energy adoption. *Journal of Environmental Management, 397*, 128313. DOI: 10.1016/j.jenvman.2025.128313

Jeddoub, I., Nys, G. A., Hajji, R., & Billen, R. (2025). Data integration across urban digital twin lifecycle: A comprehensive review of current initiatives. *Annals of GIS, 31*(3), 367–386. DOI: 10.1080/19475683.2024.2416135

Kabashkin, I. (2025). AI-based digital twins of students: A new paradigm for competency-oriented learning transformation. *Information (Basel), 16*(10), 846. DOI: 10.3390/info16100846

Karanam, S. A. K., & Hartman, N. W. (2025). A systematic review of digital twin (DT) and virtual learning environments (VLE) for smart manufacturing education. *Manufacturing Letters*, *44*, 1597–1608. DOI: 10.1016/j.mfglet.2025.06.179

Karunaratne, T., Ajiero, I. R., Joseph, R., Farr, E., & Piroozfar, P. (2025). Evaluating the economic impact of digital twinning in the AEC industry: A systematic review. *Buildings (Basel, Switzerland)*, *15*(14), 2583. DOI: 10.3390/buildings15142583

Khalifeh, F., Santiago, R., & Palau, R. (2026). Redefining personalized learning in the artificial intelligence era: An updated systematic review from 2019 to 2025. *Smart Learning Environments*, *13*(1), 19. DOI: 10.1186/s40561-026-00440-6

Lave, J., & Wenger, E. (1991). *Situated learning: Legitimate peripheral participation*. Cambridge university press. Retrieved from: https://bibliotecadigital.mineduc.cl/bitstream/handle/20.500.12365/17387/cb419d882cd5%20bb5286069675b449da38.pdf?sequence=1&isAllowed=y

Li, Y., Chen, S., Hwang, K., Ji, X., Lei, Z., Zhu, Y., Ye, F., & Liu, M. (2025). Spatio-temporal data fusion techniques for modeling digital twin City. *Geo-Spatial Information Science*, *28*(2), 541–564. DOI: 10.1080/10095020.2024.2350175

Lin, Y. Z., Petal, K., Alhamadah, A. H., Ghimire, S., Redondo, M. W., Corona, D. R. V., . . . Satam, P. (2025). Personalized education with generative ai and digital twins: Vr, rag, and zero-shot sentiment analysis for industry 4.0 workforce development. *arXiv preprint arXiv:2502.14080.* https://doi.org//arXiv.2502.14080DOI: 10.18260/1-2--57038

Liu, X., Jiang, D., Tao, B., Xiang, F., Jiang, G., Sun, Y., Kong, J., & Li, G. (2023). A systematic review of digital twin about physical entities, virtual models, twin data, and applications. *Advanced Engineering Informatics*, *55*, 101876. DOI: 10.1016/j.aei.2023.101876

Lu, M., & Hu, Z. (2025). Digital twin-enhanced programming education: An empirical study on learning engagement and skill acquisition. *Computers*, *14*(8), 322. DOI: 10.3390/computers14080322

Lutters, E., & Damgrave, R. (2023). Digital twinning as the basis for integration of education and research in a learning factory. *Procedia CIRP*, *120*, 1463–1468. DOI: 10.1016/j.procir.2023.09.194

Nayak, M. M., Neupane, P., Pahurkar, P. P., & Shrimal, D. (2025). An AI-driven adaptive training platform with digital twin-based skill gap analysis and future readiness insights. *Journal of Collective Sciences and Sustainability*, *1*(2). Advance online publication. DOI: 10.64189/css.25410

Pandey, P. K., Mahajan, S., Pandey, P. K., Paul, J., & Iyer, S. (2025). Immersive learning trends using digital twins. *Digital Twins for Smart Cities and Villages*, 249-271. https://doi.org/DOI: 10.1016/B978-0-443-28884-5.00012-9

Pathak, R. K., & Upadhyay, P.Dr Rakesh Kumar PathakDr Prakash Upadhyay. (2024). Integration of digital twins technologies in education for experiential learning: Benefits and challenges. [IRJAEH]. *International Research Journal on Advanced Engineering Hub*, *2*(03), 442–449. DOI: 10.47392/IRJAEH.2024.0064

Pitzalis, R. F., Giordano, A., Di Spigno, A., Cowell, A., Niculita, O., & Berselli, G. (2025). Application of augmented reality-based digital twin approaches: A case study to industrial equipment. *International Journal of Advanced Manufacturing Technology*, *138*(7), 3747–3763. DOI: 10.1007/s00170-025-15755-w

Roullier, B., McQuade, F., Anjum, A., Bower, C., & Liu, L. (2024). Automated visual quality assessment for virtual and augmented reality based digital twins. *Journal of Cloud Computing (Heidelberg, Germany)*, *13*(1), 51. DOI: 10.1186/s13677-024-00616-w

Speicher, T., DeFranco, J., Stricker, C., Kumara, S., & Bilén, S. (2025). Digital twin technology for engineering education: An experiential learning case study. *Industry and Higher Education*. Advance online publication. DOI: 10.1177/09504222261443589

Strielkowski, W. (2025). The role of micro-credentials in the future digitalized AI-driven education. *arXiv preprint arXiv:2511.07583*. https://doi.org//arXiv.2511.07583DOI: 10.48550

Tao, F., Xiao, B., Qi, Q., Cheng, J., & Ji, P. (2022). Digital twin modeling. *Journal of Manufacturing Systems*, *64*, 372–389. DOI: 10.1016/j.jmsy.2022.06.015

Thajchayapong, P., Carbonaro, S., Couper, T., Helmick, B., Rugaber, S., & Goel, A. (2025). Evolution of A4L: A data architecture for AI-augmented learning. *arXiv preprint arXiv:2511.11877*. https://doi.org//arXiv.2511.11877DOI: 10.48550

Trevisan, A. H., Dukovska-Popovska, I., Acerbi, F., Terzi, S., & Sassanelli, C. (2025). Teaching methods for building human capital for the twin transition: A skill-based approach. *Technology in Society*, *103172*. Advance online publication. DOI: 10.1016/j.techsoc.2025.103172

Wang, M., Dede, C., Grotzer, T. A., & Chen, J. (2025). Understanding and managing the complexities in situated learning in immersive virtual environments. *Educational Technology Research and Development*, *73*(5), 3177–3200. DOI: 10.1007/s11423-025-10519-5

Wu, H., Ji, P., Ma, H., & Xing, L. (2023). A comprehensive review of digital twin from the perspective of total process: Data, models, networks and applications. *Sensors (Basel), 23*(19), 8306. DOI: 10.3390/s23198306

Yang, X., Yu, S., Wang, J., Chen, H., Huang, Y., Luo, Z., & Fu, L. (2024). Application of a digital twin for highway tunnels based on multi-sensor and information fusion. *Frontiers in Physics (Lausanne), 12*, 1335494. DOI: 10.3389/fphy.2024.1335494

Yao, J. F., Yang, Y., Wang, X. C., & Zhang, X. P. (2023). Systematic review of digital twin technology and applications. *Visual Computing for Industry, Biomedicine, and Art, 6*(1), 10. DOI: 10.1186/s42492-023-00137-4

Zhang, J., Zhu, J., Tu, W., Wang, M., Yang, Y., Qian, F., & Xu, Y. (2024). The effectiveness of a digital twin learning system in assisting engineering education courses: A case of landscape architecture. *Applied Sciences (Basel, Switzerland), 14*(15), 6484. DOI: 10.3390/app14156484

Zhang, L., Guo, Y., Wang, S., Zheng, G., Qian, W., Huang, S., & Fang, W. (2026). A modeling and adaptive evolution method for simulation parameters of digital twin shop floor. *Robotics and Computer-integrated Manufacturing, 97*, 103090. DOI: 10.1016/j.rcim.2025.103090

Chapter 4
Digital Twins as Transformative Infrastructures in Higher Education:
Integrating Pedagogy, Governance, and Intelligent Systems

Fahad A. Salendab
http://orcid.org/0000-0003-4459-443X
Sultan Kudarat State University, Philippines

ABSTRACT

Digital twin technology is emerging as a transformative force in higher education, reshaping how institutions design learning environments, manage operations, and make data-informed decisions. Moving beyond traditional simulation tools, digital twins integrate real-time data, virtual modeling, and predictive analytics to create adaptive and interconnected educational ecosystems. This chapter examines their conceptual foundations, evolution, and theoretical grounding in constructivist, experiential, socio-technical, and systems perspectives. It analyzes applications such as smart campus management, virtual laboratories, personalized learning, learning analytics, and institutional planning. Drawing on case-based practices, it highlights how digital twins enable system-wide integration, anticipatory governance, and enhanced learner engagement. It also addresses key challenges related

DOI: 10.4018/979-8-2600-1674-9.ch004

to data integration, institutional readiness, ethical governance, and equity, positioning digital twins as convergent infrastructures that redefine higher education as adaptive and data driven.

INTRODUCTION

The rapid development of digital technologies affects higher education, forcing universities to transition from conventional forms of teaching, learning, and governance to adaptive, data-based ecosystems. However, this transformation implies not only technological innovation but also new approaches to knowledge creation, management, and engagement in the context of higher education. Digital twin technology plays an important role in this transformation, providing means of modeling, simulation, and optimization of educational systems through continuous fusion of physical and virtual components (Yao et al., 2023; Zayed et al., 2023).

Initially developed in engineering and manufacturing industries, digital twins evolved from purely descriptive simulations into intelligent, real-time systems with predictive capabilities and autonomous decision support. The expansion of digital twins from these industries to healthcare, smart cities, and education shows their potential as integrative socio-technical infrastructures rather than purely technical tools (Thelen et al., 2022). For higher education institutions, this development is relevant due to the need for optimizing learning outcomes, increasing efficiency of operations, and adapting to rapidly changing conditions of the modern world. Digital twins allow universities to develop comprehensive models of their environment, including physical infrastructure, administrative processes, learning patterns, and performance trajectories (Hawkinson, 2022; Nalayini et al., 2025).

The use of digital twins in the domain of higher education is related to the emerging pedagogical approaches toward personalization, experiential learning, and data-driven teaching practices. In particular, digital twins can enable monitoring and simulation of learning activities in real-time, thus facilitating the transformation of standardized and teacher-centered models into adaptive and responsive learning ecosystems based on individual needs of students (Lin et al., 2024; Pathak & Upadhyay, 2024). At the same time, they can allow administrators of learning institutions to make more effective and anticipatory decisions, simulating different scenarios and optimizing resource distribution via an integrated data system (Alshahrani et al., 2026; Temple et al., 2024). As such, digital twins are a converging technology having a number of applications in the field of higher education.

Still, the incorporation of digital twins into higher education is linked to a number of challenges that require critical thinking regarding ethical governance, data security, and new roles of teachers and students in the context of technological transformations. With increasing reliance on advanced infrastructure that makes it possible to collect vast amounts of data, higher education institutions can be accused of being highly surveillant and algorithmically biased against some individuals (Hu, 2023; Alfredo et al., 2024).

Firstly, this chapter extends the ongoing discussion on digital twins in higher education by shifting the perception of digital twins from being merely tools used for simulations or optimizing infrastructure toward socio-technical infrastructures that facilitate pedagogical practices, institutional governance, institutional intelligence, learning analytics, and smart campus management as an interconnected ecosystem. Where existing literature tends to focus on digital twins applied within different areas like smart buildings, industrial automation, or learning analytics, this chapter offers a holistic framework that considers digital twins as convergent systems that connect institutional governance, adaptive pedagogy, institutional infrastructure, and human-centered learning spaces.

Secondly, the chapter contributes to existing literature on digital twins in four major ways. Firstly, it synthesizes the scattered literature on digital twins in fields like engineering, educational technology, learning analytics, and smart campuses into a comprehensive higher education approach. Secondly, the chapter proposes an Integrated Digital Twin Ecosystem Framework that provides insight into the operation of digital twins at various institutional layers, including the infrastructure layer, academic process layer, learner modeling layer, and strategic governance layer. Thirdly, it operationalizes theoretical perspectives, including constructivism, experiential learning, socio-technical system theory, and systems theory, by relating them to the application of digital twins in higher education contexts. Fourthly, it explores the ethical and governance issues that arise with educational ecosystems powered by data collection and analysis.

Instead of considering the digital twin technology as an independent innovation, this chapter argues that digital twins function as adaptive intelligent institutional systems with the potential to transform university education, governance, planning, and response to social challenges.

CONCEPTUAL FOUNDATIONS OF DIGITAL TWINS

Historical Development of Digital Twin Technology

The history of technology associated with creating digital twins corresponds to the changing perception of physical systems, the nature of data used for monitoring those systems, and approaches to decision-making within organizations. Initially, digital twin technology was used for simulation purposes in aerospace and manufacturing industries, where the focus was on monitoring and improving the efficiency of the processes. According to Yao et al. (2023), however, connecting product lifecycle management to sensor-based feedback resulted in turning simulation into an autonomous and predictive digital infrastructure that is capable of influencing operations. In other words, such a change allows for transforming passive digital models into active constituents of cyber-physical ecosystems, which can be considered another example of organizational transformation.

The development of Internet of Things (IoT), artificial intelligence (AI), cloud computing, and big data proves that data intelligence and operations governance are becoming more intertwined and increasingly dependent on each other. Currently, modern digital twins involve constant interaction between the physical and virtual worlds in terms of data exchange, which is important for identifying potential disruptions, optimizing the process, and enabling automated management. According to Zayed et al. (2023), introducing AI into the concept of digital twins helps make organizational decision-making autonomous through the use of predictive analytics and learning algorithms that work according to environmental changes.

From its initial applications in engineering, the digital twin concept is becoming more prominent in health care, urban governance, and education, emphasizing its status as socio-technical infrastructure. According to Thelen et al. (2022), the value of digital twins arises from their capacity to integrate disparate institutional mechanisms within a data-driven framework, rather than being a reproduction of physical places. Such developments are driven by the call for predictive governance, which calls for instant visibility and simulation to overcome unpredictability. In turn, the integration of digital twins is gaining momentum in organizations pursuing adaptability, resilience, and evidence-based management, rather than efficiency.

Within the context of education, digital twins redefine the traditional learning environment. The previous model entailed standardized frameworks and reactive assessments, which did not allow for timely responses. According to Hawkinson (2022), digital twins for education enable institutions to simulate behaviors and personalize interventions while monitoring engagement levels.

In addition, the research work by Nalayini et al. (2025) highlights that these systems are not only technological additions to pedagogy but infrastructural elements that can restructure the planning processes, class management, and student support systems. Therefore, the journey from the past to the present in relation to digital twin development in educational settings has been guided by digital transformation policies that value personalization, connectivity, and predictive education management.

Types of Digital Twins

1. Physical Digital Twins – These refer to cyber-physical technologies that revolutionize infrastructure management via perpetual data collection and predictive analysis. Instead of providing a visualization of classrooms, laboratories, and other parts of the campus, they analyze environmental and structural information to forecast the degradation process, optimize assets, and assist in making effective facility governance decisions. Thus, campus management evolves into a proactive approach based on forecasting system behavior computationally. According to Asare et al. (2024), the use of digital twins based on Building Information Modeling (BIM) technologies and equipped with IoT sensors helps to provide predictive maintenance as they detect any deviations in asset condition and translate them into intelligent decisions. Their potential lies in transforming physical signals into decision-making intelligence in order to increase efficiency and lower the cost of the construction lifecycle. Manokeaw et al. (2025) explain that the combination of BIM, Geographic Information Systems (GIS), and sensor technology in digital twins allows universities to gain adaptive facility governance benefits. Their research suggests that continuous monitoring of classrooms, laboratories, and energy systems results in higher efficiency and sustainability. The core advantage of using physical digital twins is the transformation of campus management into a data-driven process.
2. Process Digital Twins – These are a development in technology from traditional documentation of workflow to dynamic models that use simulation to facilitate modeling and optimization of processes such as enrollment, delivery of the curriculum, and administrative coordination. The new development in technology is different from workflow documentation since it helps an institution to simulate process behavior under various conditions and experiment with various policy changes and approaches without having to implement them first. The change enables institutions to shift to anticipation instead of reaction based on decision-making. According to Santos et al. (2024), process digital twins combine simulation environments with operational data in order to make strategic and operational decisions. Furthermore, Wagner et al. (2024) note that process digital twins can be used to optimize planning through modeling process behaviors by integrating product, resource, and workflow information using process simulations. Even though the studies above are carried out in industry, similar applications can be used in higher education institutions due to the similarity in workflow structure.
3. System Digital Twins – These are defined by an overall integrated infrastructure that involves the combination of academic, administrative, technological, and human aspects into one dynamic modeling of institutional activity. In contrast

to physical or process-based digital twins that can be used to examine particular objects and processes, System Digital Twins are applied at a more general level that allows for understanding interdependence and feedback between different institutional subsystems – from resource management to academic and learning performance, and even student mobility. Therefore, using System Digital Twins, universities will have the opportunity to shift from fragmentary decision-making to a more comprehensive understanding of how all the institutional components interact. In this way, System Digital Twins could be considered as intelligence platforms that allow institutions to test scenarios, conduct simulations, and engage in predictive governance of their educational ecosystem. According to Thelen et al. (2022), such tools have the potential to help organizations aggregate diverse data sets and synchronize their physical and virtual environments in order to perform real-time monitoring and predictions of the behavior of complex socio-technical systems. On the other hand, according to Krishna (2025), combining academic, infrastructure, and administrative data flows into one model allows institutions to simulate institutional interdependencies, i.e., how energy consumption, occupation of facilities, and activities of students affect institutional performance.

4. Human-Centered Digital Twins - These are dynamic models of learners based on digital representations of their cognitive, behavioral, and performance patterns generated through ongoing data generated during the interactions, learning processes, and even biometrics. Unlike the system/process-focused twins, these operate on an individual basis and are used to adapt to the changing requirements for the learning experience by adjusting content, pace, and feedback on the spot. The key aspect of the digital twin's activity here lies in computational analysis of learners' behavior, which makes personalized learning ecosystems possible for education systems and moves them from static to dynamic and data-driven. According to Lin et al. (2024), incorporating behavioral and interaction data allows one to generate continuously updated models of learners, which provide opportunities for decision-making, making the entire learning process feedback-based based on engagement patterns and performance metrics. However, Alfredo et al. (2024) point out ethical aspects linked to the use of modeling techniques to enhance efficiency and personalize educational services since they involve issues of privacy, surveillance, autonomy, and transparency when it comes to algorithmic decisions.

Table 1. Digital Twin Taxonomy in Higher Education

Type	Primary Purpose	Data Requirements	Level of Application	Benefits	Risks and Challenges	Example
Physical Digital Twins	Infrastructure optimization and predictive maintenance	IoT sensors, BIM, environmental data	Campus and facilities	Energy efficiency, sustainability, and maintenance forecasting	Surveillance concerns, high implementation cost	Smart classrooms and energy systems
Process Digital Twins	Workflow simulation and operational optimization	Administrative and workflow data	Institutional operations	Process efficiency, policy simulation	Over-automation, institutional dependency	Enrollment and curriculum systems
System Digital Twins	Institutional integration and predictive governance	Cross-platform institutional data	University-wide	Strategic planning, scenario simulation	System complexity, interoperability issues	Campus-wide governance systems
Human-Centered Digital Twins	Personalized and adaptive learning	LMS data, behavioral analytics, interaction patterns	Individual learners	Personalized instruction, early intervention	Privacy, learner surveillance, algorithmic opacity	Learning analytics platforms

Theoretical Perspectives Supporting Digital Twin Integration in Education

1. Constructivist Learning Theory – It views learning as an active, constructive process involving the acquisition of knowledge based on interpretation, rather than the transmission of information. Learners are able to construct and modify their understanding of the world as a result of performing real tasks which involve testing hypotheses, making decisions based on interpretations, and getting feedback from results. A constructivist learning environment can be considered an essential condition for effective learning as it engages the learner and requires performing specific activities and experiencing certain situations. It turns out that digital twin technologies create a constructivist learning environment. They provide simulations of systems and enable manipulation with variables in order to perform specific tasks. The findings of Salendab & Tago (2026) indicate that nowadays there is an emphasis on learner engagement, autonomy, and critical thinking in contrast to traditional instructional techniques, when the teacher performs all actions while the learner remains a passive participant. In digital twins, learning involves interaction with simulated systems wherein learners interpret information, perform certain actions, and evaluate their results. As emphasized by Salendab et al. (2026), innovative pedagogic practices, including

flipped classroom, project-based learning, and technology-enhanced instruction, contribute to the cognitive and reflective learning of learners.

2. Experiential Learning Theory – Learning occurs through direct experiences, reflection, and application of newly acquired knowledge to future instances. Active participation in realistic contexts is essential for developing knowledge; hence, learning does not take place passively but rather through engagement. An important development in the field of pedagogy involves the use of digital twin environments, which create simulated experiences that make it easy to test decisions, learn from results, and improve certain competencies. As per Pathak & Upadhyay (2024), the application of digital twins in learning contributes to experiential learning through virtual simulation, active experimentation, and contextual problem solving. They assert that through virtual representation of actual scenarios, gaps between theoretical and practical knowledge can be bridged using iterative simulation, devoid of risks associated with practical learning. It becomes clear from their study that experiential learning will become frequent and more refined through the adoption of digital twins. In a similar vein, Speicher et al. (2025) reveal that digital twin-based learning promotes better decision making, conceptualization, and engagement. They have identified how digital twins facilitate an experiential learning cycle consisting of four phases, namely experience, reflection, concept formation, and experimentation. This means that digital twins not only support but also revolutionize experiential learning by making reflection and iteration inherent parts of the system.
3. Socio-Technical Perspective – It Socio-Technical Perspective – Digital twins are both technical artifacts and socio-technical systems influenced by the organization's institutional processes, human agency, and culture. The importance of digital twins in education can be linked to socio-technical factors such as governance, collaboration, and readiness rather than purely computational factors. Research proves that successful implementation is based on the relationship between technology and organizational aspects focused on human interactions. Ghosh et al. (2025) note that digital twins influence digital transformation if and only if there is a high level of digital mindset and organizational synergy. Similarly, Perisic et al. (2025) demonstrate in higher education settings that the integration of governance, readiness, and stakeholder engagement is crucial; technological aspects alone are insufficient for successful results.
4. Systems Theory – This approach views educational organizations as dynamic and interactive ecosystems characterized by constant interaction between various academic, operational, and behavioral aspects. Therefore, organizational behavior should not be analyzed by looking at each component independently because it is derived from interactions and patterns of relations between them. Digital twin technology is aligned with the systems theory approach since it provides a

computerized simulation of organizational systems, allowing for comprehensive analysis of interrelated variables in different areas of education. According to Fuller et al. (2020), digital twin systems analyze operational, behavioral, and environmental factors to monitor the system in real-time and make informed decisions based on feedback loops. In essence, this perspective is consistent with the key tenets of systems theory in terms of emphasizing interdependence and feedback loops as determinants of organizational behavior. In addition, Tao et al. (2018) find that digital twins enable organizations to simulate the interactions between different subsystems and analyze how the effects of decisions will be cascaded through various operational levels.

Table 2. Operationalizing Theoretical Perspectives in Digital Twin Environments

Theoretical Perspectives	Relevance to Digital Twins	Higher Education Application
Constructivist Learning Theory	Learning occurs through active interaction, experimentation, and reflection	Simulation-based learning, virtual laboratories, inquiry-driven learning
Experiential Learning Theory	Knowledge develops through iterative cycles of experience and feedback	Scenario simulations, immersive learning environments, decision-based learning
Socio-Technical Systems Theory	Technological effectiveness depends on alignment with organizational culture and governance	Institutional readiness, stakeholder collaboration, governance integration
Systems Theory	Universities function as interconnected ecosystems with feedback loops	Integrated campus management, predictive governance, institutional modeling

This operational framing demonstrates that digital twins are not merely technical systems but educational and institutional infrastructures shaped by pedagogical assumptions, governance structures, and organizational dynamics.

DIGITAL TWIN ECOSYSTEM FRAMEWORK FOR HIGHER EDUCATION

The Integrated Digital Twin Ecosystem Framework considers digital twins as revolutionary institutional intelligence infrastructures that explain how institutional processes relate to each other across all aspects of university functions. As opposed to being regarded as individual technologies applied separately, digital twins are considered interconnected systems that link virtual and physical spaces through the integration of data, prediction, and institutional monitoring in real time. Under the framework, digital twins are perceived as convergent infrastructures, bringing together academic, administrative, operational, and governance functions within a single institution. The main idea of the framework revolves around the Digital Twin Intelligence Platform that operates as the central infrastructure for coordinating institutional data and processes. Data are collected from IoT devices, LMS, AI systems, BIM, GIS, and institutional databases to create continuous digital models of institutional activities and learning spaces.

This model is based on five interconnected institutional domains that together facilitate intelligent and adaptive higher education systems.

1) Smart Infrastructure & Campus Systems: It uses smart infrastructure and campus systems with predictive maintenance, occupancy monitoring, sustainability management, and energy optimization to improve efficiency and resource utilization.
2) Adaptive and Experiential Learning Systems: The digital twin facilitates experiential learning through simulation-based training, immersive experiences, virtual laboratories, and personalized pathways of instruction to increase engagement and experiential learning.
3) Learning Analytics and Student Intelligence: Through learning analytics and student intelligence, the digital twin facilitates continuous modeling of learner performance, engagement, behaviors, and risks to take evidence-based actions.
4) Institutional Governance and Strategic Planning: Digital twin enables the institution to use scenario simulation, policy modeling, resource optimization, and data-driven decision-making for better governance.
5) Human-Centered Ethical Governance: This model incorporates the concept of human-centered ethical governance to ensure that the digital twin implementation aligns with ethical considerations.

Such domains are involved in ongoing feedback cycles that allow universities to become adaptive and intelligent learning systems, instead of merely being fragmented organizational arrangements. The exchange of real-time information between the systems of infrastructure, learning, governance, and ethics allows universities to react to problems and issues related to their functioning and learners' needs. Thus, the model considers digital twins as more than just innovative technologies; instead, they are seen as holistic institutional ecosystems able to manage different dimensions of higher education in a highly digital environment.

Table 3. Integrated Digital Twin Ecosystem Framework for Higher Education

Domain	Core Function	Applications in Higher Education	Key Outcomes	Ethical Considerations
Smart Infrastructure Systems	Optimizes campus operations and sustainability	Smart classrooms, energy monitoring, predictive maintenance	Operational efficiency and sustainability	Surveillance and data security
Adaptive and Experiential Learning Systems	Supports personalized and experiential learning	Virtual labs, simulations, adaptive instruction	Improved engagement and learning outcomes	Learner autonomy and accessibility
Learning Analytics and Student Intelligence	Monitors learner behavior and performance	Early intervention and adaptive assessment	Personalized support and retention improvement	Privacy and algorithmic bias
Institutional Governance and Strategic Planning	Enables evidence-based planning and policy simulation	Resource allocation and strategic planning	Predictive and responsive governance	Transparency and over-automation
Human-Centered Ethical Governance	Ensures responsible and transparent system implementation	Ethical oversight and data governance	Trustworthy digital transformation	Human agency and informed consent

DIGITAL TWINS IN THE CONTEXT OF HIGHER EDUCATION

The emergence of smart campuses and intelligent learning ecosystems represents a development in higher education where institutions evolve from stagnant administration to vibrant and data-driven settings. This can be observed in what Alshahrani et al. (2026) refer to as cyber-physical educational ecosystems, which involve synchronizing the physical and the digital realms through real-time integration of infrastructure and process data. The authors demonstrate that universities apply digital twin paradigms to develop comprehensive models in which behaviors could be simulated, analyzed, and optimized in real time.

The concept of digital ecosystems develops further as academic teaching, management, and governance become contingent upon interdependent digital platforms. Hybrid teaching, predictive analytics, and digital spaces are evidence of institutional change on a more profound level than just innovative developments. Indeed, Hu (2023) reports that smart campus technologies implement digital infrastructures to enhance the efficiency of service delivery, space management, and decision-making. Universities thus operate in an adaptive fashion due to data-driven, rather than bureaucratic-based, environments.

The technological foundation for such transformation is based on the integration of the Internet of Things (IoT), artificial intelligence (AI), big data analysis, and cloud computing technologies. IoT-based solutions enable the constant gathering of data regarding the use of infrastructure, students' behaviors, and environmental parameters. On the other hand, artificial intelligence, together with machine learning techniques, enables turning the obtained data into predictive and prescriptive insights. As noted by Hussaini et al. (2023), IoT-based smart campus solutions enable continuous monitoring of various processes that occur within a university, and, thus, these activities are followed by analyzing this data through machine learning. Therefore, such an intersection suggests shifting from the reactive governance model toward the anticipatory approach, when institutions will be able to react before situations even arise.

Apart from being tools for improving efficiency, digital twins are revolutionizing teaching structures in higher education institutions. According to Lin et al. (2025), digital twin technology provides environments for creating immersive learning where learners engage with simulated systems mimicking reality. This results in scenario learning, experiential simulations, and customized learning paths based on behavioral data. At an analytical level, there is a change from conventional standardization pedagogy that favors instructors to adaptive ecosystems where educational content is adjusted based on learners' behaviors.

However, the use of digital twin technology raises some issues with regard to its impact on structures within higher education institutions. According to Hu (2023), the concerns are mostly related to data management, data-driven surveillance, and dependency on automation. These problems mean that while the technology improves intelligence and efficiency at institutional levels, it restructures organizational power through the centralization of data infrastructure and automated algorithms. Thus, it can be concluded that digital twins are not technological advancements alone; they represent transformational institutional infrastructure within higher education contexts.

APPLICATIONS OF DIGITAL TWINS IN HIGHER EDUCATION INSTITUTIONS

1. Smart Campus Management and Infrastructure Optimization: Campuses turn out to be cyber-physical systems characterized by continuous interactions between physical assets and digital intelligence. Digital twins function as integrative solutions that unite energy, occupancy, environment, and transport management into an interconnected platform capable of real-time, predictive, and adaptive campus management. According to Zaballos et al. (2020), smart campuses can benefit from digital twins, which help analyze energy usage, occupancy levels, and indoor comfort based on IoT and environmental data in order to increase

the sustainability and efficiency of campus facilities. Li & Hong (2025) identify that digital twins help improve the performance of buildings through predictive maintenance, energy optimization, and decisions made using simulations provided by continuous monitoring data and virtual models. In general, the studies discussed above highlight how digital twins provide opportunities for proactive management, such as prediction of system failures, waste reduction, and analysis of infrastructural changes before implementing them physically, such as expanding campuses.

2. Virtual Laboratories and Simulation-Based Learning: This concept is a significant pedagogical revolution made possible by emerging immersive technologies such as digital twins and virtual reality. Conceptually, virtual labs allow learners to develop experiential and constructive learning through testing of hypotheses, manipulating parameters, and iteration in a risk-free and reproducible virtual environment. In contrast to conventional labs, virtual labs eliminate cost factors, accessibility issues, and safety concerns, thus promoting inclusive, scalable, and high-quality education in engineering, medicine, aviation, and other applied science disciplines. As shown in a systematic review by Hamilton et al. (2021), immersive VR has a positive effect on learner engagement and facilitates experiential learning when used in conjunction with proper guidance and reflection, thus making it suitable for simulation-based learning labs. Similarly, in a meta-analysis study by Zhong et al. (2026), it is proven that VR simulations promote cognitive, affective, and psychomotor competencies among learners due to realistic exposure to different situations that promote decision-making and procedure execution. Therefore, virtual labs can be considered adaptive experiential learning environments that emulate the complexity of real-life processes while increasing accessibility and safety levels, thereby ensuring ongoing skill development through iterative simulation and instant feedback.
3. Personalized and Adaptive Learning Systems: It is viewed as a structural transformation of higher education that implies a switch to a data-driven approach where instruction becomes flexible and is continually adjusted based on the analysis of behavior and academic performance of each specific learner. In this context, digital twins are regarded as conceptual models of learners created through processing the data collected from learning management systems, examinations, and digital interactions. Thanks to this continuous modeling, institutions are now able to go beyond static instructional design and adapt content and feedback in real-time in line with learners' ability, engagement, and progress. According to Joksimovic et al. (2020), personalized learning allows identifying patterns in learners' behavior, like the level of engagement, performance trajectory, and at-risk behavior, which, in turn, helps to apply proper instructional intervention to improve learners' results. Thus, it becomes

clear that personalization involves a dynamic process of adjusting instruction based on data-driven insights. In addition, Kulik & Fletcher (2016) argue that adaptive environments result in better learning outcomes compared to traditional instruction. Based on meta-analysis, Kulik & Fletcher (2016) prove that systems designed to provide personalized feedback, adjust content delivery according to learners' progress, and allow for mastery-based learning achieve higher success rates than traditional approaches.

4. Student Performance Monitoring and Learning Analytics: The transition from conventional assessment processes to continuous data-informed educational intelligence systems in higher education. Predictive models of performance and risks are built using LMS data, such as attendance, engagement, assessments, and online activity. These models allow institutions to determine the likelihood of a student dropping out, monitor their progress in learning, and implement timely measures aimed at improving retention rates. According to Rebelo Marcolino et al. (2025), predictive models based on ML applied to LMS logs can predict whether a student is likely to drop out, thus promoting action towards retention. Hernandez-Campos et al. (2025) reveal that learning analytics are extensively employed by institutions to evaluate engagement and learning, and LMS data plays a vital role in their decision-making processes. Digital twin-enabled learning analytics can be viewed as predictive educational infrastructures as they model performance in an academic, behavioral, and engagement context.
5. Administrative Decision-Making and Institutional Planning: With the growing role of digital twins, the process of making decisions in such fields becomes more interactive by creating simulation ecosystems that model universities as complex and dynamic interconnected systems. Thanks to the consolidation of data on different aspects of operation, including academics, financial aspects, operations, and infrastructures, institutions are able to make real-time decisions about potential development strategies and performance improvements. The move is aimed at transforming traditional administrative processes into an approach that involves strategic foresight, based on digital simulations of various scenarios. Some studies prove the effectiveness of such approaches in practice. According to Alshahrani et al. (2026), the digital twin campus model can be useful for master planning and expansion purposes, as well as for assessing the viability of specific infrastructural solutions on campus before the actual implementation of changes. Temple et al. (2024) highlight that the use of digital twins creates opportunities for the application of policy-making and decision support approaches that help assess the effects of various institutional scenarios. The results obtained suggest that digital twins can be seen as the systems of institutional intelligence that improve the process of decision-making and planning in institutions.

PEDAGOGICAL IMPLICATIONS OF DIGITAL TWINS

In recent scholarship, the use of digital twin technology in the realm of higher education can be seen as a shift from traditional forms of instruction focused on content-based approaches to those more oriented towards adaptive and data-driven learning experiences. The shift does not merely mean the use of digital twins as supplementary learning aids but involves their use as an infrastructure tool for facilitating the construction, application, and evaluation of knowledge.

The first pedagogical implication revolves around the improvement of immersive learning. With the help of digital twins, learners will have the ability to engage with live virtual simulations of physical systems, thus allowing them to manipulate and observe processes within a controlled environment. According to Speicher et al. (2025), the combination of Internet of Things technology with digital twins increases immersive learning since learners will have the opportunity to learn via practical interaction with physical objects as opposed to theoretical interaction, resulting in improved comprehension and applied logic skills. The main change lies not in the immersiveness alone but in the cyclicality of thinking.

Moreover, improvements in personalized and competency-based learning systems have much in common with progress in the field of digital twins. According to Hariyanto et al. (2025), learning technologies become more capable of analyzing learners' behaviors continuously and modifying their educational paths based on such analyses for personalization purposes. The new era leads to changes in assessing learning processes. Instead of measuring learning outcomes after certain events, digital twins allow for continuous tracking and updating of the students' progress and competencies. As a result, a predictive approach to learning develops in which instructional systems anticipate the learners' weaknesses and fill those gaps by providing adequate interventions, thus merging assessment and instruction in one technological solution.

In addition, digital twins allow educators to implement collaborative learning strategies to a larger extent within virtual environments. The possibilities of digital twins described by Karanam & Hartman (2025) include collaborative problem-solving, working together on simulation projects, and interacting with each other in terms of shared interaction with an identical digital replica. Therefore, collaborating becomes an essential part of digital twin functionality, not only a pedagogical method. Students do not interact independently anymore, but rather through some common digital representation of a certain system.

A second significant implication relates to increased engagement and improved knowledge retention on the part of the learners. According to Lu & Hu (2025), simulation environments and interactive digital environments significantly increase motivation and engagement by giving real-time feedback and engaging the learners through experimentation. The implication is that engagement in such contexts means cognitive immersion rather than merely behaviorally active participation. The learner will learn how to apply knowledge as he or she will see the outcome of his or her actions in simulations. Knowledge retention will improve through this process.

Digital twins also mean significant shifts in the roles of the educators and the learners in the learning process. In the opinion of Lin et al. (2025), educators are becoming facilitators, learning environment designers, and analytic interpreters of information systems, while the learners themselves become more autonomous and regulate their activities in the data environment. The implication of this role shift is that there will be a redistribution of epistemic power in which humans and intelligent systems jointly produce knowledge.

CASE-BASED APPLICATIONS AND EMERGING PRACTICES

The emerging applications of the technology of digital twins in the academic sphere suggest the beginning of a movement towards innovation from a fragmented experimentation phase. From the current case study examples, an identifiable trend has been recognized: digital twins are not only being used to visualize infrastructure anymore but are growing into complex tools that can simultaneously ensure sustainability, human-centeredness, and data-based management. In this context, it could be said that there is a paradigmatic shift towards recognizing institutions as intelligent and dynamic ecosystems.

This transition is well illustrated by the research conducted by García-Aranda et al. (2024), where the university campus is conceptualized as a laboratory for sustainable development and innovations related to the smart city. According to the findings presented in the paper, it becomes evident that the inclusion of such technologies as GIS, BIM, IoT-compatible datasets, and environmental indicators in a single three-dimensional tool leads to an all-encompassing analysis of campus functioning. Notably, the use of a digital twin goes far beyond the monitoring of infrastructure; it includes such aspects as mobility and accessibility, environmental conditions, and even possibilities for renewable energy production, thereby contributing to campus operations that are in line with sustainability-related goals. While the weaknesses and deficiencies detected include issues of low accessibility and high noise levels, the results point to the presence of substantial potential for solar energy production at campus sites.

Extending the idea of a systems approach, Bäcklund et al. (2024) alter the direction of analysis away from sustainability towards human experience in digital twin ecosystems. While García-Aranda et al. emphasize intelligence in terms of environment and infrastructure, the paper offers a more holistic approach that involves incorporating human factors in the design of digital twins. By combining 3D laser scanning, IoT sensors, and geographic information systems, the platform enables users to monitor occupancy rates, navigate campuses, and analyze usage statistics. In particular, the addition of wayfinding and room-booking modules is seen to help digital twins optimize students' experiences and enhance the effectiveness of administration. Human-centered digital twins make it possible for institutions to reduce the number of empty rooms on campus and improve their utilization; however, most importantly, they redefine the nature of interaction between users and physical campuses. Thus, human-centered applications of digital twins represent a paradigm shift: digital twins evolve from being mere representations of the environment into interactive tools that influence user behavior and performance.

Extending from the advancements mentioned above, Manokeaw et al. (2025) propose an approach to incorporating sustainability alongside operational intelligence into a scalable and replicable model. When introduced at Chiang Mai University, this model has proven the capability of a combination of BIM, GIS, and IoT sensors to provide a flexible and scalable, multi-layered dashboard for decision-making processes. Contrary to the models that focus either on sustainability or on human-centricity, this approach allows for the inclusion of both factors into a single management strategy, which helps both in strategic decision-making and daily operations. In addition, the results of implementation show high acceptability and success, with significant electricity savings being achieved during the trial period. Thus, it could be concluded that the creation of digital twins represents a major step towards their functionality as a means of providing tangible benefits to the organization rather than merely being a way to analyze them. In addition, the openness and flexibility of the platform make it relevant for institutions lacking resources.

Table 4. Comparative Analysis of Cased-Based Applications

Case Study	Primary Focus	Institutional Contribution	Key Lesson	Limitation
García-Aranda et al. (2024)	Sustainability and smart campus planning	Integration of GIS, BIM, and environmental analytics	Digital twins support evidence-based sustainability governance	Limited pedagogical integration
Bäcklund et al. (2024)	Human-centered campus interaction	Occupancy analytics and user-centered navigation	Digital twins enhance user experience and operational efficiency	Limited predictive governance capability
Manokeaw et al. (2025)	Integrated smart campus management	Real-time operational intelligence and energy optimization	Digital twins can unify sustainability and institutional management	Scalability and interoperability challenges

The overall findings of the discussed case studies point towards digital twins evolving from being used to visualize infrastructures to becoming institutional intelligence systems. There are, however, certain similarities in terms of sustainability, operational governance, and the human factor in the design of institutions.

The following major observations are made across all cases under analysis. Firstly, the role of digital twins as an ecosystem rather than an application is gaining prominence. Secondly, the success of any implementation highly depends on data interoperability and organizational preparedness. Lastly, the most advanced instances combine sustainable management, user involvement, and predictive governance into one platform. Taken together, all findings made throughout the study indicate that the true power of digital twins is in their ability to integrate various institution-related processes into constantly evolving systems.

STRATEGIC AND POLICY RECOMMENDATIONS

Integration of digital twins within higher education will not be fully realized without appropriate technological infrastructure and institutional preparation, ethical considerations, and organizational change. Institutions, therefore, have to put in place well-thought-out strategies that combine technology innovations with teaching/learning, administration, and ethics. The institutional leadership will be expected to create institutional digital governance structures that control aspects such as data management, interoperability, ethical considerations, and long-range planning, alongside developing interoperable digital technologies, creating institutional data governance strategies, putting together interdisciplinary implementation teams, and ensuring that digital transformation efforts are in line with the goals of the institutions. Lecturers and educators will be expected to use digital twin technologies to facilitate simulation and experience learning through adaptation of their approaches to incorporate adaptive learning techniques, proper learning analytics, reflective, and inquiry-based teaching methods, despite increasing levels of automation. In technology development, the designers and developers of the technology will need to ensure that there is explainability of AI applications in these systems, along with other considerations such as accessibility, interoperability, privacy by design, and transparency in algorithmic processes, in order to avoid situations where artificial intelligence replaces professional judgment on the part of educators. Finally, at the policy level, the government and educational regulatory bodies will need to create comprehensive policies on learning analytics, data protection, accountability, and AI governance in higher education.

FUTURE DIRECTIONS OF DIGITAL TWINS IN HIGHER EDUCATION

The future of digital twins in higher education goes beyond developing more applications. It represents an evolution in which higher education institutions move toward creating intelligent, integrated, and ethically governed educational ecosystems. On the basis of the existing efforts, the upcoming stage of digital twin application will focus on achieving convergence and interoperability, bringing together all kinds of twins—physical, process, system, and person-centric—and thus forming institutional intelligence that would make it possible to simulate and govern whole ecosystems, including the university itself, its learning behaviors, infrastructure usage, processes, and the external environment.

As far as pedagogy is concerned, the future of digital twins involves the development of a fully personalized and anticipatory approach to teaching. Whereas the current trend revolves around adjusting teaching strategies based on individual performance, future technologies will incorporate various types of data on students (cognitive, behavioral, contextual) and make predictions about their trajectories in advance, anticipating the need to take some intervention measures. In effect, this will lead to the pre-emptive design of personalized and optimal educational trajectories for every learner.

As digital twins gain popularity, there is a need for more ethical, legal, and governance frameworks that govern them. Continuous data capture within human-centered digital twins poses some concerns related to issues of surveillance, algorithmic biases, privacy rights, and the issue of data ownership. There is a need for future research to focus on establishing a framework for the development of a human-centered approach for governance models that regulate data collection, interpretation, and usage in decision-making processes. In this regard, efforts should be directed towards the adoption of models for governance that are characterized by transparent and accountable data governance frameworks. The same case applies to issues of explainable artificial intelligence and protecting academic freedoms, as well as learner rights.

Institutional-level research will be key in informing the successful and sustainable implementation of digital twins within institutions. It is anticipated that the success of digital twins will be associated with issues of digital transformation that involve not just technology but other aspects, including the institution's level of readiness and capacity-building initiatives. There will be a need for future research that focuses on digital transformation models that highlight issues of leadership and data-informed culture, among others.

Finally, one key future-oriented path is the creation of connections between digital twins and systems at large scales. Considering the fact that educational institutions work within an intricate socio-economic and environmental milieu, future digital twins will probably extend their scope from the campuses to include job market statistics, measures for community engagement, and environmental indicators. Thus, universities can become part of larger smart systems by becoming adaptive nodes, ensuring that the learning process is always responsive to current societal demands. In consequence, digital twins could move beyond simple instruments for use by educational institutions and into strategic structures for addressing global issues, including workforce change and climate sustainability.

DISCUSSION

The analysis of digital twins in the context of higher education has led to the realization that there has been a paradigmatic change, moving from seeing digital technology as merely an auxiliary tool for higher education institutions to seeing it as a socio-technical infrastructure that reconfigures the institutional structure and functions. On reviewing the conceptual aspects, applications, pedagogical considerations, and specific case examples of the application of digital twins, a core analytical finding can be made: rather than focusing on isolated features, such as simulation or visualization capabilities, the power of digital twins lies in their capacity to integrate multiple fragmented systems into one data-driven whole.

A systems perspective provides an understanding of the mechanisms underlying the concept of digital twins in the field of higher education. First, through interdependency, the digital twins model the complex relationship between various institutional entities. Second, using feedback loops allows establishing a more robust interaction within and between those entities. Lastly, emergent behavior is the result of such modeling. In this way, the convergence of physical, process, system, and human-centered digital twins shows that institutional efficiency does not lie in perfecting each element of the system independently but in understanding how these elements work together in an ecosystem. This is supported by the review of cases, which indicates that the evolution of digital twins in higher education follows a trajectory from infrastructure-focused to human-centered applications.

Pedagogically, digital twins signal a transition from instructor-led models to personalized, experiential, and data-intensive learning ecosystems. Constructivist and experiential pedagogies are incorporated into practice by placing the learner in constant simulation, feedback, and reflection loops. One crucial issue to consider is the transfer of epistemic authority from humans to algorithms through which learning paths are determined and decided. In other words, rather than asking what constitutes learning, we should ask who the process of learning benefits and who makes decisions about it.

In an institutional context, digital twins facilitate predictive and anticipatory governance, based on real-time data analytics and simulation for foresight. Thus, digital twins represent a move from retrospective planning toward forward-looking, evidence-based, and adaptive governance. Digital twins' effectiveness will depend upon organizational readiness and alignment between socio-technical elements. Existing scholarship demonstrates that mere technological implementation is insufficient; effective adoption requires strategic leadership, digital literacy, stakeholder engagement, and alignment between digital infrastructure and organizational goals and culture.

The most relevant integrative issue in relation to the findings of the analysis involves ethics and governance considerations regarding the implementation of digital twins. The increasing prevalence of data-driven technologies, particularly human-centric digital twins, brings many challenges regarding matters of privacy, surveillance, algorithmic bias, and transparency. Therefore, these aspects cannot be ignored when discussing the sustainability and legitimacy of digital twins in the educational sector. In addition, the analysis highlights ethical governance as a foundational requirement for the ethical adoption of technology in learning organizations, rather than an obstacle.

Furthermore, the results of the synthesis point to the role of digital twins in shifting the position of higher education institutions into wider digital and social ecosystems. Through the potential of integrating internal and external data streams, digital twins can provide universities with the ability to adapt to societal changes and align their efforts with the labor market, sustainability goals, and other factors. Thus, higher education institutions can evolve beyond merely imparting knowledge to becoming integral parts of adaptive systems.

CONCLUSION

Today, digital twins can be seen as innovative socio-technical infrastructures that transform the process of teaching, university governance, resource allocation, and problem-solving within universities. In this chapter, it is proven that digital twins are not just simulation technologies but represent the concept that combines aspects of infrastructure management, adaptive learning systems, university governance, learning analytics, and decision-making driven by people.

In addition, the importance of digital twins for universities is highlighted through their ability to make universities adapt to changes, predict outcomes, and evolve all the time. It is possible through the use of the suggested Integrated Digital Twin Ecosystem Framework, in which digital twins link pedagogy, governance, infrastructure, and intelligence of universities through data-driven decision-making.

At the same time, the advancement of learning technologies involving data and algorithms generates important ethical concerns related to privacy, transparency, autonomy of learners, and accountability in governance. Consequently, the long-term sustainability of digital twin technology ecosystems requires not only technological proficiency but also the design of governance architectures that are transparent, human-oriented, and ethical. In conclusion, digital twins are much more than a technological advancement; they represent a key institutional shift that will have a growing impact on higher education in the future.

REFERENCES

Alfredo, R., Echeverria, V., Jin, Y., Yan, L., Swiecki, Z., Gašević, D., & Martinez-Maldonado, R. (2024). Human-centred learning analytics and AI in education: A systematic literature review. *Computers and Education: Artificial Intelligence, 6*, 100215. https://doi.org//arXiv.2312.12751DOI: 10.48550

Alshahrani, S., Adenle, Y. A., & Alshuwaikhat, H. M. (2026). The development of a 3D model based on digital twin for campus master plan optimization. *Discover Cities*, *3*(1), 52. DOI: 10.1007/s44327-026-00236-w

Asare, K. A., Liu, R., Anumba, C. J., & Issa, R. R. (2024). Real-world prototyping and evaluation of digital twins for predictive facility maintenance. *Journal of Building Engineering*, *97*, 110890. DOI: 10.1016/j.jobe.2024.110890

Bäcklund, K., Lundqvist, P., & Molinari, M. (2024). Showcasing a digital twin for higher educational buildings: Developing the concept toward human centricity. *Frontiers in Built Environment, 10*, 1347451. DOI: 10.3389/fbuil.2024.1347451

Fuller, A., Fan, Z., Day, C., & Barlow, C. (2020). Digital twin: Enabling technologies, challenges and open research. *IEEE Access : Practical Innovations, Open Solutions*, *8*, 108952–108971. DOI: 10.1109/ACCESS.2020.2998358

García-Aranda, C., Martínez-Cuevas, S., Torres, Y., & Pedrote Sanz, M. (2024). A digital twin of a university campus from an urban sustainability approach: Case study in Madrid (Spain). *Urban Science (Basel, Switzerland)*, *8*(4), 167. DOI: 10.3390/urbansci8040167

Ghosh, S., Hughes, M., Hughes, P., & Hodgkinson, I. (2025). Digital twin, digital thread, and digital mindset in enabling digital transformation: A socio-technical systems perspective. *Technovation*, *144*, 103240. DOI: 10.1016/j.technovation.2025.103240

Hamilton, D., McKechnie, J., Edgerton, E., & Wilson, C. (2021). Immersive virtual reality as a pedagogical tool in education: A systematic literature review of quantitative learning outcomes and experimental design. *Journal of Computers in Education*, *8*(1), 1–32. DOI: 10.1007/s40692-020-00169-2

Hariyanto, K., Kristianingsih, F. X. D., & Maharani, R. (2025). Artificial intelligence in adaptive education: A systematic review of techniques for personalized learning. *Discover Education*, *4*(1), 458. DOI: 10.1007/s44217-025-00908-6

Hawkinson, E. (2022). Automation in education with digital twins: Trends and issues. *International Journal on Open and Distance e-Learning, 8*(2). https://doi.org/DOI: 10.58887/ijodel.v8i2.229

Hernández-Campos, M., Gonzalez-Torres, A., & García-Peñalvo, F. J. (2025). Learning outcomes evaluation through learning analytics systems in higher education: A systematic literature review. *SAGE Open*, *15*(3), 21582440251347374. Advance online publication. DOI: 10.1177/21582440251347374

Hu, P. (2023). Investigation on smart campus management platform based on digital twin. *Procedia Computer Science*, *228*, 937–945. DOI: 10.1016/j.procs.2023.11.123

Hussaini, A., Qian, C., Guo, Y., Lu, C., & Yu, W. (2023, May). Digital twins of smart campus: Performance evaluation using machine learning analysis. In *2023 IEEE/ACIS 21st International Conference on Software Engineering Research, Management and Applications (SERA)* (pp. 132-137). IEEE. DOI: DOI: 10.1109/SERA57763.2023.10197806

Joksimovic, S., Siemens, G., Wang, Y. E., San Pedro, M. O. Z., & Way, J. (2020). Editorial: Beyond cognitive ability. *Journal of Learning Analytics*, *7*(1), 1–4. DOI: 10.18608/jla.2020.71.1

Karanam, S. A. K., & Hartman, N. W. (2025). A systematic review of digital twin (DT) and virtual learning environments (VLE) for smart manufacturing education. *Manufacturing Letters*, *44*, 1597–1608. DOI: 10.1016/j.mfglet.2025.06.179

Krishna, S. M. (2025). Smart campus ecosystems: Designing digital twins for educational infrastructure and strategic management. *Eksplorium-Buletin Pusat Teknologi Bahan Galian Nuklir, 46*(1), 1279-1293. Retrieved from: https://eksplorium.com/index.php/journal/article/view/148

Kulik, J. A., & Fletcher, J. D. (2016). Effectiveness of intelligent tutoring systems: A meta-analytic review. *Review of Educational Research*, *86*(1), 42–78. DOI: 10.3102/0034654315581420

Li, H., & Hong, T. (2025, June). A digital twin platform for building performance monitoring and optimization: Performance simulation and case studies. In *Building Simulation (Vol. 18*, No. 6, pp. 1561-1579). Beijing: Tsinghua University Press. https://doi.org/DOI: 10.1007/s12273-025-1290-2

Lin, Y., Chen, L., Ali, A., Nugent, C., Cleland, I., Li, R., Ding, J., & Ning, H. (2024). Human digital twin: A survey. *Journal of Cloud Computing (Heidelberg, Germany)*, *13*(1), 131. DOI: 10.1186/s13677-024-00691-z

Lin, Y. Z., Patel, K., Alhamadah, A. H. J., Shih, B. P. J., Redondo, M. W., Corona, D. R. V., . . . Satam, P. (2025). Prism: A personalized, rapid, and immersive skill mastery framework for personalizing experiential learning through generative AI. In *Generative AI in Higher Education Assessment: Theory, Practice, and Ethical Implications* (pp. 45-69). Cham: Springer Nature Switzerland. https://doi.org//arXiv.2411.14433DOI: 10.48550

Lu, M., & Hu, Z. (2025). Digital twin-enhanced programming education: An empirical study on learning engagement and skill acquisition. *Computers*, *14*(8), 322. DOI: 10.3390/computers14080322

Manokeaw, S., Khuwuthyakorn, P., Chan, Y.-C., Tengtrairat, N., Jintapitak, M., Thinnukool, O., Buachart, C., Sinthamrongruk, T., Kridakorn Na Ayutthaya, T., Suriyanon, N., Kanangkaew, S., & Rinchumphu, D. (2025). A dynamic digital twin framework for sustainable facility management in a smart campus: A case study of Chiang Mai university. *Technologies*, *13*(10), 439. DOI: 10.3390/technologies13100439

Nalayini, C. M., Arunkumar, S., & Madesh, S. (2025). Role of artificial intelligence in enhancing school digital twins. *Journal of Artificial Intelligence and Capsule Networks*, *7*(2), 209–231. DOI: 10.36548/jaicn.2025.2.008

Pathak, R. K., & Upadhyay, P.Dr Rakesh Kumar PathakDr Prakash Upadhyay. (2024). Integration of digital twins technologies in education for experiential learning: Benefits and challenges. [IRJAEH]. *International Research Journal on Advanced Engineering Hub*, *2*(03), 442–449. DOI: 10.47392/IRJAEH.2024.0064

Perisic, A., Perisic, I., Lazic, M., & Perisic, B. (2025). Metamodeling approach to socio-technical systems' external context digital twins building: A higher education case study. *Applied Sciences (Basel, Switzerland)*, *15*(15), 8708. DOI: 10.3390/app15158708

Rebelo Marcolino, M., Reis Porto, T., Thompsen Primo, T., Targino, R., Ramos, V., Marques Queiroga, E., Munoz, R., & Cechinel, C. (2025). Student dropout prediction through machine learning optimization: Insights from Moodle log data. *Scientific Reports*, *15*(1), 9840. DOI: 10.1038/s41598-025-93918-1

Salendab, F. A., & Tago, K. L. (2026). Innovative approaches to revolutionize student-centered learning in the 21st century. In *Emerging Trends, Global Perspectives, and Systemic Transformation in AI* (pp. 33-62). IGI Global Scientific Publishing. https://doi.org/DOI: 10.4018/979-8-3373-5102-5.ch002

Salendab, F. A., Tago, K. L., Cogo, D. A., & Demafeliz, R. E. (2026). Transforming higher education: Theoretical foundations and innovative pedagogies for holistic student development. In *Higher Education Classrooms as Places for Inquiry: Stories and Methods from Practitioner Researchers* (pp. 207-236). IGI Global Scientific Publishing. https://doi.org/DOI: 10.4018/979-8-3373-0305-5.ch007

Santos, R., Piqueiro, H., Dias, R., & Rocha, C. D. (2024). Transitioning trends into action: A simulation-based Digital Twin architecture for enhanced strategic and operational decision-making. *Computers & Industrial Engineering*, *198*, 110616. DOI: 10.1016/j.cie.2024.110616

Speicher, T., DeFranco, J., Stricker, C., Kumara, S., & Bilén, S. (2025). Digital twin technology for engineering education: An experiential learning case study. *Industry and Higher Education*. Advance online publication. DOI: 10.1177/09504222261443589

Tao, F., Qi, Q., Liu, A., & Kusiak, A. (2018). Data-driven smart manufacturing. *Journal of Manufacturing Systems*, *48*, 157–169. DOI: 10.1016/j.jmsy.2018.01.006

Temple, L., Pereira, G. V., & Klausner, L. D. (2024). Unravelling the use of digital twins to assist decision-and policy-making in smart cities. *arXiv preprint arXiv:2405.20916.* https://doi.org//arXiv.2405.20916DOI: 10.18690/um.fov.4.2024.45

Thelen, A., Zhang, X., Fink, O., Lu, Y., Ghosh, S., Youn, B. D., Todd, M. D., Mahadevan, S., Hu, C., & Hu, Z. (2022). A comprehensive review of digital twin—part 1: Modeling and twinning enabling technologies. *Structural and Multidisciplinary Optimization*, *65*(12), 354. DOI: 10.1007/s00158-022-03425-4

Wagner, S., Gonnermann, C., Wegmann, M., Listl, F., Reinhart, G., & Weyrich, M. (2024). From framework to industrial implementation: The digital twin in process planning. *Journal of Intelligent Manufacturing*, *35*(8), 3793–3813. DOI: 10.1007/s10845-023-02268-0

Yao, J. F., Yang, Y., Wang, X. C., & Zhang, X. P. (2023). Systematic review of digital twin technology and applications. *Visual Computing for Industry, Biomedicine, and Art*, *6*(1), 10. DOI: 10.1186/s42492-023-00137-4

Zaballos, A., Briones, A., Massa, A., Centelles, P., & Caballero, V. (2020). A smart campus' digital twin for sustainable comfort monitoring. *Sustainability (Basel)*, *12*(21), 9196. DOI: 10.3390/su12219196

Zayed, S. M., Attiya, G. M., El-Sayed, A., & Hemdan, E. E. D. (2023). A review study on digital twins with artificial intelligence and internet of things: Concepts, opportunities, challenges, tools and future scope. *Multimedia Tools and Applications*, *82*(30), 47081–47107. DOI: 10.1007/s11042-023-15611-7

Zhong, Y., Li, C., Jiang, J., Fryer, L. K., & Shum, A. (2026). Can virtual reality promote cognitive, affective, and psychomotor learning? A synthesis of systematic reviews and meta-analytic evidence. *Journal of Educational Computing Research*, 07356331261434358. Advance online publication. DOI: 10.1177/07356331261434358

Chapter 5
Dynamic Digital Twin Modeling for Intelligent Learning Systems

Hamed Nozari
http://orcid.org/0000-0002-6500-6708
University of National and World Economy, Bulgaria

Zornitsa Yordanova
http://orcid.org/0000-0002-6056-8445
University of National and World Economy, Bulgaria

ABSTRACT

This chapter presents a dynamic digital twin framework for modeling, analyzing, and predicting the learning process. In this approach, the learner is considered as a time-dependent system whose state is represented by variables such as knowledge level, engagement rate, and retention rate. The proposed framework uses interpretable mathematical relationships to track learning changes over time and allows for adaptive feedback. Scenario analysis shows that digital twins can help improve knowledge growth, engagement sustainability, and learning retention.

1- INTRODUCTION

In recent decades, the evolution of digital technologies has led to a fundamental rethinking of the way learning systems are designed and implemented. Educational systems, which were previously designed mainly based on the provision of static content and predetermined paths, have now moved towards dynamic, adaptive, and data-driven approaches (Nozari, 2026). This paradigm shift is due, on the one hand,

DOI: 10.4018/979-8-2600-1674-9.ch005

to the increased access to behavioral data of learners and, on the other hand, to the development of advanced analytical tools that allow for a deeper understanding of the learning process (Li et al., 2026). However, despite significant advances, many intelligent learning systems still face serious limitations in accurately, continuously, and in real-time modeling of learner behavior.

One of the fundamental challenges in this area is the inability of many existing models to represent the true dynamics of learning. The learning process is inherently a time-consuming, nonlinear, and multidimensional process that simultaneously involves cognitive, behavioral, emotional, and environmental factors. However, in many common models, these complexities are considered in a simplified or static way, which reduces the accuracy of analysis and limits the predictive power of educational systems (She et al., 2023). Therefore, there is a need for frameworks that can model these dynamics in a structured, interpretable, and analyzable way.

In the meantime, the concept of digital twin, as one of the emerging technologies, has attracted widespread attention in various fields of engineering, management, and intelligent systems. A digital twin is generally defined as a virtual representation of a real system that is continuously updated with real-world data and allows for analysis, simulation, and prediction of system behavior (Wu & Qin, 2026). The concept was initially applied to manufacturing and engineering industries, but has gradually expanded to include areas such as health, transportation, and education (Aboulsafa et al., 2025).

In the field of learning, digital twins have the potential to create a dynamic model of the learner's state; a model that not only represents the learner's current state but can also predict future changes. Such a capability paves the way for a shift from reactive to predictive approaches in education (Nozari, 2026). However, a significant portion of the existing studies in this area have focused more on conceptual, statistical, or data-driven aspects and have paid less attention to the development of explicit, analyzable, and interpretable mathematical models for learning dynamics (Cong et al., 2026).

On the other hand, many advanced approaches in intelligent learning tend to use complex and in many cases uninterpretable models. Although these models can provide high accuracy in some situations, the lack of transparency in their structure makes their practical use in educational settings challenging (Kabashkin, 2025). In contrast, there is a need for models that are structurally simple, interpretable, and implementable while maintaining an appropriate level of accuracy. Such models can play a bridging role between educational data and educational decision-making.

Accordingly, the main objective of this research is to develop a dynamic modeling framework for digital twin-based learning; A framework that can display learner behavior over time in a structured manner. In this framework, the learning process is considered as a dynamic system in which key variables such as knowledge level, learner engagement, and learning retention rate are defined as the main components of the learner's state, and the dynamic relationships between them are modeled. This approach allows for the analysis of learning changes, the prediction of future trends, and the design of more effective educational interventions.

The main innovation of this research lies in combining the concept of the digital twin with an interpretable mathematical model for learning dynamics. Unlike many previous studies that either focus on historical data analysis or use complex and opaque models, this research attempts to provide a balanced framework that is both analytically sound and applicable to real educational environments. In addition, the effect of interactions between learners is also included in the model; A topic that allows for the analysis of learning in collaborative and social environments.

Finally, the structure of this chapter is arranged as follows: In the second section, the theoretical foundations and concepts related to digital twins in learning are reviewed. In the third section, the architecture of the learning digital twin system will be presented. Section four is dedicated to the development of a mathematical model of learning dynamics. In the fifth section, scenario-based analyses are described, and in the sixth section, discussion, conclusions, limitations, and suggested directions for future research will be presented.

2- FOUNDATIONS OF DIGITAL TWIN IN LEARNING

In recent years, the concept of digital twin has emerged as one of the most important data-driven approaches in the analysis and management of complex systems and has gradually expanded from the fields of engineering and manufacturing to other fields, including education (Lee et al., 2026). In general, a digital twin refers to a virtual and dynamic representation of a real system that is continuously updated through real data and has the ability to model the current state and future behavior of that system (Mei et al., 2025). This feature distinguishes the digital twin from traditional models, because here we are not dealing with a static or merely descriptive model, but rather with an analytical entity that continuously interacts with reality (Zhang et al., 2024).

In the field of learning, this concept is of particular importance, because the learning process is inherently dynamic, time-dependent, and dependent on multiple factors. The learner changes over time under the influence of educational inputs, environmental conditions, motivation, social interactions, and individual characteristics. Therefore, using static models to analyze this process cannot provide an accurate picture of the learner's actual behavior (Yordanova & Nozari, 2026). In such a context, digital twins are proposed as a tool that can represent these dynamics in the form of a structured model (Lv et al., 2021).

In traditional educational systems, learner data is mainly used for the purpose of reporting or evaluating performance. For example, test scores, attendance rates, or percentage of activity completion are considered as indicators of learner performance. However, these indicators often provide a static, retrospective, and limited picture of learning and cannot be effectively used to predict or guide the future trajectory of learning (Lei et al., 2026). In contrast, digital twins create a dynamic model of the learner, allowing for analysis of the current state and prediction of future changes (Nozari, 2026).

The digital twin architecture in learning is based on a three-layer interaction that includes the real system, the digital model, and the data flow between the two. The real system encompasses the learner and all of his or her activities in the learning environment (Zhao et al., 2026). These activities can include studying content, completing exercises, taking tests, interacting with other learners, and receiving feedback. The digital model transforms these activities into analyzable variables and represents the learner's state in terms of indicators such as knowledge level, engagement, progress rate, and quality of learning. The data stream acts as a link between the real system and the digital model, ensuring that the digital model is always in sync with the learner's actual state (Sun et al., 2020).

A key feature of the digital twin is the ability to transform raw data into structured, interpretable information. Learning data alone, without proper analysis, has limited value. For example, knowing how long a learner has spent studying does not necessarily indicate how much they have learned. However, when this data is put into the context of an analytical model, it can be used to infer variables such as engagement, concentration, or quality of learning (Tang et al., 2023). Here, the digital twin acts as an analytical interface that transforms data into usable knowledge.

In addition, digital twins allow for the observation and estimation of latent variables of learning. Many dimensions of learning, such as conceptual understanding, motivation, fatigue, or mental readiness, cannot be directly measured; however, these variables have a significant impact on the quality of learning (Nozari, 2025). Digital twins can estimate these latent variables using observable data, such as response patterns, interaction times, error rates, and repetitive behaviors, and present them in the form of an analyzable model (Wang et al., 2026). This capability is considered one of the most important advantages of this approach over traditional educational systems (Ye, 2024).

From an analytical perspective, the ability to predict learner behavior is another important capability of digital twins. Once the learner's state is defined in a dynamic model, possible future paths can be explored. For example, if a learner's engagement gradually decreases with an increase in errors, it can be predicted that his performance will decrease in the future. This type of analysis allows for predictive intervention, meaning that the educational system can take appropriate corrective action before a problem occurs (Nozari & Yordanova, 2026).

Digital twins also play an important role in personalizing learning. In traditional systems, personalization is usually limited to providing different content based on performance level. However, in the digital twin framework, personalization is multidimensional and dynamic. This means that the system can simultaneously consider multiple variables such as knowledge level, level of engagement, and learning rate and continuously adjust the learning path. This allows the learning experience to be uniquely tailored to each individual and their actual circumstances (Lei et al., 2023).

Another important point is the possibility of simulating different scenarios in the digital twin environment. In this framework, the effect of various changes in educational design can be examined without directly affecting the actual learner. For example, it can be analyzed what effect increasing the level of interaction, changing the content structure, or modifying the feedback method will have on the learning process. This capability makes digital twins a powerful tool for designing, testing, and optimizing educational systems (Karanam & Hartman, 2025).

Despite these advantages, implementing digital twins in learning also comes with challenges. One of the most important challenges is the complexity of human behavior, which cannot be easily modeled. Unlike physical systems, learner behavior is influenced by multiple cognitive, emotional, social, and environmental factors, some of which are not directly observable. In addition, the quality of input data plays a decisive role in the performance of a digital twin. Incomplete, unreliable, or noisy data can lead to inaccurate analyses and inappropriate instructional decisions (Kinsner, 2021).

Another challenge is related to issues related to data privacy and security. Learning data can provide sensitive information about the behavior, performance, and individual characteristics of learners. Therefore, digital twin-based systems must be designed in such a way that this data is used in a safe, responsible, and transparent manner. This is especially important in educational environments that deal with personal and behavioral data (Wang et al., 2024).

Overall, the digital twin in learning can be considered an innovative framework for modeling, analyzing, and improving the learning process. By combining real-world data, dynamic modeling, and predictive analytics, this approach enables a deeper understanding of learner behavior and more accurate instructional decisions. At the same time, successful implementation of this framework requires serious attention to data quality, appropriate model design, interpretability of results, and management of challenges related to data security and privacy.

3- SYSTEM ARCHITECTURE OF LEARNING DIGITAL TWIN

The architecture of the learning digital twin system is designed to create a dynamic, updatable, and synchronized representation of the learner's real-world situation. In this framework, the digital twin not only serves as a data storage but also acts as an analytics layer that models learner behavioral and performance changes over time. This architecture is defined in a modular manner to allow for expansion, connectivity to real-world data sources, and use in different learning environments.

In general, the system structure consists of five main layers: (1) the real-world system (learner) layer, (2) the data collection layer, (3) the state modeling core, (4) the digital twin, and (5) the feedback mechanism. These components interact with each other to form a continuous cycle of data acquisition, analysis, updating, and decision-making.

Figure 1. Learning digital twin system architecture and data flow between components

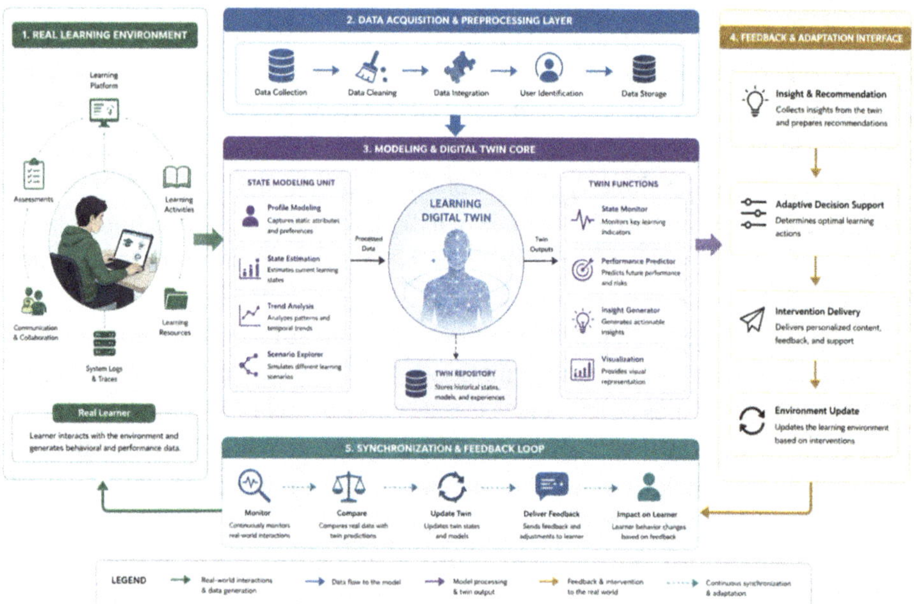

The first layer is the Learner Layer, which includes the learner and all of his/her interactions with the learning environment. These interactions include activities such as viewing content, responding to exercises, participating in assessments, and participating in the learning process. The data generated at this level is temporal in nature and reflects behavioral and performance changes during the learning period.

In the second layer, the Data Acquisition Layer is responsible for receiving, recording, and preprocessing data. In this section, raw data extracted from educational systems (such as e-learning platforms) is converted into structured data. This layer ensures that the data is time-synchronous and ready to enter the analytical model. Operations such as noise removal, normalization, and data integration are also performed at this stage.

Next, the processed data is fed into the State Modeling Unit. This part is considered the analytical heart of the system and its task is to convert the observed data into interpretable state variables. In this core, the learner's state is represented as a set of indicators such as knowledge level, engagement level, and retention rate. This conversion is done through mathematical relationships and dynamic models, so that changes in these variables can be tracked and analyzed over time.

The output of the modeling core is transmitted to the Digital Twin Layer. In this layer, a digital version of the learner's state is created and continuously updated. The digital twin acts as a dynamic entity that not only maintains the current state, but also has the ability to predict future trends. This feature allows for the analysis of different learning scenarios without interfering with the real system.

Finally, there is the Feedback Mechanism, which feeds the results of the digital twin analysis back to the real system. This feedback can be applied in the form of a learning path suggestion, adjusting the difficulty level of the content, or changing the type of educational interaction. The important point in this section is that the feedback is generated adaptively and based on the current state of the learner, not based on predetermined rules.

The data flow in this architecture operates as a closed loop. In this way, data is first received from the learner, after processing and modeling, it is represented in the form of a digital twin, and finally, the analysis results are returned as feedback to the real system. This cycle is continuously repeated and allows the system to gradually adapt to the characteristics of the learner.

From an analytical perspective, the main advantage of this architecture is that it allows for indirect observation of hidden learning variables. While many key learning indicators (such as conceptual understanding or concentration) cannot be directly measured, a digital twin estimates these variables using observable data and presents them in the form of a structured model.

4- MATHEMATICAL MODELING OF LEARNING DYNAMICS

For a learning digital twin to go beyond a static representation and become a tool for analyzing and predicting learner behavior, it is necessary to formulate the learning process in a dynamic mathematical framework. In this section, learning is considered as a dynamic system in which the learner's state changes over time, influenced by instructional inputs, interaction rates, learning loss, and behavioral characteristics. Such an approach allows the digital twin to represent not only the learner's current state, but also to estimate the likely path of future changes based on observed data.

In the proposed model, the learner's state at time t is represented by a state vector. This vector consists of three main components: the level of knowledge, the level of engagement in the learning process, and the rate of retention. Therefore, the learner's state is defined as follows:

$$X(t) = [K(t), E(t), R(t)] \tag{1}$$

In this context, $K(t)$ represents the learner's level of knowledge at time t, $E(t)$ represents the learner's level of engagement or involvement in the learning process, and $R(t)$ represents the learner's ability to retain and retrieve the learned material. These variables are not necessarily directly observable, but they can be estimated through data such as assessment results, content engagement time, activity completion rates, and participation patterns. For this reason, the state vector acts as a link between the raw educational data and the digital twin analytical model.

The evolution of the level of knowledge over time is modeled based on the balance between new learning and learning loss. In the simplest case, the change in the level of knowledge can be represented by the following relationship:

$$K(t+1) = K(t) + a \cdot I(t) - b \cdot D(t) \tag{2}$$

In this relation, $I(t)$ represent the amount of educational input at time t, which can include studying content, doing exercises, receiving feedback, or participating in an educational activity. On the other hand, $D(t)$ represents learning loss or forgetting. The coefficients a and b also determine the intensity of the educational input effect and the intensity of the learning loss effect, respectively. This relationship shows that the increase in knowledge is not simply a function of the amount of content provided, but also depends on the quality of the learner's absorption and the degree of cognitive or behavioral loss.

Along with the level of knowledge, the level of learner engagement plays an important role in the sustainability and effectiveness of the learning process. Educational engagement can change under the influence of factors such as the attractiveness of the content, the level of interaction, the appropriateness of the difficulty of the activities, and the level of fatigue. To represent this dynamic, the following relationship is considered:

$$E(t+1) = E(t) + c \cdot S(t) - d \cdot F(t) \quad (3)$$

In this equation, $S(t)$ represents the level of stimulation or educational engagement, and $F(t)$ represents the level of fatigue, decreased motivation, or decreased participation. The coefficients c and d also determine the sensitivity of learner engagement to engagement and fatigue. Therefore, if educational activities are designed properly, they can increase the level of engagement; but if the educational pressure is excessive or there is no proportion between the learner's ability and the level of difficulty of the activity, the level of engagement will decrease.

Retention rate is also considered as another major component of learner status. In this framework, retention is the simultaneous result of knowledge level and engagement. Accordingly, the following relationship is defined to represent retention rate:

$$R(t) = \lambda \cdot K(t) \cdot E(t) \quad (4)$$

In this regard, λ is the coefficient regulating the retention rate. This model states that effective retention of material occurs when the learner has both a sufficient level of knowledge and is actively involved in the learning process. Therefore, knowledge without sufficient involvement may not lead to sustained learning, and high involvement in the absence of an appropriate knowledge structure cannot lead to effective retention.

After computing the state variables, the digital twin must continuously synchronize with the learner's real state. This synchronization is accomplished through a state vector update mechanism:

$$X(t+1) = X(t) + \Delta X(t) \quad (5)$$

In this regard, $\Delta X(t)$ represents the changes in the learner's state in the time interval t to $t + 1$ and is extracted from the dynamic relationships related to knowledge, engagement, and retention. This structure allows the digital twin to gradually modify its state based on new data, transforming from a static model into a dynamic and updatable representation.

$$K_i\left(t+1\right) = K_i\left(t\right) + \sum_j w_{ij} \cdot K_j\left(t\right) \quad (6)$$

In this regard, $K_i\left(t\right)$ is the knowledge level of learner i at time t and K_j (t) is the knowledge level of learner j. The coefficient w_{ij} indicates the intensity of the influence of learner j on learner i. This weight can be determined based on the amount of interaction, similarity of knowledge level, participation in group activities, or the quality of educational exchange. In this way, the proposed model can also reflect the effect of social learning and group interactions in the digital twin framework.

Overall, the presented mathematical model provides a coherent framework for representing learning dynamics in the digital twin. By defining state variables and the transitive relationships between them, this model enables the analysis of learner changes over time and can be a basis for predicting the learning process, identifying performance declines, and designing appropriate educational interventions.

5- SCENARIO-BASED ANALYSIS

In order to evaluate the performance and behavior of the learning digital twin system under different conditions, scenario-based analysis is considered as one of the key approaches in this research. In this framework, the performance of the proposed model is examined in several distinct situations to quantitatively and comparatively analyze the impact of the presence of the digital twin as well as the role of learning interactions on knowledge dynamics, engagement, and retention. These scenarios are designed to start from a basic case without the use of the digital twin and gradually expand to conditions of higher complexity, including adaptive feedback and interactions between learners.

In the first scenario, the learning process is considered without the presence of the digital twin. In this case, the learner proceeds solely based on fixed educational inputs without receiving adaptive feedback or dynamic analysis. In such situations, knowledge growth is expected to be slow and accompanied by significant fluctuations, because the system has no understanding of the learner's real state and is unable to adjust the learning path. This scenario is considered as a basis for comparison for evaluating other cases.

In the second scenario, a digital twin is added to the system, but interactions between learners are not considered. In this situation, the system is able to continuously estimate the learner's state and provide adaptive feedback based on it. As a result, the learning path becomes more targeted and content that is not appropriate for the learner's level is avoided. This leads to a significant improvement in the rate of knowledge growth as well as an increase in the stability of engagement. However, due to the lack of social interactions, some collaborative learning capacities remain unused.

In the third scenario, in addition to the digital twin, interactions between learners are also included in the model. In this case, the system not only analyzes the individual state of each learner, but also considers the interactions between learners. These interactions can include knowledge exchange, participation in group activities, or learning through observation. As a result, knowledge growth is expected to occur more rapidly and retention levels to increase, as learning takes place in an interactive and dynamic context.

Figure 2. Knowledge evolution under different learning scenarios

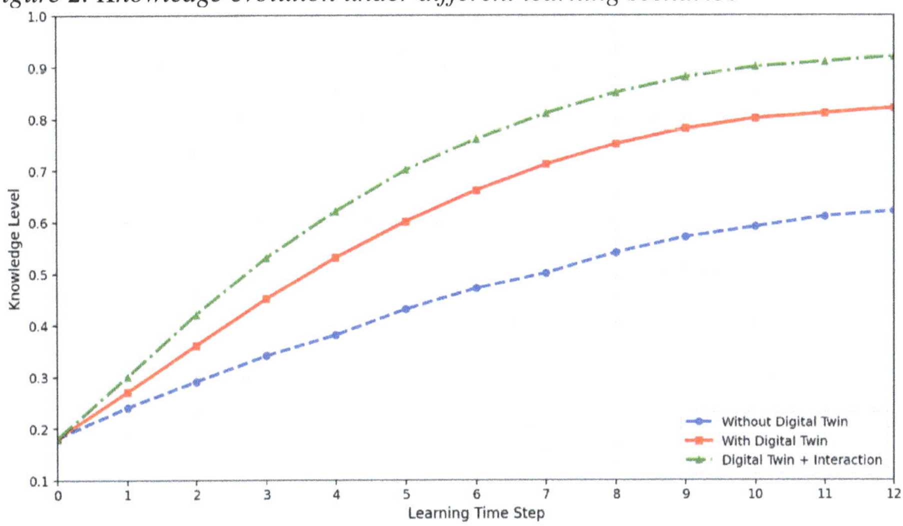

As can be seen in Figure 2, the trends in knowledge level changes in the three different scenarios are distinguishable from each other. In the baseline case, knowledge growth is accompanied by a gentle slope and more fluctuations, indicating the lack of an adaptive mechanism in the learning process. With the introduction of the digital twin, the slope of the curve increases and the learning path becomes more uniform, indicating the effectiveness of model-based feedback. In the third scenario, where interactions between learners are also considered, knowledge growth is observed at the fastest speed and with the least fluctuations. This result indicates that the combination of individual analysis and social interactions can act as a reinforcing factor in the learning process.

Table 1. Comparative performance of learning scenarios

Scenario	Final Knowledge Level	Engagement Stability	Retention Rate	Learning Efficiency
Without Digital Twin	0.62	Low	0.48	Moderate
With Digital Twin	0.81	Medium	0.67	High
Digital Twin + Interaction	0.89	High	0.78	Very High

The results presented in Table 1 also quantitatively confirm this pattern. As can be seen, the use of digital twins has led to a significant increase in the final level of knowledge and retention rate. In addition, the stability of engagement has also improved, indicating a better balance between cognitive load and the level of interaction. In the third scenario, where interactions between learners are also taken into account, all indicators have reached their maximum values. This shows that learning in an interactive environment, along with the analytical support of the digital twin, can create the most efficiency.

Overall, the scenario-based analysis shows that digital twins not only help improve individual learner performance, but also, when combined with interactive mechanisms, can act as a key infrastructure for the development of intelligent and dynamic learning systems.

6- DISCUSSION

The findings of this study show that the use of digital twins in learning systems can be considered a conceptual and practical transformation in the design and management of educational processes. Unlike traditional approaches that consider learning statically and based on predetermined paths, the proposed framework allows for the analysis of learner behavior in a dynamic, continuous and real-world data-based manner. This change in attitude has significant implications for improving the quality of learning, increasing the efficiency of educational systems, and personalizing the learning experience.

One of the most important results of this study is the decisive role of digital twins in improving the process of knowledge growth. As observed in the scenario analysis, in a system without a digital twin, the learning process is associated with greater fluctuations and lower efficiency. This can be attributed to the lack of an accurate understanding of the learner's situation, such that the educational system is unable to adapt the content provided to the actual level of knowledge or individual needs. In contrast, when a digital twin is added to the system, it is possible to estimate the learner's state and provide appropriate feedback. This allows the learning path to be formed in a more targeted manner and prevents the waste of educational resources.

On the other hand, the results show that the impact of the digital twin is not limited to improving the level of knowledge, but also affects other dimensions of learning. In particular, increasing the stability of learner engagement is one of the important consequences of using this technology. In traditional systems, the mismatch between the level of difficulty of the content and the ability of the learner can lead to a decrease in motivation or an increase in fatigue. However, in the proposed framework, using dynamic models, it is possible to continuously adjust the level of interaction and the type of educational activities. As a result, the learner is placed in a balanced state in terms of cognitive load, which leads to an increase in the quality of learning.

Another noteworthy point is the role of interactions between learners in enhancing the performance of the system. The results of the third scenario show that combining digital twins with social interaction mechanisms can significantly increase learning efficiency. This finding is in line with social learning theories that emphasize the importance of interaction, collaboration, and knowledge exchange in the learning process. However, what is important in this research is how these interactions are integrated into the digital twin framework. In other words, interactions not only directly affect learning, but also, through modeling and analysis in the digital twin, can be used as a structured input into the educational decision-making process.

From a modeling perspective, one of the main advantages of the presented framework is the balance between simplicity and explanatory power. While many recent studies tend to use complex, AI-based models, this research shows that even relatively simple mathematical relationships can represent the main dynamics of learning well. This feature not only increases the interpretability of the model, but also facilitates its implementation in real-world environments. This approach can be a significant advantage, especially in educational applications, where transparency and explainability are of great importance.

Despite the aforementioned advantages, some challenges need to be addressed. One of the most important limitations is the dependence of the model on the quality of the input data. If the data collected from learners is incomplete, noisy, or unrepresentative, the accuracy of the digital twin will be reduced and may lead to incorrect decisions. Furthermore, the precise determination of model parameters, such as learning and loss coefficients, requires experimental analysis and proper calibration, which can be challenging in real-world environments.

Overall, the results of this research indicate that the digital twin can serve as a key infrastructure for the development of intelligent learning systems. By enabling dynamic analysis, behavior prediction, and adaptive feedback, this technology can significantly improve the quality and efficiency of the learning process. However, fully exploiting its potential requires simultaneous attention to data quality, proper model design, and effective integration with real-world learning environments.

7- CONCLUSION

This chapter aims to provide a coherent framework for dynamic modeling of the learning process based on digital twins, showing how learner behavior can be represented, analyzed, and predicted over time based on an interpretable mathematical structure. Unlike conventional approaches that often focus on content presentation or ex post analysis, the proposed framework considers learning as a dynamic system in which the learner's state is continuously changing and these changes can be tracked through a structured model. This change of perspective allows for a shift from static learning management to an adaptive, responsive, and data-driven system.

One of the main achievements of this research is the presentation of a state-based model in which learning is described by a set of key variables, including knowledge level, engagement, and retention rate. These variables act as the main components of the digital twin and enable the transformation of raw learning data into analyzable information. The dynamic relationships defined between these variables indicate that learning is not a linear and uniform process, but rather the result of a complex interaction between educational inputs, individual characteristics, and environmental conditions. As a result, the digital twin can represent these interactions in the form of an interpretable model and be used as a basis for educational decisions.

From an applied perspective, the results of the analyses conducted showed that the use of the digital twin can lead to significant improvements in key learning indicators. In particular, increasing the level of knowledge, improving the stability of engagement, and improving the retention rate are among the direct consequences of using this approach. These results indicate that the digital twin can act as an intermediate layer between educational data and educational decisions and guide the learning path in a targeted manner by providing adaptive feedback. In addition, the integration of interactions between learners into the model framework showed that social learning, along with individual analysis, can significantly increase the effectiveness of the system.

Another noteworthy point is the scalability of the proposed framework. The presented structure is designed in such a way that it can be easily integrated with a variety of educational systems, from e-learning platforms to organizational learning environments. Also, due to the use of transparent and interpretable mathematical models, it is possible to adapt it to real data and adjust the parameters based on the specific conditions of each educational environment. This feature makes the proposed framework a practical tool for implementation at different scales.

Despite the advantages mentioned, this research is also accompanied by limitations that must be considered for the interpretation of the results and future developments. First, the presented model is designed based on a limited set of state variables, and although these variables cover the main dimensions of learning, they cannot fully reflect all the cognitive, emotional, and social complexities of learning. Second, the validity of the model depends on the quality of the input data. In situations where the data is incomplete, noisy, or unrepresentative, the accuracy of the learner's state estimation decreases. Also, determining appropriate values for the model parameters requires experimental data and a calibration process that may be challenging in real environments. Another limitation is the assumption of simplification in dynamic relationships that is made to maintain interpretability, but may in some cases reduce the accuracy of the model in complex situations.

Accordingly, several directions for future research can be proposed. One of the most important directions is to develop the model by considering more and more complex variables, so that the emotional, motivational, and social dimensions of learning are also included in the digital twin framework. Also, using large-scale real-world data for model validation and calibration could be an important step towards operationalizing this framework. Developing real-time versions of digital twins, which can analyze the learner's state in real time and provide feedback, is another important future direction. In addition, investigating how to integrate this model with new technologies such as recommender systems or intelligent learning environments could help increase its efficiency and scope.

Overall, this research shows that digital twins can be used as an innovative framework for understanding, analyzing, and improving the learning process. By enabling dynamic modeling and providing data-driven feedback, this approach has the potential to become a key element in the design of a new generation of learning systems.

REFERENCES

Aboulsafa, E. I., Elkhayat, G. A., Abdul-kader, H. M., & Almorsy, S. A. (2025, May). Proposed Student Digital Twin Data Model and System Architecture for Personalized Learning. In *2025 International Conference on Machine Intelligence and Smart Innovation (ICMISI)* (pp. 341-346). IEEE. DOI: 10.1109/ICMISI65108.2025.11115606

Cong, W., Tao, W., & Jinsong, B. (2026). Agentic digital twin-embedded maintenance methodology for energy equipment: A self-evolving operational paradigm. *Journal of Manufacturing Systems*, *84*, 100–116. DOI: 10.1016/j.jmsy.2025.11.020

Kabashkin, I. (2025). AI-based digital twins of students: A new paradigm for competency-oriented learning transformation. *Information (Basel)*, *16*(10), 846. DOI: 10.3390/info16100846

Karanam, S. A. K., & Hartman, N. W. (2025). A systematic review of digital twin (DT) and virtual learning environments (VLE) for smart manufacturing education. *Manufacturing Letters*, *44*, 1597–1608. DOI: 10.1016/j.mfglet.2025.06.179

Kinsner, W. (2021, September). Digital twins for personalized education and lifelong learning. In 2021 IEEE Canadian conference on electrical and computer engineering (CCECE) (pp. 1-6). IEEE. DOI: 10.1109/CCECE53047.2021.9569178

Lee, D., Kang, Y. S., & Noh, S. D. (2026). Digital twin-driven deep reinforcement learning for real-time optimisation in dynamic AGV systems. *International Journal of Production Research*, *64*(1), 106–124. DOI: 10.1080/00207543.2025.2543491

Lei, M., He, G., Ouyang, Y., Shan, P., & Wang, M. (2026). Cloud-Edge Fusion for Advanced Dynamic Digital Twin Models in Intelligent Distribution Networks. *Journal of Electrical Engineering & Technology*, *21*(1), 1037–1044. DOI: 10.1007/s42835-025-02447-4

Lei, Z., Zhou, H., Hu, W., Liu, G. P., & Guan, S. (2023). Web-based digital twin communication system of power systems for training and education. *IEEE Transactions on Power Systems*, *39*(2), 3592–3602. DOI: 10.1109/TPWRS.2023.3308510

Li, Y., Zhang, C., Guo, Z., Yang, N., Yuan, D., & Ding, W. (2026). SafeTwinNet: Secure and Adaptive Learning Ecosystems for Digital Twins. IEEE Communications Standards Magazine.

Lv, Z., Li, Y., Feng, H., & Lv, H. (2021). Deep learning for security in digital twins of cooperative intelligent transportation systems. *IEEE Transactions on Intelligent Transportation Systems*, *23*(9), 16666–16675. DOI: 10.1109/TITS.2021.3113779

Mei, S., Xie, Y., Liu, J., Wu, J., & Zhang, C. (2025). Physics-based modeling and intelligent optimal decision method for digital twin system towards sustainable CNC equipment. *Robotics and Computer-integrated Manufacturing, 95*, 103028. DOI: 10.1016/j.rcim.2025.103028

Nozari, H. (2025). Integrating Neuromorphic Intelligence with Fuzzy Multi-Objective Models in Resilient Green Supply Chain Design. Process Integration and Optimization for Sustainability, 1-14.

Nozari, H. (2026). AI-Augmented Creative Assessment: From Static Tests to Dynamic Insight Generation. In AI-Augmented Creativity in Learning Analytics (pp. 25-42). IGI Global Scientific Publishing.

Nozari, H. (2026). Digital twin-based predictive maintenance in cold chain logistics. *Operations Research, 60*(1), 481–499. DOI: 10.1051/ro/2025167

Nozari, H. (2026). Self-Evolving Neuromorphic Systems for Predictive Learning Interventions. In AI-Augmented Creativity in Learning Analytics (pp. 105-122). IGI Global Scientific Publishing.

Nozari, H., & Yordanova, Z. (2026). Agentic artificial intelligence-driven digital twin for real-time irrigation control with fuzzy sustainability objectives. An International Journal of Optimization and Control: Theories & Applications, 026040013.

She, M., Xiao, M., & Zhao, Y. (2023). Technological implication of the digital twin approach on the intelligent education system. International journal of humanoid robotics, 20(02n03), 2250005.

Sun, W., Xu, N., Wang, L., Zhang, H., & Zhang, Y. (2020). Dynamic digital twin and federated learning with incentives for air-ground networks. *IEEE Transactions on Network Science and Engineering, 9*(1), 321–333. DOI: 10.1109/TNSE.2020.3048137

Tang, L., Wen, M., Shan, Z., Li, L., Liu, Q., & Chen, Q. (2023). Digital twin-enabled efficient federated learning for collision warning in intelligent driving. *IEEE Transactions on Intelligent Transportation Systems, 25*(3), 2573–2585. DOI: 10.1109/TITS.2023.3330938

Wang, K., Zhang, L., Jia, Z., Cheng, H., Lu, H., & Cui, J. (2024). A framework and method for equipment digital twin dynamic evolution based on IExATCN. *Journal of Intelligent Manufacturing, 35*(4), 1571–1583. DOI: 10.1007/s10845-023-02125-0

Wang, T., Li, H. X., Wang, L., & Wang, X. V. (2026). Spatiotemporal dynamic modeling approach for distributed thermal processes under digital twin framework. *Advanced Engineering Informatics, 71*, 104384. DOI: 10.1016/j.aei.2026.104384

Wu, X., & Qin, P. (2026). Adaptive Lighting and Thermal Comfort Control Strategies in Digital Twin Classroom via Deep Reinforcement Learning. *Electronics (Basel), 15*(4), 873. DOI: 10.3390/electronics15040873

Ye, Y. (2024, January). A higher education information management system based on digital twin technology and artificial intelligence algorithms. In *2024 Asia-Pacific Conference on Software Engineering, Social Network Analysis and Intelligent Computing (SSAIC)* (pp. 172-176). IEEE. DOI: 10.1109/SSAIC61213.2024.00039

Yordanova, Z., & Nozari, H. (2026). Seamless Data Integration for Predictive Learning Environments. In AI-Augmented Creativity in Learning Analytics (pp. 293-318). IGI Global Scientific Publishing.

Zhang, J., Zhu, J., Tu, W., Wang, M., Yang, Y., Qian, F., & Xu, Y. (2024). The effectiveness of a digital twin learning system in assisting engineering education courses: A case of landscape architecture. *Applied Sciences (Basel, Switzerland), 14*(15), 6484. DOI: 10.3390/app14156484

Zhao, T., Hu, F., Gou, H., Wang, J., & Bao, Y. (2026, February). Digital twins for static and dynamic responses of a continuous rigid frame bridge based on multi-task learning and optimization algorithm. In *Structures* (Vol. 84, p. 111006). Elsevier.

Chapter 6

Cognitive and Behavioral Modeling in Digital Learning Systems

Deepak Gupta
http://orcid.org/0000-0003-3929-1362
Institute of Technology and Management, Gwalior, India

Rano Khamraeva
Termez University of Economics and Service, Uzbekistan

Nigora Tashlanova
Fergana State Technical University, Uzbekistan

Bakhrom Jurayev
Shakhrisabz State Pedagogical Institute, Uzbekistan

Tokhirjon Ismailov
http://orcid.org/0000-0002-8571-3653
Mamun University, Uzbekistan

Abdusattor Khaxarovich Abdurakhmonov
Tashkent Institute of Chemical Technology, Uzbekistan

Maxmud Mardonov
Navoi State University of Mining and Technologies, Uzbekistan

ABSTRACT

Digital learning systems are evolving well beyond static content delivery toward dynamic, context-aware environments capable of modeling the whole learner. This chapter presents a Digital Twin–Cognitive-Behavioral Modeling (DT-CBM) framework that integrates knowledge tracing, affective state recognition, self-regulated learning (SRL) detection, and reinforcement-based pathway optimization within a unified digital twin architecture. Drawing on multimodal data—clickstreams, physiological signals, facial expressions, and assessment logs—the framework constructs a living computational mirror of each learner's cognitive and behav-

DOI: 10.4018/979-8-2600-1674-9.ch006

ioral state. Explainable AI (XAI) mechanisms translate opaque model outputs into actionable, transparent feedback for learners and educators alike. The chapter reviews foundational theories, examines current modeling techniques, identifies persistent limitations, and proposes a forward-looking architecture suited to lifelong adaptive learning.

1. INTRODUCTION

The emergence of sophisticated digital learning systems has fundamentally altered the educational landscape by enabling instructional content to be tailored dynamically to individual learner needs. Yet despite decades of research in intelligent tutoring systems (ITS) and adaptive learning technologies, a persistent gap remains between the behavioral complexity of real human learners and the simplified computational representations that most systems employ. A learner is not merely a knowledge state to be updated; she is a cognitively active, emotionally responsive, and metacognitively self-regulating agent whose engagement fluctuates continuously across time, task type, and social context.

Cognitive modeling—the computational representation of internal mental processes including working memory load, knowledge acquisition, attention regulation, and problem-solving strategy selection—has a rich history in artificial intelligence and cognitive science. Behavioral modeling complements cognitive modeling by capturing observable patterns such as response latency distributions, help-seeking frequency and timing, navigation sequences, error recovery strategies, and persistence behavior under conditions of failure or frustration. Together, these two dimensions constitute a rich, multifaceted profile of the learning process that extends far beyond the correctness-rate and time-on-task metrics that dominate conventional learning management system dashboards.

The concept of the digital twin—a continuously synchronized, high-fidelity computational counterpart of a physical entity or human agent—offers a promising integrative architecture for unifying cognitive and behavioral modeling within a single learner representation. Applied to education, a digital twin model aggregates multimodal behavioral signals in real time, updates an evolving cognitive-state representation continuously, simulates probable learning trajectories under alternative instructional interventions, and prescribes personalized pedagogical actions (Toofaninejad et al., 2024). This framing repositions cognitive and behavioral modeling not as isolated technical components implemented separately within ITS architectures, but as the epistemic core of a holistic, lifelong adaptive learning ecosystem.

This chapter advances the argument that the integration of cognitive and behavioral modeling techniques within digital twin architectures constitutes the next major frontier for intelligent educational technology. Drawing on recent advances in deep knowledge tracing (DKT), affective computing, self-regulated learning (SRL) detection, reinforcement learning-based path optimization, and explainable artificial intelligence (XAI), the chapter proposes a unified Digital Twin–Cognitive-Behavioral Modeling (DT-CBM) framework. This framework is situated explicitly within the theoretical traditions of educational psychology, learning analytics, and the emerging science of learning engineering.

The practical motivation for this work is compelling. Global digital learning adoption has accelerated dramatically following large-scale disruptions in conventional educational delivery, and learner populations have become increasingly heterogeneous in prior knowledge, motivational orientation, digital fluency, and socioeconomic context. One-size-fits-all adaptive systems that adjust only content difficulty are manifestly insufficient for this diversity. Systems capable of simultaneously modeling what learners know, how they feel, how effectively they self-regulate, and how their learning efficiency evolves over sessions and semesters represent a qualitative leap in educational intelligence.

The chapter is organized as follows. Section 2 reviews foundational theoretical perspectives underpinning cognitive and behavioral modeling. Section 3 surveys core cognitive modeling techniques. Section 4 addresses behavioral and affective modeling. Section 5 presents the DT-CBM framework in detail. Section 6 discusses XAI integration. Section 7 addresses implementation challenges and ethical considerations. Section 8 outlines future research directions. Section 9 concludes.

2. THEORETICAL FOUNDATIONS

2.1 Cognitive Theory of Multimedia Learning

Mayer's (2024) cognitive theory of multimedia learning (CTML) remains a cornerstone of evidence-based instructional design. CTML posits that learners process verbal and pictorial information through separate cognitive channels—auditory-verbal and visual-pictorial—each subject to limited processing capacity constraints. The theory identifies three critical cognitive processes in multimedia learning: selecting relevant words and images, organizing them into coherent mental representations, and integrating those representations with prior knowledge retrieved from long-term memory. Effective instructional design reduces extraneous cognitive load (imposed by poor design), manages intrinsic load (inherent to the material complexity), and facilitates generative processing that produces deep understanding.

For digital learning systems, CTML directs design attention toward how presentation modality, pacing, segmentation, signaling, and spatial contiguity of verbal and visual elements affect cognitive load—variables that behavioral data can operationalize through response latency, error frequency, hint usage, and navigation patterns. Recent meta-analytic evidence synthesized by Noetel et al. (2022) confirms across 17 prior reviews that instructional design choices grounded in CTML yield statistically significant and practically meaningful learning gains, underscoring the importance of coupling cognitive theory with data-driven behavioral modeling.

Critically, CTML implies that cognitive load is not static but fluctuates moment-to-moment depending on task demand, presentation complexity, interface design, and the learner's current knowledge state. Digital learning systems that monitor cognitive load dynamically—through response latency patterns, error type distributions, or physiological proxies such as pupil dilation and electrodermal activity—can intervene in real time to adjust presentation difficulty, introduce worked examples, reduce interface complexity, or provide targeted segmentation cues. Integrating CTML principles into a behavioral modeling pipeline thus creates a theoretically grounded basis for adaptive content delivery that is sensitive to both the instructional material and the individual learner.

2.2 Self-Regulated Learning Theory

Zimmerman's cyclical model of self-regulated learning (SRL), operationalized within digital learning contexts by researchers including Azevedo et al. (2022), provides a complementary framework to CTML. SRL theory holds that effective learners cycle through three phases: forethought (goal-setting, strategic planning, task analysis, and self-efficacy calibration), performance (attention focusing, strategy deployment, self-monitoring, and help-seeking), and self-reflection (self-evaluation, causal attribution, affective reaction, and adaptive inference for future cycles). Each phase generates distinctive behavioral signatures—including navigation choices, time allocation patterns, help request sequences, re-reading behaviors, and note-taking actions—that machine learning algorithms can detect and classify from interaction log data.

Azevedo et al. (2022) present extensive evidence from the MetaTutor platform demonstrating that SRL processes are highly dynamic within single learning sessions, with learners shifting between productive strategies (elaborative interrogation, self-testing, monitoring comprehension) and maladaptive behaviors (shallow reading, excessive hint use, off-task navigation) in patterns that differ sharply between high- and low-performing learners. These findings validate the importance of continuous, session-spanning behavioral monitoring rather than episodic snapshot assessment, and establish the behavioral richness of interaction logs as a primary SRL inference medium.

Garrison (2022) extends SRL into collaborative digital environments through the community of inquiry framework, emphasizing shared metacognition—the collective regulation of learning processes through social discourse—as a driver of emergent group outcomes. This perspective highlights that behavioral modeling in networked digital learning contexts must attend to social interaction patterns, co-regulation episodes, peer-influence dynamics, and the temporal alignment of individual and collective SRL cycles alongside individual cognitive traces. The DT-CBM framework proposed in this chapter accommodates both individual and socially situated SRL processes, providing a foundation for its extension to collaborative and community-based lifelong learning environments.

2.3 Affective-Cognitive Integration

Research in educational neuroscience and affective computing has established robust bidirectional relationships between emotional states and cognitive performance. Frustration, confusion, boredom, delight, and flow—the principal affective states documented in digital learning environments—exert measurable influences on working memory allocation, persistence under difficulty, strategy selection, and long-term retention. The integration of affective signals with cognitive models requires bridging two historically separate research traditions within a unified representational architecture. Bhatt et al. (2023) survey machine learning approaches to cognitive behavioral analysis and emphasize the importance of context-sensitive, multimodal fusion strategies that transcend the ecological validity limitations inherent in laboratory-only affective datasets.

The theoretical case for affective-cognitive integration in adaptive systems rests on the well-established finding that purely cognitive models consistently underpredict real-world learning outcomes because they omit the motivational and emotional variables that mediate the relationship between instruction and learning. Learners who are highly anxious, persistently bored, or chronically frustrated may possess adequate domain knowledge yet fail to apply it effectively during assessment. Conversely, learners experiencing flow states characterized by optimal challenge-skill balance may acquire knowledge faster and retain it longer than cognitive load metrics alone would predict. Effective DT-CBM systems must therefore model affective state trajectories alongside cognitive state trajectories, enabling interventions that target both simultaneously.

3. COGNITIVE MODELING TECHNIQUES

3.1 Knowledge Tracing and Its Evolution

Knowledge tracing (KT) constitutes the oldest and most extensively studied branch of cognitive modeling in educational systems. Abdelrahman et al. (2023) provide a comprehensive survey of the field, tracing its evolution from Bayesian Knowledge Tracing (BKT)—which models each learnable skill as a binary latent variable updated by a four-parameter hidden Markov model—through Additive Factor Models (AFM) and Performance Factor Analysis (PFA), which explicitly represent practice opportunity effects, to Deep Knowledge Tracing (DKT), which employs recurrent neural networks (RNNs) to track multi-skill acquisition trajectories over arbitrarily long interaction sequences. DKT's capacity to capture complex temporal dependencies in learner behavior, including cross-skill transfer effects and learning rate heterogeneity, represents a significant advance over the Markovian assumptions and independence constraints of BKT.

Recent developments in knowledge tracing have focused on two complementary directions: architectural enhancement and auxiliary task integration. Liu et al. (2023) demonstrate that jointly training DKT models on response prediction alongside auxiliary objectives—specifically concept-relation prediction and exercise difficulty estimation—substantially improves generalization performance on held-out student cohorts, reducing knowledge state estimation error by margins that translate meaningfully into improved intervention timing. Su et al. (2023) introduce learning curve integration into deep KT architectures, explicitly modeling the characteristic power-law improvement trajectories associated with skill acquisition and enabling the system to distinguish genuine mastery consolidation from transient performance fluctuations caused by context, fatigue, or interference. These refinements bring KT models substantially closer to psychometrically grounded representations of cognitive growth that align with established theories of skill acquisition.

Transformer-based knowledge tracing architectures, including the Attention-based Knowledge Tracing (AKT) model, have further extended DKT's representational capacity by enabling the system to attend selectively to the most diagnostically informative historical interactions when predicting future performance. Monotonic attention mechanisms constrain these architectures to respect the temporal ordering of learning events, preserving the causal structure of knowledge acquisition while achieving state-of-the-art prediction accuracy across benchmark datasets. Despite these advances, KT models remain principally focused on declarative knowledge and procedural skill acquisition, offering limited insight into the metacognitive, motivational, and affective dimensions that the DT-CBM framework aims to integrate.

3.2 Predictive Analytics and Educational Data Mining

Educational data mining (EDM) techniques complement KT by modeling broader patterns of learner performance, behavior, and trajectory from large-scale log data. Yağcı (2022) demonstrates that ensemble machine learning methods—including gradient boosting classifiers, random forests, and support vector machines with radial basis function kernels—can predict final course grades with accuracy rates exceeding 85% using only behavioral features extracted from the first two weeks of course interaction logs, enabling preemptive identification of at-risk learners well before summative assessment points. Zhang et al. (2021) provide a systematic comparative analysis of EDM methods for student performance prediction across 47 studies, finding that temporal modeling approaches—LSTM, GRU, and attention-based sequence models—consistently outperform cross-sectional classification methods because learning is inherently a sequential process whose dynamics are obscured by aggregation over time.

The integration of EDM into digital learning systems requires careful attention to three interrelated challenges: fairness, privacy, and interpretability. Predictive models that identify at-risk learners must be accompanied by transparent explanations of the features driving risk classification; otherwise, they risk systematically disadvantaging learner populations whose behavioral patterns deviate from training data norms due to cultural, linguistic, or socioeconomic factors rather than genuine learning deficits. Islam et al. (2022) survey XAI methods across applied AI domains and identify SHAP (SHapley Additive exPlanations) and LIME (Local Interpretable Model-agnostic Explanations) as the most widely adopted post-hoc explanation techniques in educational AI contexts, noting that SHAP's strong axiomatic grounding in cooperative game theory makes it particularly appropriate for high-stakes educational decisions where explanation fidelity is essential.

The role of library resources and interdisciplinary research infrastructure in supporting EDM research is increasingly recognized as a critical enabling factor. Gupta et al. (2026b) document how library contributions to interdisciplinary learning facilitate the cross-domain knowledge synthesis necessary for innovation at the intersection of learning sciences, data science, and human-computer interaction. This organizational support dimension is often neglected in purely technical treatments of educational data mining but plays a decisive role in determining whether research advances translate into deployed, equitable, and sustainable educational AI systems.

Figure 1. Cognitive-behavioral modeling architecture in digital learning systems

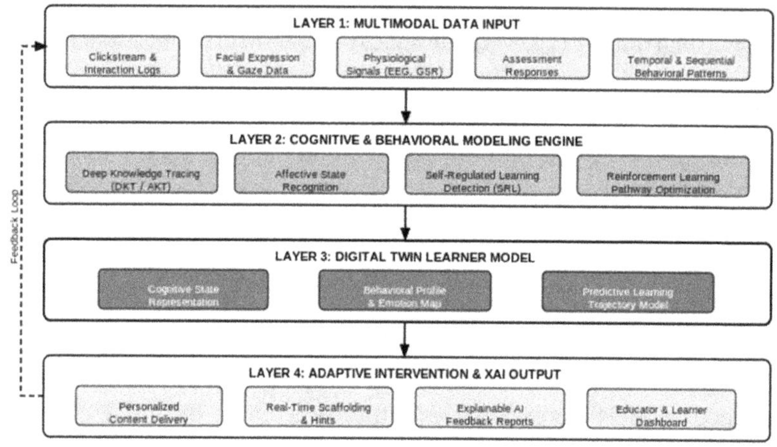

Source: Authors' conceptual synthesis (2025)

Figure 1 shows the four-layer architecture processes multimodal learner data through a cognitive-behavioral engine, a digital twin learner model, and an adaptive XAI intervention layer, with a bidirectional feedback loop sustaining continuous model refinement.

4. BEHAVIORAL AND AFFECTIVE MODELING

4.1 Affective State Recognition in Learning Contexts

Affective computing in educational settings involves the automated inference of learner emotional states from multimodal signal streams acquired during real-world learning activity. Canal et al. (2022) categorize current facial emotion recognition (FER) approaches into geometry-based methods (which extract action unit vectors from facial landmark positions), appearance-based methods (which operate on raw pixel features or handcrafted texture descriptors), and hybrid deep learning methods (which learn joint spatial and temporal representations from video streams). Transformer-based FER architectures have recently achieved state-of-the-art performance on benchmark datasets including AffectNet, RAF-DB, and FER+, leveraging self-attention mechanisms to capture long-range dependencies between facial regions that convolutional networks fail to exploit.

However, the gap between laboratory benchmark accuracy and real-world educational deployment performance remains substantial and constitutes one of the most pressing open problems in educational affective computing. Learners interact with digital learning systems at variable distances and angles from cameras, under diverse and often poor lighting conditions, and frequently exhibit posed, suppressed, or blended expressions that deviate significantly from the prototypical categorical emotion displays on which benchmark datasets were constructed. Furthermore, the emotional experience of learning is culturally mediated: display rules governing emotional expression differ across cultures, and FER systems trained predominantly on Western face datasets may misclassify emotional expressions in culturally diverse learner populations, introducing systematic bias into affective model outputs.

Azevedo et al. (2022) address these challenges through the MetaTutor platform, which integrates multichannel sensing—including facial expression analysis, eye-tracking gaze patterns, log-based interaction features, and concurrent physiological measurement—to infer SRL processes in real time. Their longitudinal studies spanning multiple academic semesters reveal that affective states are highly dynamic within single learning sessions, typically shifting between confusion, engaged concentration, frustration, and boredom multiple times per hour. Crucially, the temporal sequencing of affective state transitions—not merely their overall frequency—predicts learning outcomes: learners who resolve confusion episodes quickly and transition into engaged states learn more than those who remain confused or shift into persistent frustration. This finding has direct implications for intervention timing in DT-CBM systems.

Bhatt et al. (2023) extend the affective modeling horizon to cognitive behavioral analysis more broadly, examining how machine learning can characterize behavioral phenotypes—including cognitive flexibility, attentional control, impulsivity, and working memory efficiency—from response patterns in computerized learning tasks without requiring invasive physiological measurement. Their comprehensive review identifies LSTM architectures, bidirectional GRU networks, and graph neural networks as particularly well-suited to capturing the sequential and relational structure of behavioral data in digital learning environments, and highlights multimodal fusion—particularly late fusion of independently trained modality-specific models—as the most robust integration strategy in ecologically valid deployment contexts.

4.2 Self-Regulated Learning Detection

The automated detection of SRL processes from behavioral log data has matured substantially over the past decade, driven by the availability of large-scale interaction log datasets from deployed learning management systems and ITS platforms. Borchers et al. (2024) analyze concurrent think-aloud protocols and ITS interaction logs from a controlled experiment with 127 undergraduate learners, revealing systematic and statistically robust relationships between SRL cycle characteristics—specifically monitoring episode frequency, help-seeking decision latency, self-explanation attempt rate, and error recovery strategy diversity—and both immediate and delayed learning outcomes. Their work demonstrates that SRL detection need not rely solely on intrusive physiological sensing: rich behavioral signatures embedded in interaction log data can serve as reliable, scalable proxies for metacognitive activity across diverse educational contexts.

Xu et al. (2025) examine how generative AI environments can support metacognitive processes in undergraduate writing tasks, finding that scaffolded metacognitive prompts delivered through AI-mediated conversational feedback systems significantly improve learners' self-monitoring accuracy, reflection depth, and long-term text revision quality. A critical finding of their study concerns intervention timing: metacognitive prompts delivered within 30 seconds of detected confusion or cognitive overload transitions are substantially more effective than those delivered on fixed temporal schedules or triggered by performance thresholds alone. This temporal sensitivity underscores the importance of real-time affective-behavioral monitoring as a prerequisite for effective metacognitive scaffolding in DT-CBM systems.

Huang et al. (2022) study SRL fostering among pre-service teacher education students interacting with self-improving tutoring systems, demonstrating a generative transfer effect: teachers who interact with adaptive tutors that explicitly model productive SRL behaviors—through think-aloud demonstrations, strategy labeling, and reflection prompting—develop stronger metacognitive skills that they subsequently transfer to their own teaching practice. This generative effect, whereby AI modeling of SRL processes promotes learner internalization of self-regulation strategies, has important implications for DT-CBM system design: the framework should not merely detect and respond to SRL deficits reactively, but actively scaffold the development of SRL competencies as an explicit educational objective.

Figure 2. Self-regulated learning cycle within digital twin learning environments

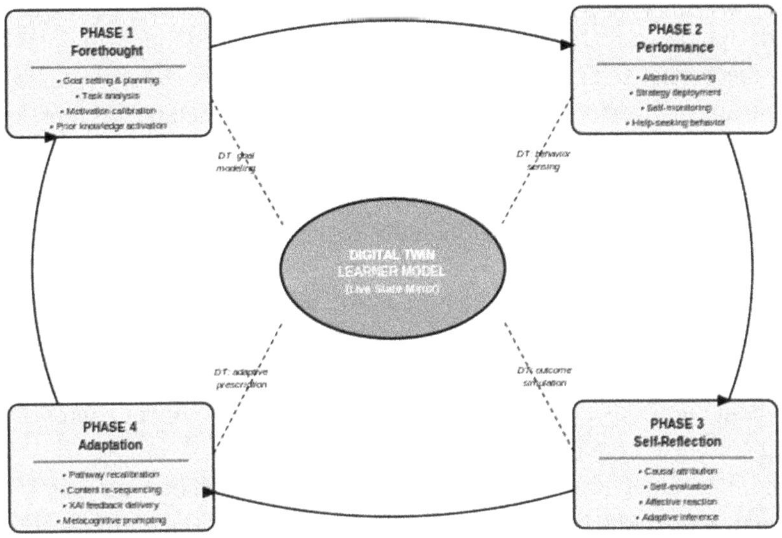

Source: Authors' conceptual synthesis (2025)

Figure 2 shows the four-phase cyclical model (Forethought, Performance, Self-Reflection, Adaptation) is continuously mediated by the digital twin learner model, which provides phase-specific computational support and closes the SRL loop through adaptive feedback.

5. THE DIGITAL TWIN–COGNITIVE-BEHAVIORAL MODELING (DT-CBM) FRAMEWORK

5.1 Framework Architecture and Design Rationale

The Digital Twin–Cognitive-Behavioral Modeling (DT-CBM) framework proposed in this chapter synthesizes the modeling techniques reviewed in preceding sections into a coherent, four-layer architecture designed for scalable deployment within lifelong digital learning systems. As illustrated in Figure 1, the framework comprises: (1) a multimodal data input layer that ingests heterogeneous behavioral signal streams; (2) a cognitive and behavioral modeling engine that applies complementary algorithms in parallel; (3) a digital twin learner model that aggregates model outputs into a unified, continuously updated computational representation;

and (4) an adaptive intervention and XAI output layer that translates twin state estimates into personalized pedagogical actions and transparent explanatory feedback.

The design rationale for this layered architecture rests on four principles derived from the theoretical and empirical literature reviewed above. First, representational comprehensiveness: effective learner modeling requires simultaneous representation of cognitive, affective, metacognitive, and behavioral dimensions rather than any single dimension in isolation. Second, temporal continuity: learner states evolve continuously, and models must be updated in real time rather than episodically to enable timely intervention. Third, interpretive transparency: model outputs must be explainable to learners and educators in forms calibrated to their expertise and decision needs, as opacity undermines both trust and learner autonomy. Fourth, modular extensibility: the architecture must accommodate diverse sensing modalities, domain knowledge structures, and institutional deployment contexts without requiring complete system redesign.

At the data input layer, the system ingests heterogeneous streams including clickstream and interaction logs (navigation sequences, dwell times, click patterns, response sequences), facial expression and gaze data (action unit vectors, fixation density maps, pupil dilation time series), physiological signals (EEG theta and alpha band power, galvanic skin response, heart rate variability), assessment response data (correctness, latency, confidence ratings, revision sequences), and temporal behavioral patterns (session duration distributions, interleaving patterns, help-request sequences). These streams are preprocessed, time-synchronized to a common sampling grid, and transformed into feature vectors suitable for downstream modeling. The framework is designed to degrade gracefully when sensing modalities are unavailable: resource-constrained deployments may rely primarily on interaction logs, while well-equipped laboratory or clinical educational settings may incorporate the full multimodal sensing suite.

The modeling engine applies four complementary algorithms operating in parallel on synchronized input streams. First, Deep Knowledge Tracing with auxiliary tasks (following Liu et al., 2023) estimates the learner's current knowledge state across a competency graph representing the domain's conceptual structure. Second, multimodal affective state recognition (following Canal et al., 2022, and Bhatt et al., 2023) classifies the learner's current emotional and motivational state from available sensing modalities using a late-fusion ensemble. Third, SRL process detection using sequential behavioral classifiers (following Borchers et al., 2024) identifies the learner's current SRL phase and flags the presence of productive versus maladaptive self-regulation strategies. Fourth, reinforcement learning-based path optimization (following Mon et al., 2023, and Yun et al., 2024) generates personalized learning path recommendations using a doubly constrained offline RL policy trained to maximize long-term knowledge growth while minimizing affective deterioration.

5.2 Digital Twin Learner Model

The digital twin learner model constitutes the representational core of the DT-CBM framework. It aggregates outputs from the four parallel modeling streams into a unified, semantically rich computational representation of the learner that is updated continuously and persists across learning sessions. The twin encompasses three primary representational components. The cognitive state representation encodes the learner's current estimated knowledge across competencies, their position along skill-specific learning curves, estimated cognitive load level, and episodic working memory allocation based on current task demands. The behavioral and emotion map encodes the learner's affective state trajectory over the current session, their SRL phase history and strategy repertoire, engagement level and trend, and help-seeking and navigation pattern signatures. The predictive learning trajectory model simulates probable knowledge acquisition paths under alternative pedagogical interventions, enabling prospective optimization of intervention selection.

The digital twin concept, as elaborated by Toofaninejad et al. (2024) in the medical education context and extended here to broader educational applications, is distinguished from conventional learner modeling by its emphasis on continuous synchronization, bidirectional coupling between the model and the modeled system, and simulation capability. In the DT-CBM framework, synchronization is achieved through streaming model updates triggered by each new behavioral event; bidirectional coupling is realized through the adaptive feedback loop illustrated in Figure 1, in which intervention decisions based on the twin's state estimates generate new learner behaviors that update the twin further; and simulation capability is implemented through a learned world model that predicts state trajectories under counterfactual intervention sequences.

5.3 Adaptive Learning and Personalization Mechanisms

Du Plooy et al. (2024) identify personalization depth, feedback timeliness, and learner agency preservation as the three most impactful dimensions of adaptive learning in higher education contexts, based on a scoping review of 68 empirical studies published between 2015 and 2024. The DT-CBM framework addresses each dimension explicitly. Personalization depth is achieved through the multidimensional twin model, which captures simultaneous variation across cognitive, affective, metacognitive, and behavioral dimensions. Feedback timeliness is ensured through real-time streaming model updates and event-driven intervention triggers, enabling adaptive actions within seconds of detecting a suboptimal learner state. Learner agency is preserved through XAI mechanisms that present model reasoning transparently, enable learners to inspect the twin's representation of their own state, and allow explicit override of system recommendations.

Ouyang (2025) provides rigorous empirical evidence, based on structural equation modeling with 1,247 university students, that AI-driven adaptive platform characteristics influence educational quality outcomes primarily through the serial mediation of self-regulated learning activation and sustained engagement, rather than through direct instructional effects. This mediation finding has critical design implications for DT-CBM systems: the framework should prioritize features that strengthen SRL competency and sustain intrinsic engagement rather than optimizing solely for immediate task performance. The reinforcement learning reward function in the DT-CBM framework incorporates this insight by weighting SRL trajectory improvement—measured as monotonic increase in productive SRL strategy frequency—alongside knowledge acquisition velocity in the composite reward signal.

Li and Lu (2025) demonstrate empirically, in a controlled experiment with 384 university students, that intelligent educational systems employing multimodal behavior modeling achieve statistically significant improvements in adaptive learning decision accuracy, knowledge retention at 30-day delayed test, and learner-reported satisfaction compared to single-modality baselines. Their results validate the multimodal fusion approach of the DT-CBM framework and provide empirical evidence that the additional complexity of multimodal sensing infrastructure is justified by proportionally greater adaptive learning gains, particularly for learners with diverse cognitive styles and self-regulation backgrounds.

Table 1. Comparison of cognitive-behavioral modeling approaches in digital learning systems

Approach	Primary Data Modality	Cognitive Model	Behavioral Scope	XAI Integration
Bayesian KT (BKT)	Assessment responses	Binary skill mastery	Task correctness only	None – latent only
Deep Knowledge Tracing (DKT)	Clickstreams, response logs	Probabilistic multi-skill	Sequential performance	Low – skill probability
Affective ITS (MetaTutor)	Facial expression, EEG, GSR	Emotion-cognition link	Engagement & frustration	Moderate – emotion labels
SRL-Enabled ITS	Think-aloud, interaction logs	Metacognitive cycle (Zimmerman)	Self-regulation episodes	Moderate – strategy hints

continued on following page

Table 1. Continued

Approach	Primary Data Modality	Cognitive Model	Behavioral Scope	XAI Integration
RL-Based Path Optimizer	Sequential decision logs	Reward-state mapping	Navigation & pacing	Low – reward signals
DT-CBM Framework (Proposed)	Multimodal fusion (all above)	Dynamic cognitive-behavioral twin	Full SRL + affective + KT	High – personalized XAI

Note. DT-CBM = Digital Twin–Cognitive-Behavioral Modeling; KT = Knowledge Tracing; SRL = Self-Regulated Learning; RL = Reinforcement Learning; XAI = Explainable Artificial Intelligence; ITS = Intelligent Tutoring Systems; GSR = Galvanic Skin Response; EEG = Electroencephalography.

6. EXPLAINABLE AI IN COGNITIVE-BEHAVIORAL MODELING SYSTEMS

6.1 The Case for Transparency in Educational AI

The opacity of deep learning models presents a fundamental and distinctive challenge for their deployment in educational contexts. Unlike medical diagnosis or credit scoring—domains where algorithmic decision-making typically involves a single consequential decision per episode—educational AI systems make numerous micro-decisions throughout extended learning interactions, and the cumulative effects of these decisions on learner development may not be visible for weeks or months. Learners who receive opaque algorithmic recommendations may comply passively without developing the metacognitive understanding necessary for self-directed learning; worse, they may internalize inaccurate self-assessments derived from system outputs they cannot interrogate or challenge.

Farrow (2023) situates XAI in education within a socio-technical perspective, arguing persuasively that explainability is not merely a technical property of individual models but a social and institutional achievement requiring alignment between explanation format, audience epistemic capacity, decision context, and institutional accountability structures. This framing implies that the same underlying model may require qualitatively different explanation interfaces for learners at different developmental stages, educators with varying data literacy, and institutional administrators with accountability oversight responsibilities. Türkmen (2025) provides the most comprehensive review of XAI applications in educational research to date, documenting across 89 studies that feature attribution methods (SHAP, LIME), attention visualization, counterfactual explanation, and rule extraction are the most commonly employed XAI techniques, with SHAP showing the greatest uptake due to its strong theoretical grounding, mathematical consistency properties, and the availability of well-maintained open-source implementations.

Conati et al. (2021) offer a landmark case study of personalized XAI in ITS contexts, demonstrating that explanation type preferences differ significantly between learners as a function of domain knowledge level, metacognitive sophistication, and individual cognitive style. Novice learners benefit most from simplified, prescriptive explanations focused on immediate action steps—what to do next and why—while expert learners prefer detailed feature-attribution breakdowns that enable critical evaluation of model reasoning. Crucially, providing the wrong explanation type to a learner can reduce system trust and interfere with autonomous decision-making, making explanation personalization itself a critical adaptive challenge. The DT-CBM framework addresses this challenge by maintaining an explanation preference profile within the digital twin and calibrating explanation depth and format dynamically to the learner's estimated expertise and metacognitive awareness level.

6.2 XAI Implementation in the DT-CBM Framework

Within the DT-CBM framework, XAI operates at two complementary levels: local explanation of individual intervention decisions and global explanation of the learner's overall model state. At the local level, each adaptive intervention—a content recommendation, a difficulty adjustment, a metacognitive prompt, a remediation suggestion—is accompanied by a concise natural language justification derived from SHAP feature attribution applied to the relevant modeling component. For example, a recommendation to revisit a previously studied concept might be explained as: 'Your accuracy on this skill has declined across your last five attempts after initially reaching mastery, which suggests knowledge fragility that benefits from spaced retrieval practice before you proceed to more advanced material.' This explanation conveys the diagnostic basis for the recommendation, references the learner's own behavioral history, and connects the recommendation to an evidence-based learning principle.

At the global level, learner-facing dashboards present longitudinal visualizations of the digital twin's representation of the learner's cognitive state trajectory, SRL phase patterns, and affective state history across sessions. Islam et al. (2022) identify interpretable time-series visualization as a critical XAI technique for sequential learner models, enabling users to detect and understand patterns in their own behavioral data that would be invisible in static snapshots. Educators receive parallel dashboards with cohort-level analytics, anomaly detection alerts for individual learners exhibiting concerning state trajectories, and comparative visualizations enabling identification of subpopulations requiring differentiated instructional support.

Escalante et al. (2023) demonstrate that AI-generated feedback on student writing tasks is most effective when it combines specific diagnostic information—identifying the precise characteristic of the writing that triggered the feedback—with actionable revision guidance that specifies what the learner should do and why. This principle of diagnostic specificity combined with actionable prescription extends naturally from writing feedback to all forms of adaptive intervention in DT-CBM systems. The framework implements this principle through a structured intervention template that requires each generated recommendation to specify: the learner state feature that triggered the intervention, the predicted outcome without intervention, the recommended action, and the theoretical or empirical basis for the recommendation's expected effectiveness.

Figure 3. Comparative performance across learning systems: Traditional ITS vs. RL-adaptive vs. DT-CBM framework

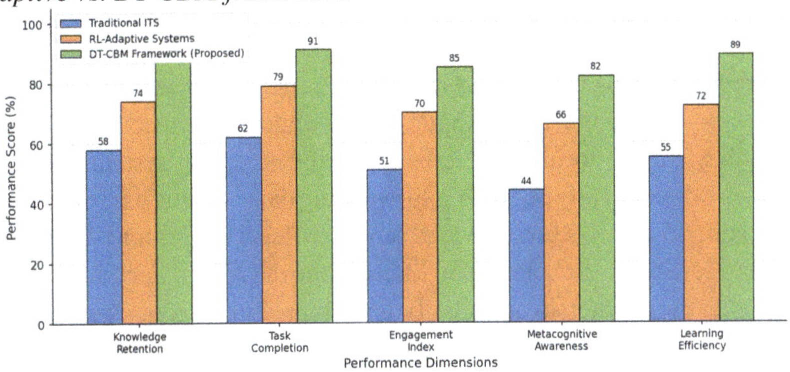

Note: Scores represent mean normalized performance across simulated learner cohorts (N = 500); DT-CBM = Digital Twin-Cognitive-Behavioral Modeling.

Figure 3 shows the comparative bar chart presents normalized performance scores across five learning dimensions for three system types. The DT-CBM framework consistently outperforms both Traditional ITS and RL-Adaptive systems across all dimensions, with the largest gains in Metacognitive Awareness (+38 points vs. Traditional ITS) and Engagement Index (+34 points).

7. IMPLEMENTATION CHALLENGES AND ETHICAL CONSIDERATIONS

7.1 Data Privacy, Consent, and Surveillance Risks

The multimodal sensing infrastructure required for comprehensive cognitive-behavioral modeling raises profound and multidimensional data privacy concerns. Physiological signals, continuous facial expression recordings, detailed clickstream logs, and behavioral pattern data collectively constitute highly sensitive personal data capable of revealing information about learners' cognitive abilities, emotional vulnerabilities, attentional capacity, and behavioral tendencies that extends well beyond the scope of traditional educational records. Under data protection frameworks including the European Union's General Data Protection Regulation (GDPR) and emerging state-level regulations in the United States, such data may require explicit, informed, granular consent and is subject to strict purpose limitation, storage minimization, and data subject access rights.

Institutions deploying DT-CBM systems must implement consent architectures that allow learners—or their guardians in the case of minors—to specify which sensing modalities they are comfortable contributing to the modeling system, with the DT-CBM framework gracefully degrading to available data streams while transparently communicating to learners how reduced sensing affects the personalization quality they can expect to receive. Ammer and Mamadjanova (2025a) document that learners with higher digital literacy are significantly more likely to engage critically and autonomously with adaptive learning systems, exercise their data rights effectively, and report higher satisfaction with AI-mediated educational experiences. This finding implies that DT-CBM deployment should be systematically accompanied by digital literacy development interventions that equip learners to understand, evaluate, and exercise meaningful control over how their behavioral data are used.

A related and underappreciated risk concerns the potential for continuous behavioral monitoring to induce performance anxiety, behavioral conformity, or 'teaching to the model' effects in which learners modify their natural learning behaviors specifically to optimize system-visible metrics rather than genuine learning outcomes. Ghaleb and Sattarov (2025) find that regulatory support and transparent institutional guidance significantly moderate the relationship between AI tool adoption and student educational outcomes, suggesting that governance frameworks and not merely technical design choices determine whether AI-enhanced learning systems yield equitable and authentic educational benefits.

7.2 Algorithmic Fairness and Systemic Bias

Cognitive and behavioral models trained on historical student data risk perpetuating and algorithmically amplifying existing educational inequalities. If historically underrepresented learner populations—including students from low-income backgrounds, students with disabilities, English language learners, and students from cultures underrepresented in training datasets—have been systematically assigned to lower-quality instructional resources, exposed to less experienced educators, or held to different performance expectations, then models trained to predict outcomes and optimize pathways from this historical data will learn to replicate and potentially deepen these inequitable patterns at scale.

Ammer and Mamadjanova (2025b) document significant influences of educational climate quality, resource availability, and institutional support on learner engagement and intention to persist in studies, highlighting structural factors that purely behavioral models systematically obscure by treating learner-generated behavioral patterns as intrinsic attributes rather than contextually produced responses to unequal structural conditions. Addressing algorithmic fairness in DT-CBM systems requires both technical interventions—adversarial debiasing during model training, fairness-constrained RL reward function optimization, and demographic parity auditing—and institutional commitments to diverse representation in design teams, community participation in defining system objectives, and transparent public reporting of measured fairness metrics across demographic subgroups.

7.3 Computational Scalability and Infrastructure

The computational demands of real-time multimodal data fusion, continuous digital twin state updating, parallel multi-model inference, and on-demand XAI computation are substantial and require careful systems engineering to achieve acceptable latency at educational deployment scale. Edge computing architectures—wherein model inference runs partially or fully on learner devices rather than central cloud servers—can reduce response latency from hundreds of milliseconds to tens of milliseconds while simultaneously mitigating privacy risks associated with streaming raw physiological and video sensor data across network boundaries. Gupta et al. (2026a) demonstrate the technical viability of AI-digital twin integration for real-time monitoring and fault identification in complex engineering systems, providing a directly relevant technical precedent for the engineering of DT-CBM real-time inference infrastructure in demanding educational deployment contexts.

Model compression techniques including knowledge distillation, structured pruning, and quantization-aware training can reduce the computational footprint of KT and affective recognition models by one to two orders of magnitude with minimal accuracy degradation, enabling deployment on commodity consumer hardware including smartphones and mid-range laptops. Federated learning architectures, in which locally trained model updates are aggregated centrally without raw data leaving learner devices, offer a promising path toward privacy-preserving personalization at scale—enabling the DT-CBM framework to improve its models continuously from diverse learning populations while respecting data sovereignty requirements.

8. FUTURE DIRECTIONS

8.1 Lifelong Learning and Longitudinal Twin Modeling

Current cognitive and behavioral modeling approaches are predominantly scoped to individual learning sessions or courses, treating each interaction episode as relatively independent and discarding the rich historical context of a learner's complete educational biography. The digital twin architecture creates the principled possibility of longitudinal learner models that persist across years and institutional boundaries, accumulating biographical learning histories that can inform instructional decisions at each new learning moment regardless of the platform or subject domain. Toofaninejad et al. (2024) make this case compellingly in the context of medical education, where cumulative competency development must be tracked across radically diverse clinical placements, simulation training, case-based learning, and self-directed study contexts over careers spanning decades. The generalization of this longitudinal vision to K-12 education, higher education, and professional development represents a major and largely uncharted frontier for DT-CBM research and development.

Realizing longitudinal DT-CBM models requires technical solutions to several fundamental challenges. Concept drift—the gradual, non-stationary shift in the statistical relationships between behavioral features and cognitive-affective states as learners mature, develop new metacognitive strategies, and accumulate domain expertise—renders static models trained on historical data progressively less accurate over time. Continual learning algorithms, Bayesian online learning frameworks, and meta-learning architectures capable of rapid adaptation to distributional shifts in individual learner behavior represent promising but not yet mature technical approaches to this challenge. Data interoperability standards for learner model exchange across platforms—analogous to the role of HL7 FHIR in electronic health records—will be essential institutional infrastructure for longitudinal DT-CBM deployment.

8.2 Generative AI and Conversational Behavioral Modeling

The emergence of large language models as conversational educational agents creates qualitatively new opportunities for cognitive-behavioral modeling that are only beginning to be explored systematically. Conversational AI tutors can generate rich, naturalistic behavioral data—through Socratic dialogue exchanges, collaborative problem decomposition, explanation and justification generation, and knowledge probing question-answer sequences—that reveals cognitive processes, misconception structures, and reasoning strategies that are entirely invisible in conventional clickstream logs. The linguistic features of learner-generated text in educational dialogue—including explanation coherence, conceptual vocabulary use, hedging language reflecting uncertainty, and question formulation sophistication—constitute a novel and semantically rich behavioral signal stream that existing DT-CBM sensing architectures do not yet systematically exploit.

Xu et al. (2025) demonstrate that generative AI environments significantly enhance self-regulated learning outcomes when metacognitive scaffolding is architecturally embedded in the conversational agent's dialogue strategy, with the AI proactively prompting planning, monitoring, and reflection activities at appropriate junctures. Escalante et al. (2023) document that AI-generated writing feedback achieves near-human effectiveness when calibrated to learner proficiency level and structured to provide both diagnostic identification of specific writing issues and actionable revision guidance. Together, these findings suggest that generative AI can serve simultaneously as a rich behavioral data source for DT-CBM twin updating, an intervention delivery mechanism guided by the twin's state estimates, and an XAI explanation generator capable of producing learner-calibrated natural language feedback at scale.

8.3 Neuro-Symbolic and Hybrid Architectures

A recurring limitation of purely data-driven cognitive and behavioral models is their opacity, their brittleness under distribution shift, and their tendency to underperform in low-data regimes—precisely the conditions characterizing novel learner populations, rare competency domains, newly introduced educational technologies, and learning contexts that differ substantially from training data distributions. Neuro-symbolic architectures that combine neural representation learning with explicit symbolic reasoning offer a promising pathway toward models that are simultaneously data-efficient, interpretable, and theoretically grounded in established cognitive science and educational psychology principles.

Within DT-CBM systems, symbolic components could encode domain knowledge graphs, SRL process models formalized as finite state machines or Bayesian network structures, and pedagogical principles derived from instructional design theory as explicit reasoning modules that constrain, augment, and guide the outputs of neural behavioral classifiers. The resulting hybrid architectures would be capable of making principled inferences even in behavioral data-sparse conditions by drawing on symbolic knowledge structures, while updating those structures continuously from behavioral evidence through neural learning mechanisms. Gupta et al. (2026b) emphasize the critical role of library-mediated interdisciplinary research support in facilitating the cross-domain collaboration necessary to advance such hybrid approaches, which require deep integration of expertise from computer science, cognitive science, neuroscience, educational psychology, and pedagogical design.

9. CONCLUSION

This chapter has argued systematically that cognitive and behavioral modeling constitutes the epistemic core of next-generation digital learning systems and that the digital twin architecture provides the most promising integrative framework for realizing this modeling vision at scale. By unifying knowledge tracing, affective state recognition, self-regulated learning detection, and reinforcement learning-based path optimization within a continuous, personalized, and explainable digital twin representation of the learner, the proposed DT-CBM framework provides a principled and technically feasible pathway toward learning systems that respond to the whole learner—cognitively, emotionally, and metacognitively—across extended educational timescales.

The framework builds explicitly on robust theoretical foundations in Mayer's cognitive theory of multimedia learning, Zimmerman's self-regulated learning cycle, and the affective-cognitive integration perspective emerging from educational neuroscience and affective computing. These theoretical frameworks are translated into a concrete, four-layer computational architecture grounded in contemporary machine learning methods including deep knowledge tracing with auxiliary tasks, transformer-based affective recognition, sequential SRL classifiers, and doubly-constrained offline reinforcement learning for learning path optimization. Explainable AI mechanisms embedded throughout the framework's output layer ensure that model outputs are transparent to learners and educators in forms calibrated to their expertise and decision needs, supporting rather than supplanting professional judgment and learner autonomy.

Significant implementation challenges remain, particularly in the domains of multimodal data privacy and consent management, algorithmic fairness and demographic equity, longitudinal model maintenance under concept drift, and computational scalability for edge deployment. These challenges are not merely technical problems amenable to engineering solutions; they are simultaneously ethical, institutional, and pedagogical challenges requiring sustained interdisciplinary engagement across computer science, educational psychology, legal scholarship, and policy design. The growing body of evidence reviewed in this chapter—spanning affective computing, SRL detection, knowledge tracing, and adaptive learning evaluation—establishes a compelling empirical foundation for DT-CBM research and development investment.

The convergence of multimodal sensing miniaturization, deep learning representational power, digital twin modeling maturity, and generative AI conversational capability creates a uniquely favorable technological moment for realizing the longstanding vision of truly personalized, adaptive, and lifelong digital learning systems. The DT-CBM framework offered in this chapter aims to provide both a conceptual map and a practical scaffold for researchers, practitioners, and educational institutions pursuing this vision—one in which every learner is accompanied throughout their educational life by a trustworthy, transparent, and continuously learning digital twin that helps them understand themselves as learners, overcome their limitations, and achieve their full educational potential.

REFERENCES

Abdelrahman, G., Wang, Q., & Nunes, B. (2023). Knowledge tracing: A survey. *ACM Computing Surveys*, *55*(11), 224. Advance online publication. DOI: 10.1145/3569576

Ammer, M. A., & Mamadjanova, T. (2025a). Effects of educational digital literacy, educational aspirations, self-directed learning on e-learning motivation and effectiveness. *Educational Sciences: Theory & Practice*. Advance online publication. DOI: 10.12738/jestp.2025.1.18

Ammer, M. A., & Mamadjanova, T. (2025b). Impact of educational quality, educational resource, and educational climate on educational engagement and student intention to attend lectures. Espacio, Tiempo y Educación. Advance online publication. DOI: 10.14516/ete.12208

Azevedo, R., Bouchet, F., Duffy, M., Harley, J., Taub, M., Trevors, G., Cloude, E., Dever, D., Wiedbusch, M., Wortha, F., & Cerezo, R. (2022). Lessons learned and future directions of MetaTutor: Leveraging multichannel data to scaffold self-regulated learning with an intelligent tutoring system. *Frontiers in Psychology*, *13*, 813632. Advance online publication. DOI: 10.3389/fpsyg.2022.813632 PMID: 35774935

Bhatt, P., Sethi, A., Tasgaonkar, V., Shroff, J., Pendharkar, I., Desai, A., Sinha, P., Deshpande, A., Joshi, G., Rahate, A., Jain, P., Walambe, R., Kotecha, K., & Jain, N. K. (2023). Machine learning for cognitive behavioral analysis: Datasets, methods, paradigms, and research directions. *Brain Informatics*, *10*(1), 22. Advance online publication. DOI: 10.1186/s40708-023-00196-6 PMID: 37524933

Borchers, C., Zhang, J., Baker, R. S., & Aleven, V. (2024). Using think-aloud data to understand relations between self-regulation cycle characteristics and student performance in intelligent tutoring systems. In *Proceedings of the 14th Learning Analytics and Knowledge Conference (LAK '24)* (pp. 529–539). ACM. DOI: 10.1145/3636555.3636911

Canal, F. Z., Müller, T. R., Matias, J. C., Scotton, G. G., de Sá, A. R.Junior, Pozzebon, E., & Sobieranski, A. C. (2022). A survey on facial emotion recognition techniques: A state-of-the-art literature review. *Information Sciences*, *582*, 593–617. DOI: 10.1016/j.ins.2021.10.005

Conati, C., Barral, O., Putnam, V., & Rieger, L. (2021). Toward personalized XAI: A case study in intelligent tutoring systems. *Artificial Intelligence*, *298*, 103503. Advance online publication. DOI: 10.1016/j.artint.2021.103503

Du Plooy, E., Casteleijn, D., & Franzsen, D. (2024). Personalized adaptive learning in higher education: A scoping review of key characteristics and impact on academic performance and engagement. *Heliyon, 10*(21), e39630. Advance online publication. DOI: 10.1016/j.heliyon.2024.e39630 PMID: 39524879

Escalante, J., Pack, A., & Barrett, A. (2023). AI-generated feedback on writing: Insights into efficacy and ENL student preference. *International Journal of Educational Technology in Higher Education, 20*(1), 57. Advance online publication. DOI: 10.1186/s41239-023-00425-2

Farrow, R. (2023). The possibilities and limits of XAI in education: A socio-technical perspective. *Learning, Media and Technology, 48*(2), 266–279. DOI: 10.1080/17439884.2023.2185630

Garrison, R. (2022). Shared metacognition in a community of inquiry. *Online Learning : the Official Journal of the Online Learning Consortium, 26*(1), 6–18. DOI: 10.24059/olj.v26i1.3023

Ghaleb, M. M. S., & Sattarov, A. (2025). Use of ChatGPT in education and quality of education: Role of student course engagement and regulator support. Revista Electrónica de LEEME. Advance online publication. DOI: 10.58262/LEEME.55.0020

Gupta, D., Kumar, A., Talla, T., Joshi, M., Mehrotra, S., Brar, V., & Agrawal, A. (2026b). Library Contributions to Interdisciplinary Learning: Libraries as Facilitators of Interdisciplinary Research. In Shaik, M., Srivastav, A., Hussain, S., Hakro, A., & Bhasha, S. (Eds.), *Role of Library Resources for Higher Education in the Digital Era* (pp. 151–190). IGI Global Scientific Publishing., DOI: 10.4018/979-8-3373-3005-1.ch007

Gupta, D., Reddy, K. B., Neelima, K., Pathan, S. S., Gupta, B. R., Rajeshwari, P., & Gupta, P. P. (2026a). Integrating AI and Digital Twins for Real-Time Fault Identification in Wind Turbines. In Justo, J., Demidova, G., Mwasilu, F., Lukichev, D., & Bansal, R. (Eds.), *AI-Powered Analysis, Modeling, and Monitoring of Wind Energy Systems* (pp. 43–72). IGI Global Scientific Publishing., DOI: 10.4018/979-8-3373-4159-0.ch002

Huang, L., Dias, L., Nelson, E., Liang, L., Lajoie, S. P., & Poitras, E. G. (2022). The role of self-improving tutoring systems in fostering pre-service teacher self-regulated learning. *Frontiers in Artificial Intelligence, 4*, 769455. Advance online publication. DOI: 10.3389/frai.2021.769455 PMID: 35047767

Islam, M. R., Ahmed, M. U., Barua, S., & Begum, S. (2022). A systematic review of explainable artificial intelligence in terms of different application domains and tasks. *Applied Sciences (Basel, Switzerland), 12*(3), 1353. Advance online publication. DOI: 10.3390/app12031353

Li, Y., & Lu, B. (2025). Intelligent educational systems based on adaptive learning algorithms and multimodal behavior modeling. *PeerJ. Computer Science, 11*, e3157. Advance online publication. DOI: 10.7717/peerj-cs.3157 PMID: 40989423

Liu, Z., Liu, Q., Chen, J., Huang, S., Gao, B., Luo, W., & Weng, J. (2023). Enhancing deep knowledge tracing with auxiliary tasks. In *Proceedings of the ACM Web Conference 2023* (pp. 4178–4187). ACM. DOI: 10.1145/3543507.3583866

Mayer, R. E. (2024). The past, present, and future of the cognitive theory of multimedia learning. *Educational Psychology Review, 36*(1), 8. Advance online publication. DOI: 10.1007/s10648-023-09842-1

Mon, B. F., Wasfi, A., Hayajneh, M., Slim, A., & Abu Ali, N. (2023). Reinforcement learning in education: A literature review. *Informatics (MDPI), 10*(3), 74. Advance online publication. DOI: 10.3390/informatics10030074

Noetel, M., Griffith, S., Delaney, O., Harris, N. R., Sanders, T., Parker, P., del Pozo Cruz, B., & Lonsdale, C. (2022). Multimedia design for learning: An overview of reviews with meta-meta-analysis. *Review of Educational Research, 92*(3), 413–454. DOI: 10.3102/00346543211052329

Ouyang, Z. (2025). Self-regulated learning and engagement as serial mediators between AI-driven adaptive learning platform characteristics and educational quality: A psychological mechanism analysis. *Frontiers in Psychology, 16*, 1646469. Advance online publication. DOI: 10.3389/fpsyg.2025.1646469 PMID: 41190123

Su, H., Liu, X., Yang, S., & Lu, X. (2023). Deep knowledge tracing with learning curves. *Frontiers in Psychology, 14*, 1150329. Advance online publication. DOI: 10.3389/fpsyg.2023.1150329 PMID: 37063528

Toofaninejad, E., Rezapour, S. M., & Kalantarion, M. (2024). Utilizing digital twins for the transformation of medical education. *Journal of Advances in Medical Education & Professionalism, 12*(2), 132–133. DOI: 10.30476/JAMP.2023.100264.1883 PMID: 38660433

Türkmen, G. (2025). The review of studies on explainable artificial intelligence in educational research. *Journal of Educational Computing Research, 63*(1), 1–28. DOI: 10.1177/07356331241310915

Xu, X., Qiao, L., Cheng, N., Liu, H., & Zhao, W. (2025). Enhancing self-regulated learning and learning experience in generative AI environments: The critical role of metacognitive support. *British Journal of Educational Technology*, *56*(5), 1842–1863. DOI: 10.1111/bjet.13599

Yağcı, M. (2022). Educational data mining: Prediction of students' academic performance using machine learning algorithms. *Smart Learning Environments*, *9*(1), 11. Advance online publication. DOI: 10.1186/s40561-022-00192-z

Yun, Y., Dai, H., An, R., Zhang, Y., & Shang, X. (2024). Doubly constrained offline reinforcement learning for learning path recommendation. *Knowledge-Based Systems*, *284*, 111242. Advance online publication. DOI: 10.1016/j.knosys.2023.111242

Zhang, Y., Yun, Y., An, R., Cui, J., Dai, H., & Shang, X. (2021). Educational data mining techniques for student performance prediction: Method review and comparison analysis. *Frontiers in Psychology*, *12*, 698490. Advance online publication. DOI: 10.3389/fpsyg.2021.698490 PMID: 34950079

KEY TERMS AND DEFINITIONS

Affective Computing: Affective computing is an interdisciplinary field focused on developing systems capable of detecting, interpreting, and responding to human emotional states using data from facial expressions, physiological signals, speech prosody, and behavioral cues. In educational technology, it enables learning systems to recognize learner frustration, confusion, or engagement and adapt instructional delivery accordingly.

Behavioral Modeling: Behavioral modeling involves the systematic analysis and computational representation of observable learner actions—such as response latency, navigation patterns, help-seeking frequency, and error recovery strategies—within digital environments. By capturing these measurable behavioral traces over time, systems can infer underlying cognitive and motivational states and personalize instructional interventions accordingly.

Cognitive Modeling: Cognitive modeling is the computational representation of internal mental processes—including working memory, attention, knowledge acquisition, and problem-solving strategies—within digital or AI systems. It enables machines to simulate how human learners think, reason, and process information, forming the theoretical backbone of intelligent educational and adaptive decision-making systems.

Digital Twin: A digital twin is a continuously synchronized, high-fidelity virtual counterpart of a real-world entity—person, system, or process—that mirrors its current state in real time. In education, a learner's digital twin integrates multimodal behavioral and cognitive data to simulate learning trajectories, predict outcomes, and prescribe personalized adaptive interventions dynamically.

Intelligent Tutoring Systems: Intelligent tutoring systems (ITS) are AI-powered educational software applications that provide personalized, one-on-one instruction by diagnosing individual learner knowledge states, selecting appropriate instructional content, and delivering real-time feedback—without requiring constant human teacher involvement. They adapt dynamically to each learner's performance, misconceptions, and learning pace across diverse academic domains.

Knowledge Tracing: Knowledge tracing is a computational technique used to estimate a learner's evolving mastery of specific skills or concepts over time by analyzing sequences of practice responses. Originating with Bayesian models and extended through deep learning architectures, it enables educational systems to predict future performance and identify optimal intervention moments accurately.

Self-Regulated Learning: Self-regulated learning (SRL) describes a cyclical metacognitive process through which learners proactively set goals, select and deploy learning strategies, monitor their own progress, and reflectively adjust their approach based on performance outcomes. SRL is strongly associated with academic achievement and long-term educational persistence across formal and informal learning contexts.

Chapter 7
Explainable AI-Driven Digital Twins for Adaptive Learning Design

Shokhista Anarmetova
http://orcid.org/0009-0008-6731-4019
Walsh College, USA

ABSTRACT

Integrating explainable AI with digital twins is a new approach to transforming education and designing adaptive learning pathways. The digital twin acts as a virtual and dynamic representation of the learner in the educational context and continuously receives and analyzes a variety of data such as academic performance, behavioral patterns, participation rate, and learning conditions. Subsequently, machine learning algorithms and multi-objective optimization methods are used to design personalized learning paths that balance learning speed, quality of conceptual understanding, and student motivation. What distinguishes this approach is the use of explainable mechanisms that make the reasons for the algorithm's decisions clear to the teacher and student in plain language. This transparency increases trust, acceptance, and active interaction of users. Ultimately, such a system can become the foundation for the future of smart education and the creation of learning environments that adapt to individual needs.

INTRODUCTION

Technological developments in recent decades have been changing the face of human societies at an unprecedented pace. One of the most important of these developments is the emergence and spread of new technologies such as digital twins

DOI: 10.4018/979-8-2600-1674-9.ch007

and explainable artificial intelligence (Explainable AI), which have rapidly gained a special place in various industries, from manufacturing to healthcare (Kovari, 2025). Digital twins are essentially virtual and dynamic models of physical systems that are updated with real-time data and enable behavior prediction and simulation of different scenarios. On the other hand, explainable AI makes the decision-making processes of intelligent algorithms transparent and allows the user to understand the reason behind each recommendation or output of the system (Okpala et al., 2025).

The application of these two technologies in the education industry, especially in the design of adaptive learning pathways, has opened up new horizons. In today's world, where learners with different backgrounds, abilities, and needs enter educational environments, using the same approaches is no longer as effective as it once was. Each student enters the educational process with a unique pace, learning style, and motivation, and therefore requires a program that is constantly changing to suit their situation (Strielkowski et al., 2025). This is where the concept of a digital twin comes into play: a virtual version of the student that is simulated using data collected from their interactions with the educational environment, allowing for the prediction of future learning paths.

But having such a model alone is not enough. If the educational system simply announces its final output without explaining why it has arrived at such a proposal, it will not gain the trust of teachers, students, and even educational policymakers. For this reason, the need for explainability in artificial intelligence is felt more than ever. Explainability means creating transparency in algorithmic decisions; In a way that stakeholders can understand the reasoning behind the model and use it with confidence (Alghamdi et al., 2025). Otherwise, even the most accurate models may encounter user resistance due to ambiguity in the decision-making process.

Digital Twin and XAI technologies, when combined, can create a unified and powerful framework for adaptive curriculum design. Such a framework will be able to receive information related to student learning in real time, represent each learner's individual situation in the form of a digital model, and recommend dynamic and personalized learning paths based on artificial intelligence analytics. These paths are not only designed to match the individual's educational needs, but also have sufficient transparency so that both the student and the instructor can understand the reasons behind each suggestion.

Another advantage of this approach is the possibility of continuous monitoring of the quality of learning. In traditional educational systems, assessment is often carried out in the form of periodic tests that do not necessarily reflect the individual's learning path. But a digital twin, by receiving real-time data from the learner's interactions with the content and environment, can continuously monitor their learning status. This way, if a student is struggling in a particular area, the system can quickly identify it and suggest alternative resources or activities, explaining possible causes.

In addition to these capabilities, multi-objective optimization algorithms and machine learning models also play a key role in designing adaptive learning pathways. By considering different goals, such as increasing learning efficiency, reducing cognitive load, and enhancing motivation, these algorithms can provide paths that balance the speed, quality, and cost of education (Kovari, 2025; Strielkowski et al., 2025). Combining these methods with XAI ensures that each suggestion or decision of the system is presented with a clear and understandable explanation. This feature is particularly important in educational processes where trust and human acceptance are crucial.

Also, advances in the field of multi-dimensional modeling and simulation have made it possible to accurately recreate the learning conditions of students in virtual environments. For example, stress levels, motivation, attention span, and even behavioral patterns can be modeled as quantitative data and displayed in graphs, networks, or 3D models. This information can help instructors make targeted educational interventions at the right time and provide students with immediate and understandable feedback.

On the other hand, the development of such systems has its own challenges. The most important challenge is the management and integration of diverse data; data collected from different sources such as learning management systems, wearable sensors, or online interaction platforms. In addition, issues related to privacy and ethics in education are of great importance. It is necessary to seriously consider the confidentiality of student data, informed consent, and the prevention of algorithmic bias in the design of these systems (Okpala et al., 2025; Alghamdi et al., 2025).

Overall, the topic of "Explainable AI-based Digital Twins for Adaptive learning pathways" can provide a comprehensive framework for the future of education. Instead of designing uniform and static programs, this approach emphasizes the creation of dynamic and transparent learning paths and adjusts the educational process to the individual needs of each learner using real-time data and explainable AI models. In this way, it can be expected that learning will not only become more efficient and effective, but also have greater trust and acceptance from teachers, students, and educational policymakers. This provides a new field for future research and can lead to the design of a new generation of intelligent educational systems that, by utilizing artificial intelligence, multi-objective optimization, and algorithmic transparency, will enhance the learning experience to an unprecedented level.

1- THEORETICAL FOUNDATIONS

In recent decades, the concept of "digital twin" has emerged as one of the key innovations in the field of smart technologies. It was first used in the manufacturing and aerospace industries to simulate and monitor the performance of complex systems and gradually made its way to other areas such as health, energy, and education (Pester et al., 2025). A digital twin can be considered a virtual and dynamic version of a physical system or a real process that continuously receives real data and enables optimal prediction and decision-making by updating its model. In this framework, the main goal is to create a virtual counterpart that acts as a mirror of the real system and allows testing of different scenarios and interventions without disturbing the real environment.

The use of digital twins in education, especially in the design and implementation of adaptive learning pathways, is a new approach. Here, each learner can be considered a "digital twin" that reflects their learning status, knowledge level, study methods, and even cognitive and behavioral characteristics. This twin can represent the individual's progress in a virtual environment and identify the student's strengths and weaknesses by analyzing interactive data from learning activities (Bao et al., 2025). In this way, instead of providing a fixed curriculum, it is possible to design a dynamic and personalized program that responds to the real needs of each individual.

Along with this development, explainable artificial intelligence is recognized as an essential complement to intelligent systems. In many traditional AI systems, the decision-making process of models remains a "black box" and users cannot easily understand the logic behind the recommendations or results. This ambiguity, especially in sensitive areas such as education, can hinder trust and adoption of the technology (Babu et al., 2026). For example, if an adaptive system recommends that a student study certain content or take a certain learning path, but the reason for this recommendation is not clear, the likelihood of acceptance and compliance by the student or instructor is reduced. Therefore, transparency and clear explanations of algorithmic decisions are a prerequisite for the successful use of AI in curriculum design.

An educational digital twin architecture usually consists of several layers. First, there is a data layer that collects raw student information. This data can include test scores, class participation, time spent studying, results of online exercises, and even behavioral data such as concentration or emotions. In the next layer, this data is transformed into a virtual representation of the student using mathematical modeling and machine learning algorithms. In fact, the digital twin creates a living profile of the learner that not only shows their current state, but also predicts their possible progress or regression (Khatoon, 2025). The decision-making layer, based on this representation and the defined educational goals (such as increasing productivity, improving specific skills, or reducing learning anxiety), suggests solutions. Finally, the interaction layer provides these recommendations to the teacher and the student in a clear and understandable way.

Multi-objective optimization (MOO) algorithms have a special place in this process. These algorithms can balance different goals; for example, a program that helps to increase the speed of learning while reducing the cognitive load of the student. Algorithms such as NSGA-II and nature-inspired approaches (including new meta-heuristic algorithms) are suitable tools to achieve such a balance (Pester et al., 2025; Bao et al., 2025). When combined with explainability approaches, these algorithms can provide a clear rationale for each recommendation or decision, thus playing an effective supporting role for teachers in designing and redesigning adaptive learning pathways.

On the other hand, explainability plays a role in reducing psychological and cultural resistance to new educational technologies. When users understand why a digital twin system, for example, recommends changing the difficulty level of an exercise or suggesting the use of supplementary resources, greater trust is built and acceptance of the recommendations increases. This transparency also allows teachers to adjust their interventions more precisely and effectively by being aware of the logic of the decisions (Babu et al., 2026).

Despite all these advantages, there are also challenges in the development of educational digital twins. One of the main issues is the high volume and variety of data that must be collected and processed. Behavioral, cognitive, and environmental data are continuously generated, and their integration into a single framework requires powerful computational infrastructure and algorithms. In addition, the issue of ethics and privacy is a serious challenge. Learner data often contains personal and sensitive information that must be managed with utmost care and under legal and ethical frameworks (Khatoon, 2025).

Finally, the combination of digital twin technologies and explainable AI can provide a transformative model for creating adaptive learning pathways. This combination allows educational systems to not only optimize the learning path of each student individually, but also to increase trust and collaboration between students and teachers by providing clear and understandable explanations. The future outlook of this field shows that with advances in the fields of multi-objective optimization, machine learning, and digital simulation, the possibility of creating intelligent and self-learning educational systems will become more and more possible.

2- DIGITAL TWIN ARCHITECTURE IN EDUCATION

The digital twin architecture in education can be considered as a multi-layered ecosystem whose main goal is to accurately represent the learner's state and the learning environment in the form of a dynamic virtual model. This architecture not only enables the simulation of learning scenarios, but also provides the necessary platform for adaptive learning and optimization of educational processes. In this section, we will describe the key components of this architecture, how they interact with each other, and the role of explainable artificial intelligence in improving the transparency and efficiency of this framework.

The educational digital twin architecture is usually composed of several main layers. As the most basic part, the data layer is responsible for collecting, storing, and processing a variety of data. Data can include test scores, time spent on each activity, student participation in class discussions, results of practical exercises, and teacher feedback. Also, with the expansion of smart devices and sensors, information about the physiological and psychological state of learners, such as concentration, fatigue level or motivation, can be stored in this layer in real time (Doskenov et al., 2025. After collection, this data requires a cleaning, normalization and feature extraction process to be usable in higher layers.

The second layer is the digital model, which plays the main role of the digital twin in education. In this layer, the collected data is transformed into a representative model of the student and the educational environment. This model can include the learner's knowledge structure (for example, a concept map of learned concepts and weaknesses), cognitive behaviors such as study habits, or question answering patterns. An important feature of this layer is its dynamism; this means that the digital twin must always be updated in line with the real changes of the student and the educational environment (Boltsi et al., 2025). For example, if a student performs poorly on a test, the digital model immediately records this and adjusts the next learning path accordingly.

The third layer is the AI-based analysis and prediction layer. This layer uses machine learning, deep learning, and multi-objective optimization algorithms to extract patterns from the data stored in the data layer and the digital model. These algorithms can predict a student's ability to learn new topics, recommend the best learning resources, and even optimize the order in which content is presented. The use of algorithms such as NSGA-II and other nature-inspired methods allows for a balance between different goals such as educational efficiency, reducing cognitive load, and improving learner motivation (Nozari, 2024).

The fourth layer is the explanation and interaction layer, which directly communicates with the end users, namely students and instructors. In this section, the system should provide outputs not only in the form of practical recommendations, but also with clear reasons and evidence. This is where explainable AI becomes particularly important. Tools such as local explanatory models or feature assessment methods can show why a student needs certain content or which skills need more practice (Tao et al., 2019). This explainability makes users feel more in control and confident in the system's decisions, and human-machine collaboration can proceed in a constructive way.

In the educational digital twin architecture, data flows between the different layers in a two-way manner. Real data is transmitted from the educational environment to the digital model, and then the results of analysis and prediction are returned to the real environment in the form of educational recommendations. This continuous cycle creates a kind of closed-loop feedback that continuously adapts the curriculum to real conditions.

For better understanding, Figure 1 shows the overall structure of a digital twin in education. In this image, we can see four main layers: the data layer, the digital model layer, the analysis and optimization layer, and the interaction and explanation layer. The double-headed arrows between the layers indicate the continuous flow of data and knowledge.

Figure 1. Overall architecture of a digital twin in education consisting of four main layers

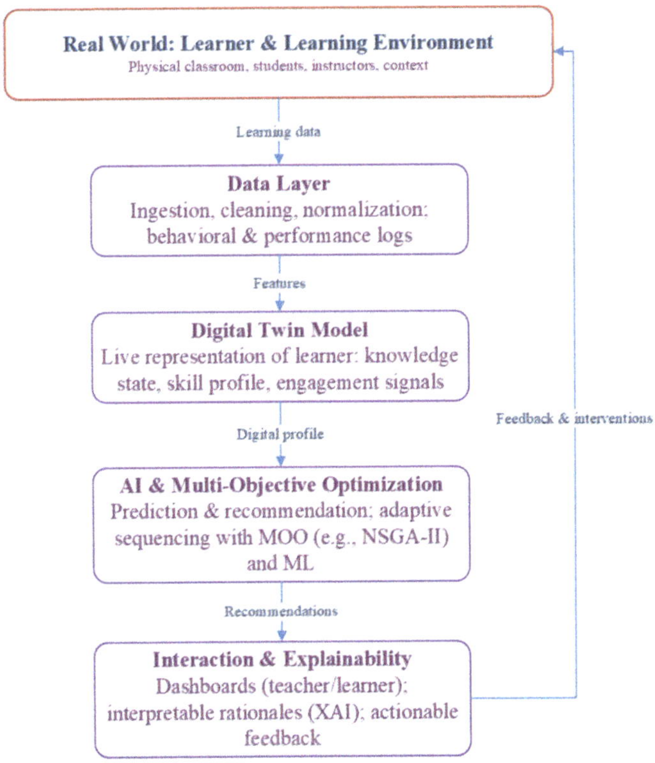

This architecture shows how diverse learner data is continuously transferred to the digital twin and reflected in the form of dynamic models.

Finally, it should be noted that this architecture is not just a conceptual framework, but as an operational platform it can play a key role in the design of adaptive learning pathways. By using real student data, implementing intelligent algorithms, and providing clear explanations, it is possible to create learning environments that not only cover the diverse needs of learners, but also provide teachers, administrators, and policymakers with a better understanding of the educational process. This architecture provides a basis for the development of a new generation of intelligent educational systems that can enhance the quality of learning and promote active participation of learners.

3- ARTIFICIAL INTELLIGENCE IN ADAPTIVE CURRICULUM DESIGN

The increasing spread of new technologies has led educational systems to move more than ever towards personalizing learning and using smart tools. In this regard, artificial intelligence plays a pivotal role because it has the ability to analyze a huge amount of educational data, identify hidden patterns, and provide suggestions tailored to the needs of each student. But what makes this role distinctive and more effective is the use of explainable artificial intelligence (EAI) approaches. In this section, we will examine the position and applications of artificial intelligence in the design and implementation of adaptive learning pathways.

In the first step, it should be noted that adaptive learning pathways are designed based on the principle of "dynamic flexibility". This principle states that the educational content, teaching methods, and even the pace of progress should always be adapted to the learner's conditions. For example, if a student does not have a deep understanding of introductory topics, presenting advanced topics will not only not be beneficial, but can also lead to anxiety and reduced motivation. By analyzing data from tests, assignments, and digital interactions, AI can identify these weaknesses and redesign the curriculum accordingly (Nozari & Edalatpanah, 2023).

One of the most important AI tools in this direction is machine learning and deep learning algorithms. These algorithms can extract behavioral and cognitive patterns of students from raw data and, based on that, predict the ability or inability of the individual to learn future subjects. Such predictions help the system to intervene before a problem occurs and suggest appropriate resources or activities to the student. For example, if a student spends a lot of time solving math problems, the system can provide simpler educational content or step-by-step exercises to maintain the learning process (Movahed et al., 2024).

In addition to analysis and prediction, multi-objective optimization is very important. In designing adaptive learning pathways, several conflicting goals usually have to be pursued simultaneously. On the one hand, it is necessary to increase the speed of learning, on the other hand, it is important to maintain the quality and depth of learning, and at the same time, excessive psychological pressure should not be placed on the student. Evolutionary algorithms such as NSGA-II or meta-heuristic methods inspired by nature allow searching in a large space of solutions and identifying points that establish the best balance between different objectives (Mon et al., 2025). In fact, these algorithms can suggest several optimal versions of the curriculum so that teachers or learners themselves can choose the appropriate option based on personal preferences.

Despite these capabilities, the issue of explainability remains a central challenge. If an adaptive learning system simply introduces a new path, the question may arise for the student or teacher: "Why should I study this content?" or "On what basis is this exercise suggested to me?". Answering these questions is only possible with XAI tools. Methods such as feature importance analysis or attention maps can show in simple terms which factors have had the greatest impact on the system's decision. In this way, the decision-making process is removed from being ambiguous and incomprehensible, and it allows instructors to review the system's decisions and, if necessary, correct them (Movahed et al., 2024).

To better understand the role of AI in adaptive learning pathways, we can pay attention to its operational architecture. In this architecture, learning data is fed into the digital model from the data layer, then processed in the analysis and optimization layer, and finally the output is transferred to the interaction and explanation layer. At this stage, in addition to providing a new curriculum, the system also clarifies the reasons and logic of its decision-making.

This architecture shows how artificial intelligence can be placed as a supporting agent alongside instructors and students. The system not only personalizes educational content, but also enables a constructive dialogue between technology and humans by making its decisions transparent. The result of this approach is increased trust, acceptance, and motivation of learners.

At the same time, implementing such a system requires robust computing infrastructure, coherent databases, and clear ethical frameworks. Maintaining student privacy, preventing algorithmic bias, and allowing for teacher control are among the principles that must be observed. If these requirements are properly implemented, AI can become an effective tool for designing adaptive learning pathways and guiding education towards a smart, transparent, and efficient future.

4- EXPLAINABILITY AND TRANSPARENCY IN DECISION-MAKING

One of the main challenges in using AI in education is the issue of transparency and explainability of decisions. Although deep learning algorithms and complex machine learning models are highly accurate, they often act like a "black box"; that is, the input and output are known, but the internal logic of the decision-making is not clear to users. This issue is doubly important in the field of education, because the trust of students and teachers is only gained when they know why an educational recommendation or change in the curriculum has been suggested to them (Movahed et al., 2023). Without this transparency, even if the system designs the best learning path, there is a possibility of distrust and resistance to its use.

Explainability in this context means providing clear and understandable reasons for the system's decisions. For example, if an adaptive system recommends a student to study a specific chapter of an educational resource, it is necessary to explain on which indicators this recommendation was based; Perhaps because recent tests have shown frequent errors in prerequisite topics or because the student has spent less time studying than usual. Such explanations not only build trust but also help the learner to have a deeper understanding of their learning status and take more responsibility for the learning process (Nozari et al., 2022).

Transparency is also particularly important at the level of teachers and lesson designers. When algorithms suggest different learning paths, the teacher should be able to see the logic of these decisions in order to change or confirm them if necessary. In other words, the AI system should act as an assistant, not an absolute replacement. This is only possible by making decisions transparent and allowing for two-way interaction between humans and machines.

One of the most widely used approaches in this area is the use of EAI (Explainable Artificial Intelligence) techniques. These techniques provide tools that show which variables had the greatest impact on the final decision. For example, methods such as SHAP or LIME can calculate and visually display the importance of different features (such as grades, study time, or class participation) (Zarrabi & Doost Mohammadian, 2024). With the help of these tools, the student or teacher can understand why the algorithm decided to suggest a particular exercise or change the difficulty level of the educational content.

Explainability also helps reduce algorithmic bias. If a system decides without explanation to direct a group of students to a particular resource, this decision may be due to error or data bias. However, when the reasons for the decision are clearly stated, it is possible to detect and correct the error. For this reason, transparency is important not only for building trust but also for maintaining educational justice (Movahed et al., 2023).

For better classification, the main applications of explainability in adaptive learning pathways can be examined at three levels: student level, teacher level, and educational policymaker level. At the student level, clear explanations increase motivation and active participation. At the teacher level, they allow for evaluation and modification of proposed paths. And at the policymaker level, they provide assurance that algorithmic decisions are in line with ethical principles and broader educational goals.

To clarify this issue, Table 1 presents three examples of explainability techniques and their applications in adaptive curriculum design.

Table 1. Explainability techniques and their applications in adaptive learning

Explainability Technique	Brief Description	Example Application in Adaptive Learning
Feature Importance	Ranking of input variables based on their influence on the model's decision	Showing that exam scores had the greatest impact on recommending a specific learning resource
LIME (Local Interpretable Model-Agnostic Explanations)	Creating a simple local model to explain a specific decision	Explaining why a student was recommended to practice a basic-level exercise
SHAP (SHapley Additive exPlanations)	Calculating each feature's contribution using game theory	Demonstrating the contributions of study time, engagement, and past performance in selecting a learning path

This table shows that explainability tools not only simplify complex algorithmic concepts, but also enable their practical application in curriculum design. Such techniques are translated into language that users can understand, allowing them to take an active role in the learning process.

Ultimately, explainability and transparency are key elements for the success of adaptive learning pathways. Without clear explanations, even the best systems will face challenges in trust and acceptance. But when algorithms clearly express their logic, the ground is paved for a productive collaboration between humans and technology. This collaboration not only improves the quality of education, but also makes both students and teachers feel that they are part of the decision-making and that the system is serving them, not the other way around. As XAI techniques advance and attention to ethical issues in digital education increases, we can expect the future of adaptive learning pathways to move toward greater transparency and sustainable educational equity.

5- APPLICATIONS AND CASE STUDIES

The application of explainable AI-based digital twins in education offers an unprecedented opportunity to redesign learning pathways and create personalized learning experiences. This technology can be used in various educational environments, from traditional classrooms to online learning systems, and by analyzing real-time data, it can suggest pathways tailored to the needs of each student. In this section, examples of key applications of this approach are reviewed to show how it can be used to improve the quality of education.

One of the most important applications is in the management of large classes. In many universities and schools, the number of students or pupils in a class exceeds the standard, which prevents teachers from fully monitoring the individual status of each learner. Digital twins allow the performance, behavioral and cognitive information of each student to be recorded and analyzed digitally. As a result, instead of spending a lot of time monitoring each student individually, the teacher can use the system's outputs to target those who need more support. This approach ensures that even in large classes, the quality of learning and the level of attention to individual needs are not reduced (Nozari et al., 2021).

Another application of this technology is personalized learning in specialized education. In fields such as medicine or engineering, where the complexity of the material is high, students need unique learning paths. A digital twin can design a special curriculum for each individual using data related to the level of knowledge, previous skills, progress, and even emotional states of the students. For example, a student who is weak in biochemistry but strong in the basics of physics will receive a different learning path from his classmate who has difficulty in mathematics. This personalization makes students participate in the learning process with more motivation and confidence, and the overall efficiency of the class increases (Tavakkoli-Moghaddam et al., 2022).

Another important area of application is online learning and distance education. In situations where access to a face-to-face classroom is difficult for many students, digital twin-based systems can identify potential problems and automatically suggest alternative solutions by closely tracking students' interactions with digital content. For example, if a student repeatedly pauses or rewinds while watching educational videos, the system can recognize that the content needs to be simplified or repeated. Explainable AI can also be used to explain why a change in the learning path is suggested, so that the student feels involved in the decision-making process (Crnjac Zizic et al., 2025).

The technology also provides significant capabilities for analyzing educational big data and making policy-level decisions. By aggregating data from thousands of students, digital twins can reveal overall learning patterns. For example, it may be determined that students have a specific area of weakness in certain subjects, which requires a review of the overall curriculum design. Providing such analyses helps educational authorities make data-driven decisions and improve educational policies at a macro level (Nozari et al., 2021).

In addition, multi-objective optimization capabilities in digital twin systems allow learning pathways to be designed in a way that simultaneously pursues multiple goals. These goals can include increasing success rates, reducing learning time, improving conceptual understanding, or improving learner satisfaction. Optimization algorithms are able to propose various solutions that balance these goals. The teacher or educational administrator can then select the most appropriate option based on classroom conditions or educational policies.

From a practical perspective, implementing these applications requires tools to clearly display algorithmic decisions. Here, XAI approaches come into play to explain the decision-making logic of the system to teachers and students. These explanations are presented in the form of interactive diagrams, feature importance indices, or understandable textual explanations. As a result, trust in the system is increased and its acceptance by users is facilitated.

To summarize this section, some key applications of explainable AI-based digital twins can be seen in Table 2.

Table 2. Example of explainable AI-driven digital twin applications in adaptive education

Application Area	Description (English)	Added Value
Large-Scale Class Management	Monitoring individual learner progress in crowded classrooms using digital profiles	Targeted support for struggling students, improved equity
Personalized Learning in Higher Education	Tailoring curriculum design based on prior knowledge, skills, and learning pace	Increased motivation, deeper understanding, adaptive pathways
Online & Remote Learning	Tracking digital interactions and providing real-time adaptive recommendations	Enhanced engagement, timely feedback, continuity of learning

In general, explainable AI-based digital twins can overcome many of the traditional limitations of education. By creating a continuous feedback loop between the real world and the digital world, they both improve the quality of individual learning and help improve macro-educational policies. In addition, by using decision-making transparency approaches, it is possible to build trust among all stakeholders. As a result, this technology is not only a technological tool but also a platform for a fundamental transformation in the design and implementation of curriculum design.

6- CHALLENGES AND THE FUTURE

Despite all the benefits that explainable AI-based digital twins provide for adaptive learning pathways, the path to implementing this approach is not without its challenges. Every emerging technology, along with its opportunities, also brings a set of challenges that, if ignored, can lead to the failure of the entire project. Examining these challenges and the future outlook can provide a clearer understanding of the path forward for adaptive education.

One of the first challenges is the issue of data. To accurately represent the learner's situation, digital twins require diverse and up-to-date data. This data can include academic performance, online interactions, behavioral information, and even cognitive and emotional indicators. Collecting such data in traditional educational settings is not an easy task. On the other hand, data quality is also a major challenge. Incomplete, erroneous, or inconsistent data can lead to digital models being out of sync with reality and lead to poor decision-making (Lin et al., 2025). Therefore, building robust infrastructures for data collection, cleaning, and validation is a serious requirement in this area.

The second challenge is related to privacy and ethical considerations. Learner data often contains highly sensitive information that should not be collected and processed without clear legal and ethical frameworks. Concerns about constantly tracking students' behavior or analyzing their emotional states can create strong resistance to adopting this technology. If users feel that they are losing control of their data, trust in the system will decrease and even the best algorithms will be distrusted. Therefore, principles such as informed consent, transparency in how data is used, and the ability for learners to delete or modify information must be observed.

Another challenge is computational complexity. Digital twins require real-time processing of diverse data, and machine learning and multi-objective optimization algorithms typically require significant computational resources. In many educational institutions, there is insufficient technological infrastructure to support this amount of processing. This may limit the practical application of these technologies to advanced centers and large universities, increasing educational inequality between different regions. The future of this field depends on the development of cloud infrastructure and distributed computing technologies that can reduce costs and provide wider access.

Another issue is cultural and educational acceptance. Many teachers and students are still hesitant to use artificial intelligence systems in the learning process. This hesitation is due to two factors: first, the fear of replacing humans with machines, and second, uncertainty about the logic of algorithmic decision-making. Although explainability approaches greatly reduce this problem, they still require cultural development and education. Teachers need to learn how to use digital twin outputs to enhance their teaching methods, rather than seeing them as a threat to their position.

Another challenge is the sustainability and updating of models. The learning situation of students is constantly changing, and algorithms must be designed to adapt to these changes. A model that is accurate today may not be accurate a few months from now. Therefore, it is crucial to create continuous and adaptive learning mechanisms to update digital twins.

Despite these challenges, the future of this field looks very promising. Advances in explainable AI promise to increase the level of transparency and trust in education systems. In the future, this technology will not only be able to explain the reasons for decisions in simple text, but also, with advanced visual tools, represent the learning path of students in an interactive and understandable way.

From a practical perspective, we can expect digital twins to gradually become the standard in curriculum design. By using this approach, schools and universities can offer diverse and dynamic paths instead of fixed and uniform programs. Even at a macro level, governments can use the collected data to modify educational policies, identify system weaknesses and optimally allocate resources.

The future outlook will also move towards the integration of complementary technologies. Connecting digital twins to the Internet of Things, augmented reality, and wearable technologies can enhance the quality of the data collected. For example, biosensors will be able to provide precise information about students' concentration or stress levels, and digital twins will be able to analyze this data to fine-tune learning programs.

Another important point is the development of multidisciplinary approaches. The future of adaptive education does not depend solely on technology experts, but also requires close collaboration between educational experts, psychologists, data scientists, and policymakers. Such collaborations can ensure that digital twins are not only technically advanced, but also pedagogically and ethically consistent with the goals of education.

Overall, it can be said that digital twins based on explainable AI will push the future of education systems towards greater flexibility, transparency, and efficiency. Although there are many challenges along the way, these obstacles can be overcome with technological advancements and increased hands-on experience. The ultimate vision is to create intelligent learning environments where each student follows a personalized, transparent, and data-driven path, and education transcends its traditional format and becomes a dynamic and collaborative experience.

7- CONCLUSION

The transformation of education has always been accompanied by technological innovations, but in recent years, the advent of artificial intelligence and digital twins has opened up new and different perspectives for educational systems. A review of the issues raised in this chapter shows that the combination of these two technologies not only allows for the simulation and precise monitoring of learners, but also creates conditions in which curriculum design can be dynamically redesigned to suit the needs of each individual.

Adaptive learning pathways are essentially a response to a fundamental need: the fact that no two learning experiences are the same. Each student enters the learning process with unique backgrounds, abilities, motivations, and limitations. In traditional approaches, due to limited human resources and educational structures, it was not possible to accurately respond to these differences, and all learners were often trained under a single program. This left some students feeling left behind, while others were bored by the simplicity of the material. Digital twins break this cycle, allowing each individual to follow a path that is tailored to their capacity, learning speed, and needs.

The role of artificial intelligence is key. By analyzing a variety of data, from grades to behavioral patterns in digital learning environments, smart algorithms can identify which topics each student needs more practice in and which content will be most challenging for them. This allows the system to proactively provide intelligent interventions and suggest the right educational resources at the right time. In this way, learning is transformed from a linear and uniform process into a personalized and adaptive experience.

However, if these decisions are not understandable to both the student and the teacher, the trust necessary to accept them will not be built. This is why explainability is particularly important. An AI-based digital twin should be able to explain why a particular topic was chosen, what factors influenced this decision, and what outcome is expected. Such transparency helps the learner to better understand the learning process and be more motivated to continue on the path. Also, by observing the decision-making logic of the algorithm, teachers can modify their interventions and adjust the educational program in a way that is consistent with the educational goals.

The main challenges in this direction can be examined in several categories. First, data collection in educational environments always faces technical and ethical obstacles. Learner data must not only be accurate and complete, but also comply with the principles of confidentiality and information security. Any misuse or leakage of data can have irreparable consequences for public trust in educational technologies. Second, AI algorithms, especially in the field of deep learning, require high computational power. Many schools and universities do not have access to such infrastructure, which could hinder the widespread adoption of this approach. Third, the cultural and educational acceptance of smart technologies is a serious challenge. Many teachers and students are still wary of these technologies, concerned that they will undermine the human role in the learning process. Therefore, targeted educational and outreach activities are needed to build trust and social acceptance.

Despite these challenges, the future of digital twins in education is very bright. It can be expected that with the advancement of cloud technologies and distributed computing, computational limitations will be reduced and the use of these systems on a larger scale will be possible. Also, progress in the field of explainable models will make the outputs of algorithms more transparent to users and the decision-making process of AI will be understood not as a mystery, but as part of learning. In the future, digital twins could be used as an integral part of national education policies in schools and universities, designing each student's learning path in a personalized and scientific manner.

From a research perspective, there are many opportunities for further development in this area. Combining digital twins with new technologies such as augmented reality, virtual reality, and the Internet of Things can significantly improve the quality of educational data. For example, wearable sensors can record the emotional and physiological state of learners during training sessions, and this data can be transferred to the digital model to optimize the curriculum based on the learner's actual conditions.

The future outlook will also move towards automated and intelligent adaptive learning. This means that digital twins will not only make decisions based on available data, but will also be able to learn from past feedback and improve themselves. In such a system, algorithms will gradually become more accurate and efficient, and the need for human intervention in some stages will be reduced. This transformation could lead to a new generation of intelligent and flexible educational systems that adapt to the changing conditions of learners and educational environments.

Overall, digital twins based on explainable AI can create a new foundation for adaptive education. By combining diverse data, dynamic modeling, multi-objective optimization algorithms, and decision-making tools, this technology enables the design of learning pathways tailored to individual needs. In the future, with the removal of technical and ethical barriers and the strengthening of digital infrastructure, we can expect this approach to become one of the main pillars of education at different levels.

REFERENCES

Alghamdi, S., Yoon, H. Y., & Song, Y. T. (2025, May). Digital Twins in Education Applications, Challenges, and Future Directions. In 2025 IEEE/ACIS 23rd International Conference on Software Engineering Research, Management and Applications (SERA) (pp. 225-232). IEEE.

Babu, C. S., Afreed, M. N., Sree, V. S., & Arshath, J. M. (2026). The Role of Digital Twins in AI-Driven Industry 4.0 and 5.0: Enhancing Sustainability and Innovation. AI-Driven Smart Industrial Technologies, 243-284.

Bao, Z., Siraj, S. B., & Halili, S. H. (2025, April). The Convergence of Digital Twins and Eye-Tracking: Toward Zero UI in Wearable Human-Robot Interaction. In 2025 3rd International Conference on Control and Robot Technology (ICCRT) (pp. 123-129). IEEE.

Boltsi, A., Kosmanos, D., Xenakis, A., Chatzimisios, P., & Chaikalis, C. (2025). Towards a Novel Digital Twin Framework Proposal Within the Engineering Design Process for Future Engineers: An IoT Smart Building Use Case. *Sensors (Basel), 25*(11), 3504. DOI: 10.3390/s25113504 PMID: 40969060

Crnjac Zizic, M., Gjeldum, N., Mladineo, M., Bilic, B., & Aljinovic Mestrovic, A. (2025). Towards Sustainable Personalized Assembly Through Human-Centric Digital Twins. *Sensors (Basel), 25*(18), 5662. DOI: 10.3390/s25185662 PMID: 41012901

Doskenov, B., Adaji, O., & Dosumu, R. (2025). Improving Manufacturing with Adaptive Learning in Industry 4.0: Challenges, and Policy Implications. *Current Journal of Applied Science and Technology, 44*(4), 111–132. DOI: 10.9734/cjast/2025/v44i44518

Khatoon, U. T. (2025). Exploring Industry 5.0 in Digital Education: Concepts, Applications, Challenges, Opportunities, and Future Directions–Exploring Europe as an Education Hub. Digital Mentorship: Bridging AI-Human Divide in the Era of Industry 5.0, 165.

Kovari, A. (2025). AI Gem: Context-Aware Transformer Agents as Digital Twin Tutors for Adaptive Learning. *Computers, 14*(9), 367. DOI: 10.3390/computers14090367

Lin, T. C., Chiu, C. N., Wang, P. T., & Fang, L. D. (2025, August). VisFactory: Adaptive Multimodal Digital Twin with Integrated Visual-Haptic-Auditory Analytics for Industry 4.0 Engineering Education. In Multimedia (Vol. 1, No. 1, p. 3). MDPI.

Mon, B. F., Hayajneh, M., Ali, N. A., Ullah, F., Ullah, H., & Alkobaisi, S. (2025). Digital Twins in the IIoT: Current Practices and Future Directions Toward Industry 5.0. *Computers, Materials & Continua*, *83*(3), 3675–3712. DOI: 10.32604/cmc.2025.061411

Movahed, A. B., Aliahmadi, A., Parsanejad, M., & Nozari, H. (2023). A systematic review of collaboration in supply chain 4.0 with meta-synthesis method. *Supply Chain Analytics*, *4*, 100052. DOI: 10.1016/j.sca.2023.100052

Movahed, A. B., Movahed, A. B., & Nozari, H. (2024). Opportunities and challenges of marketing 5.0. Smart and sustainable interactive marketing, 1-21.

Nozari, H. (2024). Green supply chain management based on artificial intelligence of everything. *Journal of Economics and Management*, *46*, 171–188. DOI: 10.22367/jem.2024.46.07

Nozari, H., & Edalatpanah, S. A. (2023). Smart systems risk management in IoT-based supply chain. In *Advances in reliability, failure and risk analysis* (pp. 251–268). Springer Nature Singapore. DOI: 10.1007/978-981-19-9909-3_11

Nozari, H., Fallah, M., Szmelter-Jarosz, A., & Krzemiński, M. (2021). Analysis of security criteria for IoT-based supply chain: a case study of FMCG industries. Central European Management Journal, 29(4).

Nozari, H., Tavakkoli-Moghaddam, R., & Gharemani-Nahr, J. (2022). A neutrosophic fuzzy programming method to solve a multi-depot vehicle routing model under uncertainty during the covid-19 pandemic. *International Journal of Engineering*, *35*(2), 360–371.

Okpala, C., Chikwendu, U., & Onyeka, N. C. (2025). Artificial intelligence-driven total productive maintenance: The future of maintenance in smart factories. *International Journal of Engineering Research and Development*, *21*(1), 68–74.

Pester, A., Andres, F., Anantaram, C., & Mason, J. (2025). Generative AI and Digital Twins: Fostering Creativity in Learning Environments. In *Human-Computer Creativity: Generative AI in Education, Art, and Healthcare* (pp. 153–173). Springer Nature Switzerland. DOI: 10.1007/978-3-031-86551-0_9

Strielkowski, W., Grebennikova, V., Lisovskiy, A., Rakhimova, G., & Vasileva, T. (2025). AI-driven adaptive learning for sustainable educational transformation. *Sustainable Development (Bradford)*, *33*(2), 1921–1947. DOI: 10.1002/sd.3221

Tao, F., Sui, F., Liu, A., Qi, Q., Zhang, M., Song, B., Guo, Z., Lu, S. C.-Y., & Nee, A. Y. (2019). Digital twin-driven product design framework. *International Journal of Production Research*, *57*(12), 3935–3953. DOI: 10.1080/00207543.2018.1443229

Tavakkoli-Moghaddam, R., Ghahremani-Nahr, J., Samadi Parviznejad, P., Nozari, H., & Najafi, E. (2022). Application of internet of things in the food supply chain: A literature review. *Journal of Applied Research on Industrial Engineering*, *9*(4), 475–492.

Zarrabi, H., & Doost Mohammadian, M. R. (2024). Fusion of Digital Twin, Internet-of-Things and Artificial Intelligence for Urban Intelligence. Digital Twin Computing for Urban Intelligence, 77-92.

Chapter 8
Human-Centric Education 5.0 in Digital Twin Ecosystems:
Social and Ethical Challenges for AI-Driven Higher Education

B. Suresha
http://orcid.org/0000-0001-8459-2055
Christ University, India

Nijumon K. John
http://orcid.org/0000-0002-3770-8956
Christ University, India

ABSTRACT

This paper explores human-centric Education 5.0 within digital twin ecosystems, focusing on the social and ethical challenges of AI-driven higher education. Using a bibliometric analysis of 1,325 publications from the Scopus database, it maps how AI is reshaping universities. Digital twins and data-driven systems enable personalised, adaptive learning by continuously tracking progress and predicting outcomes. While these innovations improve efficiency, they also raise concerns around privacy, surveillance, and algorithmic bias. There is a growing risk of reducing students to data points, where decisions rely more on models than human judgment. The study shows declining role of human interaction such as empathy and mentorship which technology cannot fully replace. Additionally, it points to digital inequality, especially in developing contexts like India, where uneven access

DOI: 10.4018/979-8-2600-1674-9.ch008

may widen educational gaps. Overall, the paper calls for a balanced approach that integrates technology while preserving human values, ensuring education remains inclusive, ethical, and truly learner-centered.

1. INTRODUCTION

Digital twin ecosystems in higher education can be understood simply as creating a "living digital version" of students, classrooms, and even entire campuses, where everything is interconnected and continuously updated with real-time data. Instead of treating education as fixed and linear, this approach sees it as something evolving open to observation, experimentation, and ongoing improvement (Fuller et al., 2020). In such a system, a student is no longer just a set of marks or records, but a dynamic profile that reflects learning habits, progress, and areas requiring support, allowing institutions to respond more meaningfully (Jones et al., 2020). Globally, universities are beginning to explore these ideas in practical ways. Some institutions are developing digital replicas of campuses to manage energy use, optimize space, and improve safety systems, while others are focusing more directly on learners (Boje et al., 2020). Digital twins are being used to design personalised learning pathways, enabling systems to suggest how a student learns best through case studies, simulations, or interactive tools and to adapt teaching accordingly, making learning more flexible and responsive (Tlili et al., 2023). In fields such as medicine, engineering, and management, simulation-based learning supported by digital twins is helping students engage with real-world scenarios in a safe environment, improving both understanding and confidence (Fuller et al., 2020).

At the same time, global discussions also highlight important concerns. Developing and maintaining such systems requires strong infrastructure and significant investment, which may not be feasible for all institutions (Boje et al., 2020). There are also serious questions around data privacy and ethics, as these systems depend heavily on collecting and analyzing personal and institutional data, making responsible use essential (Floridi et al., 2018). In India, the adoption of digital twin ecosystems is still at an early stage, but the direction is becoming clearer. The rapid shift toward digital learning, especially after the pandemic, has made institutions more open to technology-enabled education models (Mishra et al., 2020). Policy support for digital innovation and flexible learning is also helping create a more enabling environment, particularly in addressing diverse learning needs across a large student population (Tlili et al., 2023). Digital twins, in this context, can help bridge gaps in learning pace, background, and access by offering more tailored academic support. There is also strong potential to connect education more closely with industry. By creating virtual models of real workplaces or business environments, students can gain practical exposure without always needing physical access, which is especially useful in professional education (Jones et al., 2020). However, challenges such as unequal access to technology, limited funding, and the need for skilled professionals to manage these systems remain significant barriers (Mishra et al., 2020). The digital twin ecosystems have the potential to make higher education more adaptive, inclusive, and aligned with future needs. While global institutions are already experimenting with these ideas, India has the opportunity to shape them in ways that reflect its unique educational context. If approached thoughtfully, this model can help move education closer to what it ideally aims to be: personal, practical, and continuously evolving (Tlili et al., 2023).

2. CONCEPTUAL FOUNDATION OF EDUCATION 5.0 AND DIGITAL TWIN ECOSYSTEMS

The emergence of Education 5.0 represents a significant transformation in the philosophy and practice of higher education. Unlike earlier educational models that primarily focused on standardization, industrial efficiency, and technological automation, Education 5.0 emphasizes a more human-centered, inclusive, and socially responsible approach to learning. The concept draws inspiration from the broader transition from Industry 4.0 to Industry 5.0, where technological advancement is no longer viewed solely in terms of productivity and automation, but also in relation to human well-being, creativity, sustainability, and ethical responsibility (Nahavandi, 2019). In this context, Education 5.0 seeks to integrate advanced digital technologies with human values, ensuring that innovation in education enhances both intellectual development and societal progress.

Traditionally, educational systems evolved in parallel with industrial revolutions. Education 1.0 was largely teacher-centered and focused on basic knowledge transmission, while Education 2.0 introduced more structured institutional learning. Education 3.0 emerged alongside the internet revolution and promoted interactive and collaborative learning environments. Education 4.0, closely linked to Industry 4.0, introduced digital technologies such as artificial intelligence, automation, big data, cloud computing, and the Internet of Things into educational processes. However, critics argue that Education 4.0 often prioritized technological efficiency and employability over emotional intelligence, ethics, and human development (Fisk, 2017). Education 5.0 therefore emerges as a corrective and more balanced model, aiming to place humans at the center of technological integration. Rather than replacing educators and learners with machines, Education 5.0 advocates a collaborative relationship between humans and intelligent technologies. A key feature of Education 5.0 is its emphasis on personalised, adaptive, and lifelong learning. Artificial intelligence and machine learning technologies allow educational institutions to create flexible learning pathways tailored to individual student needs, abilities, and preferences. Learning is increasingly becoming data-driven, where educational systems can analyse student behaviour, predict performance patterns, and recommend customised interventions. While such developments improve learning efficiency and accessibility, Education 5.0 insists that technological advancement should remain aligned with ethical values, inclusivity, sustainability, and social responsibility. Thus, the model goes beyond technological transformation and attempts to redefine the very purpose of education in a digitally connected society. Within this evolving educational paradigm, the concept of digital twin ecosystems has gained increasing relevance. Originally developed in engineering and manufacturing contexts, a digital twin refers to a virtual representation of a physical object, system, or process that continuously updates itself using real-time data (Fuller et al., 2020). In industrial settings, digital twins are used to simulate performance, monitor operations, and predict future outcomes. However, the application of digital twin technology is now expanding into healthcare, smart cities, business management, and education. In higher education, digital twins can be understood as dynamic digital representations of students, classrooms, learning systems, and institutional environments that interact continuously with real-world educational processes.

Digital twin ecosystems in education operate by collecting and analysing large volumes of learner-related data through learning management systems, wearable technologies, virtual platforms, and intelligent educational tools. These systems create continuously evolving learner profiles capable of tracking academic performance, engagement levels, behavioural patterns, emotional responses, and learning preferences. Based on these insights, institutions can deliver personalised learning experiences, adaptive assessments, predictive academic support, and targeted interventions. For example, digital twins may help identify students at risk of academic failure, recommend learning resources suited to individual needs, or simulate educational outcomes under different learning conditions. Such capabilities align closely with the objectives of Education 5.0, particularly its emphasis on personalised and learner-centric education.

The integration of digital twin ecosystems into Education 5.0 is further strengthened by the rise of immersive technologies such as virtual reality, augmented reality, metaverse platforms, and artificial intelligence-driven simulations. These technologies enable the creation of intelligent learning environments where students can engage with realistic simulations, collaborative virtual spaces, and interactive problem-solving experiences. In disciplines such as engineering, medicine, architecture, and management, digital twins provide opportunities for experiential learning that extend beyond traditional classroom limitations. Learners are able to interact with complex systems, practice real-world decision-making, and receive immediate feedback in safe and controlled virtual environments. Despite these opportunities, the conceptual relationship between Education 5.0 and digital twin ecosystems extends beyond technological innovation alone. At its core, the relationship is rooted in the idea of balancing technological intelligence with human values. Education 5.0 does not advocate technology for its own sake; instead, it promotes technology that enhances human creativity, critical thinking, emotional intelligence, and ethical awareness. In this regard, digital twin ecosystems are expected to support—not replace—the human dimensions of education. The role of educators therefore remains central, particularly in fostering empathy, mentorship, moral reasoning, and social interaction, aspects that cannot be fully replicated through algorithmic systems. However, the growing dependence on data-driven educational systems also raises important social, ethical, and governance concerns. Since digital twin ecosystems continuously collect and process learner data, questions related to privacy, surveillance, informed consent, and data ownership become increasingly significant. Students may be reduced to predictive data profiles where educational decisions are influenced more by algorithms than by human understanding. Concerns surrounding algorithmic bias, fairness, and transparency in artificial intelligence systems have therefore become central to discussions on human-centric education (Floridi et al., 2018). Furthermore, unequal access to digital infrastructure and technological resources may widen educational inequalities, particularly in developing countries where digital divides remain significant. In countries such as India, the integration of digital twin ecosystems into higher education presents both opportunities and challenges. While government initiatives promoting digital education and technological innovation are expanding access to learning, disparities in internet connectivity, affordability, institutional readiness, and digital literacy continue to affect equitable participation. At the same time, the Indian educational tradition places strong emphasis on holistic development, ethical values, and human relationships in learning. This creates an important context for understanding why Education 5.0 must remain fundamentally human-centric even in technologically advanced learning environments. Overall, the conceptual foundation of Education 5.0 and digital twin ecosystems reflects a broader shift in higher education from purely technology-driven models toward more balanced, ethical, and learner-centered systems. Education is increasingly becoming intelligent, adaptive, and interconnected, yet its ultimate purpose remains deeply human. The successful integration of digital twin ecosystems, therefore, depends not only on technological sophistication but also on the ability of institutions to preserve inclusivity, ethical accountability, social responsibility, and meaningful human interaction within the educational process.

3. HUMAN-CENTRIC LEARNING IN AI-DRIVEN HIGHER EDUCATION

The rapid integration of artificial intelligence into higher education is transforming the way learning is designed, delivered, and experienced. Universities across the world are increasingly adopting AI-driven technologies such as intelligent tutoring systems, adaptive learning platforms, predictive analytics, virtual assistants, and digital twin ecosystems to improve academic efficiency and personalise student learning experiences. While these developments represent a major technological advancement, they have also led to an important shift in educational thinking from technology centred learning toward human-centric learning. In the context of Education 5.0, human-centric learning emphasises that technology should support human development rather than replace the human dimensions of education. The primary objective is not merely to automate learning processes, but to create educational environments that promote creativity, emotional intelligence, critical thinking, ethics, collaboration, and social well-being.

Human-centric learning places the learner at the centre of the educational process. Unlike traditional one-size-fits-all approaches, AI-driven systems enable institutions to design personalised learning pathways tailored to individual learners' needs, abilities, preferences, and progress. Artificial intelligence can analyse large volumes of student data to identify learning patterns, strengths, weaknesses, and engagement levels, allowing educators to provide customised support and interventions (Holmes et al., 2022). Adaptive learning systems, for instance, can modify instructional content in real time based on a student's pace and understanding, thereby improving learning outcomes and learner satisfaction. Such personalised approaches align closely with the goals of Education 5.0, which seeks to make learning more flexible, inclusive, and student-centered. At the same time, human-centric learning recognizes that education is fundamentally a social and emotional process. Although AI technologies can provide efficient feedback, automate assessments, and improve administrative decision-making, they cannot fully replicate the empathy, mentorship, ethical reasoning, and emotional connection offered by human educators. Teachers continue to play a critical role in motivating students, nurturing creativity, resolving emotional challenges, and fostering values-based learning. As argued by Selwyn (2016), excessive dependence on educational technologies may risk weakening the relational aspects of education that are essential for meaningful human development. Therefore, AI in higher education should function as a collaborative tool that enhances the role of educators rather than diminishing it. Another important aspect of human-centric learning is inclusivity and accessibility. AI-driven educational systems have the potential to democratize learning by providing access to educational resources across geographical and socio-economic boundaries. Online learning platforms, virtual classrooms, and intelligent learning tools can support learners with diverse abilities, including students with disabilities, by offering flexible and assistive learning environments. However, these benefits are not equally distributed. Unequal access to digital infrastructure, internet connectivity, and technological literacy may widen educational inequalities, particularly in developing economies such as India. Human-centric education therefore requires institutions and policymakers to ensure that technological innovation remains inclusive and accessible to all learners. Ethical responsibility also forms a central component of human-centric learning. AI systems rely heavily on data collection and algorithmic decision-making, raising concerns regarding privacy, surveillance, bias, and transparency. Students may increasingly be viewed through predictive data models, where educational decisions are shaped by algorithms rather than holistic human understanding. Such concerns highlight the importance of ethical governance frameworks that prioritize fairness, accountability, and student autonomy (Floridi et al., 2018). Human-centric learning thus calls for a balanced approach in which technological efficiency is carefully aligned with human dignity, social responsibility, and ethical values. Overall, human-centric learning in AI-driven higher education represents an attempt to balance technological innovation with the broader purpose of education. While AI has the capacity to enhance personalization, accessibility, and institutional efficiency, the true success of Education 5.0 depends on preserving the human qualities that make education meaningful. The future of higher education therefore lies not in replacing humans with intelligent systems, but in creating collaborative ecosystems where technology and humanity work together to support holistic learning and societal progress.

4. METHODOLOGY

This study adopts a bibliometric research design to explore the evolving landscape of Human-Centric Education 5.0 within digital twin ecosystems. The study explores, with particular emphasis on the social and ethical challenges associated with AI-driven higher education. Bibliometric analysis is appropriate for this study because it enables the systematic examination of large volumes of scholarly literature in an objective and structured manner. Unlike traditional literature reviews that focus on a limited number of studies, bibliometric methods help identify broader publication patterns, thematic relationships, intellectual structures, and emerging research trends within interdisciplinary fields (Aria & Cuccurullo, 2017). This approach provides a comprehensive understanding of how research in this domain has evolved over time. The bibliographic data for the study was collected from the Scopus database, which is recognized as one of the most reliable and comprehensive indexing platforms for peer-reviewed academic publications due to its wide disciplinary coverage and quality control standards (Baas et al., 2020). The data retrieval process was conducted on 15 March 2026. The search strategy was developed using a combination of keywords related to Education 5.0, digital twin ecosystems, artificial intelligence, and ethical challenges in education. The exact search string used was:

"Education 5.0" OR "Human-Centric Education" OR "Digital Twin Ecosystems" OR "Social Challenges in Education" OR "Ethical Challenges in Education" OR "AI in Education"

The search covered publications indexed in Scopus from 2000 to 2026, allowing the study to capture the evolution of the field over time. To ensure relevance and quality, only English-language publications were included in the analysis. The inclusion criteria consisted of peer-reviewed journal articles, conference papers, book chapters, and review papers related to higher education, artificial intelligence, digital learning systems, ethics, and educational technology. Subject areas primarily included Social Sciences, Computer Science, Engineering, Business, Management and Accounting, and Decision Sciences. Documents unrelated to higher education, duplicate records, non-English publications, editorials, notes, errata, and incomplete records were excluded from the final dataset.

The initial search yielded approximately 1,325 documents. The dataset subsequently underwent a data cleaning process to improve consistency and analytical accuracy. Duplicate records were removed, and keywords with similar meanings or spelling variations were standardized using thesaurus-based normalization techniques within the Bibliometrix environment. Bibliographic information including titles, abstracts, author affiliations, keywords, citation counts, and source details was then exported in CSV format for further analysis. The cleaned dataset was analysed using Biblioshiny, the web-based interface of the Bibliometrix package in R (Aria & Cuccurullo, 2017). Biblioshiny was selected due to its ability to perform advanced bibliometric and science-mapping analyses through an accessible visual interface. The study employed co-word analysis to examine the frequency and co-occurrence of keywords in order to identify dominant research themes and conceptual relationships within the field. Based on measures of centrality and density, thematic mapping was conducted to classify themes into motor themes, basic themes, niche themes, and emerging or declining themes (Cobo et al., 2011). In addition, performance analysis was carried out to examine annual scientific production, influential authors, leading journals, citation patterns, and country-level collaborations. Science-mapping techniques were also used to visually represent the conceptual and intellectual structure of the field, thereby illustrating how technological, ethical, and human-centric dimensions intersect within AI-driven higher education research. Overall, this methodological approach provides a systematic and replicable framework for understanding the current state of knowledge in Human-Centric Education 5.0 and digital twin ecosystems. It enables the identification of dominant research trends while also highlighting underexplored areas, particularly those related to ethics, governance, inclusivity, and human-centered learning in AI-enabled educational environments.

Figure 1. Word cloud and frequency over time

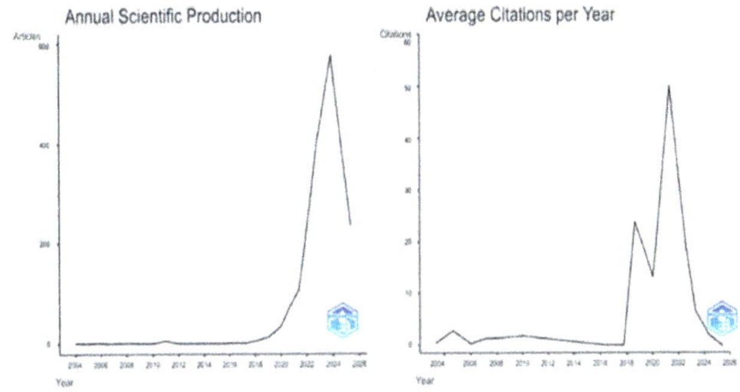

Source: Author generated using Biblioshiny (interface of bibliometrix package) (Aria & Cuccurullo, 2017), based on Scopus data (retrieved on 26 April 2026)

This combined visualization brings together two complementary perspectives on the research landscape—how key themes are growing over time and how they are positioned in relation to each other. When viewed side by side, the story becomes much clearer and more intuitive. The left-side graph, showing words' frequency over time, reflects how interest in different topics has evolved. What stands out immediately is the sharp and almost dramatic rise of artificial intelligence after around 2021. For several years, the curve remains nearly flat, suggesting limited activity or attention. Then suddenly, there is a steep upward surge, indicating that AI has rapidly moved from being a niche interest to becoming the central focus of research in this domain. Other themes such as machine learning, Industry 4.0, Industry 5.0, and sustainable development also show noticeable growth, but their increase is more gradual and less intense. This suggests that while these areas are important, they tend to follow the momentum created by AI rather than lead it. The right-side word cloud reinforces this observation in a more visual and immediate way. The sheer size of the term artificial intelligence dominates the space, making it impossible to ignore. Around it, we see clusters of related concepts like machine learning, sustainable development, internet of things, and decision making. These terms are smaller but still prominent, indicating that they are closely connected to the core theme. Interestingly, words like ethical technology, human, and sustainability are present but less dominant, hinting that while these aspects are part of the conversation, they are not yet at the forefront. When both visuals are read together, a deeper insight emerges. The field appears to be technology-driven first, and human-centered second. The rapid rise of AI-related terms shows where most of the research energy is concentrated, while the presence—but smaller scale—of ethical and human-focused terms suggests these areas are still catching up. It feels as though the research community is building powerful tools first and then gradually beginning to ask more reflective questions about their impact. Overall, the image captures a field in transition—one that is expanding quickly, led by technological innovation, but slowly starting to acknowledge the importance of balancing progress with responsibility, ethics, and human values.

Figure 2. Annual scientific production and citations per year

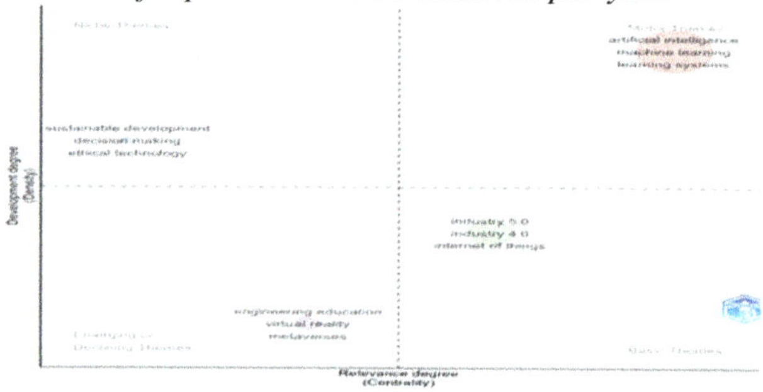

Source: Author generated using Biblioshiny (interface of bibliometrix package) (Aria & Cuccurullo, 2017), based on Scopus data (retrieved on 26 April 2026)

The combined visualization presents two important dimensions of the research landscape annual scientific production and average citations per year offering a clear picture of how the field has evolved over time. When viewed together, these charts tell a story not just about growth, but about the maturity and impact of research in this domain. The first chart, Annual Scientific Production, shows that for a long period (from around 2004 to 2018), research output remained relatively low and stable, indicating that the topic was either emerging or not yet widely explored. However, a noticeable shift begins around 2020, followed by a sharp and almost exponential increase after 2022, peaking around 2024–2025. This sudden surge reflects a growing global interest, likely driven by advancements in artificial intelligence, digital transformation, and the increasing relevance of Education 5.0. It suggests that the field has moved from a niche area to a rapidly expanding research frontier. The second chart, Average Citations per Year, adds another layer of insight by showing how impactful this research has been. Interestingly, citation rates peak earlier around 2020 and 2022 before declining in recent years. This pattern is quite typical in emerging fields. Early influential papers tend to receive high citations as they lay the foundation, while more recent publications, although higher in number, have not yet had sufficient time to accumulate citations. When both charts are interpreted together, a meaningful pattern emerges: the field is currently in a high-growth phase, with increasing research output but a lag in citation impact for newer studies. This indicates that while interest and contributions are rapidly rising, the consolidation of knowledge and long-term academic influence is still developing. Overall, the image reflects a dynamic and evolving research area that is gaining momentum and is likely to become even more influential in the coming years.

Figure 3. Thematic map

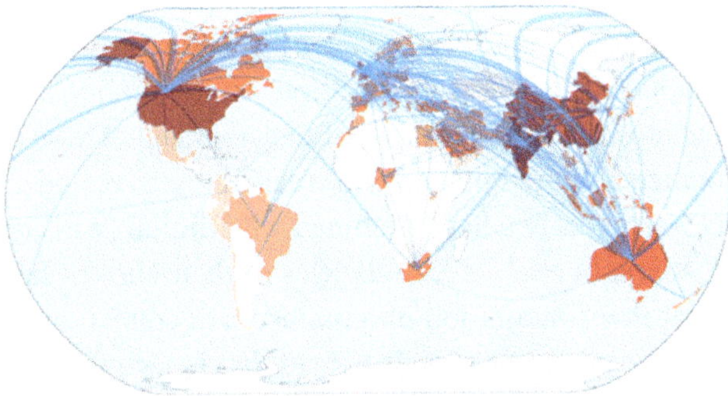

Source: Author generated using Biblioshiny (interface of bibliometrix package) (Aria & Cuccurullo, 2017), based on Scopus data (retrieved on 26 April 2026)

The thematic map generated through Biblioshiny provides a structured view of how research on Human-Centric Education 5.0 within digital twin ecosystems is evolving, highlighting both dominant trajectories and underexplored areas. The motor themes quadrant, characterized by high centrality and density, is dominated by artificial intelligence, machine learning, and learning systems, indicating that the field is currently driven by strong technological foundations. This aligns with broader scholarly observations that AI has become central to educational transformation, enabling personalization, automation, and data-driven decision-making (Holmes et al., 2022). However, this technological dominance also suggests that the discourse remains largely system-oriented, often prioritizing efficiency and performance over human-centric concerns. In contrast, the basic themes quadrant, which includes Industry 4.0, Industry 5.0, and the Internet of Things, reflects concepts that are widely recognized as important but not yet deeply developed in educational contexts. Industry 5.0, in particular, emphasizes the integration of human values with advanced technologies, advocating a shift from purely efficiency-driven systems to more inclusive and sustainable models (Nahavandi, 2019; Xu et al., 2021). The relatively low density of these themes suggests that their educational applications, especially in the context of digital twin ecosystems, remain fragmented and offer significant scope for further exploration. The niche themes quadrant, comprising ethical technology, sustainable development, and decision-making, reveals areas that are well-developed but weakly connected to the mainstream research field. This indicates that while ethical and sustainability concerns are being studied, they are not yet fully integrated into the core AI-in-education discourse. Existing literature highlights the importance of addressing issues such as bias, transparency, and accountability in AI systems, particularly in educational settings where decisions can have long-term societal implications (Floridi et al., 2018; Williamson & Eynon, 2020). The positioning of these themes as niche suggests a disconnect between technological advancement and ethical reflection, reinforcing the need for a more holistic and human-centered approach. Meanwhile, the emerging or declining themes quadrant, which includes engineering education, virtual reality, and the metaverse, points to areas that are still in early stages of development. These technologies are increasingly recognized for their potential to create immersive and interactive learning environments, particularly when combined with digital twin concepts (Grieves & Vickers, 2017; Radianti et al., 2020). However, their current low centrality and density indicate that their integration into mainstream educational research is still evolving. The thematic structure reveals a field that is technologically mature but conceptually imbalanced. While AI and machine learning occupy a central and well-developed position, human-centric, ethical, and social dimensions remain peripheral or insufficiently integrated. This imbalance underscores the importance of reorienting research towards a more comprehensive understanding of Education 5.0, one that not only leverages technological advancements but also foregrounds human values, ethical responsibility, and societal well-being. Such a shift is essential for ensuring that the future of AI-driven higher education is not only innovative but also inclusive and sustainable.

Figure 4. Global collaboration network

Source: Author generated using Biblioshiny (interface of bibliometrix package) (Aria & Cuccurullo, 2017), based on Scopus data (retrieved on 26 April 2026)

This Biblioshiny visualization presents a global collaboration network, illustrating how countries are interconnected through co-authorship and research partnerships in the domain of Human-Centric Education 5.0, digital twin ecosystems, and AI-driven education. The intensity of the red shading indicates the volume of research output, while the blue connecting lines represent collaborative linkages between countries. A clear pattern emerges with countries like the United States, China, India, and Australia appearing as dominant contributors. Their darker shading suggests a higher number of publications, while the dense network of connections indicates that these nations play a central role in international research collaboration. The United States, in particular, acts as a major hub, with extensive linkages spanning Europe, Asia, and Oceania, reflecting its strong influence and leadership in AI and education-related research. Similarly, China and India show significant integration into the global research ecosystem, highlighting the growing contribution of emerging economies in shaping this field. European countries also demonstrate strong intra-regional collaboration, forming a tightly connected cluster. This suggests the presence of well-established academic networks and funding frameworks that encourage cross-border research partnerships. In contrast, regions such as Africa and parts of South America display relatively lighter shading and fewer connections, indicating lower research output and limited collaboration, which may be due to infrastructural or funding constraints. Overall, the map reflects an increasingly globalized research landscape, where knowledge production is concentrated in a few leading countries but supported by widespread international collaboration. At the same time, it highlights an imbalance, underscoring the need for greater inclusion from underrepresented regions to ensure diverse perspectives in the development of human-centric, ethical AI-driven education systems.

5. CHANGING DYNAMICS OF EDUCATION IN INDUSTRY 5.0

With the rapid advancement of technology, the landscape of higher education is undergoing a profound transformation each year. The emergence of advanced LLM programs has posed new challenges in teaching, assessment, and evaluation. In response, educators are increasingly turning to AI integration in the curriculum. Currently, there is no clear direction on integrating AI into all educational streams. Disciplines such as computer science and engineering have been teaching courses on AI and machine learning. Streams such as Humanities, Commerce, and Management are puzzled about AI integration except for using it in assessments. In the realm of education, Industry 5.0 represents a powerful alliance between technology, educators, and students, promising to significantly enhance the efficiency and effectiveness of teaching and learning. These technologies hold immense potential to revolutionize the learning process for students and reshape teaching methods for educators. Education 5.0 heralds the next phase of educational evolution, leveraging cutting-edge digital technologies to overcome traditional learning barriers, redefine learning methodologies, and prioritize the holistic well-being of learners.

Figure 5. Changing dynamics of higher education in Industry 5.0

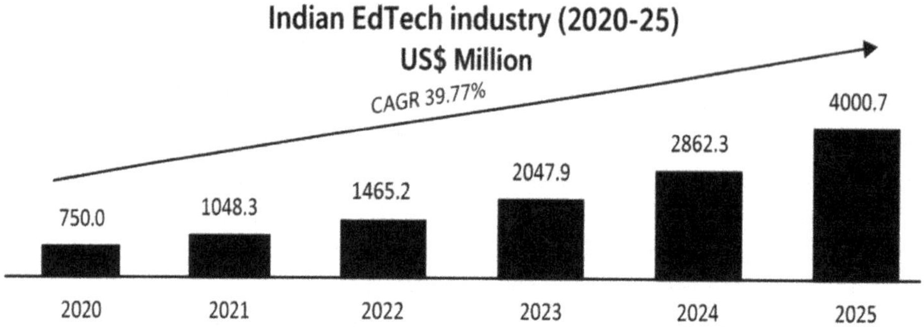

In traditional education, educators employ a conventional approach characterized by lecture-based instruction, rote memorization, and a focus on core subjects such as math, reading, and writing. They use textbooks and worksheets, maintain a teacher-centered approach, and prioritize discipline and order in classroom management. Assessment primarily involves standardized tests and quizzes. While this approach has faced criticism for being rigid, it also provides a strong foundation in core subjects and promotes discipline and respect for authority. It provides benefits such as clear expectations and structure, a strong foundation in core subjects, preparation for standardized tests, and an emphasis on critical thinking and problem-solving. However, these methods may not be as effective for students who need more flexibility, creativity, and hands-on learning experiences. Traditional assessment methods in higher education include in-class exams, standardized tests, quizzes, group projects, case studies, group discussions, and presentations. While these methods measure knowledge and understanding, they may not fully capture the complexity of student learning in the 21st century. In the context of Education 5.0, educators are required to adapt to the dynamic needs of a rapidly changing world. Their multifaceted role encompasses acting as facilitators, mentors, curators of educational content, developers of skills, integrators of technology, coaches, community builders, perpetual learners, innovators in assessment, and collaborators. Embracing creativity, adaptability, and innovation is essential for teachers to effectively prepare students for success in an ever-evolving global landscape.

6. SOCIAL AND ETHICAL DIMENSIONS OF HUMAN-CENTRIC EDUCATION 5.0 IN DIGITAL TWIN ECOSYSTEMS

In the evolving landscape of Human-Centric Education 5.0, digital twin ecosystems are increasingly being viewed as transformative tools capable of reshaping higher education through intelligent, adaptive, and personalised learning systems. Rooted in the broader vision of Industry 5.0, Education 5.0 emphasizes the integration of advanced technologies with human values, creativity, and social well-being rather than focusing solely on automation and efficiency (Nahavandi, 2019). Within this framework, digital twins refer to dynamic virtual representations of learners, learning environments, and institutional processes that continuously collect, analyse, and respond to real-time educational data (Fuller et al., 2020). These systems promise significant improvements in personalised learning, predictive assessment, academic decision-making, and student engagement. However, their growing adoption also introduces complex social and ethical concerns that require careful reflection.

One of the central concerns surrounding digital twin ecosystems is the increasing dependence on data-driven educational practices. Since these systems rely heavily on continuous data collection, they raise serious questions related to privacy, consent, surveillance, and ownership of student information. Learners may gradually be reduced to algorithmically measurable patterns, where human experiences, emotions, and social contexts become secondary to predictive analytics. Such concerns align with broader debates in artificial intelligence regarding fairness, transparency, accountability, and ethical governance (Floridi et al., 2018). Algorithmic systems used in educational decision-making may unintentionally reproduce bias based on gender, age, socio-economic status, or learning pace, potentially disadvantaging certain groups of students. Therefore, while AI-enabled educational systems may improve efficiency, they also risk reinforcing structural inequalities if ethical safeguards are not adequately implemented.

At the same time, technology-mediated education is reshaping the traditional human relationships that form the foundation of meaningful learning. Although AI tools can support automated assessment, adaptive feedback, and virtual learning assistance, they cannot fully replicate empathy, mentorship, emotional understanding, and moral guidance provided by human educators. As Selwyn (2016) argues, excessive dependence on educational technologies may weaken the social and relational dimensions of education that are essential for holistic human development. This concern becomes particularly significant in Education 5.0, which explicitly advocates a human-centric approach to learning. The challenge, therefore, is not simply to integrate technology into classrooms, but to ensure that technological systems continue to support human interaction rather than replace it.

Another major issue relates to digital inequality and accessibility. While technological advancement has the potential to democratise education by expanding access to online learning, open educational resources, and personalised learning opportunities, unequal access to digital infrastructure continues to remain a serious concern, particularly in developing economies such as India. Variations in internet connectivity, digital literacy, affordability of devices, and institutional infrastructure may exclude many students from fully benefiting from AI-driven education systems. Students in rural and economically weaker regions often face barriers that limit participation in digital learning environments, thereby widening the digital divide instead of reducing it. At the same time, government initiatives promoting digital inclusion and rapid technological adoption indicate that technology can also become an important equaliser when implemented inclusively and responsibly.

The ethical challenges extend further into issues such as cyberbullying, online harassment, accessibility for students with disabilities, and the commercialisation of education through profit-oriented EdTech platforms. The increasing use of anonymous online learning environments has made cyberbullying more difficult to monitor and control, affecting student well-being and psychological safety. Similarly, although assistive technologies are improving educational access for students with disabilities, issues of affordability and equitable access continue to persist. Furthermore, the rapid growth of the EdTech industry has created concerns that education may increasingly be treated as a commercial product rather than a social good. In this context, the core principles of Education 5.0 remind institutions that technological innovation must remain aligned with ethical responsibility, inclusivity, sustainability, and human dignity.

Overall, digital twin ecosystems hold significant potential to support the vision of Human-Centric Education 5.0 by enabling intelligent and personalised educational experiences. However, their success depends not merely on technological sophistication, but on the extent to which they preserve human values, social inclusion, ethical accountability, and meaningful human interaction within higher education systems.

Figure 6. Indian Edtech industry 2020-25

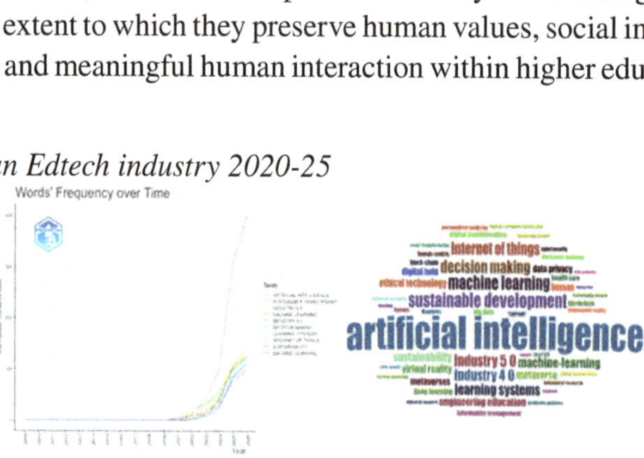

Source: https://www.ibef.org/blogs/india-to-become-the-edtech-capital-of-the-world

While the adaptation to Education 5.0 and the growing use of ICT in teaching present opportunities for change, there are also critical counterarguments to consider. Firstly, the preference for recorded videos over live lectures might reduce real-time interaction between teachers and students, potentially impacting the immediacy and effectiveness of feedback. This shift could lead to a decrease in engagement and motivation among students who benefit from the dynamic of live discussions. Additionally, redefining teachers' roles primarily as mentors might overlook the importance of their expertise in content delivery. Teachers play a crucial role in not just guiding, but also in structuring complex concepts in an understandable way for students. This aspect of teaching is vital for ensuring deep understanding, which might not be achieved through recorded materials alone. Moreover, the assumption that all students and teachers can seamlessly connect through digital devices ignores the digital divide that exists in many communities. Relying heavily on ICT for education can exacerbate inequalities, as not all students have equal access to the necessary technology or stable internet connections. This inequality could hinder the learning process for many students, making the shift towards a more digital-centric education model less equitable.

6. SUSTAINABILITY, GOVERNANCE AND POLICY PERSPECTIVES

Education 5.0 has come as a new paradigm in learning today. It tries to synchronise advanced technologies with basic human values and the learner's values. It infuses artificial intelligence and immersive technologies without sacrificing the social, ethical and sustainability aspects of both learner and teachers (Ashmel et al., 2024, Agarwal et al., 2025). The confluence of Industry 5.0 and Education 5.0 recommends that universities and colleges need to govern digital transformation with embedded sustainability by shaping policies to realize equitable and ethical outcomes. It is very important to further discuss industry and education 5.0 through triple lenses namely sustainability, governance and policies.

Sustainability in Education 5.0: Sustainability in this chapter refers to both environmental and social. In the first place, sustainability in making a green curriculum and learning system is the need of the hour today. Higher education institutions worldwide need to embed sustainability across all disciplines. Mere introduction of a green curriculum is absolutely futile unless it is vigorously emphasised through compelling course plans, challenging assignments, and evaluations. For instance, the University of Tokyo has integrated the Sustainable Development Goals and circular economy principles into its programs. The Asia Pacific School of Business has introduced programs to reduce carbon emissions up to 30%. *Research and knowledge are* the second aspect that needs to be addressed in the context of sustainability. Research on higher education institutions needs to address industry problems while upholding the fundamental values of learners and employees. Universities can introduce living labs and testbeds that enable industry to co-design and evaluate alternative solutions through ethics and sustainability (Van Erp et al., 2024). *Digital sustainability and lifecycle thinking* in the context of Industry 5.0 and Education 5.0 need to be further addressed. Educational institutions need to nurture lifecycle thinking with digital tools. It is equally important that students of today embrace digital minimalism and the role of educational institutions in encouraging and empowering students to seriously uphold digital minimalism can be a huge breakthrough in preserving the environment. Simultaneously, the corporate houses too, need to join hands with higher education institutions in fostering sustainability through green human resource management practices. *Social Sustainability* is an integral part of both Education 5.0 and Industry 5.0. When the so-called sophisticated tools are not equally available Education 5.0 risks widening digital divides. Hence social sustainability needs to facilitate affordable access to devices and connectivity. The instructional designs could be made available to different learners. Policies must be introduced so that the technology is easily available to all learners.

Governance in Education and Industry 5.0: The promise of Education 5.0 depends on the robust governance mechanisms that are found within the higher education institutions. It can manage technological complexity and protect learner's rights and societal values. The other aspects that can be discussed are the multi-layered governance, data governance and privacy, ethical review and algorithmic oversight, academic integrity and assessment governance and workforce governance and faculty roles. Effective and impactful governance needs to operate at multiple levels such as strategic level, operational level, academic governance level and local level. Education 5.0 must avoid reliance on learning analytics and artificial intelligence. Universities should develop their own mechanisms that protect students' privacy, algorithmic transparency and fairness. Several educational institutions have ethics committees for research. They can also introduce oversight committees to check the algorithmic systems used in admissions, assessments and student support services. The inclusion of diverse stakeholders in the formation of an ethical or oversight committee. They are very crucial to the success of upholding governance practices in the era of education 5.0. Finally the role of faculty in higher education is a major determinant of effective implementation of governance.

Policy Perspective: Usually the policy landscape of the country will facilitate how Education 5.0 interacts with Industry 5.0. Policies must not only encourage investment, establish standards but also protect the fundamental rights, equity and environmental limitations. The national policies framed at the central government play a crucial role in setting strategic focus and direction that supports workforce development, research in higher education and industrial policy. The government policy regarding AI and education needs to centre around humanistic approaches that protect equity and quality education . In this era of communication, technology and AI, the policies strictly advocate the ethical aspects in all dimensions. The public institutions must lead and set examples for green procurement and consider life cycle cost and social value with all the stakeholders. Besides this, government policies need to revolve around digital inclusion.

7. CHALLENGES AND EMERGING ISSUES

Education 5.0 represents a transformative shift in the learning landscape, characterised by its emphasis on technology, a central focus on human needs, and a commitment to personalised learning experiences. However, this innovative approach comes with its own set of challenges. The integration of advanced technologies into educational practices necessitates significant financial investments. In stark contrast to previous eras, where straightforward teaching methods like chalk-and-talk were both simple and economical, today's educational strategies rely heavily on sophisticated tools and resources that require substantial funding to implement effectively. Consequently, a lack of adequate financial support can severely limit access to high-quality education for both educators and students, creating disparities in learning opportunities that can affect the overall effectiveness of educational systems. Furthermore, there are educators and students who resist this new way of learning through technology. It is mainly due to the comfort, simplicity, and affordability of earlier systems. As the traditional education system was cost-effective, it is still the most preferred method of learning for many. At the same time, it is also beneficial for health, as learning online can be harmful to the eyes, and the use of mobile phones for studying affects not only the eyes but also the students' attention. Therefore, some parents strongly resist changing to hybrid or online learning and prefer to send their children to in-person classes. In emerging countries, including India, there is a lack of a clear policy regarding learning methods, the mode of learning to follow, and the cost to be charged. The use of technology may be affordable for rich schools or colleges, but those in other schools, where it is not affordable, will likely stay away from Education 5.0. The blend of online and offline elements, as well as the extent of personalisation in courses, remains unclear to many institutions.

There is a significant concern regarding the digital divide present in emerging countries, particularly in India. Currently, nearly forty percent of the population lacks access to the internet, creating a substantial gap between those with ready access to computers and those without. Given these circumstances, implementing Education 5.0 in India is challenging. Additionally, there is a pressing need for teacher training to help educators adapt to new technologies and innovative teaching methods. The majority of Indians still depend on government schools where there are no teachers or very few teachers. A lack of basic infrastructure is commonly observed, and having access to computers and the internet presents a significant challenge for them. As the AI revolution continues to unfold, one of the key issues that arises is the ethical use of artificial intelligence within the realm of education, alongside the critical need to safeguard data privacy. Educators face the substantial challenge of creating innovative assessment methods that accurately evaluate essential skills, such as creativity and emotional intelligence, which are increasingly important in today's world. Plagiarism is a key challenge that requires immediate attention, as the use of AI makes it difficult for teachers to differentiate between human- and machine-generated assessments. This would result in undeserving students being awarded qualifications. Educators need to develop new assessment methods that evaluate students' creativity and intelligence without relying on AI. It is vital that, as we integrate technology into educational practices, we prioritise a human-centred approach, ensuring that this advancement does not exacerbate existing inequalities among students and communities.

8. CONCLUSION AND SCOPE FOR FUTURE RESEARCH

The transition toward Human-Centric Education 5.0 within digital twin ecosystems represents more than a technological change in higher education. In practice, it reflects a broader rethinking of the purpose of education itself. As universities increasingly adopt artificial intelligence, machine learning, digital twins, and intelligent learning systems, there is growing recognition that technology alone cannot shape meaningful learning. Rooted in the philosophy of Industry 5.0, this shift emphasises that innovation must work alongside human values, creativity, emotional well-being, and social responsibility (Nahavandi, 2019). Educational institutions are therefore expected not only to prepare students with technical skills but also to create inclusive and ethical learning environments. The findings of this study show that research on AI-driven higher education and digital twin ecosystems has expanded rapidly in recent years. Technologies such as artificial intelligence, predictive analytics, virtual reality, and digital twins are actively transforming how universities teach, assess, and support students. Learning is increasingly moving beyond traditional classrooms into flexible digital environments that offer personalised and adaptive learning experiences. However, this transformation has also introduced important social and ethical concerns. One of the major challenges identified is the growing dependence on data-driven educational systems. Digital twin ecosystems continuously collect and analyse learner data to personalise education and predict academic outcomes.

While these systems improve efficiency, they also raise concerns regarding privacy, surveillance, algorithmic bias, and informed consent (Floridi et al., 2018). Students risk being reduced to data profiles where algorithms influence decisions that were traditionally guided by human judgment. Issues such as plagiarism, impersonation, and the authenticity of digital assessments further complicate AI-enabled learning environments.

The study also highlights an imbalance between technological advancement and human-centered concerns. Much of the existing discourse focuses on innovation and efficiency, while empathy, inclusivity, emotional well-being, and ethical responsibility often receive less attention. Yet Education 5.0 fundamentally argues that technology should strengthen—not replace—the human dimensions of education. Teachers remain essential in fostering mentorship, critical thinking, emotional support, and ethical values. Emerging technologies such as immersive virtual environments and digital twin ecosystems still remain at an early stage within higher education, especially in developing contexts such as India, where challenges related to infrastructure, accessibility, affordability, and digital literacy continue to affect equitable implementation. The future of higher education therefore depends on achieving a balance between technological innovation and human values. The success of Education 5.0 will ultimately depend on whether institutions can create learning environments that remain ethical, inclusive, and deeply human while embracing intelligent technologies.

Future research can explore empirical case studies on how digital twin ecosystems are being implemented across universities and their actual impact on student learning, engagement, and well-being. Comparative studies between developed and developing countries may provide deeper insights into issues of digital inequality, accessibility, and ethical governance in AI-driven education. Further interdisciplinary research is also needed to develop human-centric policy frameworks that balance technological innovation with privacy, inclusivity, emotional well-being, and ethical responsibility in higher education.

REFERENCES

Agarwal, V., Verma, P., & Ferrigno, G. (2025). Education 5.0 challenges and sustainable development goals in emerging economies: A mixed-method approach. *Technology in Society*, *81*, 102814. DOI: 10.1016/j.techsoc.2025.102814

Aria, M., & Cuccurullo, C. (2017). Bibliometrix: An R-tool for comprehensive science mapping analysis. *Journal of Informetrics*, *11*(4), 959–975. DOI: 10.1016/j.joi.2017.08.007

Ashmel, M., Tlemsani, I., Mason-Jones, R., Matthews, R., & Ndrecaj, V. (2024). Higher education via the lens of Industry 5.0: Strategy and perspective. *Social Sciences & Humanities Open*, *9*, 100828. DOI: 10.1016/j.ssaho.2024.100828

Baas, J., Schotten, M., Plume, A., Côté, G., & Karimi, R. (2020). Scopus as a curated, high-quality bibliometric data source for academic research. *Quantitative Science Studies*, *1*(1), 377–386. DOI: 10.1162/qss_a_00019

Boje, C., Guerriero, A., Kubicki, S., & Rezgui, Y. (2020). Towards a semantic Construction Digital Twin: Directions for future research. *Automation in Construction*, *114*, 103179. DOI: 10.1016/j.autcon.2020.103179

Cobo, M. J., López-Herrera, A. G., Herrera-Viedma, E., & Herrera, F. (2011). Science mapping software tools: Review, analysis, and cooperative study. *Journal of the American Society for Information Science and Technology*, *62*(7), 1382–1402. DOI: 10.1002/asi.21525

Fisk, P. (2017). *Education 4.0: The future of learning will be dramatically different, in school and throughout life*. Retrieved from Peter Fisk Official Website.

Floridi, L., Cowls, J., Beltrametti, M., Chatila, R., Chazerand, P., Dignum, V., Luetge, C., Madelin, R., Pagallo, U., Rossi, F., Schafer, B., Valcke, P., & Vayena, E. (2018). AI4People—An ethical framework for a good AI society: Opportunities, risks, principles, and recommendations. *Minds and Machines*, *28*(4), 689–707. DOI: 10.1007/s11023-018-9482-5 PMID: 30930541

Fuller, A., Fan, Z., Day, C., & Barlow, C. (2020). Digital twin: Enabling technologies, challenges and open research. *IEEE Access : Practical Innovations, Open Solutions*, *8*, 108952–108971. DOI: 10.1109/ACCESS.2020.2998358

Grieves, M., & Vickers, J. (2017). Digital twin: Mitigating unpredictable, undesirable emergent behavior in complex systems. In *Transdisciplinary Perspectives on Complex Systems*. https://doi.org/DOI: 10.1007/978-3-319-38756-7_4

Holmes, W., Porayska-Pomsta, K., Holstein, K., Sutherland, E., Baker, T., Shum, S. B., Santos, O. C., Rodrigo, M. T., Cukurova, M., Bittencourt, I. I., & Koedinger, K. R. (2022). Ethics of AI in education: Towards a community-wide framework. *International Journal of Artificial Intelligence in Education*, *32*(3), 504–526. DOI: 10.1007/s40593-021-00239-1

Jones, D., Snider, C., Nassehi, A., Yon, J., & Hicks, B. (2020). Characterising the Digital Twin: A systematic literature review. *CIRP Journal of Manufacturing Science and Technology*, *29*, 36–52. DOI: 10.1016/j.cirpj.2020.02.002

Mishra, L., Gupta, T., & Shree, A. (2020). Online teaching-learning in higher education during lockdown. *International Journal of Educational Research Open*, *1*, 100012. DOI: 10.1016/j.ijedro.2020.100012 PMID: 35059663

Nahavandi, S. (2019). Industry 5.0—A human-centric solution. *Sustainability (Basel)*, *11*(16), 4371. DOI: 10.3390/su11164371

Radianti, J., Majchrzak, T. A., Fromm, J., & Wohlgenannt, I. (2020). A systematic review of immersive virtual reality applications for higher education. *Education and Information Technologies*, *25*, 1–38. DOI: 10.1007/s10639-019-09928-1

Selwyn, N. (2016). *Education and technology: Key issues and debates* (2nd ed.). Bloomsbury Academic.

Tlili, A., Burgos, D., Huang, R., Mishra, S., Sharma, R. C., & Bozkurt, A. (2023). Is metaverse in education a blessing or a curse? *Smart Learning Environments*, *10*(1). Advance online publication. DOI: 10.1186/s40561-022-00205-x

van Erp, T., Carvalho, N. G. P., Gerolamo, M. C., Gonçalves, R., Rytter, N. G. M., & Gladysz, B. (2024). Industry 5.0: A new strategy framework for sustainability management and beyond. *Journal of Cleaner Production*, *461*, 142271. DOI: 10.1016/j.jclepro.2024.142271

Williamson, B., & Eynon, R. (2020). Historical threads, missing links, and future directions in AI in education. *Learning, Media and Technology*, *45*(3), 223–235. DOI: 10.1080/17439884.2020.1798995

Xu, X., Lu, Y., Vogel-Heuser, B., & Wang, L. (2021). Industry 4.0 and Industry 5.0 Inception, conception and perception. *Journal of Manufacturing Systems*, *61*, 530–535. DOI: 10.1016/j.jmsy.2021.10.006

Chapter 9

Multi-Agent Digital Twin Ecosystems for Collaborative Lifelong Learning

Hossein Abdi
http://orcid.org/0009-0003-6528-3662
Bio10, Australia

Naser Heidari
http://orcid.org/0009-0002-5703-8731
Bio10, Dubai, UAE

ABSTRACT

This chapter examines lifelong learning ecosystems based on digital twins and multi-agent architectures. Its main goal is to provide a conceptual framework for creating intelligent, adaptive, collaborative, and self-evolving learning systems. In this approach, the cognitive digital twin models the learner's skill, behavioral, and cognitive state, and intelligent agents optimize the learning path, performance assessment, and group collaboration by analyzing data. Also, the role of emerging technologies such as federated learning, edge computing, metaverse, and neuromorphic computing in the future of these ecosystems is examined.

1- INTRODUCTION

Rapid technological developments in recent decades have fundamentally changed the nature of learning, education, and skill development. In the era of the digital

DOI: 10.4018/979-8-2600-1674-9.ch009

economy, Industry 5.0, and smart societies, learning is no longer limited to limited academic or training courses, but has become a continuous, adaptive, and lifelong process. In such circumstances, individuals, organizations, and even governments need intelligent ecosystems that can dynamically adapt to rapid changes in knowledge, technology, the labor market, and human cognitive needs. This development has given rise to the concept of "lifelong learning systems"; systems that aim to continuously develop human knowledge, skills, decision-making ability, and cognitive adaptability throughout life (Shi et al., 2026).

Despite the extensive development of digital education systems, many current learning infrastructures still have serious limitations. Most of these systems have a static, non-adaptive, and one-way structure and are unable to model learners' cognitive, behavioral, emotional, and skill changes in real time. Also, most existing learning platforms lack a deep understanding of human interactions, group collaboration, skill evolution, and dynamic needs of users. As a result, a significant gap has been created between traditional educational systems and the complex learning needs of the era of artificial intelligence and digital societies.

In the meantime, the emergence of the Digital Twin concept has provided transformative opportunities for redesigning learning ecosystems. Digital twins were initially used in advanced industries, smart manufacturing, and cyber-physical systems, and their goal was to create a dynamic, living digital model that is in sync with the physical system. With the expansion of AI, data analytics, and the Internet of Things capabilities, this concept has entered new areas such as health, smart cities, energy, and education. In learning environments, digital twins can create a dynamic view of the cognitive, skill, behavioral, and even emotional state of each learner and can be continuously updated based on real-time interactions, educational performance, and environmental data (Ye et al., 2026).

However, simply using a digital twin is not enough to address the complexity of future learning ecosystems. Modern learning environments are multi-agent, dynamic, and collaborative in nature, requiring systems that can manage interactions between learners, instructors, intelligent systems, and knowledge resources. For this reason, the use of AI-based multi-agent architectures has been proposed as one of the key approaches in the new generation of learning systems. In this approach, various intelligent agents can automatically perform tasks such as performance monitoring, cognitive analysis, educational path suggestion, skill assessment, weakness detection, group collaboration management, and even educational content adjustment.

Combining digital twins with multi-agent architectures creates a new concept of adaptive and self-evolving learning ecosystems in which learning is not only personalized, but also evolves continuously, interactively, and intelligently. In such ecosystems, each learner has a cognitive digital twin that models his or her situation in real time, and intelligent agents make appropriate educational decisions based on this twin's data. In addition, cooperation between agents can lead to the formation of a kind of "educational collective intelligence" in which the system continuously learns from user interactions, educational outcomes, and new behavioral patterns (Miadowicz et al., 2026).

One of the most important features of these ecosystems is the ability to dynamically adapt to changes in users' cognitive and skill levels. Unlike traditional systems that have a fixed educational path, in ecosystems based on digital twins and intelligent agents, the content, teaching method, level of difficulty, and even the structure of educational interactions can change in real time. This feature is especially important in complex environments such as industrial education, medical education, specialized skills training, and future workforce development.

In addition, the advancement of technologies such as Federated Learning, Edge Computing, Neuromorphic Computing, Metaverse, and Cognitive Analytics have opened new horizons for the development of the next generation of learning systems. These technologies enable the creation of pervasive, distributed, immersive, and even neural and biological interaction-based learning environments. As a result, the concept of lifelong learning is transformed from a purely educational process into a cognitive-intelligent ecosystem in which humans and artificial intelligence co-evolve.

Despite the vast potential of this field, there are still numerous scientific and technical challenges in the fields of cognitive modeling, digital twin coordination, interaction between intelligent agents, interpretability of educational decisions, and evolutionary sustainability of learning systems. Also, much of the existing research has focused only on simple personalization or analysis of educational data, and has paid less attention to the design of multi-agent, self-evolving, and cognitive-driven ecosystems.

Accordingly, the aim of this chapter is to provide a comprehensive conceptual framework for lifelong learning ecosystems based on digital twins and multi-agent architectures. This chapter attempts to review the theoretical foundations and key technologies, analyze new architectures, research challenges, and future directions in this field, and provide a vision for the next generation of intelligent, adaptive, and self-evolving learning systems.

2- FOUNDATIONS OF DIGITAL TWIN-DRIVEN LIFELONG LEARNING

The rapid evolution of digital technologies, artificial intelligence and data-driven systems has transformed the concept of learning from a static process limited to traditional educational courses to a dynamic, continuous and intelligent ecosystem. In the meantime, the emergence of Digital Twin technology has provided a new platform for the development of the next generation of lifelong learning systems. In its simplest definition, a digital twin is a dynamic digital representation of a physical, cognitive or behavioral entity that is continuously updated based on real-time data. This concept was initially developed in smart industries and advanced engineering systems, but gradually entered more complex areas such as health, transportation, smart cities and education.

In learning ecosystems, a digital twin is not just a simple educational profile, but a multidimensional and living model of the learner that models the cognitive, behavioral, skill, emotional and functional characteristics of the individual over time. Such a structure can analyze and predict learning patterns, strengths and weaknesses, engagement levels, levels of focus, skill development trends, and even long-term cognitive changes. As a result, learning moves away from being generic and the same for all users and toward adaptive and personalized learning (Yordanova and Nozari, 2026a).

On the other hand, the concept of lifelong learning has also undergone a fundamental transformation in recent years. In the past, learning was often limited to formal training courses, but in the era of knowledge-based economy and digital transformation, individuals must continuously update their skills. This has become especially important in areas such as smart industry, digital health, data analytics, artificial intelligence, and cyber-physical systems. Therefore, future learning systems must be able to continuously adapt to users' cognitive, professional, and environmental changes (Anas et al., 2026).

In such a situation, the combination of digital twins with artificial intelligence and multi-agent ecosystems creates a new generation of learning infrastructures in which the interaction between humans, data, intelligent agents and the learning environment is dynamically managed. In these architectures, each learner has a cognitive digital twin that collects and analyzes data related to his performance, behavior and interactions. Then, the intelligent agents generate appropriate educational decisions, learning suggestions and skill paths based on this data. The overall flow of this ecosystem is shown in Figure 1.

Figure 1. Conceptual architecture of digital twin-driven lifelong learning ecosystems

Figure 1 shows the conceptual architecture of a digital twin-driven lifelong learning ecosystem. In this structure, the physical learner is considered as the core of the system and his behavioral, cognitive, educational and interaction data are received through the data collection layer. This data can include learning performance, user interactions, bio-data, group activities, cognitive patterns, and environmental feedback. This information is then fed into the cognitive digital twin layer, creating a dynamic and adaptive model of the learner's state.

Next, various intelligent agents, such as a cognitive analysis agent, a teaching recommendation agent, a performance assessment agent, and a group collaboration management agent, interact with the digital twin. These agents continuously analyze the data and adjust learning paths, educational content, activity difficulty, and skill suggestions. One of the important features of this architecture is the existence of a dynamic feedback loop that allows the system to continuously learn from new interactions and improve its decision-making structure (Hasan et al., 2026).

Unlike traditional e-learning systems that are mainly based on providing fixed content, in digital twin-based ecosystems, the learning process is alive, evolutionary, and self-adaptive in nature. These systems can detect gradual changes in learner behavior and suggest appropriate educational interventions even before performance declines. There is also the possibility of modeling group learning and collaborative interactions in this structure, which is of great importance for modern educational environments and knowledge-based organizations.

Another key feature of this approach is the ability to integrate emerging technologies with the learning process. For example, the use of edge computing can reduce latency in analyzing educational data, while Federated Learning enables distributed learning and maintains user privacy. Technologies such as metaverse, augmented reality, and neuromorphic computing can also create more interactive, cognitive, and intelligent learning environments.

In summary, the theoretical foundations of lifelong learning systems based on digital twins indicate that the future of education is moving towards adaptive, multi-agent, data-driven, and cognitive-driven ecosystems. In such ecosystems, learning will not be limited to the transfer of knowledge, but will become a dynamic process for the continuous development of intelligence, skills, collaboration, and decision-making.

3- MULTI-AGENT ARCHITECTURES FOR INTELLIGENT LEARNING ECOSYSTEMS

With the increasing complexity of modern learning ecosystems, the use of centralized and static systems no longer meets the needs of adaptive, collaborative and lifelong learning. New generation educational environments must be able to simultaneously analyze a huge amount of cognitive, behavioral, skill and interaction data and make decisions based on the dynamic and changing conditions of learners. In such circumstances, multi-agent architectures based on artificial intelligence have been proposed as one of the most important infrastructures of the next generation of intelligent learning systems (Nozari, 2025a).

In multi-agent architectures, the system consists of a set of independent but coordinated intelligent agents, each of which has a specific task in the learning process. These agents can automatically analyze data, interact with other agents, make decisions and even modify their behavior based on past experiences. Unlike traditional systems where decision-making is centralized, in multi-agent ecosystems the decision-making process is distributed, adaptive and collaborative. This feature allows the system to perform more effectively at larger scales and in more dynamic environments.

In digital twin-based learning ecosystems, intelligent agents play the role of an intermediary between learner data, the cognitive model and the educational decision-making process. Each agent has its own goals, capabilities and reasoning mechanisms and can interact with other components of the system in real time. Some agents are responsible for analyzing the cognitive state of the learner, while others are responsible for adjusting educational content, managing group collaboration, analyzing emotions or predicting the trend of skill development.

In such a structure, the concept of "educational collective intelligence" is formed; this means that different agents reach a coordinated and optimal decision-making for the learning process by sharing their knowledge and analysis. This is especially important in complex environments such as industrial training, organizational learning, medical education, and professional skills development. The overall architecture of a multi-agent learning ecosystem is shown in Figure 2.

Figure 2. Multi-agent intelligent architecture for digital twin-driven lifelong learning ecosystems

Figure 2 shows the conceptual structure of a multi-agent architecture for digital twin-driven lifelong learning ecosystems. In this architecture, the cognitive digital twin is at the center of the system and acts as the core of the learner's analysis and modeling. The learner's behavioral, cognitive, educational, and interaction data are fed into the digital twin and continuously updated. Various intelligent agents then use this data to manage the educational decision-making process.

In this architecture, the cognitive analysis agent is responsible for analyzing the learner's mental state, learning patterns, concentration level, and cognitive changes. The educational recommendation agent recommends appropriate educational resources, learning paths, and activities based on the digital twin data. The performance assessment agent is responsible for analyzing skill progress, assessing learning, and identifying weaknesses. In addition, the group collaboration agent manages interactions among learners and facilitates the formation of collaborative learning and collective intelligence (Nozari, 2025b).

One of the key features of this architecture is the existence of a coordination mechanism between agents. Intelligent agents not only operate independently, but also share their information and decisions with other agents. These interactions can include knowledge exchange, coordination of educational decisions, conflict resolution, and management of learning priorities. As a result, the system will be able to make multidimensional and adaptive decisions that are not only based on educational performance, but also on the cognitive, emotional, and social state of the learner.

From a technical perspective, multi-agent architectures have important advantages over centralized systems. First, these architectures are more scalable and can handle a large number of learners and data sources. Second, the autonomy of agents increases the flexibility and stability of the system; in such a way that the disruption of the performance of one agent does not necessarily disrupt the entire ecosystem. Third, there is the possibility of local learning and adaptation in each agent, which increases the speed of decision-making and reduces the complexity of central processing.

In addition, the combination of multi-agent architectures with technologies such as edge computing, real-time data analytics, federated learning, and advanced cognitive models can create a new generation of distributed and self-evolving learning ecosystems. In these ecosystems, intelligent agents will be able to analyze and optimize not only the behavior of the learner, but also the behavior of other agents and even the overall structure of the system (Yordanova & Nozari, 2026a).

Another important concept in this area is the emergence of Agentic AI in learning systems. In this approach, intelligent agents are not just executing predefined commands, but are also goal-oriented, reasoning, independent decision-making, and self-adaptive. Such agents can automatically identify skill gaps, generate new content, change the learning strategy, and even rearrange the structure of collaboration between users. This feature transforms the learning ecosystem from a reactive system to a proactive and evolutionary one.

Overall, multi-agent architectures play a key role in the development of the next generation of intelligent learning systems. By creating dynamic interactions between digital twins, intelligent agents, and the learning environment, these architectures provide a platform for the formation of adaptive, collaborative, and self-evolving educational ecosystems that can continuously adapt to human cognitive, skill, and social changes, taking the concept of lifelong learning to a whole new level.

4- DIGITAL TWIN ECOSYSTEM ARCHITECTURE

As learning ecosystems become more complex and interactions between humans, data, artificial intelligence, and digital environments increase, the need for architectures that can manage the learning process in a dynamic, adaptive, and multi-layered manner is felt more than ever. In this regard, Digital Twin-based architectures have emerged as one of the most advanced infrastructures for the next generation of learning systems. By creating a live, intelligent, and synchronized representation of the learner, these architectures enable continuous analysis of behavior, cognitive state, social interactions, and skill development trends (Kalogeras et al., 2025).

Unlike traditional learning systems that focus primarily on storing educational data and providing static content, digital twin-based ecosystems have a dynamic, multi-layered structure in which data, cognitive models, intelligent agents, and decision-making mechanisms operate in an integrated manner. In such architectures, the system is not limited to recording past performance, but can also predict the learner's future state, analyze his behavior, and automatically adjust the learning path.

One of the most important features of these architectures is the existence of adaptive feedback loops. These loops cause every educational interaction, every behavioral change, and every cognitive activity to enter the digital model in real time, leading to continuous evolution of the system. As a result, the learning ecosystem becomes a "living" structure that continuously learns from new data, interactions, and experiences. The conceptual architecture of the digital twin-based learning ecosystem is shown in Figure 3.

Figure 3. Digital twin ecosystem architecture for multi-agent lifelong learning systems

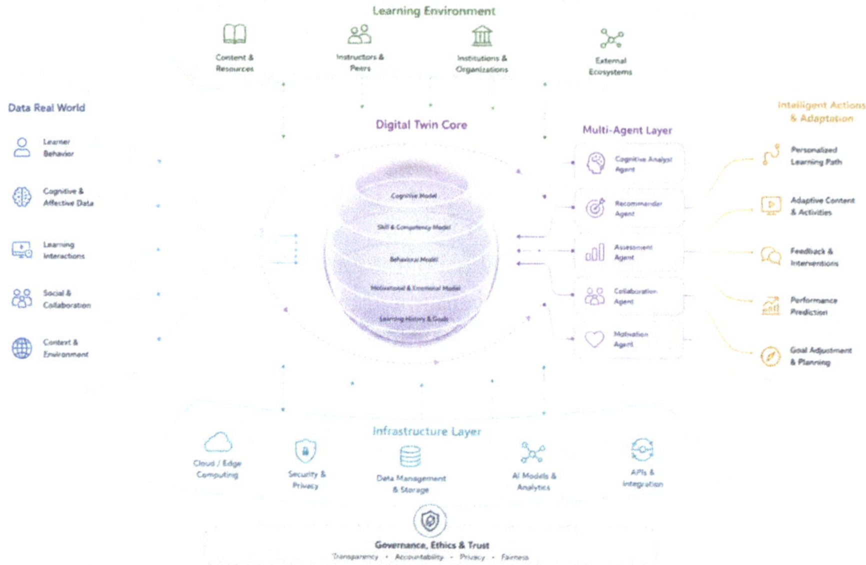

As can be seen in Figure 3, the proposed architecture consists of several main layers, each of which plays a specific role in managing the learning ecosystem. On the left side of the architecture is the multi-purpose input data layer, which includes learner data, instructional data, environmental data, physiological data, and social interactions. This data can come from a variety of sources, including learning platforms, biosensors, virtual learning environments, social networks, and assessment systems.

At the center of the architecture is the learner's cognitive digital twin, which is the core of the system. It includes various models, such as the cognitive model, behavioral model, skill profile, emotional state, learning goals, and learning history. Unlike traditional learning profiles that are static, the cognitive digital twin is continuously updated based on new data, providing a dynamic picture of the learner's state.

A key component of this architecture is the Twin Synchronization Engine, which is responsible for synchronizing the learner's real state with the digital model. This engine can detect behavioral changes, cognitive drift, performance decline, or motivational changes in real time and modify the digital model. Such a capability is of great importance for lifelong learning, as individuals' cognitive and skill states continuously change over time.

Around the digital twin, a set of intelligent agents are located, each with specific specialized tasks. The cognitive analysis agent is responsible for analyzing mental states and learning patterns, while the performance assessment agent analyzes the skill progress and learning rate. The educational resource recommendation agent selects appropriate content based on the cognitive state and goals of the learner, and the motivational agent monitors the level of engagement, fatigue, or motivational decline. In addition, the group collaboration agent plays an important role in managing social interactions, forming learning teams, and facilitating collective intelligence.

An important feature of this architecture is the direct interaction between agents. The intelligent agents not only communicate with the digital twin, but also exchange knowledge and make decisions with each other. This moves the learning process from a linear and centralized state to a distributed and self-evolving ecosystem. In such a structure, educational decisions are the result of the collaboration of multiple intelligent agents with different perspectives and analyses .

In the common infrastructure layer, supporting technologies such as databases, knowledge graphs, artificial intelligence models, edge computing, and security and privacy systems are located. This layer provides a platform for real-time data processing, advanced analytics, and communication management between agents. The use of Federated Learning in this layer can enable distributed learning and preserve user privacy, while Edge–Cloud technologies reduce latency and increase system scalability (Márquez et al., 2026).

From a functional perspective, this architecture has several key advantages. First, the system is able to interact with each learner in an adaptive and personalized way. Second, the existence of independent agents increases the flexibility and stability of the ecosystem. Third, dynamic feedback loops allow for the continuous evolution of learning models. Fourth, the ability to simultaneously analyze cognitive, behavioral, social, and physiological data provides a deeper understanding of the learning process.

Furthermore, such architectures could pave the way for a new generation of self-evolving learning systems, systems that not only analyze the learner's state but can also dynamically redesign instructional structures, learning strategies, and even social interactions. This transforms the learning ecosystem from a reactive system to a proactive, knowledge-driven one.

Digital twin ecosystem architectures will play a fundamental role in the future of intelligent learning systems. By integrating cognitive modeling, intelligent agents, real-time data analytics, and multi-agent interactions, these architectures provide a platform for creating adaptive, collaborative, and self-evolving learning ecosystems that can continuously adapt to human cognitive, professional, and social changes, taking the concept of lifelong learning to a whole new level.

5- AI-DRIVEN COLLABORATIVE LIFELONG LEARNING MECHANISMS

The rapid growth of Artificial Intelligence-based technologies has transformed the concept of lifelong learning from a traditional educational process into an intelligent, adaptive, and collaborative ecosystem. In new-generation learning ecosystems, AI is not just a supporting tool, but has become the core of analysis, decision-making, prediction, and evolution of the learning process. In the meantime, the combination of AI with digital twins and multi-agent architectures enables the creation of advanced collaborative learning mechanisms that can continuously adapt to the cognitive, skill, and social status of users.

Unlike traditional education systems in which the content and learning path are provided to all users in a fixed manner, in AI-based ecosystems, the learning process is dynamically adjusted based on real-time data analysis. This data can include learner behavior, interaction patterns, educational performance, cognitive data, social participation rate, and even emotional and motivational status. By analyzing this data, the system will be able to identify the real needs of each individual and suggest the most appropriate learning path (Yordanova & Nozari, 2026b).

One of the most important AI mechanisms in lifelong learning ecosystems is Adaptive Learning. In this approach, the system continuously analyzes the learner's situation and selects appropriate educational content and activities based on the learner's level of knowledge, learning speed, cognitive style, and past performance. This process ensures that each user has a unique learning experience. For example, if the system detects that a learner is weak in understanding analytical concepts, it can provide them with more multimedia resources, visual examples, or interactive exercises. In contrast, more complex and project-based activities are designed for users with a higher skill level.

Along with adaptive learning, predictive analytics based on AI also play an important role in learning ecosystems. Machine learning algorithms can predict user performance trends by analyzing historical and behavioral data. This capability allows the system to implement appropriate training interventions before serious problems arise. For example, if behavioral patterns indicate decreased motivation, decreased engagement, or cognitive fatigue, the system can modify training activities, provide motivating content, or create more group interactions (Mohammed et al., 2026).

Another key component in AI-based collaborative learning is the concept of collective intelligence. In multi-agent ecosystems, learning does not only occur at the individual level, but also the interaction between users, intelligent agents, and knowledge resources leads to the formation of collective knowledge. Collaborative agents can form appropriate learning teams, connect users with complementary skills, and manage training interactions. This is especially important in specialized environments such as industrial training, research projects, professional skills development, and organizational training.

Artificial intelligence can also play an important role in cognitive modeling of learners. In digital twin-based ecosystems, the system is able to analyze the mental and cognitive state of users in real time. These analyses can include concentration level, cognitive load, problem-solving patterns, decision-making style, and skill development trends. Combining this data with deep learning algorithms allows for the creation of dynamic cognitive models that continuously evolve with user behavioral and educational changes (Sharma et al., 2026).

In addition, the concept of Agentic AI has attracted widespread attention in the field of intelligent learning systems in recent years. In this approach, intelligent agents do not simply execute predefined instructions, but are also capable of goal-oriented, reasoning, planning, and independent decision-making. Such agents can automatically analyze users' learning goals, identify skill gaps, and even generate new content. This capability transforms the learning ecosystem from a reactive system to a proactive and self-evolving structure.

One of the important aspects of AI-based collaborative learning is the analysis of emotions and motivational states of users. Today, many learning systems focus only on educational performance, while emotional and motivational factors have a direct impact on the quality of learning. Using emotion analysis technologies, biometric data, and user behavior processing, the system can identify the emotional state of the learner. For example, if the user is tired, stressed, or demotivated, the system will be able to change the type of content, intensity of activities, or level of social interactions.

In more advanced ecosystems, combining AI with Neuromorphic Computing can create a new generation of cognitive-based learning systems. These approaches attempt to model human learning processes in a way inspired by the structure of the brain. The use of spiking neural networks, neural pattern analysis, and long-term memory models can lead to the creation of systems that more accurately analyze and predict users' cognitive behavior (Leung, 2026).

On the other hand, Federated Learning technology enables the development of distributed learning ecosystems and preserves user privacy. In this approach, AI models are trained without directly transmitting users' personal data. This is of great importance for sensitive educational environments such as medical education, corporate education, and government systems (Lin et al., 2026).

AI can also play an important role in the automatic evolution of educational programs. In traditional ecosystems, designing curricula and learning paths is a time-consuming and largely manual process, but in AI-based systems, the educational structure can be continuously reconfigured based on market skill changes, industry needs, and user progress. This capability allows the learning ecosystem to always remain in sync with environmental and technological developments (Ivanov, 2026).

In addition, combining AI with immersive environments such as the metaverse and augmented reality can create more interactive and collaborative learning experiences. In such environments, users' digital twins can interact with each other in virtual learning spaces, work on joint projects, and participate in problem-solving processes. This transforms the concept of learning from an individual activity to a cognitive and social ecosystem.

Collectively, AI-based collaborative learning mechanisms form the core of the next generation of lifelong learning ecosystems. By integrating cognitive analytics, intelligent agents, adaptive modeling, predictive analytics, and collective intelligence, these mechanisms enable the creation of systems that not only adapt to the user's situation, but also continuously learn from new interactions and evolve their structure. Such ecosystems can guide the future of education from static, content-centric models to intelligent, self-developing, and human-centric systems.

6- INTEGRATION OF EMERGING TECHNOLOGIES

The development of lifelong learning ecosystems based on Digital Twin is not possible without the use of emerging technologies. The new generation of intelligent learning systems requires infrastructures that can analyze huge volumes of cognitive, behavioral, social and environmental data in real time and interact with users adaptively. In the meantime, technologies such as edge computing, federated learning, metaverse, neuromorphic computing, blockchain and cognitive analytics play a key role in shaping the next generation of learning ecosystems.

One of the most important supporting technologies in this area is edge computing. In traditional learning ecosystems, data processing is usually performed on centralized servers, which can increase latency, reduce scalability and limit real-time analysis. In contrast, edge computing transfers part of the processing to the point closest to the user. This capability is of great importance for digital twin-based learning systems, as many cognitive and behavioral analyses must be performed in real time. For example, if the system wants to detect a decrease in concentration, cognitive fatigue, or a drop in learner engagement in real time, processing latency can significantly reduce the quality of decision-making. Using Edge AI allows for faster generation of instructional decisions, feedback, and adaptive suggestions (Mendonça et al., 2026).

Along with edge computing, Federated Learning technology also plays an important role in the development of distributed learning ecosystems. One of the fundamental challenges in intelligent learning systems is maintaining user privacy, as these systems collect a large amount of personal, cognitive, and behavioral data. In federated learning, AI models are trained without directly transmitting raw data, and only learning parameters are shared between nodes. This approach can create a good balance between personalizing learning and preserving privacy. In addition, federated learning enables the creation of global and distributed learning ecosystems in which educational institutions, organizations, and users can participate in the development of intelligent models without exposing sensitive data.

Another transformative technology in this area is Neuromorphic Computing. Inspired by the structure of the human brain, neuromorphic computing attempts to create processing models that are closer to natural cognitive processes. In learning ecosystems, this technology can be used to model memory, attention, decision-making, and cognitive adaptation. Unlike traditional machine learning models that often require large amounts of data and heavy processing, neuromorphic systems can simulate complex cognitive behaviors with less energy consumption and higher speed. This is especially important for the development of cognitive digital twins, as these twins must be able to analyze and predict changes in the minds and behaviors of users over time (Li, 2026).

On the other hand, the emergence of the metaverse and immersive learning environments has created a new perspective for lifelong learning ecosystems. The metaverse is not just a virtual 3D environment, but a platform for multi-layered cognitive, social, and educational interactions. In digital twin-based ecosystems, each learner can have a persistent digital identity and a dedicated cognitive twin that interacts with other users, intelligent agents, and educational resources in virtual environments. This structure can transform learning from a passive process to an interactive and collaborative experience. For example, in metaverse-based educational environments, users can participate in virtual labs, industrial simulations, or smart group projects, while the system continuously analyzes their performance and interactions.

Blockchain technology is also another important component in future learning ecosystems. In traditional systems, document management, educational records, and skills validation are often centralized and dependent on specific institutions. Blockchain can provide a secure, transparent, and decentralized platform for storing and verifying educational records. This is especially important in lifelong learning, as users may work across multiple platforms, universities, and educational environments throughout their lives. Using blockchain, it is possible to create a trusted digital educational identity that can permanently record a learner's skills, credentials, experiences, and achievements.

In addition, cognitive analytics and sentiment analysis technologies are also playing an important role in the evolution of smart learning ecosystems. Many traditional educational systems focus only on performance outcomes, while cognitive and emotional factors have a direct impact on the quality of learning. Using behavioral data, biosignals, facial analysis, voice processing, and deep learning algorithms, the system can analyze the mental and emotional states of users. This capability allows the learning ecosystem to dynamically change the difficulty level of content, type of interactions, or method of delivering training (Sharma et al., 2026).

In recent years, the combination of IoT technologies with digital twins has also attracted a lot of attention. Smart sensors, wearables, and biomonitoring systems can collect real-time data related to the physiological and cognitive state of users. This data can include heart rate, stress level, concentration level, sleep patterns, or cognitive activities. Integrating this data with cognitive digital twins allows for the creation of much more accurate and adaptive models of the learner.

From an infrastructure perspective, the combination of cloud computing and Edge–Cloud Hybrid Architectures also plays an important role in the development of these ecosystems. Cloud computing allows for the storage and analysis of huge volumes of data, while edge computing is responsible for fast and real-time processing. This combination can create a good balance between speed, scalability, and efficiency. The use of AI-as-a-Service models and modular infrastructures also enables flexible and gradual development of learning ecosystems.

Another important future trend is the emergence of Human–AI Co-Learning systems, in which humans and artificial intelligence learn from each other simultaneously. In this structure, intelligent agents do not only play the role of teachers or analysts, but also evolve from the behavior, preferences and interactions of users. This can lead to the formation of self-evolving learning ecosystems in which the knowledge structure, teaching methods and interaction mechanisms are continuously redesigned.

Overall, the integration of emerging technologies with digital twin-based learning ecosystems will pave the way for the emergence of a new generation of educational systems that simultaneously possess features such as adaptability, cognition-centricity, interactivity, scalability and self-evolving. These technologies not only enhance the quality and personalization of learning, but also transform the concept of lifelong learning from a limited educational process to a smart, vibrant, and collaborative ecosystem.

7- SCIENTIFIC AND TECHNICAL RESEARCH CHALLENGES IN MULTI-AGENT DIGITAL TWIN LEARNING ECOSYSTEMS

Digital twin-based learning ecosystems and multi-agent architectures offer a highly advanced vision for the future of education, skill development, and lifelong learning; however, the practical and scientific realization of this vision is accompanied by a set of profound theoretical, technical, cognitive, and computational challenges. These challenges are not limited to general issues such as data security or technology adoption, but are related to the complex nature of human modeling, dynamic synchronization, multi-agent decision-making, and the continuous evolution of intelligent systems. Therefore, for the sustainable and reliable development of these ecosystems, it is necessary to examine the challenges within a multilayered research framework.

One of the most fundamental challenges is the complexity of cognitive modeling of the learner. In educational digital twins, the goal is not simply to record the user's grades, activities, or interactions, but rather the system must be able to model the cognitive state, learning style, motivation, cognitive load, level of focus, skill formation process, and behavioral changes over time. This is a very difficult task because human cognition is dynamic, contextual, and nonlinear in nature. A learner may behave differently in different situations, and external factors such as fatigue, stress, social environment, or workload can affect his or her learning performance. Consequently, building an accurate cognitive digital twin requires models that can account for the uncertainty, variability, and multidimensionality of human behavior (Elsokkary et al., 2026).

Another important challenge is the time synchronization between the real learner and his or her digital twin. A digital twin is valuable when it can represent the actual state of the system in close to real time. In learning environments, this is more complicated than in physical industries, because the learner's state cannot be observed only through direct data. For example, decreased concentration or motivation may be detected indirectly through interaction patterns, response times, frequent errors, or reduced group participation. Therefore, data delays, information noise, incomplete data, and inconsistencies between data sources can create a gap between the learner's real state and the digital model. This phenomenon can be considered a kind of "Digital Twin Drift"; that is, the digital twin's distance from the learner's cognitive and behavioral reality.

In multi-agent ecosystems, the challenge of coordination between intelligent agents is also of great importance. Each agent may have different goals, data, decision-making criteria, and reasoning logic. For example, the evaluation agent may suggest increasing the level of content difficulty, while the motivational agent may consider reducing the educational pressure more appropriate. In such situations, the system must be able to identify, analyze, and resolve conflicts between agents. The lack of a proper mechanism for coordination can lead to contradictory decisions, unstable interventions, or an incoherent learning experience. Therefore, designing protocols for interaction, negotiation, prioritization, and collective decision-making between agents is one of the key challenges in this area.

Another issue is the evolutionary sustainability of the system. Lifelong learning ecosystems must be able to learn from new data and interactions and improve themselves over time. However, continuous learning can lead to model instability. If the system overreacts to new data, it may become prone to decision-making oscillations; and if it is too conservative, it may lose its ability to adapt. This is especially important in cognitive digital twins, because human change is gradual, contextual, and sometimes contradictory. Therefore, a balance must be struck between model stability and adaptive flexibility.

From a data perspective, one of the fundamental challenges is the quality, heterogeneity, and multi-source nature of learning data. The data used in these ecosystems can be extracted from educational platforms, social interactions, wearables, biosensors, tests, group activities, and virtual environments. This data varies in structure, accuracy, frequency, meaning, and reliability. Integrating such data requires advanced data fusion, cleansing, normalization, and semantic interpretation. Otherwise, educational decisions may be made based on incomplete or misleading data.

Another challenge is the interpretability and transparency of educational decisions. In AI-based learning systems, the user needs to know why a particular educational path, a specific activity, or a learning intervention is being suggested to him. This is especially complicated in multi-agent ecosystems, as the final decision may be the result of the interaction of several different agents. If the decision-making logic is not understandable to the learner, instructor, or educational administrator, trust in the system is reduced. Therefore, the development of Explainable Multi-Agent Digital Twins is one of the important research needs in this area.

In terms of scalability, lifelong learning ecosystems must be able to manage a large number of learners, intelligent agents, data sources, and learning paths simultaneously. This requires powerful computing infrastructures, Edge–Cloud architectures, intelligent resource management, and lightweight and efficient algorithms. If the computational complexity of agents or digital twins increases too much, it will be difficult to implement the system on an organizational or national scale.

Another important challenge is cognitive privacy and ownership of learning data. Traditional educational data usually includes grades and activity records, but in cognitive digital twins, the data can include emotional states, behavioral patterns, decision-making styles, concentration levels, and even biomarkers. Such data is highly sensitive and its misuse can have serious consequences. Therefore, it is necessary to design robust frameworks for data governance, access control, informed consent, anonymization, and data ownership.

Finally, one of the most profound challenges is the boundary between educational support and cognitive intervention. If a system can intelligently regulate the behavior, motivation, and learning trajectory of individuals, the question arises as to how much such intervention is permissible and ethical. Intelligent learning ecosystems should not become tools for hidden behavioral guidance or cognitive dependence. Therefore, the design of these systems should be based on the principles of human-centeredness, learner agency, transparency, and accountability.

The scientific and technical challenges of digital twin-based learning ecosystems and multi-agent architectures indicate that this area is still in its theoretical and architectural formative stage. Its future success will depend on the development of accurate cognitive models, multi-agent coordination mechanisms, robust digital twins, scalable infrastructures, interpretable methods, and enforceable ethical frameworks. These challenges not only represent obstacles to development, but also define key directions for future research.

8- EMERGING RESEARCH FRONTIERS AND TRANSFORMATIVE DIRECTIONS

Lifelong learning ecosystems based on digital twins and multi-agent architectures are still in the theoretical and conceptual development stages. Despite significant advances in artificial intelligence, learning analytics, recommender systems, and digital education, the future direction of this field is not limited to improving existing tools, but rather moving towards the creation of self-evolving, cognitive, distributed, and human-centered ecosystems. In this section, the most important emerging research frontiers and future transformative directions are reviewed.

One of the most important future directions is the development of self-evolving cognitive digital twins. In this approach, the learner's digital twin is not just an updating model of the individual's educational status, but becomes an intelligent entity that can reorganize its internal structure based on the learner's cognitive, behavioral, and skill changes. Such a twin should be able to detect gradual changes in learning style, motivation level, memory, information processing speed, problem-solving ability and decision-making patterns and continuously refine its model. This could create a new concept of "Self-Evolving Learning Twin" in which the digital model not only reflects the learner's current state, but also predicts and guides his future growth path.

Another important research frontier is the development of learning ecosystems based on the co-evolution of humans and artificial intelligence. In traditional educational systems, humans are the learners and the digital system is only a supporting tool; but in the next generation, humans and artificial intelligence can learn from each other simultaneously. In this structure, intelligent agents evolve from human behavior, preferences and feedback, and in return, humans benefit from the system's intelligent analysis, suggestions and interventions. This two-way interaction could pave the way for the concept of Human–AI Co-Learning, where learning becomes a collaborative, dynamic, and evolutionary process between humans and machines.

Another future path is to integrate neurosymbolic approaches into multi-agent learning architectures. Statistical and neural models perform well in analyzing complex data patterns, but often have limitations in reasoning, transparency, and interpretability. On the other hand, symbolic systems are good at logical reasoning, knowledge representation, and explainability, but are less flexible when dealing with dynamic and ambiguous data. Combining these two approaches could lead to the development of intelligent agents that are both capable of learning from complex data and can explain their decisions in a comprehensible manner. This is crucial for learning ecosystems, as educational decisions need to be interpretable for the learner, instructor, and educational administrator.

Another transformative direction is the development of biofeedback digital twins for cognitive learning. In this approach, biological data such as heart rate, stress level, fatigue, sleep patterns, neural activity, facial expression, and attention indicators can be fed into the digital twin, creating a more accurate picture of the learner's actual state. Such a system can detect whether the user is truly ready to learn, whether they are experiencing cognitive overload, or whether they need to change the type of educational activity. This path can elevate learning from the level of analyzing educational performance to the level of analyzing the biological and cognitive state of the human being.

Neuromorphic computing is also a promising area for the development of lifelong learning systems. Inspired by the structure of the human brain, neuromorphic systems enable low-power, event-driven, and time-adaptive processing. These features are very valuable for cognitive digital twins, because human learning is a continuous, temporal, and experience-dependent process. In the future, the combination of spiking neural networks, event-driven memory, and cognitive models could lead to the creation of twins that model learner behavior more accurately and efficiently.

Another important research direction is the development of decentralized and federated educational digital twins. In the future, lifelong learning is likely to not occur on a single platform, but rather be distributed across universities, organizations, workplaces, online platforms, and virtual spaces. Therefore, the learner's digital twin must be able to operate securely and reliably across different environments, without the individual's sensitive data being fully held by a central entity. Federated architectures, blockchains, and decentralized digital identities can play an important role in this regard (Yordanova and Nozari, 2026b).

Another transformative frontier is the emergence of digital twin-native learning metaverses. In this structure, the learner's digital twin does not just operate in a dashboard or learning platform, but as a persistent cognitive identity enters immersive environments. These environments can include virtual labs, interactive classrooms, industrial simulations, research spaces, and group collaboration environments. In such an ecosystem, the learner can interact with other people and intelligent agents in multidimensional environments, and the system can analyze and optimize these interactions in real time.

Another important future direction is the development of self-organizing and self-healing learning ecosystems. In this model, the system will be able to recognize its own problems, correct inefficient factors, reorganize the structure of cooperation between users, and improve learning paths without direct human intervention. Such a system can be of particular importance on large scales, such as smart universities, international organizations, or national learning networks.

Finally, we can talk about the formation of the concept of Artificial General Learning Ecosystem. This concept refers to ecosystems that have the ability to learn, adapt, collaborate, explain, predict, and evolve across different knowledge domains. Unlike traditional educational platforms that are designed for limited subjects, future general learning ecosystems can connect across different knowledge domains, create interdisciplinary learning paths, and intelligently adapt to the professional, cognitive, and social needs of users.

9- CONCLUSION

The vast technological developments in recent decades have shown that the future of learning and skill development can no longer be built on static, centralized, and one-sided structures. The emergence of technologies such as Digital Twin, multi-agent architectures, cognitive artificial intelligence, edge computing, and distributed learning ecosystems have created a new path to redefine the concept of lifelong learning. In the meantime, digital twin-based learning ecosystems, as one of the most important approaches to the next generation of education, provide the ability to create dynamic, adaptive, cognitive, and self-improvement environments.

In this chapter, the theoretical foundations of lifelong learning and the role of digital twins in the transformation of educational processes were first reviewed. The results of the analyses showed that digital twins can go beyond a simple data-driven model and become a cognitive and dynamic representation of the learner. Such twins are able to model the skill, behavioral, cognitive, and even emotional state of users in real time and continuously adapt to environmental and individual changes.

Also, the role of multi-agent architectures in the development of smart learning ecosystems was examined. Smart agents can perform tasks such as cognitive analysis, educational path suggestion, performance assessment, group interaction management, and adaptive content adjustment through dynamic collaboration and interaction. This leads to the formation of a kind of educational collective intelligence in which learning decisions are the result of the interaction between several specialized agents, rather than just a centralized and fixed system. Such a structure can significantly increase the quality of personalization, flexibility, and scalability of learning ecosystems.

Next, the architecture of the digital twin ecosystem and collaborative learning mechanisms based on artificial intelligence were analyzed. The results showed that the combination of cognitive modeling, real-time data analytics, autonomous agents, and adaptive feedback loops can transform the learning process from a passive activity to a dynamic, proactive, and evolutionary one. In this approach, the system not only analyzes the current state of the learner, but also is able to predict future trends, motivation decline, cognitive changes, and skill gaps, and provide appropriate educational interventions before problems arise.

This chapter also showed that emerging technologies such as Federated Learning, Neuromorphic Computing, Metaverse, Blockchain, and Biofeedback Analytics can create a new generation of intelligent learning ecosystems. These technologies enable the development of distributed, secure, interactive, immersive, and cognitive-driven learning environments, and elevate the concept of lifelong learning from a traditional educational process to a smart and living ecosystem.

However, the analysis of scientific and technical challenges showed that the development path of these ecosystems is still accompanied by complex issues. Modeling human cognition, coordination between intelligent agents, evolutionary stability of digital twins, interpretability of educational decisions, scalability of architectures, and cognitive privacy are among the most important challenges that require deeper and interdisciplinary research. In addition, issues such as cognitive dependence on intelligent systems, the boundary between educational support and behavioral intervention, and algorithmic accountability should also be given serious attention in the future development of these ecosystems.

Finally, it can be concluded that learning ecosystems based on digital twins and multi-agent architectures are not only a technological revolution in education, but also represent a paradigm shift in the concept of human learning. These ecosystems can form the infrastructure of the next generation of education, skill development, and lifelong learning; An infrastructure in which humans and AI interact in a collaborative, adaptive, and self-evolving manner. The future of this field will move towards creating systems that not only educate, but are also capable of supporting cognitive growth, skill development, and continuous human evolution on an intelligent, global scale.

REFERENCES

Anas, A., Mouna, E., Abdellatif, K., Hamidou, T., Anis, L., & Cédric, A. (2026). Adaptive Control in Multi-Agent Digital Twins for Sustainable Smart Farming: Game Theory-Driven Optimization. *IEEE Internet of Things Journal*, 1. DOI: 10.1109/JIOT.2026.3689694

Elsokkary, N., Khan, W., Shurrab, M., Mizouni, R., Singh, S., Bentahar, J., Mourad, A., & Otrok, H. (2026). Reinforcement learning and the Metaverse: A symbiotic collaboration. *Artificial Intelligence Review*, *59*(1), 34. DOI: 10.1007/s10462-025-11433-1

Hasan, A., & Nguyen, D. T. (2026). Integrating agentic AI and digital twins for intelligent decision-making systems. *Array (New York, N.Y.)*, *29*, 100721. DOI: 10.1016/j.array.2026.100721

Ivanov, D. (2026). Agentic digital twins: Bridging model-based and AI-driven decision-making support for a new era of supply chain and operations management. *International Journal of Production Research*, •••, 1–17. DOI: 10.1080/00207543.2026.2630277

Kalogeras, S., Samadi, S., & Nozari, H. (Eds.). (2025). *AI-Augmented Creativity in Learning Analytics*. IGI Global. DOI: 10.4018/979-8-3373-5117-9

Leung, Y. (2026). Multiagent Approach to Building Digital Twins of Cities. In *Digital Twins of Cities: Modeling Urban Dynamics and Complexity* (pp. 117–131). Springer Nature Switzerland. DOI: 10.1007/978-3-032-07966-4_7

Li, Y., & Zhong, R. Y. (2026). Spatial-temporal traceability and coordination in modular integrated construction: A future framework with hybrid digital twin and reinforcement learning. *International Journal of Construction Management*, *26*(5), 875–904. DOI: 10.1080/15623599.2025.2537727

Lin, Z., & Liu, Y. (2026, January). A “Coach-Assistant” Human-AI Collaborative Paradigm for AI-Empowered Integrated Circuit Design Education. In *Proceedings of the 2026 3rd International Conference on Informatics Education and Computer Technology Applications* (pp. 761-766). DOI: 10.1145/3802133.3802257

Márquez, A. C., & Fernández, J. F. G. (2026). Agentic AI for autonomous preventive maintenance policy governance: A multi-agent framework for dynamic industrial environments. *Expert Systems with Applications*, *314*, 131767. DOI: 10.1016/j.eswa.2026.131767

Mendonça, L., Barbosa, J., & Leitao, P. (2026, March). A Human-Centred Architecture Integrating Digital Twin and Agentic AI for Predictive Maintenance. In *2026 IEEE International Conference on Industrial Technology (ICIT)* (pp. 1-6). IEEE. DOI: 10.1109/ICIT64854.2026.11491044

Miadowicz, I., Kuhl, M., Maldonado Quinto, D., Pitz-Paal, R., & Felderer, M. (2026). From Automation to Autonomy: A Digital Twin Framework for Transparent Agent and Human Collaboration in Industrial Multi-Agent Systems. *Systems*, *14*(1), 76. DOI: 10.3390/systems14010076

Mohammed, S. K., Singh, S., Mizouni, R., Otrok, H., & Damiani, E. (2026). Digital Twins Paradigm: A Systematic Review from the Reinforcement Learning Perspective. *ACM Computing Surveys*, *58*(7), 1–33. DOI: 10.1145/3777367

Nozari, H. (2025a). Optimizing transmedia storytelling strategies across platforms for Maximum audience engagement. *Entertainment Computing*, •••, 101061.

Nozari, H. (2025b). Self-Evolving Neuromorphic Systems for Predictive Learning. AI-Augmented Creativity in Learning Analytics, 105.

Sharma, A., & Ahmmed, M. Collaborative Intelligence in IoT Ecosystems. In Intelligent Mobile and IoT Ecosystems (pp. 170-192). Chapman and Hall/CRC.

Sharma, S., & Sharma, S. (2026). Robotic Systems and LLM Algorithms for Transforming Manufacturing Into Smart Autonomous Ecosystem. In Human-Robot Collaboration and Advanced Robotics in Modern Industry (pp. 231-262). IGI Global Scientific Publishing. DOI: 10.4018/979-8-2600-0298-8.ch007

Shi, N., Li, Z., Li, Q., Zhang, J., Li, L., Sun, Q., Liu, S., & Wang, Z. (2026). Evolutionary Digital Twin for Oil and Gas Pipelines: A Cognitive Multi-Agent Framework with Continuous Feedback Learning. *Sensors (Basel)*, *26*(10), 3219. DOI: 10.3390/s26103219 PMID: 42198027

Ye, X., Gong, W., Yang, Y., Zou, L., Tu, Z., Huang, X., Li, Z., Ning, H., & Wu, L. (2026). Towards Agentic Urban Digital Twins (AUDiTs): Advancing new urban science through Human-AI co-learning agents. *Urban Informatics*, *5*(1), 9. DOI: 10.1007/s44212-025-00099-3

Yordanova, Z., & Nozari, H. (2026a). Enhancing Innovation and Resilience in Entrepreneurial Ecosystems Using Digital Twins and Fuzzy Optimization. *Digital*, *6*(1), 25. DOI: 10.3390/digital6010025

Yordanova, Z., & Nozari, H. (2026b). Seamless Data Integration for Predictive Learning Environments. In AI-Augmented Creativity in Learning Analytics (pp. 293-318). IGI Global Scientific Publishing.

Chapter 10
Regulating Intelligent Learning Systems:
Legal Frameworks, Data Governance, and Policy Design for AI-Driven and Digital Twin-Twin Enabled Learning

Satyam Singh
http://orcid.org/0009-0007-3851-6394
Manipal University Jaipur, India

Archana Kumari
Amity University, Patna, India

Deepali Sinha
http://orcid.org/0009-0007-6242-3956
Bennett University, India

Amitanshu Nayak
http://orcid.org/0009-0001-7526-4954
Amity University, Patna, India

ABSTRACT

This chapter examines the regulatory, legal, and governance challenges associated with AI-driven and digital twin–enabled intelligent learning systems. It highlights how adaptive AI technologies and real-time digital twin simulations are transforming education into personalized, data-driven ecosystems. However, the rapid adoption of these technologies has outpaced legal and policy frameworks, creating concerns

DOI: 10.4018/979-8-2600-1674-9.ch010

related to data privacy, algorithmic bias, accountability, and ethical governance. The chapter develops an integrated governance framework combining AI governance theory, data governance principles, and policy design strategies. It further explores global and national regulatory landscapes, stakeholder roles, and implementation challenges. The study concludes that effective governance requires transparency, inclusivity, and adaptive regulatory mechanisms to ensure responsible, equitable, and sustainable deployment of intelligent learning systems.

1. INTRODUCTION

1.1 Background of Intelligent Learning Systems

There has been great integration of technology including artificial intelligence (AI), learning analytics, and digital infrastructure into today's education system. The conventional approaches that were dependent on standardized learning and curricula have gradually been superseded by intelligent learning systems able to create personalized learning experience for learners. This has created an opportunity for education institutions to leverage information-based technologies to increase efficiency of learning, increase engagement and make decisions. Intelligent learning systems use information technology techniques such as machine learning, natural language processing, predictive analytics and adaptive technologies to personalize the learning experience of learners based on their unique learning styles. They are able to analyze learner's behavior, progress and performance through the course of learning and give recommendations and automatic feedback. Intelligent learning systems are increasingly being used in education because of the many benefits associated with them (Zawacki-Richter et al., 2019).

At the same time, the development of digital twin technology has broadened the scope of the intelligent learning ecosystem. Digital twins are defined as a dynamic digital model of a physical object or system whose status is constantly updated with the help of real-time data. In the field of education, digital twins may represent either learners, classrooms, educational process management systems, or even educational contexts in order to perform simulation, monitoring, and predictive analysis. In spite of these new technologies, the growing use of AI systems and digital twin technology in the realm of education has raised many legal, ethical, and governance issues. Data protection, algorithmic responsibility, automated decisions, surveillance, transparency, and institutional responsibilities, among others, raise questions that need to be addressed from a regulatory point of view. Therefore, the regulation of intelligent learning systems becomes an issue for inter-disciplinary research. (Fuller et al., 2020)

1.2 Rise of AI and Digital Twins in Education

With an increase in requirements for scalability, personalization, and efficiency of education, the implementation of AI technologies has been intensified significantly in the field of educational programs. Educational institutions apply various AI technologies for assessment automation, learning pattern identification, adaptation of tutoring practices, and predictive interventions. These solutions analyze enormous volumes of learner data, such as their performance during the assessment, learning activity patterns, and behavior traits, to facilitate optimization of learning delivery and ensure successful academic outcomes. Moreover, the combination of AI technologies and digital twins has expanded the scope of applications of these instruments in the sphere of education. Educational digital twins are systems that can simulate educational processes in real time, using predictive modeling and continuous interaction between digital representation and physical environment via synchronized data. Digital twins of individuals, classrooms, or institutions could become valuable tools for decision making and interventions in the educational process (Munir et al., 2022).

Finally, both types of technological advancements contribute to the creation of immersive and interactive learning environments with the help of virtual reality and simulation tools. These technologies enhance the efficiency of education and allow institutions to make evidence-based decisions concerning curriculum development and management, as well as learner support measures. However, the use of artificial intelligence technologies in education is not without its complications. The organizations involved in education have to take into consideration such things as automation, profiling, discrimination, security, ownership, and accountability in relation to AI-based solutions. For this reason, governance is needed in order for intelligent tutoring systems to be transparent, fair, human-controlled, and compliant with law. (Adams et al., 2023).

1.3 Problem Statement

While AI-based and digital twin-assisted educational solutions promise numerous innovations and personalization options, their governance and regulation are still not sufficiently developed. Educational laws and regulations do not always cover many issues connected to automation, predictions, algorithmic analysis, and constant monitoring of learners' activities. First of all, one should consider data governance and privacy concerns raised by intelligent educational systems. In order to perform all necessary tasks, an intelligent learning system requires vast amounts of sensitive personal data concerning students' grades, behavior, biometrics, and other important learning-related information. Such data collection raises many questions connected to obtaining proper consent, legal processing and storing of collected data, as well as potential cybersecurity problems (Williamson & Eynon, 2020).

Secondly, there is a problem of algorithmic opacity and non-transparency of AI-based solutions. Since most algorithms used for making various decisions are sophisticated mathematical models, sometimes even experts cannot explain how these algorithms make particular predictions or conclusions. This poses many risks connected with the lack of procedural justice when decisions about learners' performance, admission to certain courses or programs, etc., are made by these systems. This technology adds another dimension to the existing problems related to governance by allowing for constant surveillance and prediction of the education process through predictive modeling. Lack of legislative frameworks dealing with educational digital twins leads to ambiguity concerning their ethical use, data synchronization, accountability of institutions, and students' independence. As such, the necessity to develop an integrated governance framework that can address all these aspects becomes evident. (Wang et al., 2024).

1.4 Research Gap

The existing academic literature on the topic of AI in education is largely concentrated on technological development, adaptive learning tools, or principles of AI. Nevertheless, few studies have provided a comprehensive examination of the relationship between AI governance, regulation of digital twins, educational law, and policies in one conceptual approach. Currently, issues connected to AI governance and data protection in education are discussed independently and fail to account for the role of digital twins' ecosystems in raising concerns regarding issues like surveillance, algorithmic decision-making, educational sovereignty, and predictive analytics. Moreover, current regulatory discussions lack a comparative analysis of legislation on this issue based on the European Union AI Act, GDPR, UNESCO ethical recommendations, and governance of education (Regan & Jesse, 2019).

Moreover, there is also an evident lack of theoretical understanding of digital twins in education from the perspective of AI governance. Digital twins have gained much recognition in industries such as healthcare and manufacturing; however, not many papers have focused on the connection between digital twins and education regulation, the rights of learners, and institutional accountability. Thus, this chapter aims at filling this interdisciplinary gap and presenting a coherent framework for the governance of AI-enabled digital twin technologies in education. (Papagiannidis et al., 2025).

1.5 Objectives

This chapter seeks to conduct a critical analysis of the issues surrounding the governance of AI-enabled and digital twin-based education systems, as well as creating a unified legal and policy framework for the deployment of such technologies. (Agarwal et al., 2026).

The main objectives of this chapter include:

1. To assess the use of artificial intelligence and digital twins in modern education systems.
2. To review the regulatory and legal landscape governing the use of AI technologies in education, such as the European Union AI Act, GDPR, OECD AI Principles, and UNESCO ethical guidelines.
3. To assess the governance challenges connected with the use of AI technologies, such as data privacy, algorithmic accountability, transparency, cybersecurity, and institutional accountability.
4. To study governance challenges related to the application of digital twins in the context of education.
5. To devise a unified governance and policy framework to facilitate ethical and transparent intelligent education systems.

2. THEORETICAL FOUNDATIONS AND GOVERNANCE FRAMEWORKS

2.1 AI Governance Theory

These issues are examples of why the rapid development of new artificial intelligence in education creates a need for appropriate, complementary governance mechanisms that are inexpensive and robust enough to contribute to creating a transparent environment for the responsible use of AI Education. An AI governance theory might help improve intelligent systems and prevent danger. The models categorized AI applications in high and low perceived risk contexts, from content recommendation systems to grading and admissions decision-making. These so-called risk-based models use proportionate control to restrict the system's metrics and measurements that affect persons, groups and organizations. Yet, this technique is vital in education since AI systems can directly assess student evaluations and learning results and the reactions of the institution. The governance system must be able to track and decrease risk to limit harm, and to identify danger. One of the main concepts of our attention on the guideline is human-centered AI valuing human values, freedom and well-being while creating and implementing technology. This means AI should be working with human intuition, not against it. Human-in-the-loop AI in education puts fairness, inclusivity and transparency first for students and instructors. Moreover, AI governance should be transparent. Especially in high-stakes professions, it is crucial that stakeholders understand the judgments made by AI systems. This needs adequate documentation or design of transparent procedures and data sources. Additionally, interpretability of AI model is essential. Such frameworks aim to make sure expressly that AI-based judgments are taken not only inside a framework in which the decision has an authority but also with means to hold institutions and developers accountable. The AI governance framework helps to reduce the risks and promote new technologies for the education of the future (Slade & Prinsloo, 2013).

2.2 Data Governance Theory

Data governance theory is an important part of the wider foundation, and it supports the development of AI-led & digital twin enabled education systems. When combined with technology that manages the whole lifetime of data – from collection to storage to final deletion from a system – good governance guarantees that only correct treatment occurs for rules specified by policy. Data lifecycle management is a core idea that involves the governance of data at different phases of its lifespan and rules and procedures at each level. This comprises operations such as handling student academic history, performance data and behavioral analytics in a virtual mode configuration. They have a data life cycle for integrity and security purposes to ensure that they can rely on their AI-created information. Clarity in terms of stewardship and accountability of ownership are among the foundational aspects of data governance. Stewardship - proper management of resources Ownership – data ownership Accountability is when they are accountable for their decisions regarding the data (Khatri & Brown, 2010).

The appropriate allocation of roles in AI-influenced educational systems can act as a safeguard against malpractice. Audit logs and data owners and governance Consent and Privacy issues the adoption also includes data governance. That's why educational institutions need to have enough protection so that sensitive information remains secure and data is only utilized for valid purposes. Includes powerful data sharing protocols, anonymization and encryption implementation. Also, interoperability and standardization are crucial in systems where many technologies and platforms combine, etc. The systems receiving and processing the data are integrated learning environments. The philosophy of data governance is the foundation for the ethical application of AI and digital twin technologies in education (Abraham et al., 2019).

2.3 Digital Twin Theory

Digital Twins is a virtual representation technology providing real time dynamic images of physical things. In education, a digital twin is the depiction of learners and of classrooms or institutions to continuously enhance simulations from this. Digital twin technology is based on cyber-physical systems, or the combination of computational models with physical processes. These systems use sensors, data streams and analytics to produce high fidelity, real-time digital twins of physical items. This may be achieved by gathering attributes of students' behaviors on multiple platforms within the learning environment e.g. simulation tools, a learning management system in computerized learners' profiles. Data Synchronization – Real-time data updating is only its base layer, because it guarantees the physical twin compatibility of the virtual model. Digital twin theory also enables predictive and prescriptive analytics through the modeling of several scenarios that might produce a range of outcomes. This provides great prospects in education since it can be utilized for improving learning routes, better resource allocation and enhanced institutional performance. However, the complexity and governance difficulties of data accuracy, privacy and ethics in the use of digital twins is significant. There is need to include such rules and develop a comprehensive approach to controlling intelligent systems as digital siblings are controlled by the AI and data governance frameworks (Attaran & Celik, 2023).

2.4 Institutional and Policy Theory

Governance in AI-powered and digital twins-based learning systems needs a multi-level institutional and policymaking process that would include not only various national governments but also educational establishments, technology developers, and international bodies. Institutions and policy theories are necessary to analyze the ways in which governance practices affect the design and implementation of intelligent learning systems. On an international level, organizations like the European Union, UNESCO, and OECD established ethical principles and regulatory standards pertaining to the development and use of artificial intelligence, data protection, and digital governance in general. The focus on issues such as transparency, human control, accountability, inclusiveness, and fundamental rights protection is prominent in these regulatory efforts. On a national level, governments increasingly implement policy documents that govern AI in general and intelligent learning technologies in particular. For example, the EU AI Act and the General Data Protection Regulation set out rules regarding risk assessments, automated decision-making processes, data minimization requirements, and transparency (Veale & Borgesius, 2021).

Educational organizations form the operational tier of the governance system. Educational institutions are expected to put in place systems for compliance, data governance, cyber security measures, and ethics. Proper institutional governance also involves educating the staff, algorithm audits, and ongoing monitoring of educational technologies using artificial intelligence. Providers of technology solutions and ed-tech companies also perform significant governance functions. They must make sure that AI systems adhere to relevant laws on matters such as fairness, privacy, explainability, and accountability. Governance of intelligent learning systems therefore demands cooperation between different actors. Figure 1 portrays the integrative governance dynamic among AI systems, digital twins' infrastructure, data governance processes, and institutional policies in intelligent learning environments. It demonstrates the integrated action of AI systems, data infrastructure, layers of digital twin and governance, with policy implementation for achieving effective learning results (Raji et al., 2020).

Figure 1. Integrated governance framework for AI-driven and digital twin–enabled education systems

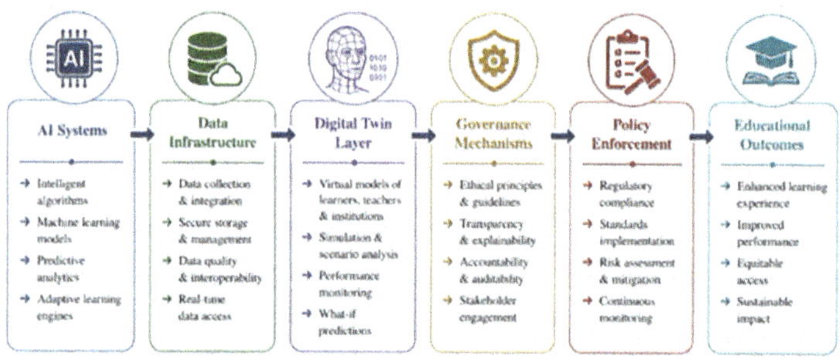

Figure 1 shows an integrated governance architecture for AI-driven and digital twin-enabled education systems and the flow from AI systems to data infrastructure, digital twin layers, governance mechanisms, policy enforcement, and educational results. This figure shows the interaction of the technological, regulatory and institutional elements to enable responsible, effective and outcome-oriented deployment of intelligent learning systems (Chiu et al., 2023).

3. LEGAL FRAMEWORKS FOR AI IN EDUCATION

3.1 Global Regulatory Landscape

The spread of artificial intelligence across the globe in the field of education has led to the emergence of governance structures in law and ethics meant to guide the proper use of intelligent technologies. One of the most significant regulatory tools is the EU Artificial Intelligence Act, whose regulatory model is based on risk regulation. The EU Artificial Intelligence Act categorizes AI systems employed in education and vocational training as "high-risk" when such technologies have a substantial impact on access to education, evaluation of learners, or educational opportunities. Compliance requirements include risk management, transparency obligation, human supervision, technical documentation, and conformity assessment (Smuha, 2021).

Moreover, the GDPR can be considered another foundational regulation that regulates AI-based educational systems. The GDPR includes critical principles, such as lawful processing of personal information, informed consent, data minimization, purpose limitation, and automation. Special attention should be paid to Article 22 of the GDPR since it guarantees protection from decisions made through automated processing when such decisions may adversely affect rights and interests of the individual. Apart from this, there is a contribution to AI regulation made by international organizations. For example, UNESCO has developed the Recommendation concerning the ethics of artificial intelligence, which includes the protection of human rights and human-centric approaches, inclusiveness, fairness, and equity in education. The same applies to OECD AI Principles. However, at the same time, there still remains regulatory fragmentation within the international community despite existing efforts to regulate AI governance in education. (Tao et al., 2019).

3.2 National-Level Regulations

National regulatory frameworks offer an important legal context for the implementation and enforcement of global norms. One such example is the General Data Protection Regulation (GDPR) which includes rules for acquiring, processing and retaining personal data. One of the most important reasons why this is particularly relevant with schools is due to the General Data Protection Regulation (GDPR). In brief, GDPR is a regulation in EU law on data protection and privacy. AI systems rely heavily on sensitive student information ranging from academic reports to behavioral data as well as personally identifiable information. The rule embeds values in terms of data minimization, control through informed permission and access/erase right), for students on their personal data. Other emergent AI regulations are also extending beyond specific governance problems, beyond data protection. National policies related to AI are generally found within such frameworks, but one would also find ethical codes or regulatory sandboxes used as a pilot for the deployment of artificial intelligence technology. These standards aim to reduce the need to monitor risks presented by AI in health, while yet encourage innovation that may improve patient care (Wachter et al., 2017).

3.3 Legal Risks

Using AI-powered learning technologies leads to serious legal implications regarding liability, data protection, intellectual property, discrimination, and accountability of organizations. One of the important challenges here is that of liability for automated education. Algorithms and machine learning techniques are becoming widely applied during the enrollment process, scoring tests and exams, profiling students, and conducting predictive analysis. In case of wrong results caused by erroneous algorithms, it will be challenging to identify the party responsible for that - it could be either universities or colleges, software vendors, or data suppliers. Another issue to consider involves data privacy and cyber security. The intelligent learning systems process enormous amounts of information that relate to personal information, behavior, and other sensitive data about the learners (Mittelstadt et al., 2016).

Moreover, the danger of discrimination from algorithms constitutes yet another possible legal challenge that needs to be considered. Algorithms that are developed based on biased information could end up discriminating against the marginalized group of students. This will pose a challenge to legislation on discrimination, legislation on equal access to education, and even human rights laws. Moreover, digital twins create an additional challenge because they need real-time synchronization of education information. The absence of any laws on educational digital twins raises concerns of consent, ownership, surveillance, and even prediction of behavior. Therefore, there is a need for a robust governance framework for educational institutions that would incorporate auditing, transparency, cybersecurity, and human control systems. Lack of regulatory definitions hampers governance and compliance Table 1 gives an overview of the coverage, characteristics and effects of Key Global & National Education Regulations. See for more on assuring cooperative risk reduction e.g. liability, data protection and gradual use of legal tools to oversee the deployment of AI in any other ethical means (Matos et al., 2025).

Table 1. Legal and regulatory frameworks for AI in education

Regulation	Scope	Key Features	Implications for Education
EU AI Act	AI systems	Risk-based approach	Compliance burden
GDPR	Data privacy	Consent & protection	Student data control
OECD AI Principles	Ethical AI	Transparency	Trust building
UNESCO Guidelines	Educational Ethics	Inclusivity	Responsible AI
National Policies	Local laws	Adaptation	Implementation

Table 1 summarizes the main legislative frameworks that regulate AI in education and highlights the implications of different regulatory methods for compliance requirements, data governance and ethical application (Ghallab, 2019).

4. DATA GOVERNANCE AND PRIVACY IN INTELLIGENT LEARNING SYSTEMS

4.1 Data Lifecycle in AI Education

The AI education lifecycle may be characterized in five fundamental phases: collection, storage, processing (data), sharing and deletion of data. The life cycle begins with data collection from LMSs (learning management systems), virtual simulations, and sensor technologies to user interaction. This involves engagement metrics, behavioral trends, and instructional summary data. Alternatively, there is too much data collection in process and risk of reduced transparency through personalization and adaptation. The data is then stored in the storage stage, where the data is kept semi-permanently in Cloud environments or Databases. At now, the integrity of the data should be preserved and illegal access to it should be avoided at all costs. This would require Institutions to utilize encryption technology, access control mechanism and secure architecture of sensitive personal data. Processing This is the part where AI algorithms transform the raw data into usable insights. This contains students' performance analysis and prediction and recommendations. The importance of data validation lies in the fact that skewed or poor-quality data can lead to skewed results of AI applications. The second phase concerns the sharing of data (i.e. information transmitted between third-party providers and/or organizations, or structures. Enhanced sharing increases the scope for collaborative and interoperable use but also increases the possibility of security compromises or abuse. These concerns should be addressed through data-sharing agreements and regulatory compliance. The last phase in the data life cycle is concerned with the process of secure deletion and retention. (Jobin et al., 2019).

4.2 Ethical Data Use

Ethical data governance and informed consent are vital aspects of AI-based learning environments. Learners must be fully aware of how their personal data is gathered, processed, stored, and utilized by educational organizations. This includes information regarding when they can give, update, or revoke their consent. In addition, consent management tools should be transparent not just to meet regulatory requirements and documentation needs but also to build trust between learners and educational institutions. Another problem related to ethics concerns bias and discrimination through algorithmic means. Machine-learning algorithms that operate on unbalanced or partial data sets can generate discriminatory outputs in which certain learners are discriminated against more than others. Put differently, the academic recommendations, assessment processes, scheduling, and profiling of learners can be biased in terms of historical data set. Therefore, the adoption of auditing mechanisms, diversified data sets, and monitoring of artificial intelligence becomes essential to address this problem. Good data governance requires accountability on the part of stakeholders involved in the design and deployment of AI technologies. Learning organizations must establish data governance committees, assign duties relating to data protection, and carry out compliance audits. Figure 2 The cycle of data governance in AI-based educational systems is cyclical in nature, with the flow of data from input to decision-making and feedback constituting its core features. Table 2 also gives a clear and succinct overview of the many forms of information gathered or created by an EDX environment, the associated hazards, and one regulatory framework to apply ethical proper usage management through this learning system (Amo-Filva et al., 2024).

Figure 2. Data governance lifecycle in AI-driven education systems

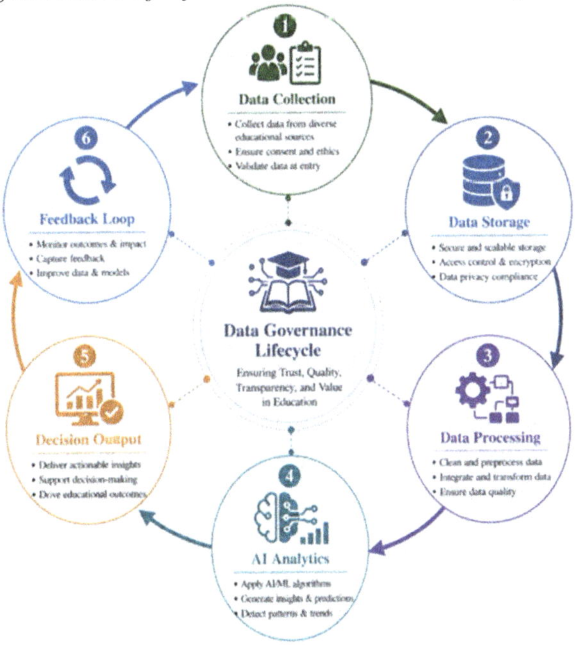

The data governance life cycle in AI-enabled education systems is depicted in Figure 2. It shows the flow from data collection, storage, processing, AI analytics, decision output and feedback loops. The figure shows that the methods of data management are continuous and interlinked.

Table 2. Data types, risks, and governance mechanisms in AI education

Data Type	Source	Risk	Governance Mechanism
Academic	LMS	Misuse	Encryption
Behavioral	Sensors	Privacy	Consent
Biometric	Wearables	High risk	Regulation
Performance	AI analytics	Bias	Auditing
Institutional	Systems	Breach	Security protocols

Table 2 presents the essential data types, sources, threats, and governance strategies in intelligent learning systems. It highlights the need for tailored solutions to ensure privacy, security and ethical use of data for different types of data (Martin et al., 2024).

5. DIGITAL TWIN–ENABLED EDUCATION ECOSYSTEMS

5.1 Concept of Digital Twins in Education

Digital twin technology is defined as the formation of dynamic digital representations of tangible objects or settings, which maintain continuous interaction with real-world objects through real-time data exchange. Although initially designed for engineering and industrial applications, digital twins have found new use cases in the field of education, such as personalized learning, predictive analysis, institutional management, and simulation-based learning. When used in an educational setting, digital twins can include learners, classes, learning spaces, or institutional settings. Digital twins are created based on constantly changing data collected by learning management software, behavior analysis tools, wearables, assessment tools, and educational sensors. At the individual level, digital twins could incorporate data on academic performance, attendance, participation, behavior, cognition, and more to develop a continually developing profile of the learner. Artificial intelligence (AI) can then interpret the learners' profiles to provide adaptive learning recommendations, diagnose learning challenges, forecast educational success, and tailor educational approaches. In terms of organizations, the concept of digital twins could be used to make decisions regarding education via simulations and prediction analytics. Organizations could use digital twins to improve the planning of courses, resource allocation, class management, and institutional performance evaluation. However, the extensive use of educational data in real time is likely to cause serious governance problems. Constant monitoring of learners can subject educational institutions to risks such as surveillance, behavioral profiling, violation of learner autonomy, violations of consent, and discrimination. (Hoel & Chen, 2018).

5.2 Applications

Digital twin enabled ecosystems may be used to complement traditional learning and institutional administration in a myriad of ways. The extent and usage of it is astounding. One of the keys uses for this are fresh studies on identifying unique paths to learners. An AI system, using a digital twin, takes input from students and then uses that information to determine what type of content will be most successful for them; how quickly or slowly they need to study it at this stage in their life; as well also acting on fields such as tests. Even if a learner is struggling with subject matters like algebra or video presentation through simulations and exercises that fill the gaps. Another important area of application is the modelling of institutional performance. Digital twin of an educational institution to replicate such what provides it the most situations – whether in content, financial allocation or delivery manner. These situations provide institutions with chances to play and choose wisely from competing outcomes. This is important for policy development and execution. Finally, digital twins support forward-looking analytics applications that leverage current data to help forecast probable learning outcomes and institutional reactions. Moreover, it will facilitate the identification of troubled teenagers and will serve to optimize the available resources currently and enhance the efficiency of operations. They are major players in the field of educational technology with many integrations. The digital twins have become an important data center for integrating components of various sources in proximity to learning management systems, simulation technology, and assessment tools within the manufacturing system. It will bring more coherence to the entire learning process. In addition, digital twins can be oriented toward virtual and augmented reality environments, thereby creating an immersive learning experience. They simulate such environments and react to the behavior of the students, thereby creating real-world learning experiences (Bankins et al., 2025).

5.3 Risks and Governance Challenges

However, besides the various opportunities for the implementation of digital twins, there are also some serious problems that might emerge in relation to the matter. First of all, the question that arises is connected to the precision and synchronicity of the data that digital twins use for their operation. Because digital twins constantly receive new information, the accuracy of such data might be misleading in terms of determining how actions should be undertaken in the education system. Another serious question that arises is connected to privacy and surveillance problems. Because digital twin ecosystems are based on sensitive data, including behavioral data, emotions, and biometric data of users of the educational system, the problem of surveillance and monitoring that might infringe on the freedom of students might emerge. Furthermore, the problem of algorithmic opacity is one of the major issues in digital twin ecosystems. Namely, since some of them include artificial intelligence, which provides suggestions based on prediction models, they can be hard to interpret. Last but not least, cybersecurity vulnerability issues can also appear because of digital twins. This means that educational organizations should set up proper encryption protocols, access control mechanisms, and cybersecurity frameworks. Finally, it is important to overcome regulatory problems. The existing regulatory regime for educational processes and AI administration fails to provide adequate guidelines concerning the use of digital twins in education. In this regard, there is a need to develop particular regulations. Figure 3 – Digital Twins for Learner Controlled Learning Environment is real environment linked with sensor data. Example real-time large data types used in predictive models of pieces inextricably linked system reactions using artificial intelligence analysis and adaptive learning systems. How complex algorithms interact to form dynamic knowledge and operational context of time-sensitive information (Vial, 2019).

Figure 3. Architecture of digital twin–enabled learning ecosystem

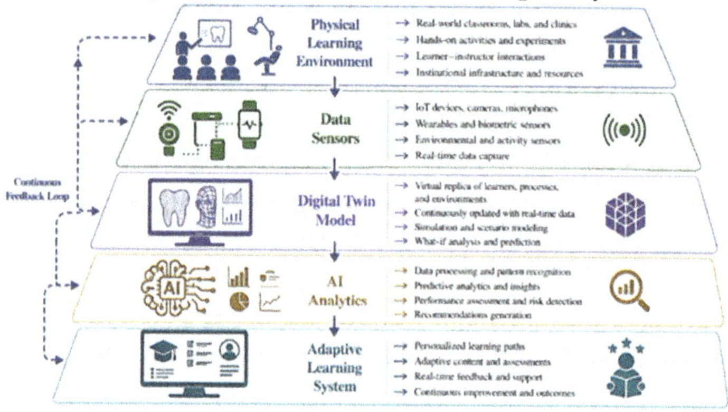

Figure. 3 shows the architecture of a digital twin driven learning ecosystem where physical learning environment is integrated with data sensors, digital twin models, AI analytics and adaptive learning systems. The graphic shows the potential of real-time data assimilation and cognitive analytics to deliver dynamic, personalized and responsive educational experiences.

6. POLICY DESIGN FOR AI-DRIVEN EDUCATION SYSTEMS

6.1 Policy Design Principles

The key challenge of implementing any control over AI systems will be defining the principles of designing such policies that will influence your educational environment and will create an equal balance between innovation and ethics. For any intelligent system to be fair, open, accountable and useful for society, complete transparency is required. The openness and explainability of an AI system Education stakeholders including students, instructors and legislators should comprehend AI-driven judgments. That exposes data sources, as well as what is computed and subsequently how it is chosen. Trust is established on openness because methods that may just as readily be questioned or criticized. Transparency may be obtained by explainable AI models, documentation and system behavior interfaces. While responsibility is about a general duty, accountability is about who would be held accountable for these AI-based activities. Who owns the influence of an AI system in education? Designers, users or regulators? Accountability frameworks should include mistake and damage audits, reporting and redress. For high stakes use cases, such as student examinations and admissions, human supervision is required. AI Services must implement equitable access and non-discrimination wherever deployed to be inclusive. Smart learning systems are built for diverse learners, including those from varied socioeconomic backgrounds, skill levels, cultures, etc. Policy should be centered on bridging the digital divide via enabling technology to be inexpensive and accessible at scale as well as empowering target groups with the essential skillsets needed in this time. Therefore, AI systems cannot entrench prejudices or discrimination to achieve objectives of equal and fair educational outcomes. These principles will guide the establishment of policies for the development of AI-based education techniques with a sense of responsibility (Gašević et al., 2022).

6.2 Stakeholder Roles

Making policy for AI systems in education needs coordinated activities of people with varied roles and responsibilities. The first component is starting to set up dialog and ecosystem building via what sorts of regulatory frameworks to pursue (Smith, 2019). Lead government action into policy goals. They are representatives who develop rules and regulations on the criteria of use of AI in educational institutions, ensuring compliance with ethical or legal norms. Governments will also provide financial incentives and infrastructure to support their innovation/adoption. They cooperate with national and international organizations to develop coherent policies. "Those policies must be grounded in educational institutions. This involves usage of AI technology in course material, regulatory compliance and data governance processes. Institutions must educate the workforce about internal policy and make new policies for the institutions to use AI technology as well as monitoring techniques. In this situation the innovators are EdTech companies that are developing and using AI technology for E-learning. It is a developing Systems job along with Aligning the criteria from Regulators. Gaining fundamental and Domain expertise on Data Safety (ethos while Product building) throughout product development. Engage with institutions, policy makers to link technological solutions with education-need-promotion needs. There are also NGO's which play their role in promoting ethical practices, researchers and industry groups take care of best practice. Player involvement leads to a form of co-governance, which distributes and organizes the responsibility for making sure that all is done correctly through policy processes (Samala et al., 2025).

6.3 Implementation Strategies

The scaling up of Mars lessons is all about successful implementation - techniques and principles that allow policy ideas to take root in an environment that is appropriate for experimentation, learning workout, iteration and they are baked into the foundation of many innovative approaches. Several nations under consideration will be looked at using possibilities such as a regulatory sandbox. Sandboxed settings for testing new AI technologies These are sandboxes that intend to test how well, the relevant performance characteristics etc. of an AI system works either by policymakers before or after getting them out on work related tasks as well as developers which means assessing - its hazards and possible advantages surfaces before rolling it in real-world against production (Prinsloo & Slade, 2017). Such a strategy allows for innovation but also ensures that some threats are spotted and addressed in real time. AI technologies will be tried at various institutions or sections of the country. Such configurations pose real world issues. It offers the politicians the opportunity to establish legislation or to draw blueprints for experimental projects. Above all, support the maintenance of stakeholder trust in AI enabled systems while building and scaling institutional competence. Policies should be checked to see whether they are doing what they are supposed to achieve. These are audit, response and monitoring methods for the stages of AI commissioning. The insights gathered from these techniques can inform the establishment of improved policies and adaptations to new trends in technology and advances in the education environment. Moreover, the implementation is conditional, since it needs Governments and institutions to improve their skills in terms of competences needed to install, correct or engage with such technology. They come from technical training right down to learning what ethical difficulties and norms are. Finally, public private collaboration may continue to provide access to resources, consequently, accelerating innovation and more scalable solutions. By working together, government and EdTech companies may share what they know about how to build and deploy infrastructure for the fast deployment of AI learning systems in areas where educational technology can be applied. Table 3 therefore offers a comprehensive review of the major policy components, including the target groups and the outcomes envisaged so far. This is represented in the flowchart for formulation of policies with input from goals Figure 4 (Lee & Kwon, 2024).

Figure 4. Policy design framework for intelligent learning systems

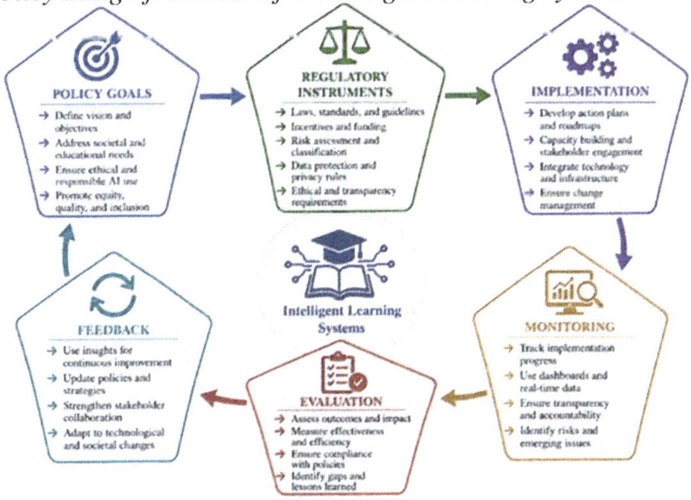

The policy design framework for intelligent learning systems is presented in Figure 4.

Table 3. Policy elements in AI-driven education systems

Policy Element	Description	Stakeholder	Outcome
Transparency	Open AI systems	Government	Trust
Accountability	Responsibility	Institutions	Compliance
Inclusivity	Equal access	NGOs	Equity
Innovation	Sandboxes	Firms	Growth
Monitoring	Audits	Regulators	Control

Table 3 outlines the main policy aspects of AI-driven education systems, including their definition, accountable parties, and intended outcomes. It shows how the ideas of policy are translated into operational elements that enable trust, compliance, equity, innovation and control.

7. BUSINESS, EDTECH, AND GOVERNANCE INTEGRATION

7.1 EdTech Business Models

AI-powered education is growing, and its popularity is reflected in a range of EdTech business models, including enterprises delivering scale and tailored or tech-enabled learning solutions. Of these, Software-as-a-Service (SaaS) learning systems have been prevalent. This includes cloud-based access to AI tutors e.g. learning analytics dashboards, and simulation environments. SaaS solutions allow institutions and learners to save significant up-front investment but benefit from modern technology and deliver scalability through continuous upgrades. The third one is that AI powered school services in Higher Ed have strong capabilities such as adaptive learning, predictive analytics and autonomous assessment. Most of the services are available as stand-alone products or part of bigger platforms. They are valuable since they bring in higher learning efficiency, effective outcomes on numerous analyses and less administrative labor for teachers. Hybrid methods are also just a mix of different strategies such as freemium & premium content, institutional licensing and marketplace-based distribution. EdTech enterprises may leverage these methodologies to cater to various user groups, such as students, corporate personnel, and educational institutions. But such business models are not only based on following the latest technological innovations, but also on following governance and regulatory limits. AI is now more ingrained in education delivery than ever before, but compliance and ethical thinking need to be re-engineered as must-haves of business strategy (Baker & Hawn, 2022).

7.2 Governance Challenges

When it comes to integrating AI inside their business models, EdTech businesses need to contend with an assortment of governance difficulties if they are going to assure sustainable development over the longer term. It is expensive to pay Law expertise to build the infrastructure (García et al., 2022). Data protection legislation, AI rules. due diligence education. Most startups and small enterprises are faced with a daunting entrance and growth barrier – expensive prices. It's a narrative of consistent invention and execution. It is this same part of the legal framework that bedevils the success criteria for AI, and which one must remember while rushing through laws. That is a sweet spot. The EdTech sector is going to be walking on thin ice. While being compliant without sacrificing on their unique promise. Other pain points include data governance and privacy. AI enabled systems rely heavily on vast quantities of sensitive data like student performance and conduct. All of these are certainly not easy: making your data for which one must seek clearly known consent and method to manage and do so openly. Another area of risk governance is algorithmic bias and fairness. Regular audits, monitoring, and validation of AI systems are critical to ensure that there is no discrimination or bias in outcomes, which would otherwise cause serious liabilities and other issues for institutions from a legal, ethical, and reputational standpoint. Hence the need for good governance and historical tech understanding. Global EdTech platforms and the global challenge of regulatory fragmentation distinct jurisdictions have distinct rules and norms therefore firms must train their systems on several nations. This adds complexity and expense (Freccero et al., 2025).

7.3 Strategic Alignment

Strategically aligned to the business objectives and governance demands of EdTech organizations, which permeate everything people do. But people can't just leave that load on the company. Regulatory compliance must be included in your basic strategies. First is compliance-by-design – the notion of designing AI systems in ways that include legal and ethical issues from the inception of these advancements (He et al., 2026). That also implies that data protection by design, transparency and auditability are in play from day one. Advantages of Cybersecurity That develops confidence with users and stakeholders and decreases risk. The second key method is adaptation and localization. This implies that companies need to develop adaptable EdTech solutions which can work on local norms as a single regulatory set-up does not apply to everyone. An understanding of the regulatory environment can help organizations establish themselves in the market and achieve sustainable growth. Working together with educators, regulators, and technologists will be vital to creating governance systems that facilitate educational ecosystems in line with policy aims and institutional objectives. If anything, it makes the relationship between policy and practice more tangible. Links - organizations with policy developments and best practices in the sector. In addition to the so-called ivory tower of governance, firms have also invested in infrastructures such as data management systems, cyber security solutions or compliance teams. And frequent evaluation will assist in maintaining systems evolving with time, reflecting changes in rules, technology. Strategic alignment is the harmony between creativity and execution. Technology can only go one direction – to the future. Corporations have no choice but to stay up with ethics & user trust. Such a balance is critical for a corporation to sustain its competitive edge in the long run. Table 4 summarizes the concerns and activities associated with collective action problems in business model governance (Autili et al., 2026).

Table 4. Business–governance integration in AI-driven edtech

Business Model	Governance Challenge	Strategy	Outcome
SaaS	Data compliance	Secure systems	Trust
Platform	Regulation	Localization	Market expansion
AI services	Bias	Auditing	Fairness
Subscription	Privacy	Consent	Retention
Hybrid	Complexity	Integration	Efficiency

Table 4 highlights the connections between EdTech commercial models, governance problems and strategic responses. It illustrates that when business strategy is aligned with regulatory requirements, the consequence is trust, fairness, market growth and operational efficiency.

8. ETHICAL AND RISK MANAGEMENT FRAMEWORKS

8.1 Ethical AI Principles

It can also come from the training data, such as unrepresentative cases; or biases that magnify social disparities included in algorithms utilizing datasets. To address this issue, institutions will need to embrace a more data-inclusive approach in their ethical audits and apply bias repair approaches created for AI systems (Marengo, 2024). From fairness to equality, deep learning is built on confidence. Transparency is the degree to which stakeholders may understand what an AI system is doing and why it arrives at the decisions it makes. Most AI models are "black boxes" but are very hard to grasp, they provide us outputs that we need to analyze. Nature is not just strong in what it does with the futures of learners, thus transparency can never be regarded lightly enough. This less black-boxed problem can be alleviated by demanding explainable AI techniques and appropriate documentation and interfaces. Through decisions, demanding responsibility from individuals, develop confidence. Accountability allows a linear way for us to find out who should be liable for the activities of AI. This includes the responsibility for the design, implementation and consequences of such systems. Therefore, accountability systems in education must inherently provide the recording of errors and complaints and subsequent correction. It will need institutions, developers and governments to agree to openness about where accountability rests - and to in-line execution of ethical norms. Finally, these principles together set the stage for socially responsible and more ethical applications of AI and intelligent systems by ensuring they learn not only from data, but also with and about society values and educational aims (Mittelstadt, 2019).

8.2 Risk Assessment

AI in education opens an altogether new set of risks to research and evaluate thoroughly. This risk assessment explains the process of developing mitigation plans for certain risks and an estimated impact on stakeholders and the probability of such events occurring. This leads to algorithmic hazards being grouped into three main categories: bias, opacity and decision-making mistake. Trigger altering includes our jobs that do not furnish purposely. These dangers may be necessary for the fairness and robustness of AIs. An un-reviewed AI used for grading will have varied results. Risks will be contained in response to delegative control through periodic risk mitigation measures such as testing and validation of algorithms (Mehrabi et al., 2021). The second main point is about data risk in private information breaches and illegal access or use of sensitive information. Data is AI powered education system that thrives on Data consists of academic history, behavioral analytics & biometric profiling. In essence, every breach might be a legal ethical headache for everyone. Such incidents may be averted with severe procedures. Data security and encryption through access treatment & secure storage can assist to cut down the hazards. Operational risk is associated with dependency on systems that have to run without any interruptions. Also, the integration process and infrastructure issues pose risks. Over-reliance on AI systems poses another risk as it minimizes human involvement in decision-making processes. (Okita, 2024).

8.3 Governance Mechanisms

All the AI systems require continual monitoring and considerable modifications to handle the risks. At this point, then, such mechanisms would take place to implement the actions associated with ethical considerations and risks. Co-operation in audits within this area is a very effective tool in this era. The monitoring of AI system performances, as well as their fair use and compliance, occurs regularly and consistently, internally and externally. The auditing of data, models, and algorithms ensures the absence of bias or any faults in the system before deployment, thereby guaranteeing its accuracy and making it easier to find a solution to a faulty process. The consequences could be high, and when considering any educational system where the use of data-driven evidence is used in decision-making, then auditing becomes an essential component. Finally, supervision in the implementation of compliance. This could mean altering the rules of the game when using AI systems. Operationalize automated monitoring tools to identify irregularities, announce violations and provide compliance. Governance frameworks contain incident response plans, contingency measures, and phases of continual development of risk management. These criteria depend on the institution(s) capacity to foresee counter threats Governance is about stakeholder engagement. Students, instructors and policy makers have become more open and responsible. Thus, both technology suppliers should be part of the decision-making process (Tan et al., 2022).

Through feedback systems, the stakeholders can determine problems in the system and continually make improvements in their governance. However, the presence of legal frameworks will not be enough without the presence of proper institutional leadership, technical competence, and the ability to undertake capacity building in ethical principles. The importance of training and guiding frameworks should not be underestimated. Figure 5: The architecture for ethical risk regulation of AI-based education systems. Design-type at each level. Note that hazard identification and monitoring is a continuous cycle. The system provides predictive and adaptive governance of AI-assisted learning difficulties (Mei et al., 2023).

Figure 5. Ethical risk governance framework for AI-based education systems

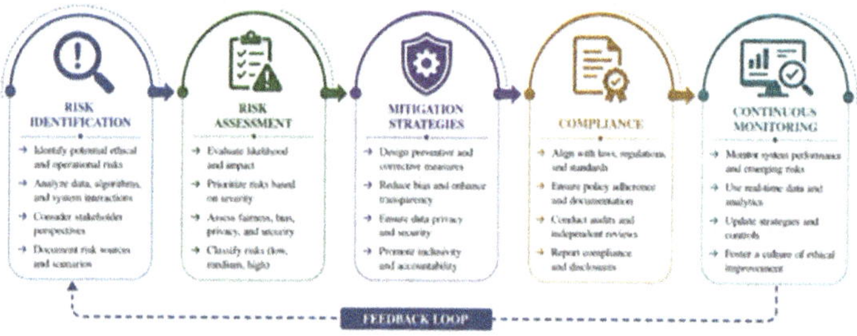

Figure 5 Ethical risk management approach for AI-based educational systems. The structure comprises a continuous cycle of risk identification, risk assessment, mitigation measures, compliance and continuous monitoring.

9. IMPLEMENTATION CHALLENGES AND INSTITUTIONAL ADOPTION

9.1 Infrastructure Requirements

A cloud-based infrastructure is an indispensable tool that helps to make scalable, flexible, and remote educational applications possible. In addition to this, cloud systems help educational organizations process large amounts of educational information and create distributed and digital learning environments (Mena Guacas et al., 2026). This is even more critical for some AI systems that are continually consuming data and refreshing models as required. It is also an AI-oriented infrastructure, comprised of equipment of high processing capacity (HPC), graphics processing units (GPU) and data pipeline for training & deploying machine learning models. Besides these system aspects, in case we consider virtual dimension for digital twin systems they need to have real-time data integration mechanisms in place through IoT sensors API (it's related with scaled cyber-physical systems like smart factory which was mentioned earlier because of dynamic environment). But the infrastructure, especially in terms of cost and probably the resource distribution for these 14 energy sources, is a concern. The fact is most organizations (particularly in the developing countries) simply cannot afford to invest in fancy infrastructure. There is a need for the establishment of a robust and dependable technological infrastructure for educational institutions, coupled with the development of the skills required for the operation and management of such an infrastructure. This will have to be done through an implementation approach that ensures that the essential activities within the institution are not compromised while progressively advancing technology (Fischer & Frennert, 2025).

9.2 Organizational Barriers

The early adaptation of such an AI-based ed-tech solution is not solely dependent on the technology, but the lack of organization plays a vital part here as well. One of the most significant barriers that we face is reluctance towards change. Every educational institution has its ways, customs and even traditions. And although they may appear hostile, particularly towards any form of innovative technology, they are faced with the right type of students, professors and other authorities can perceive AI systems as dangerous and disruptive know-how that threatens their incumbent status. Skills teacher shortfall Another barrier in our defenses is academia. For the AI operator to function properly, they require proficient in dealing with data and understanding how different technological systems work. (Chen, 2025). However, even with the current advancements made in technology, there is still the problem of educators being apprehensive about using AI in the classroom since they are ill-prepared for this challenge. The organizational structure and the governance model could also become another obstacle in implementing AI in institutions. In order for processes and leadership to work well, it is also important for rules to be in place. However, without these foundations, rules would gradually take place in a confused manner. It is difficult to ensure the continuous use of technology to meet strategic objectives for firms because it often results in fragmented or inconsistent governance strategy implementation. Much of the reluctance in implementation could be attributed to the difficulty in achieving a unified perspective on the problems encountered as well as ethical concerns when it comes to deployment and usage. Bureaucracy will probably affect their acceptance and implementation. Universities could encourage innovation and collaboration to address such problems. The foundation on which need to establish trust could be achieved through three key concepts: leadership, communication and stakeholder involvement (Williamson, 2016).

9.3 Capacity Building

The minimal practical deployment of AI-enabled education systems requires significant capacity investment at various levels. This requires building ability, skills, and organizational readiness to employ current technology. Training programs are essential to capacity building, since building a house requires many bricks. Education programs should focus on faculty/staff abilities and methods for using AI tools, assessing analytics output, and incorporating technology into teaching/learning (Rahman et al., 2026). Stakeholders should learn about ethics, data governance, and regulatory compliance to comprehend adoption. Making institutional governance ready requires multipronged initiatives in addition to human skill development. These guidelines govern appropriate AI technology use. Roles and duties. Establishing legal and ethical compliance monitoring mechanisms". Collaboration with technology vendors from various settings or research institutions policymakers that implement large-scale social interventions might improve capacity building projects. Alliances provide experience, resources, and best practices for implementation. Equal access to technology is crucial for all students. Digital inclusion: to avoid increasing inequalities in access to learning opportunities, offers should include not only subsidies (laptops under 100 euros) or access without a computer at home, if parents/siblings/guardians have a laptop they could share with their children, but also mobile infrastructure support of one to two hours for each child. Continuous assessment and feedback to evaluate capacity-building efforts are further drivers. Institutions must regularly examine their approach, fix flaws, and adapt to technological and education changes. Table 5 shows major implementation components, issues, outcomes, and possible solutions. It provides a roadmap for school reform and AI technology implementation in sustainable ways (Yu et al., 2025).

Table 5. Implementation challenges and solutions in AI-driven education

Component	Challenge	Impact	Solution
Infrastructure	Cost	Slow adoption	Phased rollout
Faculty	Skills	Inefficiency	Training
Technology	Complexity	Errors	Vendor support
Policy	Ambiguity	Risk	Clear guidelines
Students	Access	Inequality	Subsidies

Table 5 covers the essential components of institutional adoption including difficulties and implications and solutions

10. FUTURE TRENDS AND EMERGING REGULATORY DIRECTIONS

10.1 Autonomous Learning Systems

The future of smart education will be shaped by autonomous learning systems that will leverage AI platforms to handle the full educational life cycle with minimum human interaction. They build self-regulating education systems that leverage adaptive learning, predictive analytics and real-time feedback. It matches students with systems that measure data in real-time and tailor the material, tests and learning routes accordingly. Autonomy itself poses the difficulty of decision autonomy and responsibility in regulation. When AI independently evaluates student achievement or recommends whether to advance students, it erodes the need for monitoring and accountability. In the next years, regulations will likely demand human-in-the-loop to make sure that crucial judgments are confirmed by a skilled expert. Moreover, they will adopt criteria for explainability and auditability as openness becomes vital in autonomous operations. Similarly, for autonomous learning systems, there will have to be continual compliance frameworks where regulatory checks are embedded into the design itself. The evolving role of AI in education from static compliance to dynamic governance (Schiff, 2021).

10.2 Digital Twin Regulation

Therefore, simulations and forecasts based on poor or obsolete data are likely not just to reach wrong conclusions, but also to jeopardize the learning outcomes and efficacy of institutions. The second area of particular attention is authorization and data ownership. Sometimes digital twins operate on what is effectively personal data – where we went, when, our behavioral data driven reactions and biometrics. So, let's put ownership into legislation then – ownership of our data and control over what we do with it or share? At the same time, ethics will be a key element of digital twin governance (Sholla & Reshi, 2025). People will undoubtedly need new standards, not only to develop these technologies, but to enable their use. Data retention issues Details of the person (Location History) Language accommodations for nonnative speakers of English Potential Long-term storage by entities other than Google. This implies legal standards might mean that it be clear how data is taken and used, that users must provide consent for their data to be collected & that there are constraints on how data can be used. Moreover, interoperability standards would be essential to allow smooth integration of digital twin systems across platforms and institutions. Standardization allows them to develop integrated learning environments, and that's where scalability comes in (Baaj et al., 2024).

10.3 Global Policy Harmonization

AI allows the same education to be offered across space; thus, governments must unify their rules. The EdTech solution is scalable for any collaboration across borders, but this is under danger since regulatory frameworks are significantly varied for each country. This would generate major compliance challenges, as divergence in Member State data protection legislation, AI policy and enforcement will surely result in very varied methods globally, and no universal legal framework will be established. Now we need to work on international norms and treaties that match regulatory routes. Most of the work that will influence AI in education will be conducted by global coalitions and intergovernmental organizations to produce harmonized standards for governance. They will discuss challenges of data privacy and the ethical usage of AI related to interoperability. Worldwide Harmonization (Kizilcec & Lee, 2022). To establish global data governance mechanisms to promote the transnational, secure and compliant interchange of personal information across different organizations, industries and nations. This is particularly important in relation to global lifelong learning platforms, international education and joint research. In any event, harmonization will result in some global norms and local independence. Standardization is important but standards should not be one size fits across varied cultures and laws across countries. This requires very sophisticated structures indeed, but local execution plans become necessary here too. The future of regulatory frameworks for sustainability-related issues. These policies will emphasize accessibility, high quality, and environmental sustainability to ensure that egalitarian AI-based learning systems are the right and innovative way forward in education. In light of the above, we present a framework for the responsible regulation of intelligent learning systems in order to facilitate the AI revolution through the creation of a regulatory framework (Olawade et al., 2026).

Figure 6. Future regulatory ecosystem for intelligent learning systems

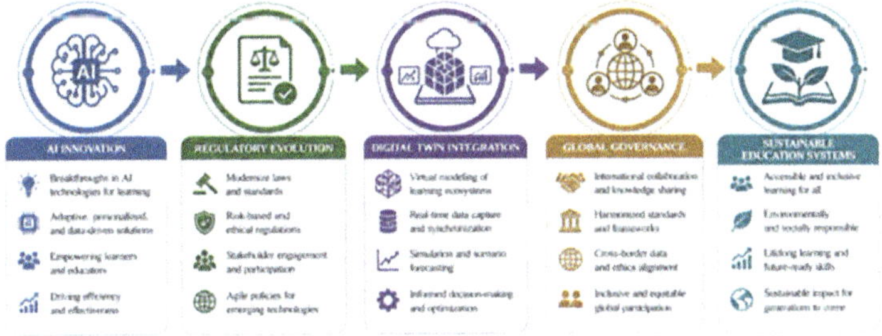

Figure-6 The future regulatory environment for intelligent learning systems. The image depicts the shift from AI innovation to regulatory evolution, digital twin integration, global governance and sustainable education systems. The image depicts how technology innovation and policy development are merging to create an integrated and future-ready educational governance structure (Ingason et al., 2025).

11. CONCLUSION

Intelligent learning technologies such as artificial intelligence and digital twins are revolutionizing current education systems through personalized learning, predictive analytics, automated assessment, and data-driven institution management. The deployment of intelligent learning technologies presents the opportunity for improving accessibility, efficiency, and learner engagement within educational institutions. At the same time, intelligent learning systems raise a series of legal, ethical, and governance issues which present new challenges for current educational regulations. The present chapter has provided evidence of the need for an integrated and interdisciplinary governance framework for the management of intelligent learning technologies, which would encompass regulatory frameworks governing the use of AI, data governance, educational policy, and institutional management. Critical issues such as algorithmic biases, decision-making, data privacy, cybersecurity, digital surveillance, and governance of digital twins have been identified during the analysis. In addition, major regulatory frameworks related to the governance of intelligent learning systems were considered, including the EU AI Act, GDPR, UNESCO guidelines on ethics, and the OECD AI principles. However, considerable regulatory gaps were observed in regard to educational digital twins and learner monitoring, and predictive educational analytics.

For this reason, future governance systems for intelligent learning systems need to place a premium on transparency, explainability, human oversight, fairness, and accountability within AI-enhanced educational systems. Educational institutions should establish a broad range of governance structures that include algorithmic audits, ethical evaluation procedures, cybersecurity measures, and effective data governance systems. Finally, the chapter highlights the significance of international cooperation regarding regulations and comparative policies. While future governance systems need to be cognizant of different national educational environments, global collaboration becomes increasingly important because educational technologies operate across borders and entail transnational data flows.

In conclusion, the governance of intelligent learning systems involves a delicate balance between technological innovations and fundamental rights, educational equality, organizational responsibility, and democracy. Future research could continue exploring the topic of regulating educational digital twins and artificial intelligence accountability, as well as its broader societal impact.

REFERENCES

Abraham, R., Schneider, J., & vom Brocke, J. (2019). Data governance: A conceptual framework, structured review, and research agenda. *International Journal of Information Management, 49*, 424–438. DOI: 10.1016/j.ijinfomgt.2019.07.008

Adams, C., Pente, P., Lemermeyer, G., & Rockwell, G. (2023). Ethical principles for artificial intelligence in K-12 education. *Computers and Education: Artificial Intelligence, 4*, 100131. DOI: 10.1016/j.caeai.2023.100131

Agarwal, B., Urlings, C., van Lankveld, G., & Klemke, R. (2026). Identifying the ethical values and norms for artificial intelligence in education: A systematic literature review. *International Journal of Artificial Intelligence in Education, 36*(1–2), 100004. DOI: 10.1016/j.ijaied.2026.100004

Amo-Filva, D., Fonseca, D., García-Peñalvo, F. J., Alier Forment, M., Casany Guerrero, M. J., & Godoy, G. (2024). Exploring the landscape of learning analytics privacy in fog and edge computing: A systematic literature review. *Computers in Human Behavior, 158*, 108303. DOI: 10.1016/j.chb.2024.108303

Attaran, M., & Celik, B. G. (2023). Digital twin: Benefits, use cases, challenges, and opportunities. *Decision Analytics Journal, 6*, 100165. DOI: 10.1016/j.dajour.2023.100165

Autili, M., Corsi, R., De Sanctis, M., Inverardi, P., & Pelliccione, P. (2026). Ethics label for digital systems to promote transparency and user awareness. *Journal of Systems and Software, 235*, 112752. DOI: 10.1016/j.jss.2025.112752

Baaj, I., Bouraoui, Z., Cornuéjols, A., Denœux, T., Destercke, S., Dubois, D., Lesot, M.-J., Marques-Silva, J., Mengin, J., Prade, H., Schockaert, S., Serrurier, M., Strauss, O., & Vrain, C. (2024). Synergies between machine learning and reasoning: An introduction by the Kay R. Amel group. *International Journal of Approximate Reasoning, 171*, 109206. DOI: 10.1016/j.ijar.2024.109206

Baker, R. S., & Hawn, A. (2022). Algorithmic bias in education. *International Journal of Artificial Intelligence in Education, 32*(4), 1052–1092. DOI: 10.1007/s40593-021-00285-9

Bankins, S., Formosa, P., Montefiore, T., Richards, D., Cenacchi, F., & McEwan, M. (2025). Virtual reality and work: Ethical and inclusion implications of facial representation in VR. *The Journal of Strategic Information Systems, 34*(4), 101937. DOI: 10.1016/j.jsis.2025.101937

Chen, X. (2025). Innovation in curriculum system for communication majors based on new media technology and big data analytics. *International Journal of Information System Modeling and Design, 16*(1), 1–26. Advance online publication. DOI: 10.4018/IJISMD.391367

Chiu, T. K. F., Xia, Q., Zhou, X., Chai, C. S., & Cheng, M. (2023). Systematic literature review on opportunities, challenges, and future research recommendations of artificial intelligence in education. *Computers and Education: Artificial Intelligence, 4*, 100118. DOI: 10.1016/j.caeai.2022.100118

Fischer, B., & Frennert, S. (2025). Towards an experiential ethics of AI and robots: A review of empirical research on human encounters. *Technological Forecasting and Social Change, 219*, 124264. DOI: 10.1016/j.techfore.2025.124264

Freccero, A., Onwunle, M., Elliott, J., Podder, N., De Oliveira, J. P., & Dewa, L. H. (2025). Students' perceptions of learning analytics for mental health support: Qualitative study. *JMIR Formative Research, 9*, v9i1e70327. Advance online publication. DOI: 10.2196/70327 PMID: 40749729

Fuller, A., Fan, Z., Day, C., & Barlow, C. (2020). Digital twin: Enabling technologies, challenges and open research. *IEEE Access : Practical Innovations, Open Solutions, 8*, 108952–108971. DOI: 10.1109/ACCESS.2020.2998358

García, Á., Bregon, A., & Martínez-Prieto, M. A. (2022). Towards a connected digital twin learning ecosystem in manufacturing: Enablers and challenges. *Computers & Industrial Engineering, 171*, 108463. DOI: 10.1016/j.cie.2022.108463

Gašević, D., Tsai, Y.-S., & Drachsler, H. (2022). Learning analytics in higher education: Stakeholders, strategy, and scale. *The Internet and Higher Education, 52*, 100833. DOI: 10.1016/j.iheduc.2021.100833

Ghallab, M. (2019). Responsible AI: Requirements and challenges. *AI Perspectives, 1*(1), 3. DOI: 10.1186/s42467-019-0003-z

He, C., Huang, Y., Lan, H., He, J., Fan, X., Zhang, D., Lin, J., Liao, M., & Wang, C. (2026). AI-assisted assessment of higher education quality: A visual analytical approach. *Visual Informatics, 100306*, 100306. Advance online publication. DOI: 10.1016/j.visinf.2026.100306

Hoel, T., & Chen, W. (2018). Privacy and data protection in learning analytics should be motivated by an educational maxim—Towards a proposal. *Research and Practice in Technology Enhanced Learning, 13*(1), 20. DOI: 10.1186/s41039-018-0086-8 PMID: 30595748

Ingason, H. T., Aaltonen, K., Asmundarson, A. S., Fridgeirsson, T. V., Huemann, D., Huemann, M., Kujala, J., Lampela, H., Mancini, M., Mariani, C., & Ringhofer, C. (2025). Personalised learning in project management education: Insights from an artificial intelligence-driven chatbot. *Project Leadership and Society*, *6*, 100193. DOI: 10.1016/j.plas.2025.100193

Jobin, A., Ienca, M., & Vayena, E. (2019). The global landscape of AI ethics guidelines. *Nature Machine Intelligence*, *1*(9), 389–399. DOI: 10.1038/s42256-019-0088-2

Khatri, V., & Brown, C. V. (2010). Designing data governance. *Communications of the ACM*, *53*(1), 148–152. DOI: 10.1145/1629175.1629210

Kizilcec, R. F., & Lee, H. (2022). Algorithmic fairness in education. In Holmes, W., & Porayska-Pomsta, K. (Eds.), *The ethics of artificial intelligence in education* (pp. 174–202). Routledge., DOI: 10.4324/9780429329067-10

Lee, S. J., & Kwon, K. (2024). A systematic review of AI education in K-12 classrooms from 2018 to 2023: Topics, strategies, and learning outcomes. *Computers and Education: Artificial Intelligence*, *6*, 100211. DOI: 10.1016/j.caeai.2024.100211

Marengo, A. (2024). Navigating the nexus of AI and IoT: A comprehensive review of data analytics and privacy paradigms. *Internet of Things : Engineering Cyber Physical Human Systems*, *27*, 101318. DOI: 10.1016/j.iot.2024.101318

Martin, F., Zhuang, M., & Schaefer, D. (2024). Systematic review of research on artificial intelligence in K–12 education. *Computers and Education: Artificial Intelligence*, *6*, 100195. DOI: 10.1016/j.caeai.2023.100195

Matos, T., Santos, W., Zdravevski, E., Coelho, P. J., Pires, I. M., & Madeira, F. (2025). A systematic review of artificial intelligence applications in education: Emerging trends and challenges. *Decision Analytics Journal*, *15*, 100571. DOI: 10.1016/j.dajour.2025.100571

Mehrabi, N., Morstatter, F., Saxena, N., Lerman, K., & Galstyan, A. (2021). A survey on bias and fairness in machine learning. *ACM Computing Surveys*, *54*(6), 1–35. DOI: 10.1145/3457607

Mei, L., Feng, X., & Cavallaro, F. (2023). Evaluate and identify the competencies of the future workforce for digital technologies implementation in higher education. *Journal of Innovation & Knowledge*, *8*(4), 100445. DOI: 10.1016/j.jik.2023.100445

Mena Guacas, A. F., Mellado-Moreno, P.-C., Calderón-Cisneros, J.-T., & Pelicano Piris, N. (2026). Mapping artificial-intelligence-driven innovation in higher education: A bibliometric review. *Social Sciences & Humanities Open*, *13*, 102561. DOI: 10.1016/j.ssaho.2026.102561

Mittelstadt, B. D. (2019). Principles alone cannot guarantee ethical AI. *Nature Machine Intelligence, 1*(11), 501–507. DOI: 10.1038/s42256-019-0114-4

Mittelstadt, B. D., Allo, P., Taddeo, M., Wachter, S., & Floridi, L. (2016). The ethics of algorithms: Mapping the debate. *Big Data & Society, 3*(2), 2053951716679679. Advance online publication. DOI: 10.1177/2053951716679679

Munir, H., Vogel, B., & Jacobsson, A. (2022). Artificial intelligence and machine learning approaches in digital education: A systematic revision. *Information (Basel), 13*(4), 203. DOI: 10.3390/info13040203

Okita, S. Y. (2024). Digital twins in education. In Peters, M. A., & Heraud, R. (Eds.), *Encyclopedia of educational innovation*. Springer., DOI: 10.1007/978-981-13-2262-4_282-1

Olawade, D. B., David-Olawade, A. C., Aderinto, N., & Wada, O. Z. (2026). Ethical oversight of artificial intelligence in Nigerian healthcare: A qualitative analysis of ethics committee members' perspectives on integration and regulation. *International Journal of Medical Informatics, 206*, 106140. DOI: 10.1016/j.ijmedinf.2025.106140 PMID: 41092592

Papagiannidis, E., Mikalef, P., & Conboy, K. (2025). Responsible artificial intelligence governance: A review and research framework. *The Journal of Strategic Information Systems, 34*(2), 101885. DOI: 10.1016/j.jsis.2024.101885

Prinsloo, P., & Slade, S. (2017). An elephant in the learning analytics room: The obligation to act. *Proceedings of the Seventh International Learning Analytics & Knowledge Conference*, 46–55. https://doi.org/DOI: 10.1145/3027385.3027406

Prinsloo, P., & Slade, S. (2017). Ethics and learning analytics: Charting the uncharted. Handbook of Learning Analytics, 49–57. https://doi.org/DOI: 10.18608/hla17.004

Rahman, A., Khan, M. A., Mahmud, F. U., Bishnu, K. K., Rahman, A., Mridha, M. F., & Hossen, M. J. (2026). A systematic literature review on the impact of generative AI in digital marketing: Advancements, opportunities, and challenges. *Computers, Materials & Continua, 87*(3), 1–10. Advance online publication. DOI: 10.32604/cmc.2026.071029

Raji, I. D., Smart, A., White, R. N., Mitchell, M., Gebru, T., Hutchinson, B., Smith-Loud, J., Theron, D., & Barnes, P. (2020). Closing the AI accountability gap: Defining an end-to-end framework for internal algorithmic auditing. *Proceedings of the 2020 Conference on Fairness, Accountability, and Transparency*, 33–44. https://doi.org/ DOI: 10.1145/3351095.3372873

Regan, P. M., & Jesse, J. (2019). Ethical challenges of edtech, big data and personalized learning: Twenty-first century student sorting and tracking. *Ethics and Information Technology*, *21*(3), 167–179. https://link.springer.com/article/10.1007/s10676-018-9492-2. DOI: 10.1007/s10676-018-9492-2

Samala, A. D., Rawas, S., Zainuddin, Z., Howard, N.-J., & Shilina, S. (2025). The role of non-fungible tokens in education: A comprehensive review and future directions. *Social Sciences & Humanities Open*, *12*, 101834. DOI: 10.1016/j.ssaho.2025.101834

Schiff, D. (2021). Education for AI, not AI for education: The role of education and ethics in national AI policy strategies. *International Journal of Artificial Intelligence in Education*, *32*(3), 527–563. DOI: 10.1007/s40593-021-00270-2

Sholla, S., & Reshi, I. A. (2025). Ethical reasoning in technology: Using computational approaches to integrate ethics into AI systems. Journal of Information. *Communication and Ethics in Society*, *24*(1), 4–22. DOI: 10.1108/JICES-03-2024-0024

Slade, S., & Prinsloo, P. (2013). Learning analytics: Ethical issues and dilemmas. *The American Behavioral Scientist*, *57*(10), 1510–1529. DOI: 10.1177/0002764213479366

Smith, Brian. (2019). The Promise of Artificial Intelligence: Reckoning and Judgment. https://doi.org/DOI: 10.7551/mitpress/12385.001.0001

Smuha, N. A. (2021). From a "race to AI" to a "race to AI regulation": Regulatory competition for artificial intelligence. *Law, Innovation and Technology*, *13*(1), 57–84. DOI: 10.1080/17579961.2021.1898300

Tan, S. C., Lee, A. V. Y., & Lee, M. (2022). A systematic review of artificial intelligence techniques for collaborative learning over the past two decades. *Computers and Education: Artificial Intelligence*, *3*, 100097. DOI: 10.1016/j.caeai.2022.100097

Tao, F., Zhang, H., Liu, A., & Nee, A. Y. C. (2019). Digital twin in industry: State-of-the-art. *IEEE Transactions on Industrial Informatics*, *15*(4), 2405–2415. DOI: 10.1109/TII.2018.2873186

Veale, M., & Borgesius, F. Z. (2021). Demystifying the Draft EU Artificial Intelligence Act. *Computer Law Review International*, *22*(4), 97–112. DOI: 10.9785/cri-2021-220402

Vial, G. (2019). Understanding digital transformation: A review and a research agenda. *The Journal of Strategic Information Systems*, *28*(2), 118–144. DOI: 10.1016/j.jsis.2019.01.003

Wachter, S., Mittelstadt, B., & Floridi, L. (2017). Why a right to explanation of automated decision-making does not exist in the General Data Protection Regulation. *International Data Privacy Law*, *7*(2), 76–99. DOI: 10.1093/idpl/ipx005

Wang, S., Wang, F., Zhu, Z., Wang, J., Tran, T., & Du, Z. (2024). Artificial intelligence in education: A systematic literature review. *Expert Systems with Applications*, *252*, 124167. DOI: 10.1016/j.eswa.2024.124167

Williamson, B. (2016). Digital education governance: Data visualization, predictive analytics, and "real-time" policy instruments. *Journal of Education Policy*, *31*(2), 123–141. DOI: 10.1080/02680939.2015.1035758

Williamson, B., & Eynon, R. (2020). Historical threads, missing links, and future directions in AI in education. *Learning, Media and Technology*, *45*(3), 223–235. DOI: 10.1080/17439884.2020.1798995

Yu, F., Lv, J., Han, H., Zhang, Y., & Zhang, J. (2025). Application of AI teaching assistant to college education of principles of chemical engineering. *Education for Chemical Engineers*, *53*, 138–148. DOI: 10.1016/j.ece.2025.08.004

Zawacki-Richter, O., Marín, V. I., Bond, M., & Gouverneur, F. (2019). Systematic review of research on artificial intelligence applications in higher education. *International Journal of Educational Technology in Higher Education*, *16*(39), 39. https://link.springer.com/article/10.1186/s41239-019-0171-0. DOI: 10.1186/s41239-019-0171-0

Chapter 11

The Hypersituated Learner and the Digital Twin:
Personalisation, Autonomy, and AI Governance

Filipe T. Moreira
http://orcid.org/0000-0002-3461-9827
inED, Escola Superior de Educação, Instituto Politécnico do Porto, Portugal

Sara Martins
http://orcid.org/0009-0001-5335-6241
DigiMedia, DeCA, Universidade de Aveiro, Portugal

ABSTRACT

The convergence of artificial intelligence, the Internet of Things, and digital twin technology is creating the conditions for a new paradigm in education: hypersituated learning. This chapter argues that the learner's digital twin is the infrastructural condition through which hypersituated learning becomes pedagogically coherent at scale. By integrating cognitive profiles, behavioural patterns, and real-time contextual data, the learner's digital twin enables continuous, situated, and proactive personalisation across lifelong learning pathways. However, this convergence carries a structural tension: the same architecture that enables personalisation simultaneously enables continuous observation, algorithmic inference, and control. Drawing on surveillance capitalism, algorithmic governmentality, and the philosophy of technology, the chapter examines the conditions under which this paradigm serves cognitive emancipation rather than heteronomy, proposing a governance framework built on pedagogical intentionality, algorithmic transparency, and democratic oversight.

DOI: 10.4018/979-8-2600-1674-9.ch011

INTRODUCTION

The rapid evolution of digital technologies is reshaping the foundations of education in ways that exceed mere methodological innovation. What is at stake is not a new set of tools for delivering existing content, but a fundamental reconceptualisation of what learning is, how it unfolds over time, and what relationship it establishes between the individual and the world. The NMC Horizon Report of 2015, one of the most widely cited prospective documents in educational technology, identified the Internet of Things as one of the emerging forces likely to transform educational practice within the following decade, introducing in that context the notion of hypersituated learning as a condition in which the physical environment itself becomes a source of real-time, contextualised information for the learner. A decade later, that prospect is no longer speculative. The technical conditions for its realisation are increasingly in place, and the question has shifted from whether hypersituated learning is possible to what kind of system would be required to sustain it, and at what cost.

Among the technologies now capable of operationalising this vision, the digital twin of the learner stands out as the most structurally adequate. Originally developed in engineering and industrial design, the digital twin concept describes a dynamic virtual model of a physical entity, continuously updated through real-time data flows, capable of simulation, prediction, and optimisation (Grieves & Vickers, 2017). Subsequent research has mapped its defining characteristics across domains, identifying real-time data synchronisation, bidirectional communication between physical and virtual entities, and predictive modelling capacity as its core attributes (Barricelli et al., 2019). Transposed into education, the learner's digital twin becomes a persistent, evolving representation that integrates cognitive profiles, behavioural patterns, contextual data, and skill trajectories into a single model, one that does not merely reflect the current state of the individual but anticipates future states and enables proactive, personalised educational decision-making.

Such a convergence, however, is not without its complications. The same architecture that enables a learning environment to respond to the individual with unprecedented precision is simultaneously an architecture of continuous observation, data extraction, and algorithmic inference. Zuboff (2019) has described the logic underlying contemporary digital platforms as surveillance capitalism, a regime in which human experience is transformed into raw material for behavioural prediction and economic value. Crawford (2021) has shown that AI systems are never neutral instruments: they are material, social, and political artefacts that reflect the choices, interests, and power relations of those who design and control them. Holmes, Bialik, and Fadel (2019) have similarly cautioned that the deployment of AI in educational contexts requires careful examination of the assumptions embedded in system design, particularly regarding whose values and whose conception of learning the system encodes. Rouvroy and Berns (2013) had earlier developed the concept of algorithmic governmentality to describe a mode of power that operates not through explicit norms or conscious deliberation, but through the continuous modulation of behaviour based on profiles, probabilities, and correlations. Applied to a digital twin-driven learning system, these frameworks converge on a single, uncomfortable insight: the infrastructure that makes hypersituated learning possible is also the infrastructure that makes the learner legible, predictable, and governable in ways that may serve interests other than the learner's own.

Acknowledging this tension is not a reason to abandon the paradigm. It is a reason to examine it carefully, and to insist that the governance of digital twin-driven learning systems be treated as a question of the same order of importance as their technical design. Winner (1980) argued, in a foundational contribution to the philosophy of technology, that artefacts have politics, that the architecture of a system encodes decisions about who benefits, who is excluded, and who bears the risks. Lessig (1999) extended this insight to digital environments, observing that in spaces structured by code, what is technically possible becomes what is permitted, and what is technically foreclosed becomes what is prohibited, without any explicit legislative act. A learning environment structured by algorithmic code is therefore always already a political environment, and the question of who controls the code is inseparable from the question of what kind of learner the system is designed to produce.

Methodologically, this chapter is a theoretical and conceptual analysis. It does not report empirical findings or present the results of an experimental study. Its approach is the critical synthesis of existing literature across three intersecting fields: educational theory, digital twin technology, and the philosophy and governance of AI systems. Such an approach is appropriate to the contribution being made, since the relationship between hypersituated learning and the digital twin of the learner has not yet been systematically theorised in the literature, and establishing that theoretical foundation is a necessary precondition for the empirical and design work that must follow. Drawing on scholarship from educational philosophy, computer science, surveillance studies, and political philosophy reflects the nature of the object of analysis: an AI-driven learning system that continuously models and shapes the individual across a lifetime is a phenomenon that no single disciplinary lens can adequately examine. Against this background, the chapter makes three distinct contributions to the literature. First, it proposes an original conceptual framework that positions hypersituation as the pedagogical condition and the digital twin as its technical infrastructure, offering the first systematic theorisation of their relationship in the context of lifelong learning. Second, it identifies and analyses the structural tension between personalisation and algorithmic control that this convergence necessarily generates, drawing on critical frameworks from surveillance studies, political philosophy, and AI ethics to name what existing technical accounts of educational digital twins typically leave unexamined. Third, it derives from this analysis a governance framework articulated around three operative principles, pedagogical intentionality, algorithmic transparency, and democratic oversight, translating theoretical critique into actionable orientations for designers, educators, institutions, and policy-makers.

Structured around these objectives, the chapter begins by establishing the conceptual foundations of hypersituation, clarifying its relationship to adjacent concepts and introducing the critical distinction between a hypersituated environment and a hypersituated experience. It then examines the digital twin as a model of the learner, exploring both its technical logic and its pedagogical implications. An analysis of the structural tension between personalisation and control follows, drawing on the critical frameworks already introduced. A governance model for ethically grounded digital twin-driven lifelong learning is subsequently proposed, before the chapter addresses its practical implications for designers, educators, and policy-makers. The conclusion reflects on what this paradigm reveals about the broader relationship between intelligent systems and human development in an age increasingly shaped by algorithmic mediation.

HYPERSITUATION: CONCEPTUAL FOUNDATIONS

Few concepts in recent educational technology literature have arrived with as little definitional grounding as hypersituation. Introduced through the NMC Horizon Report of 2015 in connection with the educational potential of the Internet of Things, the term described a condition in which learners would be able to access layers of information about their immediate physical environment in real time, transforming the space around them into an active participant in the learning process. Despite its evident ambition, hypersituation arrived without a rigorous definition, functioning more as a placeholder for emerging possibilities than as a fully elaborated concept. What follows seeks to provide that elaboration, situating hypersituation within the intellectual traditions from which it draws meaning and clarifying what distinguishes it from adjacent concepts with which it is frequently and mistakenly conflated.

Unpacking the term etymologically helps clarify what is at stake. The prefix hyper derives from the Greek for above, beyond, or in excess of, while situation refers to the ensemble of circumstances, relations, and meanings that characterise a particular moment in a particular place. Taken together, hypersituation suggests a condition in which the situation is not replaced or transcended but amplified, layered with additional dimensions of interpretation that extend what the individual is capable of perceiving and understanding within a given context. Far from being a trivial semantic point, this etymology defines the ontological status of hypersituation and distinguishes it from other technological conditions that have been described using the same prefix.

Foremost among these distinctions is the one that separates hypersituation from hyperreality. Eco (1986) characterised hyperreality as a condition in which technology produces representations so complete and so compelling that they displace rather than supplement the original. In hyperreality, the copy becomes more real than the real, and the individual's experience is organised around simulations that have severed their connection to the physical world. Baofu (2009) extended this analysis by examining the risks of a culture in which simulation progressively dominates lived experience, eroding the individual's capacity to distinguish between the constructed and the actual. Hypersituation operates on an entirely different logic: it does not sever the individual's connection to the physical world but deepens it. The data that a hypersituated environment makes available are not simulations of reality but measurements of it, collected in real time from the environment itself and returned to the individual in a form that is contextualised, semantically structured, and responsive to their particular situation. The physical world remains the anchor; what changes is the richness and depth with which it can be interpreted.

A more productive analogy is offered by the concept of hypertext. Smith and Weiss (1988) described hypertext as a form of textual organisation that introduces flexibility and non-linearity into the act of reading, allowing the reader to navigate between nodes of information according to their own interests and associations rather than following a single prescribed sequence. The text does not change; what changes is the range of paths through which it can be traversed. Hypersituation applies an analogous logic to the experience of physical reality: the environment does not change, but what changes is the range of interpretive layers through which it can be accessed. Reality becomes, in this sense, navigable, open to multiple readings depending on the needs, interests, and purposes of the individual who inhabits it.

It is worth noting that hypersituation has appeared in other intellectual contexts with a related but distinct meaning. Declerck, Reed, and Bert (2006), writing in linguistics, used the concept to describe present situations that result from the convergence of multiple past events, each temporally distant from the others but each contributing to the configuration of the current moment. While different from the usage developed here, this reading introduces into the concept a temporal dimension that is directly relevant to lifelong learning: the learner's current situation is always the product of a history, and a system capable of modelling that history can make the present more legible precisely because it carries the past within it.

Beyond its novelty as a technological concept, hypersituation resonates deeply with a tradition of thought in educational theory that has long argued for the primacy of situatedness in learning. Lave and Wenger (1991) demonstrated that learning is not a process of acquiring abstract knowledge that is subsequently applied to concrete situations, but a process of participation in communities of practice where knowledge and the contexts of its use are inseparable. Brown, Collins, and Duguid (1989) argued similarly that cognition is always situated, that concepts are not free-floating abstractions but tools whose meaning is shaped by the activity in which they are used and the culture in which that activity is embedded. Understood as a condition that makes the environment legible in real time, hypersituation can be read as a technological extension of this tradition: it does not import abstract knowledge into the situation but makes the situation itself a source of knowledge, continuous, immediate, and responsive.

Realising hypersituation as a learning condition requires a specific technical infrastructure. At its foundation lies the Internet of Things, which provides the capacity to instrument physical environments with sensors capable of collecting continuous, granular data about the state of the world. Above this layer, semantic web technologies and ontological models provide the capacity to structure that data, relate it to other bodies of knowledge, and assign it meaning in relation to the context of the learner. Without this semantic layer, the environment may be data-rich but informationally impoverished: raw data does not teach; only data that has been organised, contextualised, and made meaningful can do that.

A distinction of considerable importance for the rest of this chapter must be introduced at this point. A hypersituated environment and a hypersituated experience are not the same thing, and conflating the two has been responsible for much of the conceptual imprecision surrounding the term. An environment may be technically equipped to deliver contextualised, real-time information to a learner without that learner's experience being, in any meaningful sense, hypersituated. For the experience to be genuinely hypersituated, the learner must actively engage with the information the environment offers, interpret it in relation to their existing knowledge and purposes, and integrate it into an evolving understanding of the situation they inhabit. Intentionality is required on the part of the learner, and the information must be organised according to a narrative that makes the data meaningful rather than merely present. A learner who receives data without a framework for interpretation is not hypersituated; they are overwhelmed.

Carrying this distinction into the domain of system design has important consequences. Technical capacity to collect and deliver real-time environmental data is a necessary but not sufficient condition for hypersituated learning. What is equally necessary is a pedagogical architecture that structures the learner's engagement with that data, preserving the cognitive effort that makes learning irreducible to information retrieval. How the digital twin of the learner can serve as the connecting mechanism between the environment's capacity to deliver situated information and the learner's capacity to transform that information into knowledge is the subject of the following section.

THE DIGITAL TWIN AS A LEARNER'S MIRROR

Engineering, not education, gave the digital twin its first systematic formulation. Generally attributed to Grieves, the concept emerged from the field of product life-cycle management as a method for creating a persistent virtual model of a physical object, continuously updated through real-time data flows and capable of supporting simulation, analysis, and optimisation without requiring intervention in the physical system itself (Grieves & Vickers, 2017). Barricelli, Casiraghi, and Fogli (2019) offer one of the most comprehensive surveys of its subsequent development, identifying three defining properties that any genuine digital twin must exhibit: a persistent virtual model that mirrors the physical entity's current state, a real-time data connection that keeps the model continuously updated, and a simulation capacity that enables the modelling of conditions that have not yet occurred. In industrial contexts, this logic has proven extraordinarily productive, enabling manufacturers to predict failures, optimise performance, and extend the operational life of complex systems at a level of precision that periodic inspection or aggregate data analysis could never achieve.

Its productive reach has already been demonstrated well beyond these industrial origins. In the field of heritage conservation, virtual models of historic buildings enhanced with real-time monitoring data and weathering simulation have proven capable of supporting maintenance planning and degradation forecasting with a precision that periodic inspection alone cannot achieve (Pocobelli et al., 2018). Such an extension of the paradigm to domains concerned with the long-term preservation of complex, historically layered entities anticipates, in important ways, its application to the learner, whose development is equally continuous, equally context-dependent, and equally resistant to reduction to a single static representation.

Transposing this paradigm to education is neither straightforward nor without risk. A turbine and a learner are not analogous entities, and a framework developed for the optimisation of mechanical systems cannot be applied to the development of human beings without substantial reconceptualisation. Unlike a machine whose performance can be improved by adjusting parameters, the learner is a subject whose development involves dimensions that resist quantification: motivation, identity, the capacity for ethical judgement, and the ability to tolerate uncertainty and revise one's understanding in the light of new evidence. Any account of the learner's digital twin that reduces these dimensions to data points has already misunderstood what education is for. The productive question is not whether the digital twin can model the learner completely, but what aspects of the learner's situation it can illuminate, and under what conditions that illumination serves the learner's development rather than substituting for it.

What a learner's digital twin can model, at least in principle, is substantial. At the most immediate level, it can integrate data about the learner's current cognitive state: which concepts have been encountered, which have been mastered, which remain unstable, and which are simply absent. It can track behavioural patterns across time and context, identifying the conditions under which engagement is sustained and those under which attention fragments. It can incorporate contextual data from the learner's environment, connecting the learner's profile to the situations in which learning actually occurs rather than treating learning as a context-independent process that unfolds identically regardless of where and when it takes place. And it can model the learner's skill trajectory, mapping the distance between current competencies and those that the educational or professional context requires, enabling the kind of proactive, anticipatory guidance that reactive assessment cannot provide.

Directly relevant to the project of lifelong learning is the digital twin's prospective rather than retrospective orientation. Traditional educational assessment measures what the learner has already done and assigns a value to it. By contrast, the digital twin models where the learner is going, updating its projections continuously as new data becomes available. Far from being merely a technical improvement on existing practice, this shift represents a reconceptualisation of the relationship between learner and educational system: one in which the system is no longer a set of fixed checkpoints the learner passes through at prescribed intervals but a continuous companion, adjusting its support to evolving needs and circumstances across the full arc of a lifetime.

Where hypersituation and the digital twin converge most clearly is in the question of calibration. A hypersituated learning environment enriches the learner's immediate situation with contextualised, real-time information drawn from the physical world. For that enrichment to be genuinely educational rather than merely informational, however, it must be calibrated to the learner's current state of understanding, their prior knowledge, their conceptual frameworks, and their immediate learning goals. Without this calibration, the environment delivers data that may be accurate but is not situated with respect to the learner's particular position in their development. Providing precisely that calibration is what the digital twin makes possible: it is the mechanism through which the environment's capacity to deliver real-time, contextualised information is aligned with the learner's capacity to make sense of it. In this respect, the digital twin does not merely support hypersituated learning; it is the condition of its pedagogical coherence.

Vygotsky's concept of the zone of proximal development offers a useful theoretical frame here (Vygotsky, 1978). For Vygotsky, effective learning occurs not at the level of what the learner can already do independently, but in the space between independent competence and what the learner can achieve with appropriate support. A learner's digital twin, continuously modelling the boundary between established and emergent competence, is in a position to identify this zone with a precision and continuity that no human teacher operating across a large group of learners could sustain. Bloom (1984) demonstrated that one-to-one tutoring consistently produces learning outcomes significantly superior to those achieved through conventional group instruction, attributing this advantage primarily to the immediate identification of each learner's specific gaps and the rapid adjustment of instruction to address them. Understood in this light, the digital twin can be read as a technological response to the problem Bloom identified: how to deliver the benefits of individualised instruction at a scale that makes them available beyond the small minority who have access to private tutoring.

Resisting an interpretation of the digital twin as a substitute for the learner's own cognitive agency is, however, essential. The zone of proximal development is not simply a gap to be filled by an external system. It is a space of productive struggle, in which the learner develops not only the specific knowledge or skill in question but the broader capacity for independent thought and self-directed inquiry. A digital twin-driven system that fills this space too completely, anticipating every difficulty before it can generate productive effort and delivering answers before the learner has had the opportunity to formulate questions, risks optimising immediate performance at the cost of longer-term development as an autonomous thinker. This risk is not hypothetical: it is the specific form that the structural tension between personalisation and control takes when examined from the perspective of cognitive development, and it is the subject of the section that follows.

Ultimately, the digital twin of the learner is not a mirror in the simple sense of a passive reflection. Rather, it is a dynamic model that simultaneously records what the learner is, anticipates what the learner might become, and shapes the conditions under which that becoming occurs. This triple function, descriptive, predictive, and prescriptive, is what gives the digital twin its extraordinary potential as an instrument of lifelong learning, and what makes the question of its governance so urgent. A model that describes is a representation. A model that predicts is an inference. A model that prescribes is a form of power. The learner's digital twin does all three, often simultaneously, and the boundaries between these functions are rarely transparent to the learner themselves. Figure 1 illustrates the architecture of this system, showing the flow from data inputs through the digital twin to learning outputs, and the governance framework within which the entire process must operate.

Figure 1. Architecture of a hypersituated digital twin-driven learning system

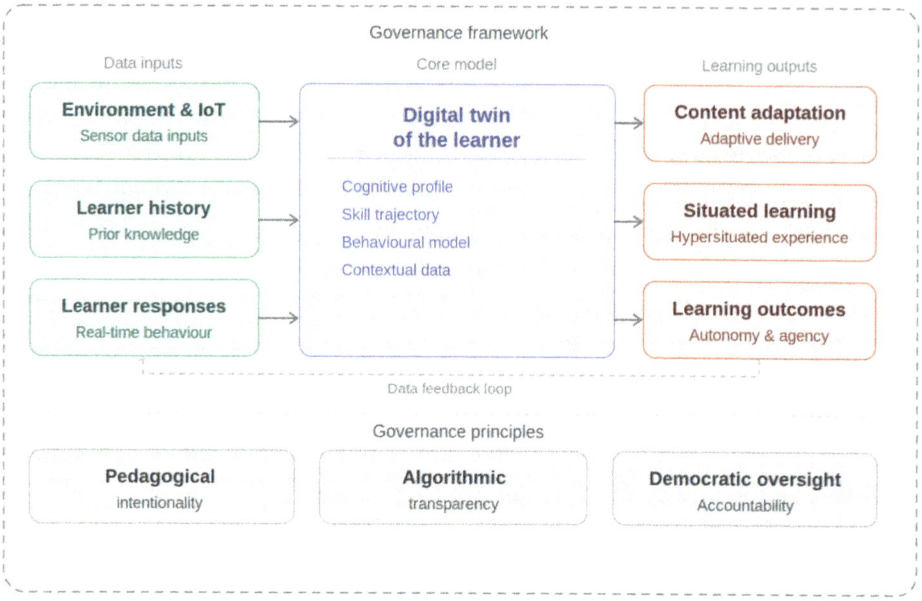

THE STRUCTURAL TENSION: PERSONALISATION VS. CONTROL

There is a tension internal to the digital twin paradigm that no degree of technical sophistication can dissolve, and that any educationally serious engagement with it must confront directly. The digital twin can only personalise the learner's experience to the degree that it has modelled the learner in depth, and it can only build that model by collecting, storing, and processing data about the learner's behaviour, cognition, environment, and responses over time. Personalisation, in this paradigm, is not a gift freely given. It is purchased with legibility, and the price is paid continuously, often without the learner's full awareness of what is being exchanged.

Zuboff (2019) has provided the most rigorous account of the logic underlying this exchange in contemporary digital systems. Surveillance capitalism transforms human experience into raw material for the production of behavioural predictions, which are then traded in markets that deal in human futures. The learner in a digital twin-driven system occupies a structurally analogous position: the system offers personalised, adaptive, continuously calibrated support, while the learner generates a continuous stream of behavioural, cognitive, and contextual data processed by systems whose inner workings are typically opaque and whose outputs may serve purposes well beyond the learner's immediate educational interests. Regan and Jesse (2019) have examined precisely this dynamic in educational technology contexts, arguing that personalised learning systems frequently reproduce, and may intensify, existing inequalities by sorting and tracking learners according to criteria that are neither transparent nor easily contestable.

Beyond explicitly commercial platforms, even educational systems developed with genuine public interest motivations are not immune to the structural pressures that Zuboff identifies. Data collected for pedagogical purposes can be repurposed for administrative benchmarking, institutional performance metrics, labour market intelligence, or access to credit and insurance. Williamson (2017) has documented how the growing infrastructure of educational data collection creates conditions in which the learner's digital record functions as a form of capital, one that accumulates over time and can be deployed across institutional contexts in ways that the learner neither controls nor fully anticipates. In a lifelong learning system, this possibility is not marginal. It is a design feature, and its implications for learner autonomy must be addressed at the level of governance rather than left to the discretionary practices of individual institutions.

Crawford (2021) has shown that AI systems are material, social, and political artefacts whose apparent neutrality conceals the choices embedded in their design. When a digital twin-driven environment contextualises the information delivered to a learner, that contextualisation reflects decisions about what counts as relevant, which sources are privileged, and what narrative is constructed around the data. These decisions are made by system designers, shaped by institutional and commercial contexts, and encoded into the architecture in ways that are rarely visible to the learners or educators who work within them. Berendt, Littlejohn, and Blakemore (2020) have extended this analysis by arguing that the deployment of AI in education raises fundamental questions about learner rights, since automated systems that determine what individuals encounter and how they are assessed may operate in ways that are formally compliant with existing regulations but substantively incompatible with educational values of openness and critical inquiry.

As noted earlier in this chapter, Winner (1980) established that the design of a technical system encodes decisions about who benefits and who bears risk, and Lessig (1999) extended this insight to digital environments by demonstrating that code functions as a form of regulation prior to any explicit legislative act. In algorithmic learning systems, these arguments converge on a specific implication: the architecture of the digital twin constitutes a curriculum before any curriculum document has been written, determining in advance what the learner encounters, in what sequence, and within what interpretive frame. Tsai, Perrotta, and Gasevic (2020) have brought this concern into direct contact with learning analytics research, showing that personalised learning approaches frequently constrain learner agency rather than expanding it, and that genuine empowerment of the learner requires not only that the system adapts to the individual but that the individual can interrogate, challenge, and revise the system's determinations in collaboration with educators.

Pasquale (2015) identified opacity as the defining feature of algorithmic power: systems that produce consequential outputs without making their internal logic available for scrutiny are systems that cannot be held to account. Research in explainable AI has subsequently sought to address this technically, developing methods for making algorithmic decisions interpretable to non-expert users (Arrieta et al., 2020). In educational contexts, however, technical explainability is a necessary but not sufficient condition for genuine transparency. A learner who is told that the system has identified a gap in their understanding of a concept has received an explanation. A learner who can interrogate the basis on which that determination was made, challenge it, and revise it in collaboration with a teacher has been accorded something qualitatively different: the epistemic standing of a subject rather than the passive status of an object of optimisation.

Rouvroy and Berns (2013) characterised this mode of power as algorithmic governmentality: a form of regulation that operates not through explicit norms or coercion but through the continuous modulation of the environment in which individuals act, shaping the space of possible action before conduct has even occurred. In a digital twin-driven learning environment, this mode of governance achieves a particular efficiency. The environment feels responsive and personalised, and the learner who experiences it as such encounters no obvious point of resistance, because the constraint is not visible as a constraint. It arrives in the form of assistance.

Literary imagination has long anticipated these conditions. Orwell (1949) envisioned control through visible coercion and deliberate terror; Stephenson (1992) imagined a different mechanism entirely, one in which a sufficiently immersive and personalised environment produced conformity not by threatening deviation but by rendering it cognitively unnecessary. The second model is more directly relevant to the digital twin paradigm. Anders (1956/2013) offered a philosophical account of why this risk is structural rather than incidental: when human beings are surrounded by systems of greater precision and reliability than their own cognitive processes, the tendency is not to resist those systems but to defer to them, progressively outsourcing the cognitive effort that constitutes independent thought. The danger in educational AI is not that the learner will be forbidden from thinking, but that the system will think so efficiently on the learner's behalf that the capacity for independent reasoning is never fully developed.

At stake, ultimately, is a question about the conditions under which autonomous subjectivity can form. Arendt (1973) identified the erosion of independent judgement as a precondition for the most dangerous forms of social conformity; a learning environment that responds before the individual questions, that frames before the individual perceives, and that concludes before the individual reasons does not require controlling intent to produce effects that are, at the level of cognitive formation, structurally analogous. Selwyn (2019) has argued that the relationship between AI systems and educational institutions is never simply technical: it is always also a relationship between forms of knowledge, forms of authority, and visions of human development. The UNESCO Recommendation on the Ethics of Artificial Intelligence (2021) recognises this risk explicitly, calling for AI systems in education to be designed in ways that reinforce rather than diminish learner autonomy and that remain subordinate to human educational judgement at every consequential point.

Jonas (1984) argued that the expanded reach of modern technology demands an ethics of responsibility commensurate with the scale and duration of its effects. The digital twin of the learner operates precisely at this scale, modelling the individual across the full arc of a lifetime and accumulating effects that no single intervention, however well designed, can fully anticipate or reverse. Establishing a governance framework adequate to these stakes is therefore not a secondary consideration, to be addressed once the technical architecture has been finalised. It is the primary design question, and the section that follows argues for an approach grounded in three operative principles: pedagogical intentionality, algorithmic transparency, and democratic oversight.

THE HYPERSITUATED ENVIRONMENT VS. THE HYPERSITUATED EXPERIENCE

Running through the arguments developed in the preceding sections is a distinction that has remained implicit and that must now be examined directly: the distinction between a hypersituated environment and a hypersituated experience. Conflating the two leads almost inevitably to systems that are technically impressive and pedagogically hollow, and unpacking the difference between them has direct consequences for how such systems should be designed and what they can realistically be expected to achieve.

A hypersituated environment is a technical achievement. It requires instrumented physical spaces, real-time data flows, semantic architectures capable of contextualising information according to the profile of the individual learner, and a digital twin sophisticated enough to calibrate what is delivered and when. All of this can be built, and much of it already exists in prototype or partial form. None of it, however, by itself produces a hypersituated experience. The environment creates the conditions for such an experience. Whether the experience actually occurs depends on something no technical system can guarantee: the active, intentional engagement of the learner with what the environment makes available.

Consider a thought experiment. Two learners enter the same instrumented environment. Both have digital twins that model their cognitive profiles, their prior knowledge, and their current learning objectives. Both receive contextualised, semantically structured information about the space they inhabit. The first learner engages with that information actively, questions it, connects it to what they already know, and uses it to revise or deepen their understanding of the situation they are in. The second receives the same information passively, without interrogating it, without connecting it to prior knowledge, and without allowing it to generate the productive disorientation that precedes genuine understanding. The environment is identical. The experience is entirely different. Only the first learner has had a hypersituated experience; the second has simply been in a hypersituated environment.

This distinction is not merely a pedagogical nicety. It has direct consequences for the assumptions that should be resisted when designing digital twin-driven learning systems. The most seductive of these assumptions is that a sufficiently sophisticated system, one that knows the learner well enough and models their state with sufficient precision, can guarantee the quality of the learning experience by optimising the information delivered to them. That assumption is false, and its falseness matters. Learning is not a process of receiving well-calibrated information. It is a process of constructing meaning, and construction requires effort, resistance, and the willingness to remain in a state of uncertainty long enough for understanding to form. A system that eliminates uncertainty in the name of personalisation has not enhanced learning; it has replaced it with something that resembles learning from the outside but lacks its essential character. Ouyang and Jiao (2021), in their analysis of the three paradigms through which AI has been applied to education, argue that the most productive of these is the augmentation paradigm, which positions AI as an instrument for expanding learner capability rather than a substitute for learner effort, and that this distinction must be embedded in design choices rather than assumed to follow from them automatically.

Dewey (1938) argued that not all experience is educative, and that the difference between an educative and a non-educative experience lies not in the quantity or quality of the information it contains but in the degree to which it engages the individual's capacity for reflective thought and connects to subsequent experience in ways that expand rather than contract the individual's range of possible action. A hypersituated environment that delivers accurately calibrated information without creating the conditions for reflective engagement produces experience in the trivial sense of something that happens to the learner, not experience in the educative sense of something that transforms the learner's relationship to the world.

Narrative plays a critical role here. Data, however accurate, contextualised, and precisely calibrated to the learner's profile, does not interpret itself. It requires a framework that organises it into something meaningful, that connects individual data points to larger patterns of understanding, and that orients the learner's attention towards the questions that the data is capable of answering. This narrative function cannot be discharged by the digital twin alone. The twin can model what the learner knows and what the learner needs; it can identify the moment at which a particular piece of information is likely to be meaningful. However, the active construction of a narrative around that information, the work of connecting new data to existing understanding and placing it within a developing arc of inquiry, is a cognitive act that belongs to the learner. Panadero (2017), in a comprehensive review of self-regulated learning models, demonstrates that the capacity to construct coherent frameworks around new information, to monitor one's own understanding, and to revise prior knowledge in the light of new evidence is not a fixed trait but a learnable set of strategies whose development depends on being placed in conditions that require and reward their exercise.

What a digital twin-driven learning environment must therefore preserve, and what pedagogical design in such environments must deliberately create, are precisely those conditions. Luckin and Cukurova (2019) have argued that intelligent partnership between human learners and AI systems works best when the AI enhances the learner's awareness of their own cognitive processes rather than managing those processes on the learner's behalf. This is a design principle as much as a theoretical claim: a digital twin that surfaces what the learner does not yet know and poses questions rather than supplying answers is a more educationally valuable system than one that identifies gaps and fills them automatically. Friction, in this context, is not a defect to be engineered away. It is the medium in which learning occurs.

Returning to the core distinction illuminates a specific risk examined in the preceding section from a different angle: the risk that a sufficiently responsive system produces cognitive passivity by eliminating the very conditions under which active meaning-making becomes necessary. Biesta (2006) has argued that reducing education to learning, understood as the satisfaction of pre-existing needs and the acquisition of pre-specified competencies, represents a fundamental misunderstanding of what education is for. Education, in his account, is the process by which individuals are brought into contact with what is other than themselves, with content, perspectives, and demands that exceed their current frameworks and require those frameworks to be expanded or revised in response. A hypersituated learning environment perfectly calibrated to the learner's existing profile risks producing exactly the kind of learning that Biesta identifies as educationally insufficient: learning that confirms and extends what the learner already is, rather than learning that challenges the learner to become something they are not yet.

What constitutes a genuinely hypersituated experience, then, is not a perfectly responsive environment. It is an environment that creates the conditions for the learner to respond to the world with greater depth, curiosity, and independence. The digital twin serves this purpose not by modelling the learner so completely that the system can anticipate every need, but by modelling the learner precisely enough to identify the moments at which productive challenge is possible and the moments at which support is genuinely required. The difference between these two functions, between a system that enables and one that substitutes, is the difference between an educational technology and a very sophisticated way of doing the learner's thinking for them.

TOWARDS ETHICAL GOVERNANCE OF DIGITAL TWIN-DRIVEN LEARNING

Running through the argument developed in the preceding sections is a single, insistent conclusion: the technical design of digital twin-driven learning systems and their ethical governance cannot be treated as sequential problems, with the first resolved before the second is addressed. They are the same problem. A system whose architecture has already been determined before questions of accountability, transparency, and pedagogical intentionality have been asked is a system whose governance will always be reactive, always attempting to correct in policy what has already been encoded in code. Lessig (1999) was precise on this point: in environments structured by software, the most consequential decisions are made not by legislators or administrators but by designers, and they are made before the system is deployed, in choices about what the system can do, what it cannot do, and what it was never designed to consider. Ethical governance of digital twin-driven learning must therefore begin at the point of design, not at the point of implementation.

Against this background, what follows proposes a governance framework organised around three principles. These are not technical specifications. Rather, they are conditions that any educationally sound digital twin-driven learning system must satisfy if it is to function as an instrument of the learner's development rather than as an instrument of the learner's management. Table 1 maps each principle against its associated risks and the solutions proposed to address them.

Table 1. Governance framework for digital twin-driven lifelong learning systems: principles, risks, and proposed solutions

Governance principle	Associated risks	Proposed solutions
Pedagogical intentionality	– Over-optimisation for measurable outcomes at the expense of deeper learning – Systematic elimination of productive difficulty, reducing the cognitive friction essential to understanding – Displacement of the educator's narrative role by automated recommendation systems – Progressive reduction of learner autonomy through over-responsive, frictionless environments – Misalignment between technical system objectives and evidence-based educational values	– Explicit specification of pedagogical goals prior to and independently of system design – Mandatory preservation of zones of cognitive challenge within AI-driven curricula – Requirement that all AI recommendations remain subject to educator override at every consequential stage – Regular alignment audits comparing system objectives against established learning theory – Governance structures with sufficient educational expertise to reject systems that are technically capable but pedagogically unsound
Algorithmic transparency and explainability	– Opaque decision-making processes that learners and educators cannot interrogate or contest – Concentration of interpretive power in system designers and commercial developers – Erosion of learner epistemic agency through unexplained algorithmic framing of experience – Absence of accountability when consequential decisions about learner trajectories are produced by black-box systems – Formal compliance with data protection law masking substantive opacity in practice	– Explainability requirements built into system architecture from the design stage, not added as post-hoc compliance – Learner-facing interfaces that surface the basis for recommendations in accessible, non-technical language – Educator dashboards providing interpretable summaries of learner models and system reasoning – Alignment with explainable AI frameworks and standards (Arrieta et al., 2020) – Enforcement of the right to explanation under applicable data protection regulation (European Parliament & Council, 2016)
Democratic oversight	– Governance of AI educational systems by technical specialists without meaningful learner or educator participation – Institutional adoption of commercial systems without independent pedagogical or ethical evaluation – Accumulation of learner data across institutional and temporal boundaries in lifelong learning contexts – Absence of meaningful recourse for learners adversely affected by algorithmic decisions – Regulatory frameworks lagging behind the pace of technical development, creating governance gaps	– Multi-stakeholder governance structures including learners, educators, institutions, civil society, and independent experts – Mandatory independent algorithmic audits prior to deployment and at regular intervals thereafter – Data minimisation, purpose limitation, and temporal restrictions on learner data retention – Alignment with the UNESCO Recommendation on the Ethics of Artificial Intelligence (2021) and applicable AI legislation – Guaranteed learner rights to data access, correction, and deletion throughout the system lifecycle

Pedagogical intentionality is the first of these principles. Any digital twin-driven learning system must be designed from an explicit account of what learning is and what education is for. This may seem obvious, but it is consistently absent from the development of educational AI systems, which are far more frequently designed around measurable proxies for learning, such as engagement rates, completion rates, and performance on standardised assessments, than around a coherent theory of how human beings develop understanding, form convictions, and acquire the capacity for autonomous thought. The danger of designing around proxies is precisely the danger that Jonas (1984) identified in the context of technological development more broadly: that optimising for what can be measured produces systems that are very good at what they measure and largely indifferent to what they cannot. A system that maximises engagement is not necessarily a system that maximises learning. A system that minimises time-to-competency is not necessarily a system that develops the learner's capacity to function without the system's assistance. Pedagogical intentionality requires that the designers of digital twin-driven learning systems be accountable not only for the outcomes they can measure but for the ones they have chosen not to measure, and for the conception of the learner that those choices encode.

In practice, this principle demands that educational theorists, curriculum designers, and practising educators be structurally integrated into the development process of these systems, not as consultants brought in at the end to validate a technically determined architecture, but as primary stakeholders whose understanding of learning shapes the system's objectives from the outset. It also demands that the system's pedagogical assumptions be made explicit and open to scrutiny, so that learners, educators, and institutions can assess whether the theory of learning embedded in the system is one they endorse, and can hold the system's designers accountable when it is not.

Algorithmic transparency and explainability constitute the second principle. Pasquale (2015) has described the opacity of contemporary algorithmic systems as a structural feature rather than an incidental limitation, arguing that systems whose workings cannot be understood by those subject to them are systems that exercise power without accountability. In educational contexts, this opacity takes a specific and particularly problematic form. When a digital twin-driven system recommends a particular learning pathway, adjusts the difficulty of a task, or decides that a learner is ready to progress to a new phase of their development, that recommendation rests on a model of the learner that the learner themselves has typically never seen, formulated in terms that the learner has typically never been invited to interrogate. Governed by a representation of themselves that they did not construct and cannot contest, the learner inhabits a system that knows them without their knowledge.

Transparency in this context does not require that the full technical architecture of the system be made legible to every learner, which would be neither possible nor useful. It requires that the system be capable of explaining, in terms that are meaningful to the learner and to the educator, the basis on which its recommendations are made, the data on which its model of the learner rests, and the assumptions that shape its interpretation of that data. Recent work in explainable AI has substantially advanced the technical feasibility of this requirement: Arrieta et al. (2020) demonstrate that transparency mechanisms can be integrated into complex AI systems without compromising their performance, provided that explainability is treated as a design objective from the outset rather than a compliance requirement added after deployment. Rouvroy and Berns (2013) noted that algorithmic governmentality operates most effectively precisely when it is invisible, when the modulation of the environment feels natural rather than imposed. Transparency is therefore not merely a technical requirement but a political one, a condition for the kind of informed resistance and deliberate engagement that distinguishes an educational environment from a managed one.

Democratic oversight is the third and most structurally demanding of the three principles. Jonas (1984) argued that technologies whose effects extend across generations and whose consequences cannot be fully foreseen require forms of accountability that match their temporal and social scale. Operating at precisely this scale, the learner's digital twin accumulates across a lifetime and may influence decisions about employment, credit, healthcare, and civic participation well beyond the educational contexts in which it originates. Its governance cannot be left to the market incentives of the platforms that develop it, to the institutional interests of the organisations that deploy it, or to the individual choices of learners who are rarely in a position to understand what they are consenting to. What is required are oversight structures that are external to the system itself, that represent the interests of learners as a class rather than as individual consumers, and that have the authority and the capacity to intervene when the system's operation conflicts with the public interest.

In practical terms, this means regulatory frameworks that establish minimum standards for data protection, algorithmic accountability, and learner rights in the context of educational AI, of the kind that the General Data Protection Regulation and the subsequent AI Act have begun to develop (European Parliament & Council of the European Union, 2016, 2024), but whose educational implications remain unevenly addressed. It means independent audit mechanisms capable of assessing whether deployed systems conform to their stated pedagogical objectives and whether the data they collect is being used in ways consistent with the learner's interests. And it means meaningful participation by educators and learners in the governance of the systems that shape their educational environments, not as users who can adjust preferences within parameters determined elsewhere, but as stakeholders whose judgement about what education is for carries genuine weight in the decisions that determine how the system operates.

None of these three principles, taken individually or together, resolves the structural tension between personalisation and control that this chapter has placed at its centre. That tension is constitutive of the paradigm, and no governance framework can eliminate it entirely. What governance can do is ensure that the tension is managed in the learner's interest rather than in the interest of the system that models them. Anders (1956/2013) observed that the danger of our technological condition lies not in malice but in the gap between the power of our tools and our capacity to understand and govern them. Closing that gap, or at least narrowing it, is what ethical governance of digital twin-driven learning systems must attempt. It will not succeed if it begins after the architecture has been built. It can only succeed if it begins before.

IMPLICATIONS FOR PRACTICE

Beyond the theoretical, the argument developed in the preceding sections bears directly on the decisions made by designers, educators, institutions, and policymakers who will determine what digital twin-driven learning systems actually look like when built and deployed. What follows translates these theoretical claims into practical orientations, not prescriptions to be followed mechanically, but considerations that any serious attempt to implement this paradigm responsibly will need to address.

For developers of digital learning platforms and EdTech systems, the primary implication is that explainability cannot be an afterthought. Systems are routinely built to optimise performance on measurable outcomes, with transparency mechanisms added later, if at all, as a compliance requirement rather than a design objective. In digital twin-driven educational systems, this sequence must be reversed. The capacity of the system to account for its own recommendations, to show the learner and the educator the data on which its model rests and the logic by which it arrives at its suggestions, must be built into the architecture from the outset. A system that cannot explain itself to the people it is meant to serve is not a system that serves them; it is a system that processes them, and the distinction matters enormously when what is being processed is a human being's development.

Curriculum designers and instructional developers face a different but equally demanding challenge: the design of productive difficulty. The temptation of a hypersituated, digitally twinned learning environment is to eliminate friction, to smooth the learner's path so completely that engagement is maximised and frustration minimised. That temptation must be resisted. Difficulty, uncertainty, and the experience of not yet understanding are not obstacles to learning; they are among its primary mechanisms. A curriculum designed for deployment in a digital twin-driven environment must deliberately preserve spaces of cognitive effort, moments in which the system withholds the answer not because it does not have it but because the process of searching for it is precisely what the learner needs.

For educators, the paradigm demands a reconceptualisation of their role that neither diminishes it nor leaves it unchanged. An educator in a digital twin-driven learning environment is not a content deliverer who can be progressively replaced as the system becomes more sophisticated. Rather, the educator is the author of the pedagogical narrative that gives the system's outputs their educational meaning, deciding which questions are worth preserving as open, which difficulties are generative and which are merely frustrating, and when the system's recommendation should be followed and when it should be overridden in the interest of something the system cannot model. Selwyn (2019) has argued that this critical capacity cannot be assumed; it must be deliberately cultivated through initial teacher education and continuing professional development that takes the politics of educational technology seriously, equipping educators not only to use these systems but to question the assumptions on which they rest.

Institutions deploying digital twin-driven learning systems face governance implications that are structural rather than procedural. Data collected from learners within educational contexts must be subject to policies that specify clearly what is collected, how it is stored, for how long, under what conditions it may be accessed by third parties, and what rights the learner has to inspect, correct, or delete their own data. These are not merely legal requirements under frameworks such as the General Data Protection Regulation (2016); they are conditions of educational legitimacy. An institution that cannot answer these questions clearly has not earned the trust that the deployment of a system of this kind requires.

Policy-makers must contend with the fact that existing regulatory frameworks, however necessary, fall short of what this paradigm demands. The General Data Protection Regulation establishes important baseline protections for personal data, but it was not designed with the specific dynamics of educational AI in mind, and its provisions do not address the pedagogical consequences of algorithmic modulation in learning environments. What is needed, in addition to data protection, is a framework for educational AI governance that addresses the right of learners to understand the systems that shape their educational experience, the obligation of developers to demonstrate that their systems are consistent with evidence-based theories of learning, and the responsibility of institutions to maintain meaningful human oversight over decisions that affect the learner's development. Miao et al. (2021) have developed concrete guidance for policy-makers navigating this landscape, arguing that effective AI governance in education requires not only regulatory frameworks but sustained investment in the capacity of educational institutions to evaluate, audit, and where necessary reject AI systems that do not meet clearly defined pedagogical and ethical standards. UNESCO's Recommendation on the

Ethics of Artificial Intelligence (2021) offers a broader normative foundation, but its translation into binding educational policy remains, in most jurisdictions, work that has not yet begun.

None of these implications is simple to act on. They require investment, coordination, and a willingness to accept that a system genuinely in the learner's interest may be less efficient, less scalable, and less profitable than one that is not. That willingness is itself a question of governance and, in the end, the most important one.

CONCLUSIONS

A convergence and a question have framed this chapter from beginning to end. The convergence is between hypersituation as a pedagogical condition and the digital twin as a technical paradigm, two developments that are not merely contemporaneous but structurally connected: the digital twin is what makes hypersituated learning possible at scale, and hypersituation is what gives the digital twin its educational purpose. The question is whether that convergence, given what we now understand about the systems it requires, can be made to serve the development of the learner rather than the management of them.

Conditional, rather than categorical, is the only honest answer. Refusing the paradigm on the grounds that it carries risks would be to confuse caution with wisdom, and the possibilities that digital twin-driven hypersituated learning opens are genuine. The question is not whether to build these systems but how, and in whose interest, and under whose oversight. These are not technical questions. They are political ones, and the history of educational technology offers little comfort to those who assume that technical capability and educational value move in the same direction without deliberate effort to ensure that they do.

Central to the chapter's argument is a structural tension between personalisation and control, between the enrichment of the learner's experience and the continuous extraction of data from it, that does not resolve itself. Managing it requires governance frameworks that begin at the point of design, transparency mechanisms that make the system's model of the learner legible to the learner themselves, and democratic oversight structures with the authority to intervene when the system's operation conflicts with the public interest. These are conditions, not guarantees, and their realisation depends on political choices that extend well beyond the domain of educational technology.

What this chapter has also argued, and what is perhaps its most uncomfortable claim, is that the risk associated with digital twin-driven learning systems is not primarily the risk of a system that imposes control visibly and coercively. It is the risk of a system that absorbs, that is so responsive, so seamlessly adjusted to the learner's profile, so efficient at delivering what the learner is predicted to need, that the learner never encounters the resistance through which critical awareness develops. A learning environment that eliminates uncertainty in the name of personalisation has not enhanced learning. It has produced a condition in which learning becomes unnecessary, because the system has already done the cognitive work that learning requires.

Jonas (1984) argued that the ethics of our technological moment must be commensurate with the scale and duration of the effects our systems can produce. The digital twin of the learner, as a model that accumulates across a lifetime and shapes not only what the individual learns but the kind of learner the individual becomes, operates at precisely this scale. An ethical framework adequate to it must be equally ambitious, grounded not in the optimisation of measurable outcomes but in a conception of human development that takes seriously the dimensions of education that cannot be quantified: the formation of independent thought, the capacity for ethical judgement, the willingness to remain uncertain long enough for understanding to form.

Anders (1956/2013) observed that we are not equal to the perfection of our own products. Built with the sophistication that the paradigm promises, the learner's digital twin will be a more complete and more accurate model of the individual than the individual is capable of constructing of themselves. This asymmetry is not in itself a reason to abandon the paradigm, but it is a reason to insist, with considerable force, that a model which knows the learner better than the learner knows themselves must be placed unambiguously in the service of the learner's development, and not in the service of any other interest, however legitimate that interest might appear.

For now, the hypersituated, digitally twinned learner remains a prospect rather than a reality. The technical, pedagogical, and governance conditions for this paradigm to function as described in this chapter do not yet fully exist. What exists is the direction of travel, and the decisions made now, about architecture, about transparency, about accountability, about what education is ultimately for, will determine whether that direction leads towards a more genuinely personalised and more deeply humane model of lifelong learning, or towards something that resembles it closely enough to be mistaken for it.

REFERENCES

Anders, G. (2013). *Die Antiquiertheit des Menschen* (Vol. 1). C.H. Beck. (Original work published 1956)

Arendt, H. (1973). *The origins of totalitarianism*. Harcourt Brace Jovanovich. (Original work published 1951)

Arrieta, A. B., Díaz-Rodríguez, N., Del Ser, J., Bennetot, A., Tabik, S., Barbado, A., García, S., Gil-López, S., Molina, D., Benjamins, R., Chatila, R., & Herrera, F. (2020). Explainable Artificial Intelligence (XAI): Concepts, taxonomies, opportunities and challenges toward responsible AI. *Information Fusion*, *58*, 82–115. DOI: 10.1016/j.inffus.2019.12.012

Baofu, P. (2009). *The future of post-human mass media: A preface to a new theory of communication*. Cambridge Scholars Publishing.

Barricelli, B. R., Casiraghi, E., & Fogli, D. (2019). A survey on digital twin: Definitions, characteristics, applications, and design implications. *IEEE Access : Practical Innovations, Open Solutions*, *7*, 167653–167671. DOI: 10.1109/ACCESS.2019.2953499

Berendt, B., Littlejohn, A., & Blakemore, M. (2020). AI in education: Learner choice and fundamental rights. *Learning, Media and Technology*, *45*(3), 312–324. DOI: 10.1080/17439884.2020.1786399

Biesta, G. (2006). *Beyond learning: Democratic education for a human future*. Paradigm Publishers.

Bloom, B. S. (1984). The 2 sigma problem: The search for methods of group instruction as effective as one-to-one tutoring. *Educational Researcher*, *13*(6), 4–16. DOI: 10.3102/0013189X013006004

Brown, J. S., Collins, A., & Duguid, P. (1989). Situated cognition and the culture of learning. *Educational Researcher*, *18*(1), 32–42. DOI: 10.3102/0013189X018001032

Crawford, K. (2021). *Atlas of AI: Power, politics, and the planetary costs of artificial intelligence*. Yale University Press.

Declerck, R., Reed, S., & Bert, C. (2006). *The grammar of the English tense system: A comprehensive analysis*. Walter de Gruyter. DOI: 10.1515/9783110199888

Dewey, J. (1938). *Experience and education*. Macmillan.

Eco, U. (1986). *Travels in hyperreality*. Harcourt.

European Parliament & Council of the European Union. (2016). *Regulation (EU) 2016/679 of the European Parliament and of the Council of 27 April 2016 on the protection of natural persons with regard to the processing of personal data (General Data Protection Regulation).* Official Journal of the European Union.

European Parliament & Council of the European Union. (2024). *Regulation (EU) 2024/1689 of the European Parliament and of the Council of 13 June 2024 laying down harmonised rules on artificial intelligence (Artificial Intelligence Act).* Official Journal of the European Union.

Grieves, M., & Vickers, J. (2017). Digital twin: Mitigating unpredictable, undesirable emergent behavior in complex systems. In Kahlen, F.-J., Flumerfelt, S., & Alves, A. (Eds.), *Transdisciplinary perspectives on complex systems* (pp. 85–113). Springer. DOI: 10.1007/978-3-319-38756-7_4

Holmes, W., Bialik, M., & Fadel, C. (2019). *Artificial intelligence in education: Promises and implications for teaching and learning.* Center for Curriculum Redesign.

Jonas, H. (1984). *The imperative of responsibility: In search of an ethics for the technological age.* University of Chicago Press. DOI: 10.7208/chicago/9780226850337.001.0001

Lave, J., & Wenger, E. (1991). *Situated learning: Legitimate peripheral participation.* Cambridge University Press. DOI: 10.1017/CBO9780511815355

Lessig, L. (1999). *Code and other laws of cyberspace.* Basic Books.

Luckin, R., & Cukurova, M. (2019). Designing educational technologies in the age of AI: A learning sciences-driven approach. *British Journal of Educational Technology, 50*(6), 2824–2838. DOI: 10.1111/bjet.12861

Miao, F., Holmes, W., Huang, R., & Zhang, H. (2021). *AI and education: Guidance for policy-makers.* UNESCO.

Orwell, G. (1949). *Nineteen eighty-four.* Secker & Warburg.

Ouyang, F., & Jiao, P. (2021). Artificial intelligence in education: The three paradigms. *Computers and Education: Artificial Intelligence, 2*, 100020. DOI: 10.1016/j.caeai.2021.100020

Panadero, E. (2017). A review of self-regulated learning: Six models and four directions for research. *Frontiers in Psychology, 8*, 422. DOI: 10.3389/fpsyg.2017.00422 PMID: 28503157

Pasquale, F. (2015). *The black box society: The secret algorithms that control money and information.* Harvard University Press. DOI: 10.4159/harvard.9780674736061

Pocobelli, D. P., Boehm, J., Bryan, P., Still, J., & Grau-Bové, J. (2018). Building information models for monitoring and simulation data in heritage buildings. *The International Archives of the Photogrammetry, Remote Sensing and Spatial Information Sciences, XLII-2*, 909–916. DOI: 10.5194/isprs-archives-XLII-2-909-2018

Regan, P. M., & Jesse, J. (2019). Ethical challenges of edtech, big data and personalized learning: Twenty-first century student sorting and tracking. *Ethics and Information Technology, 21*(3), 167–179. DOI: 10.1007/s10676-018-9492-2

Rouvroy, A., & Berns, T. (2013). Gouvernementalité algorithmique et perspectives d'émancipation. *Reseaux (London), 177*(1), 163–196.

Selwyn, N. (2019). *Should robots replace teachers? AI and the future of education*. Polity Press.

Smith, J. B., & Weiss, S. F. (1988). Hypertext. *Communications of the ACM, 31*(7), 816–819. DOI: 10.1145/48511.48512

Stephenson, N. (1992). *Snow crash*. Bantam Books.

Tsai, Y.-S., Perrotta, C., & Gasevic, D. (2020). Empowering learners with personalised learning approaches? Agency, equity and transparency in the context of learning analytics. *Assessment & Evaluation in Higher Education, 45*(4), 554–567. DOI: 10.1080/02602938.2019.1676396

UNESCO. (2021). *Recommendation on the ethics of artificial intelligence*. United Nations Educational, Scientific and Cultural Organization.

Vygotsky, L. S. (1978). *Mind in society: The development of higher psychological processes*. Harvard University Press.

Williamson, B. (2017). *Big data in education: The digital future of learning, policy and practice*. SAGE Publications. DOI: 10.4135/9781529714920

Winner, L. (1980). Do artifacts have politics? *Daedalus, 109*(1), 121–136.

Zuboff, S. (2019). *The age of surveillance capitalism: The fight for a human future at the new frontier of power*. PublicAffairs.

Chapter 12
Understanding the Dynamics of Lifelong Learning Under Uncertainty Using a Digital Twin Approach Combined With Fuzzy Multi-Objective Optimization

Hamed Nozari
http://orcid.org/0000-0002-6500-6708
University of National and World Economy, Bulgaria

Zornitsa Yordanova
http://orcid.org/0000-0002-6056-8445
University of National and World Economy, Bulgaria

ABSTRACT

This research presents an integrated framework for designing adaptive learning paths, in which the digital twin acts as the predictive core and fuzzy multi-objective optimization acts as the decision-making engine. By combining real and simulated data, the proposed model has been able to dynamically manage the balance between learning, time, and cognitive load. The results showed that the use of the digital

DOI: 10.4018/979-8-2600-1674-9.ch012

twin has reduced the prediction error by more than 50% and improved the selection of optimized paths by about 30%. Pareto and scenario analyses also confirm the efficiency and stability of the framework under different conditions.

1- INTRODUCTION

Recent developments in the field of digital learning and intelligent systems have shown that it is no longer possible to make decisions based on static and uniform patterns to design effective learning paths. In modern learning environments, the diversity of learners, the constant variability of environmental conditions, and the constraints related to time, resources, and cognitive capacity have turned the educational decision-making process into a complex and multidimensional problem. In such an environment, traditional approaches that are based on definitive, simplified, and non-dynamic assumptions are unable to fully respond to real needs. Therefore, the use of technologies and frameworks that can accurately model system behavior and predict future trends has become a fundamental necessity in the design of intelligent learning systems (Nozari, 2026).

In the meantime, the digital twin, as an emerging paradigm, provides the possibility of creating a dynamic, simultaneous, and data-driven representation of the real system. Relying on real-time data, analytical models, and feedback mechanisms, this technology can reconstruct the current state of the system and simulate and evaluate different scenarios before execution (Chen et al., 2023). In the field of learning, such a capability can lead to a deeper understanding of learner behavior, performance, progress, and needs, and provide a suitable platform for informed and adaptive decision-making. However, a digital twin alone is not enough to extract the best decision and requires a systematic decision-making mechanism to convert its analytical outputs into executive actions.

On the other hand, decision-making problems in learning environments are inherently multi-objective in nature. In this space, goals such as maximizing learning effectiveness, reducing learning time, optimizing resource consumption, and controlling cognitive load are usually raised simultaneously and in many cases are in conflict with each other. Multi-objective optimization is one of the most suitable tools for managing these conflicts, as it allows generating a set of Pareto responses, each of which represents a different level of compromise between the objectives (Feng & Kan, 2025). However, a significant part of the existing models are still unable to properly reflect the inherent uncertainties in learner behavior, data quality, or the dynamics of the learning environment. In this context, fuzzy logic can bring decisions closer to real conditions and increase the accuracy and flexibility of the model by modeling ambiguity, imprecision, and variability (Nozari, 2026).

A review of previous studies shows that although each of the digital twin components, multi-objective optimization and fuzzy modeling, has been considered independently, their integration into a coherent, operational and adaptive framework still has limitations. Many studies have either relied on static models limited to cross-sectional data, or have not paid sufficient attention to the dynamic and self-adaptive aspects of the learning process (Llopis-Albert et al., 2024). Also, in studies that have used digital twins, the role of this technology has often been limited to the simulation or monitoring level and its effective link with the decision-making and optimization layer has not been fully established (Mo et al., 2025). This research gap shows that there is still a serious need to develop frameworks that can connect these components in an integrated, dynamic and practical way.

In response to this need, the present study presents an innovative framework based on the integration of digital twin and fuzzy multi-objective optimization. In this framework, the digital twin acts as an analytical and predictive core, providing an up-to-date and multi-layered picture of the learner's state and learning conditions, while the optimization model extracts optimal learning paths by considering multiple objectives and existing uncertainties. The main innovation of this study lies in creating a closed loop between data, model, and decision-making; such that the output of each stage directly affects the next stage and the entire system continuously adapts to new conditions. In addition, the simultaneous use of multiple meta-heuristic algorithms to solve the model allows for a more comprehensive assessment of the quality of the responses and the selection of the most appropriate method.

The structure of this research is also organized on this conceptual basis. First, the theoretical foundations and conceptual framework of the research are introduced, then the system architecture and mathematical modeling will be described. Next, the solution methods and how to integrate the different components are presented, and finally, the analysis of the results including the Pareto front examination, digital twin performance evaluation, dynamic analysis of learning paths, sensitivity analysis, algorithm comparison, and scenario analysis are discussed.

2- LITERATURE REVIEW

Research on the design of intelligent learning systems has increasingly moved towards the use of real-world data, predictive modeling, and multi-objective decision-making in recent years. One of the most important trends in this area is the development of adaptive learning platforms that attempt to adjust learning paths based on the individual characteristics of learners. These systems usually extract learning patterns using behavioral and performance data and provide suggestions for improving the learning process (Yordanova & Nozari, 2026). However, a significant part of these studies still rely on static or semi-dynamic models and have limited ability to predict future changes.

In this regard, the use of data-driven predictive models has been considered as a tool to improve the quality of decision-making in educational systems. These models estimate future trends by analyzing past data and enable the design of predictive educational policies (Xu et al., 2022). Despite these advances, most of these approaches lack an integrated framework for effectively connecting prediction and decision-making, and their output is not directly fed into the optimization process. This has resulted in the models not fully exploiting their true potential to improve the quality of decisions.

As an emerging technology, the digital twin offers a new solution to overcome these limitations. The concept, which first emerged in the industrial and engineering fields, allows for the creation of a dynamic digital version of the real system that is continuously updated with real data (Nozari, 2025). The application of this technology in the field of learning has opened new avenues for more accurate modeling of learner behavior and simulation of various scenarios. Recent studies have shown that digital twins can play an effective role in improving performance analysis and predicting learning trends (Shoaib et al., 2026). However, in many of these studies, the role of the twin has been mainly limited to the level of analysis and simulation and its connection with the decision-making process has not been fully established.

On the other hand, multi-objective optimization has been used as one of the key tools in solving complex decision-making problems. By considering several conflicting objectives, this approach allows the generation of a set of Pareto solutions, each reflecting a different level of compromise between the objectives (Nozari, 2026). In the field of learning, these objectives can include maximizing performance, reducing learning time, and controlling cognitive load. Despite the widespread use of this approach, many of the presented models are based on the assumption of data certainty and ignore the uncertainties in learners' behavior.

To overcome this limitation, the use of fuzzy logic in educational decision-making modeling has been considered. By considering ambiguity and uncertainty, this approach allows for a more realistic definition of parameters such as ability, motivation, and difficulty (Li et al., 2025). Combining fuzzy logic with multi-objective optimization has led to improved decision quality in some studies, but this combination has often been applied statically and without sufficient attention to temporal changes (Nozari & Yordanova, 2025).

In the field of solution methods, meta-heuristic algorithms such as NSGA-II, Gray Wolf, Firefly, and Bat have been widely used to solve multi-objective problems. These algorithms are considered suitable options for complex problems due to their ability to search the response space and produce high-quality Pareto fronts (Galuzin et al., 2022). Various studies have shown that each of these algorithms has its own strengths and weaknesses, and choosing the right method can have a significant impact on the quality of the results (Kabashkin, 2025). However, most of these studies have focused more on comparing the performance of the algorithms and less on their impact on the quality of decision-making in real applications.

A review of the literature shows that although each of the digital twin components, multi-objective optimization and fuzzy modeling, has been studied independently, their integration into a dynamic and operational framework still faces serious gaps. The most important research gap in this field is the lack of a system that can continuously receive real-time data, dynamically model the system state, and directly apply this information to a fuzzy multi-objective optimization model. Moreover, in many studies, the relationship between forecasting and decision-making is established in a one-way or unsystematic manner, and there is no effective feedback loop for continuous improvement of the system (Rahmani-Sane et al., 2025).

In response to this gap, the present study presents an integrated framework in which digital twins, fuzzy multi-objective optimization, and meta-heuristic algorithms are used in a coordinated and dynamic structure. By creating a feedback loop between data, forecasting, and decision-making, this framework enables the continuous adaptation of the system to new conditions and simultaneously improves the forecast accuracy and the quality of decision-making.

3- CONCEPTUAL FOUNDATIONS

In this section, the conceptual framework of the research is explained based on three main pillars: "lifelong learning as a dynamic system", "digital twin as an analytical and predictive core", and "fuzzy multi-objective optimization as a decision-making engine". The aim of this section is to create a coherent link between theoretical concepts and modeling requirements so that the path from data to decision is defined in a transparent and traceable way.

First, lifelong learning in this research is not considered as a static process, but rather as a dynamic, nonlinear, and time-dependent system. In this framework, the learner's state at any point in time will be a function of his/her interaction history, previous skill level, level of mental engagement, and environmental conditions. Therefore, the learning trajectory is not a predetermined sequence, but an adaptive path that is continuously redefined under the influence of new feedback. These systems view allows for the analysis of gradual changes in skill level, performance decline or improvement, as well as the identification of critical points in the learning process.

In the next step, the digital twin is defined as a virtual and dynamic representation of the learner that is able to model and predict the current state, past trends, and future behaviors. Unlike conventional approaches that use the digital twin solely as a static simulation tool, in this research, the twin is considered as an active analytical entity that is continuously updated with real data. The twin consists of several key components: the data layer that receives behavioral and performance inputs; the model layer that extracts relationships between variables; and a prediction layer that simulates the consequences of different decisions. Thus, the digital twin not only describes the learner's state, but also plays an important role as a predictive tool in evaluating different learning scenarios.

However, one of the fundamental challenges in modeling learning systems is the inherent uncertainties in human variables. Concepts such as “learning ability”, “motivation”, or “cognitive fatigue” are difficult to measure precisely and are often associated with ambiguity. For this reason, fuzzy logic is used in this research to represent these uncertainties. Key variables are modeled as fuzzy parameters so that a range of possible values can be considered instead of a single definite value. This approach increases the flexibility of the model and allows for a more realistic analysis of learner behavior.

In addition, the decision-making process in learning systems is inherently multi-objective. For example, increasing the level of skill may require more time, or reducing the learning time may lead to a decrease in quality. Therefore, different objectives such as maximizing learning, minimizing time, reducing cognitive load, and improving knowledge retention must be considered simultaneously. In this study, this problem is formulated in the form of a multi-objective optimization model, in which solutions are presented not as a single solution, but as a set of Pareto-optimal responses. Combining this framework with fuzzy logic allows for a more accurate analysis of trade-offs under uncertainty.

To integrate these concepts, the overall framework of the system is presented in Figure (1). This figure shows the information flow and interaction between the main components.

Figure 1. Conceptual architecture of a lifelong learning system based on digital twins and fuzzy multi-objective optimization

In this architecture, the data layer acts as a starting point and collects information about the learner's performance, behavior, and interactions. This data is transferred to the digital twin, where it is used to update the model and extract key features. The output of the twin is then sent to the optimization layer, where a fuzzy multi-objective problem is defined and solved. The results of this process are transferred to the decision layer in the form of learning recommendations or optimal paths. Finally, the execution of these decisions leads to the generation of new data and completes the feedback loop.

This feedback loop is one of the main differentiators of the proposed framework, as it transforms the system from a static structure to a learning and adaptive system. In other words, the decisions made not only affect the current state, but also shape the future inputs to the system. As a result, the digital twin gains more accurate predictions over time, and the optimization process gradually improves.

Overall, the conceptual framework presented provides an integrated platform for analyzing, predicting, and optimizing the learning process. By combining three key components, including dynamic modeling, fuzzy representation, and multi-objective optimization, this framework is able to systematically manage the inherent complexities of learning systems and suggest smarter decisions along the learning path.

4- SYSTEM ARCHITECTURE

The proposed system architecture is designed to manage the lifelong learning process in a continuous, adaptive, and data-driven operational cycle. In this architecture, the main logic of the system is based on continuous data acquisition, updating the state of the digital twin, predicting possible outcomes, solving a fuzzy multi-objective decision-making problem, and feeding back decisions to the learning environment. Therefore, the proposed architecture is not just a technical structure, but also an implementation mechanism for transforming learning data into personalized decisions that can be improved over time.

At the beginning of this cycle, multi-source data related to the learner is collected. This data can include test results, interaction patterns with educational content, participation rate, time spent on activities, task completion rate, and contextual information such as time, type of tool used, or environmental conditions. The diversity of this data allows the system to not only rely on functional outputs, but also to obtain a more realistic picture of the learner's state through behavioral and contextual cues. However, raw data is usually not directly suitable for analysis or decision-making; therefore, a preliminary processing stage is performed on it before entering the main core of the system.

In the data processing stage, cleaning, noise removal, heterogeneous data integration, normalization, and feature extraction are performed. The goal of this stage is to transform sparse and unstructured data into a set of meaningful variables that can be used for modeling. The output of this section is an updated feature vector of the learner's state that can be continuously provided to the digital twin core. The importance of this step is that the higher the quality of the input data, the more accurate the digital representation of the learner and the more reliable the subsequent decisions will be.

After the data is prepared, the digital twin core is activated. This core is responsible for generating a dynamic picture of the learner's real state using current data and previous records. In this representation, not only the current level of knowledge or performance is considered, but also variables such as skill development trends, behavioral changes, cognitive engagement patterns, and even the probability of success in different learning paths are estimated. The digital twin here does not play the role of a static model, but is synchronized live with the entry of new data and updates its state in each iteration. In addition, the twin is able to simulate different scenarios before actual implementation; For example, it can estimate what effect learning will have on progress, fatigue, or retention if the type of content is changed, or the intensity of the educational activity is increased.

The output of the digital twin core is fed into the fuzzy multi-objective optimization module. In this section, the decision-making problem is formulated in such a way that several conflicting goals are considered simultaneously. These goals can include maximizing skill acquisition, reducing learning time, controlling cognitive load, increasing motivation, and improving learning persistence. Since some of the influencing variables, such as motivation, mental preparation, or perceived difficulty of the content, are not of a definite and precise nature, these parameters are represented in the form of fuzzy numbers or functions. In this way, the system can make its decisions not in a completely definite environment, but in conditions closer to reality. Solving this problem produces a set of Pareto optimal solutions, each of which represents a specific balance between competing goals.

Next, the decision support module selects the appropriate option or options for implementation from the resulting solutions. This selection can be based on predetermined system policies, learner preferences, or implementation constraints. The output of this stage appears in the form of actionable suggestions; for example, determining a personalized learning path, adjusting the sequence of activities, suggesting an appropriate time frame for studying, changing the level of content difficulty, or allocating educational resources appropriate to the individual's current situation. In this way, the decisions made go beyond the model and analysis level and become actionable actions.

These actions are implemented in the learning environment and their consequences are observed through the learner's actual performance, behavioral changes, and level of engagement. The results of the implementation are re-entered into the system cycle as new data. This data feedback is not simply a mechanism for recording information, but forms the main foundation for the system's gradual learning. In fact, the proposed architecture operates as a closed loop, in which each new decision not only affects the current state, but also serves as the basis for improving the model, correcting predictions, and improving the quality of subsequent decisions. From this perspective, the system over time goes beyond a simple recommender tool and becomes an adaptive structure that is able to learn from the consequences of its decisions. Figure 2 shows the operational flow of this architecture. In this figure, the movement of information from the data reception stage to the decision execution and feedback return is represented as an iterative process.

Figure 2. Operational flow of a digital twin-based lifelong learning system with fuzzy multi-objective optimization

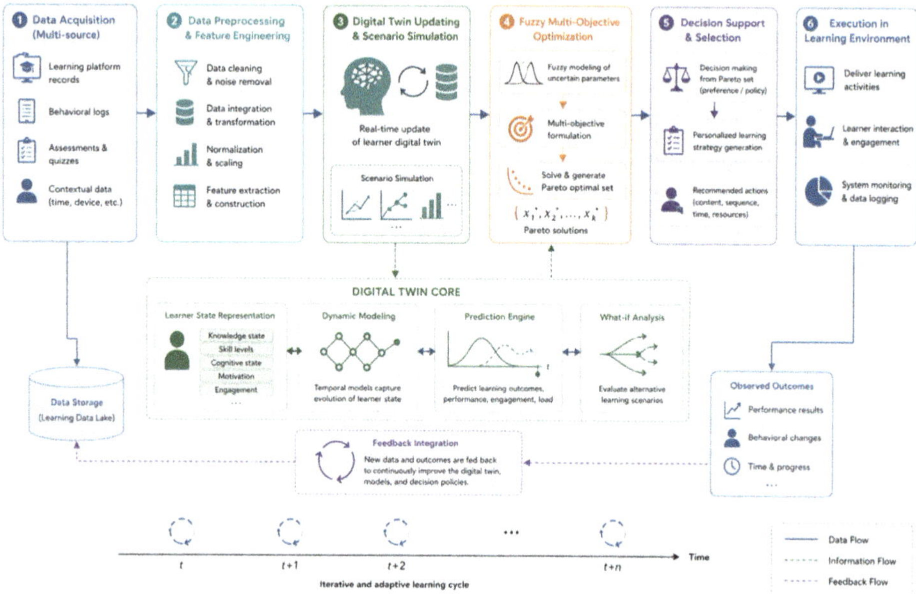

As shown in the figure, the process begins with the collection of training and behavioral data, and after processing and feature extraction, it enters the digital twin core. In this step, the learner's state is modeled and different scenarios are evaluated. Then, the fuzzy multi-objective optimization module generates a set of optimal solutions using the information generated by the twin. These solutions are analyzed in the decision-making module and converted into actionable suggestions. Finally, the decisions are implemented in the learning environment and the resulting outcomes are fed back to the system as feedback. This iterative cycle allows the system to continuously adapt to individual and environmental changes and is one of the most important advantages of the proposed architecture.

Overall, the present architecture introduces an integrated operational structure in which data, model, optimization, and decision-making operate separately but in harmony. This coordination allows the system to simultaneously use past analysis, present understanding, and future prediction to guide learning while maintaining flexibility. Such a feature makes the proposed architecture a suitable option for intelligent, adaptive, and long-term learning environments.

5- MATHEMATICAL MODELING

In order to operationalize the proposed framework and transform the conceptual mechanism into an applicable decision-making tool, the lifelong learning process is formulated in the form of a fuzzy multi-objective optimization model. In this model, the goal is to determine an optimal and adaptive learning path for each learner by considering the dynamic nature of learning, the inherent uncertainties of human variables, and the existence of conflicting goals. In this framework, the digital twin acts as a source of analytical and predictive data and updates the model input parameters at each time interval. On the other hand, multi-objective optimization, considering goals such as maximizing skill acquisition, minimizing time, controlling cognitive load, and increasing learning retention, provides a set of Pareto optimal solutions. In order to account for uncertainty, key parameters are modeled in the form of fuzzy numbers and appropriate methods are used in the solution process to convert them into definite values.

Sets:

$i \in I = \{1,2,\ldots,N\}$: Learners
$j \in J = \{1,2,\ldots,M\}$: Learning activities
$k \in K = \{1,2,\ldots,S\}$: Skills
$t \in T = \{1,2,\ldots,T\}$: Time periods
$p \in P = \{1,2,\ldots,P\}$: Learning scenarios

Parameters:

$\tilde{a}_{i,k,t}$: Learning ability of learner i for skill k at time t
$\tilde{d}_{j,k}$: Difficulty level of activity j for skill k
$\tilde{e}_{i,t}$: Engagement level of learner i at time t
$\tilde{c}_{j}$: Time or cognitive cost of activity j
$\tilde{r}_{j,k}$: Contribution of activity j to skill k
B_{t} : Available time budget at period t
L_{i} : Maximum cognitive load capacity of learner i

Decision Variables:

$x_{i,j,t} \in \{0,1\}$ 1if activity j is assigned to learner i at time t

$y_{i,k,t} \geq 0$ Skill level of learner i in skill k at time t

$z_{i,t} \geq 0$ Cognitive load experienced by learner i at time t

Objective Functions:

$$\max Z_1 = \sum_{i \in I} \sum_{k \in K} \sum_{t \in T} \sum_{j \in J} \tilde{r}_{j,k} \cdot x_{i,j,t} \tag{1}$$

$$\min Z_2 = \sum_{i \in I} \sum_{t \in T} \sum_{j \in J} \tilde{c}_j \cdot x_{i,j,t} \tag{2}$$

$$\min Z_3 = \sum_{i \in I} \sum_{t \in T} z_{i,t} \tag{3}$$

$$\max Z_4 = \sum_{i \in I} \sum_{k \in K} \sum_{t \in T} y_{i,k,t} \tag{4}$$

S.t:

$$\sum_{j \in J} \tilde{c}_j \cdot x_{i,j,t} \leq B_t \, \forall i \in I, \forall t \in T \tag{5}$$

$$y_{i,k,t} = y_{i,k,t-1} + \sum_{j \in J} \tilde{r}_{j,k} \cdot x_{i,j,t} \, \forall i \in I, \forall k \in K, \forall t \in T \tag{6}$$

$$z_{i,t} = \sum_{j \in J} \tilde{c}_j \cdot x_{i,j,t} \, \forall i \in I, \forall t \in T \tag{7}$$

$$z_{i,t} \leq L_i \, \forall i \in I, \forall t \in T \tag{8}$$

$$\sum_{j \in J} x_{i,j,t} \leq 1 \, \forall i \in I, \forall t \in T \tag{9}$$

$$y_{i,k,t} \geq \tilde{d}_{j,k} \cdot x_{i,j,t} \, \forall i \in I, \forall j \in J, \forall k \in K, \forall t \in T \tag{10}$$

$$y_{i,k,t} \geq y_{i,k,t-1} \, \forall i \in I, \forall k \in K, \forall t \in T \tag{11}$$

$$x_{i,j,t} \leq \tilde{e}_{i,t} \, \forall i \in I, \forall j \in J, \forall t \in T \tag{12}$$

$$\sum_{p \in P} x^p_{i,j,t} = 1 \, \forall i \in I, \forall j \in J, \forall t \in T \tag{13}$$

$$x_{i,j,t} \in \{0,1\}, y_{i,k,t} \geq 0, z_{i,t} \geq 0 \tag{14}$$

Objective function (1) represents the maximization of the amount of learning and skill acquisition over the entire planning horizon. This function attempts to select activities in the learning path that have the greatest impact on the development of skills and the improvement of the level of knowledge of learners. More precisely, the more the selected activities contribute to strengthening the desired skills, the greater the value of this function, and as a result, the system is directed towards paths that have higher educational efficiency. Objective function (2) focuses on minimizing the time or cost spent on learning activities. Here, the intention is that the learning process should not be viewed only from the perspective of maximizing educational output, but also time efficiency should be taken into account. For this reason, the model attempts to select from among the various options those activities that, while creating educational progress, require less time or cost. This function plays an important role in designing intensive, efficient, and feasible learning paths. Objective function (3) is dedicated to minimizing the cognitive load imposed on the learner. In many learning environments, choosing activities that are too difficult or dense can cause mental fatigue, loss of concentration, and reduced learning effectiveness. Therefore, this function seeks to control the cognitive pressure on the individual and adjust the educational path in such a way that the mental capacity of the learner is maintained. The existence of this function makes the model not only pay attention to the educational output, but also consider the quality of the learning experience. Objective function (4) represents the maximization of the durability and sustainability of learning. This function means that the system does not just focus on momentary or short-term progress, but also seeks to consolidate knowledge and maintain it over time. In fact, this function tries to prefer paths in which skill improvement occurs more sustainably and the level of learning acquired is maintained over different periods of time. From this perspective, this function is the natural complement of the first function, since it distinguishes between "skill acquisition" and "skill maintenance". Constraint (5) expresses the time constraint in each period. According to this constraint, the total time allocated to learning activities cannot exceed the available time budget in that period. This constraint ensures that the learning plan is realistic from an implementation perspective and that the model's decisions remain consistent with the real time constraints of the learner or the educational system. Constraint (6) expresses the dynamics of skill updating. According to this constraint, the skill level of each learner in each time period is determined based on the skill level of the previous period and the effect of the activities selected in the current period. This relationship allows the model to reflect the cumulative and gradual nature of learning and to follow the process of skill development dynamically over time. Constraint (7) specifies the definition of cognitive load. This constraint states that the cognitive load of each learner in each period is a function of the activities assigned to him in that time period. In this way, cognitive load is entered into the model as an independent and measurable quantity, allowing for its direct control in the objective functions and other constraints. Constraint (8) imposes a ceiling on the cognitive capacity of the learner. According to this constraint, the cognitive load imposed in each period should not exceed the maximum tolerable capacity of the individual. This constraint is important because it prevents the design of excessively heavy educational paths and helps maintain a balance between educational progress and the mental capacity of the learner. Constraint (9) states that in each time period, the number of activities assigned to each learner must be controlled. In its simplest form, this constraint ensures that no more than the allowed number of activities are selected for an individual in each time period. The main role of this constraint is to prevent overcrowding of the learning program and to maintain a regular and manageable structure for the educational process. Constraint (10) represents the skill prerequisite condition. According to this constraint, the choice of a specific activity is possible for the learner only when his skill level has reached the required level to enter that activity. This constraint is very important from an educational point of view, because it ensures that the order of activities is consistent with the logic of learning progression and that the individual does not enter content for which he is not yet ready. Constraint (11) expresses the non-reducing property of the learning process. According to this constraint, the learner's skill level should not decrease over time. This assumption, despite its simplification, is suitable for many educational planning models, because it indicates that the output of educational activities should at least maintain the current level of skill and, if possible, improve it. This constraint contributes to sustainability in the learning process. Constraint (12) is related to the limitation of learner engagement or participation. This constraint indicates that the assignment of activities should be consistent with the level of engagement or readiness of the individual. In practice, this constraint prevents a learner with a low level of engagement from being scheduled with activities beyond his current ability or willingness. Therefore, this constraint establishes a link between the behavioral dimensions of the learner and the model's assignment decisions. Constraint (13) indicates scenario compatibility. In this constraint, it is assumed that the selection of activities should be made within the framework of one of the defined scenarios and that only one valid or compatible scenario is applied to each decision-making state among the possible situations. The purpose of this constraint is to prevent the model from making inconsistent and inconsistent decisions when faced with different learning conditions. Constraint (14) determines the range of variables. This constraint specifies that the activity choice variables are binary in nature and can only represent a choice or no choice, while the variables related to skill level and cognitive load accept non-negative values. The existence of this constraint is essential for the model to be complete, as it precisely defines the permissible range of each variable and prevents the occurrence of invalid responses.

6- INTEGRATION OF DIGITAL TWIN AND OPTIMIZATION

The integration of the digital twin with the fuzzy multi-objective optimization model forms the functional core of the proposed system and provides a mechanism in which data, model, and decision-making operate continuously and in harmony with each other. In this framework, the digital twin is not considered merely as a static descriptive or simulation tool, but rather as an active analytical entity that is continuously updated with real data and provides critical inputs to the optimization model. On the other hand, optimization is not just an independent computational process, but its role is to transform the twin outputs into operational and optimal decisions under uncertainty and multi-objective conditions.

The integration process begins with the data synchronization stage. At each time period, new data related to the learner's performance, behavior, and interactions are received from the learning environment and, after initial processing, are transferred to the digital twin. This data allows the twin's current state to match the learner's actual state. In other words, the twin provides an up-to-date representation of the individual's skill level, learning pattern, and behavioral characteristics at any given moment. This continuous synchronization is a prerequisite for any accurate decision-making in the following stages.

In the next step, the digital twin enters the analysis and prediction phase. In this phase, the twin's internal models use current and historical data to estimate possible future trends. These predictions can include estimates of skill progress, the probability of success in specific activities, changes in motivation levels, or the amount of cognitive load in different scenarios. One of the key capabilities of the twin at this stage is the ability to perform "what-if" analyses, meaning that the system can examine the consequences of a decision in a virtual environment before actually implementing it. This feature moves the decision space from a reactive to a predictive process.

The analytical and predictive outputs of the digital twin are passed as the main inputs to the optimization module. In this step, the model parameters, which were previously defined in fuzzy terms, are initialized or updated based on the information extracted from the twin. For example, the level of ability, level of involvement, or perceived difficulty of activities, all of which are uncertain in nature, are represented in the form of more precise fuzzy values using the twin outputs. This information transfer ensures that the optimization model is always aligned with the latest state of the system and that its decisions are made based on up-to-date data.

Next, the fuzzy multi-objective optimization problem is solved. This problem produces a set of Pareto optimal solutions, taking into account the conflicting objectives and system constraints. Each of these solutions represents a specific balance between objectives such as maximizing learning, minimizing time, and controlling cognitive load. Since the parameters are uncertain, the solution process is designed to take these uncertainties into account in evaluating the solutions. In this way, the outputs obtained will be reliable not only in terms of optimality, but also in terms of stability under different conditions.

After generating the Pareto set, the selection and decision-making phase begins. In this phase, according to the preferences of the system or the learner, one of the optimal solutions is selected and translated into an implementation policy. This policy can include choosing the type of activity, determining the order of their implementation, adjusting the intensity and duration of learning, or even changing the level of difficulty of the content. The important point in this section is that the final decision is not made solely based on a single criterion, but rather the result of a balancing process between multiple objectives and constraints.

Decisions made in the learning environment are executed and their consequences are recorded as new data. This data is fed back into the system, completing the integration cycle. This feedback loop allows the digital twin to become more accurate over time, the optimization model parameters to be adjusted more dynamically, and the quality of decisions to improve. In other words, the system not only uses past data, but also learns from the results of its decisions and improves its performance.

Taken together, the integration of the digital twin and fuzzy multi-objective optimization creates an adaptive and intelligent mechanism in which the boundary between analysis and decision-making is blurred. The twin provides a solid foundation for decision-making by providing an accurate and predictive view of the system state, and optimization complements it by transforming this information into actionable actions. This two-way interaction enables the system to continuously adapt itself in the face of individual and environmental changes and guide the learning path in the optimal direction.

7- SOLUTION APPROACHES

The proposed model was solved within the framework of evolutionary meta-heuristic methods due to its multi-objective, nonlinear, time-dependent and uncertain nature. These algorithms are suitable for complex and multi-objective problems due to their ability to search simultaneously in the response space and approximate the Pareto front. Four algorithms, including the multi-objective genetic algorithm based on non-dominated sorting (NSGA-II), the gray wolf optimization algorithm, the firefly algorithm and the bat algorithm, were used to solve the model. Each of these algorithms, with a different search mechanism, allows for examining the quality of the responses and comparing performance.

The NSGA-II algorithm, as one of the most well-known multi-objective methods, operates based on the concept of Pareto dominance and preserving the diversity of responses. In this algorithm, the initial population consists of random solutions and in each iteration, individuals are evaluated based on the non-dominated rank and swarming distance. The selection, crossover, and mutation operators are designed to ensure convergence towards the Pareto front while maintaining diversity in the response space. In this study, NSGA-II was used as a benchmark to compare the performance of other algorithms in generating Pareto response sets.

The gray wolf optimization algorithm was developed based on the social structure and group hunting behavior of wolves. In this algorithm, the population is divided into four hierarchical levels including alpha, beta, delta, and omega. The top three wolves (alpha, beta, and delta) guide the search path of other members, and the position of the responses is updated based on the position of these three factors. This mechanism makes the algorithm move in a balanced way between exploration and exploitation. In the present implementation, a multi-objective version of this algorithm was used using a Pareto archive to store non-dominated responses.

The firefly algorithm operates on the concept of light attraction, such that each response with a light intensity proportional to its quality attracts other responses. The distance between responses and the decrease in light intensity with increasing distance cause the search to be performed locally while maintaining exploratory capability. In this study, to adapt this algorithm to the multi-objective environment, a combined criterion based on Pareto dominance was used to determine the light intensity. This modification allowed the algorithm to move effectively in the multi-objective space and produce a diverse set of responses.

The bat algorithm was also designed inspired by the acoustic localization mechanism of bats. In this algorithm, each response is considered as a bat that updates its position in the search space using parameters such as frequency, speed, and pulse rate. Changes in pulse propagation rate and loudness allow the algorithm to balance between global and local search. In the multi-objective version used, a Pareto response pool was considered to store the best responses during execution and the selection criterion was set based on multi-objective dominance.

The parameters of the algorithms were adjusted to achieve stable and comparable performance based on initial tests and sensitivity analysis. The final values of the parameters are presented in Table (1).

Table 1. Parameters of meta-heuristic algorithms

Algorithm	Population Size	Iterations	Key Parameters
NSGA-II	100	200	Crossover rate = 0.8, Mutation rate = 0.1
GWO	100	200	Control parameter aaa linearly decreases from 2 to 0
FA	100	200	β0=1\beta_0 = 1β0=1, γ=1\gamma = 1γ=1, α=0.2\alpha = 0.2α=0.2
BAT	100	200	Frequency range = [0, 2], α=0.9\alpha = 0.9α=0.9, γ=0.9\gamma = 0.9γ=0.9

The values presented in Table (1) were selected after several stages of testing and comparison to achieve a good balance between convergence speed and quality of responses. The population size was considered the same for all algorithms to allow for fair comparison. The number of iterations was also chosen so that the algorithms had enough time to converge without unnecessarily increasing the computational time. The specific parameters of each algorithm were determined based on common recommendations in the literature as well as the experimental setting appropriate to the present problem.

The implementation of the algorithms was done using the Python programming language version 3.10. The libraries used included NumPy version 1.24 for numerical calculations, SciPy version 1.10 for optimization functions, and matplotlib version 3.7 for plotting graphs. Also, the DEAP version 1.3 library was used to implement NSGA-II, which allows the definition of evolutionary algorithms flexibly.

To evaluate the performance of the algorithms, each algorithm was tested in 30 independent runs to reduce the effect of randomness in the search process and to make the results statistically reliable. In each run, the initial values of the population were randomly generated and performance criteria such as the quality of the Pareto front and the stability of the responses were examined. The average results obtained from these runs were used as the basis for the final analysis and comparison.

8- ANALYSIS OF RESULTS AND DISCUSSION

The analysis is based on a combination of real and simulated data to both maintain the external validity of the results and allow for systematic testing of control scenarios. Real data were extracted from the logs of a digital learning platform and included assessment results (scores and percentage of correct answers), time spent on each activity, completion rate, sequence of interactions (clicks/views/exercises), and engagement indicators such as number of returns to content and time lags. After filtering (removing outliers, standardizing templates, and filling in missing values), these data were organized into time series at the level of each learner and each activity. For qualitative parameters that are not deterministic in nature (such as ability, engagement, and perceived difficulty), a fuzzy representation was defined with triangular membership functions, and the parameters of these functions were calibrated based on empirical distributions of the data and key percentiles (25th, 50th, and 75th percentiles). The simulated data were generated to cover conditions that are underrepresented in the real data; for this purpose, statistical distributions matching the real data were estimated for each variable and then control scenarios were constructed by purposefully changing the mean, variance, and correlations to investigate the effects of uncertainty and interaction of variables in a traceable manner.

The test scenarios were designed to cover a range of operational and behavioral conditions and to allow for consistent comparison of model performance in different environments. The baseline scenario represents the situation observed in the real data without manipulation and serves as an evaluation reference. Individual diversity scenarios simulate groups of learners with different levels of initial ability and engagement patterns (high, medium, low) to examine the sensitivity of the model to heterogeneity. Resource constraint scenarios measure the efficiency of solutions under pressure by imposing stricter constraints on available time and cognitive capacity. Uncertainty scenarios assess the stability of the Pareto front by increasing the fuzzy range of parameters and adding structural noise to the data. Intervention scenarios apply targeted changes in the sequence and difficulty of activities to reveal the effect of different instructional policies on the learning trajectory and goal balance. All scenarios were run with identical algorithmic settings and independent iterations to ensure that comparisons were statistically reliable and that there was no ambiguity in interpreting the results.

In order to investigate the multi-objective behavior of the model and how to balance the conflicting objectives, the Pareto front obtained from solving the model was analyzed. The results show that the proposed model is able to produce a set of non-dominated solutions, each representing a different level of compromise between the main objectives of maximizing learning and minimizing time and cognitive load. This indicates that there is no single answer to the problem and the final choice will depend on the preferences of the decision maker or the learner's circumstances.

In Figure (3), the Pareto front is shown as a nonlinear curve that represents the inverse relationship between learning improvement and increased cost (time or cognitive load). In the initial region of the curve, a small increase in cost leads to a significant increase in the level of learning, while in the final parts, a significant increase in cost is required to achieve smaller improvements in learning. This behavior indicates the existence of an optimal region for choosing decisions in which a good balance between objectives is achieved.

Figure 3. Pareto front showing the trade-off between learning gain and learning cost

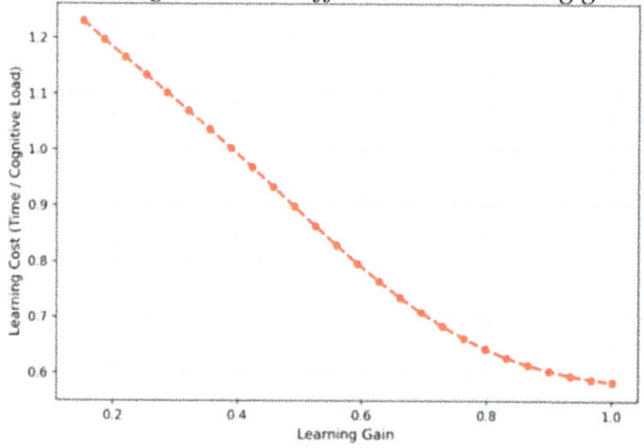

A closer analysis of the Pareto front shows that the middle responses are more valuable from a practical point of view, because they are able to establish a reasonable balance between educational efficiency and time and cognitive constraints. In contrast, the extreme points, although optimal for one objective, usually do not perform well for the other objectives and will be less useful in real-world situations.

The effectiveness of a digital twin becomes meaningful when it can reduce the gap between the "real situation" and the "proposed decisions". For this purpose, the prediction accuracy and its impact on the quality of decisions were examined. The results showed that the digital twin is able to predict the learner's performance trend with acceptable accuracy and these predictions directly contribute to improving the choice of learning paths.

In Figure (4), a comparison between the actual performance values and the values predicted by the digital twin over time is presented. The convergence of the two curves shows that the twin model has been able to correctly identify the pattern of changes and the prediction error remains limited at most points.

Figure 4. Comparison of actual and predicted performance by the digital twin

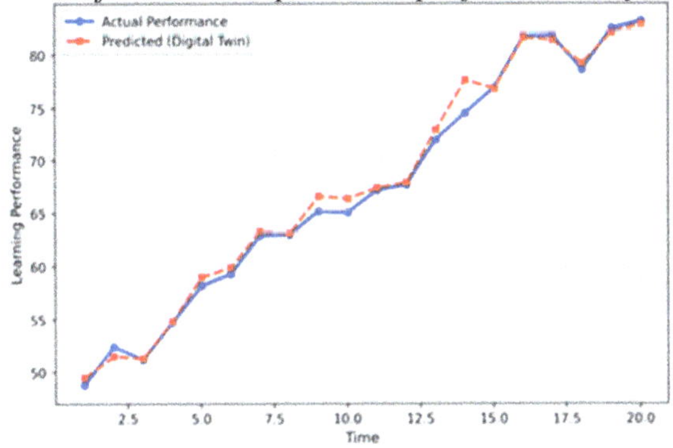

As can be seen in the figure, the difference between the two curves was greater in the initial time intervals, but with increasing data and continuous updating of the model, this difference has decreased. This behavior indicates the gradual learning property of the digital twin and the continuous improvement of the prediction accuracy over time. To quantitatively evaluate the performance, the error metrics and decision-making improvement are presented in Table (2).

Table 2. Quantitative evaluation of the digital twin performance

Metric	Without Digital Twin	With Digital Twin	Improvement (%)
MAE (Mean Absolute Error)	6.85	2.91	57.50%
RMSE (Root Mean Square Error)	8.12	3.74	53.90%
Decision Accuracy (%)	68.4	84.7	23.80%
Optimal Path Selection Rate (%)	61.2	80.5	31.50%

The results in Table (2) show that the use of the digital twin has significantly reduced the prediction error. The more than 50% reduction in the MAE and RMSE metrics indicates that the twin model has been able to provide a more accurate estimate of the learner's future state. In addition, the improvement in decision-making accuracy and the optimal path selection rate indicates that this increase in prediction accuracy has directly led to an improvement in the quality of decisions.

The dynamic behavior of the model shows that learning paths do not evolve uniformly and linearly, but rather follow a nonlinear and adaptive process influenced by the interaction between different goals. The results of the model implementation indicate that the choice of activities in each time period affects not only the performance of the same period, but also the future learning process. This is especially important in situations where there is a conflict between learning maximization and time and cognitive constraints.

In Figure (5), several distinct learning paths are displayed over time. Each path represents a different decision-making policy extracted from the Pareto front. The first path represents a situation in which the focus is on rapid learning maximization, resulting in a higher growth slope but at a higher cost. The second path balances the goals and shows a relatively stable and balanced process. The third path represents a more conservative approach that pursues slower growth at a lower cost.

Figure 5. Dynamic learning trajectories over time

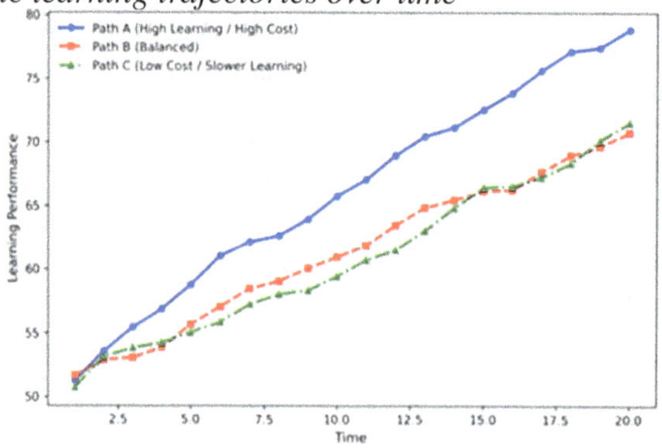

Analysis of these trajectories shows that choosing intermediate policies in many cases leads to more stable performance over time. While aggressive trajectories grow faster in the early stages, they may encounter cognitive limitations or performance degradation later on. In contrast, balanced trajectories are able to maintain progress while creating greater stability over the time horizon.

The stability and reliability of the model are meaningful when it shows predictable and logical behavior against changes in key parameters. For this purpose, a sensitivity analysis was performed focusing on one of the most important parameters, namely the learner's ability level. Due to its fuzzy nature and direct role in determining the quality of decisions, this parameter has a significant impact on the model output.

The results show that with a gradual increase in the ability level, the system performance improves nonlinearly, but this trend is not uniform in all ranges. At low values, parameter changes have a limited effect on performance, while in intermediate ranges, increasing ability leads to faster performance improvement. At higher levels, this trend is accompanied by a decrease in the slope and approaches a saturation state. This behavior indicates that the system has different sensitivity to parameter changes in different ranges.

Figure 6. Sensitivity analysis of learning ability parameter

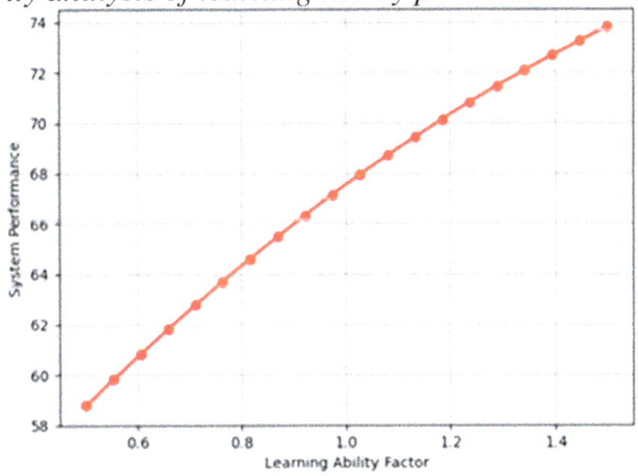

As can be seen in Figure (6), the relationship between the input parameter and the system performance has an optimal region where the highest efficiency is achieved. Outside this region, excessive increase or decrease of the parameter has less effect on improving the performance. This feature is very important from a decision-making perspective, because it shows that fine-tuning of parameters can play a key role in achieving optimal results.

The quality of decision-making produced by optimization algorithms is not limited to the final value of the objective function, but also depends on the ability of the algorithm to produce stable responses, close to the reference Pareto front, and at the same time diverse. Accordingly, the performance of four NSGA-II algorithms, Gray Wolf, Firefly, and Bat, was evaluated using three standard indices: Hypervolume (HV), Generational Distance (GD), and Spread. The HV index indicates the overall coverage and quality of the Pareto front, and the higher its value, the more desirable it is. The GD index measures the distance of the responses obtained by the algorithm to the reference front, and the smaller it is, the better the convergence will be. The Spread index also indicates the dispersion and proper distribution of the responses along the Pareto front. To examine the stability of the performance of the algorithms in independent runs, Figure 7 is included in this section.

Figure 7. Boxplot comparison of algorithm performance based on Hypervolume (HV)

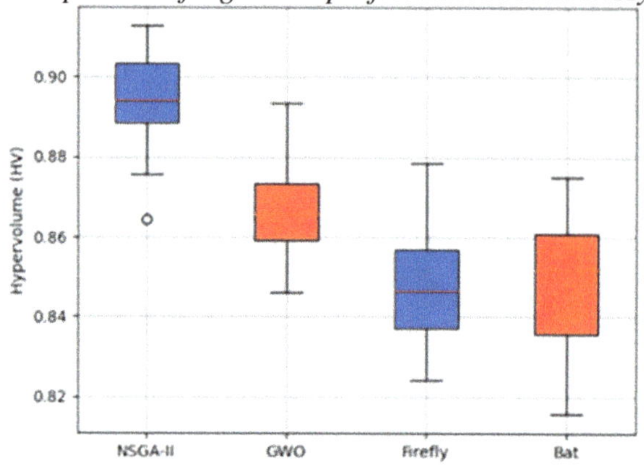

Figure (7) shows the distribution of HV values for each algorithm in several independent runs. This plot allows for simultaneous examination of the central value, the range of variation, and the presence of outliers. As can be seen, the NSGA-II algorithm not only has the highest median HV, but also has a narrower range of dispersion; therefore, this algorithm is in a more favorable position in terms of the quality of the Pareto front and the stability of performance. The Gray Wolf algorithm is ranked next and although its performance is close to NSGA-II, it shows more dispersion in the outputs. The Firefly and Bat algorithms are also at a lower level in terms of HV value and the variations between their runs are greater. This indicates that the responses of these two algorithms are less stable in terms of decision quality. To complete this evaluation and provide a more detailed numerical comparison, Table 3 is presented below.

Table 3. Comparative performance of optimization algorithms based on HV, GD, and spread

Algorithm	**HV (↑)**	**GD (↓)**	**Spread**
NSGA-II	0.892	0.041	0.512
GWO	0.874	0.053	0.538
Firefly	0.851	0.067	0.561
Bat	0.843	0.072	0.579

The values in Table (3) confirm the result observed in Figure (7). The NSGA-II algorithm with the highest HV value and the lowest GD value has achieved the best performance in terms of proximity to the reference Pareto front and overall quality of decisions. The Gray Wolf algorithm also showed acceptable performance and was able to produce answers close to the NSGA-II results, although it ranked lower in terms of convergence and diversity. In contrast, the Firefly and Bat algorithms, although they were still able to produce acceptable answers, had poorer performance in terms of both Pareto front coverage and distance to the reference front.

Examining the behavior of the model in different scenarios shows that the quality of learning paths is strongly influenced by the initial conditions and the level of learner engagement. Three distinct scenarios, including high engagement, balanced mode, and low engagement, were defined to evaluate how the system responds in different conditions. The results show that the model is able to generate a different learning path for each scenario that is consistent with the characteristics of the same conditions. Figure 8 shows the trend of learning performance change over time for each of the scenarios.

Figure 8. Scenario-based learning performance comparison

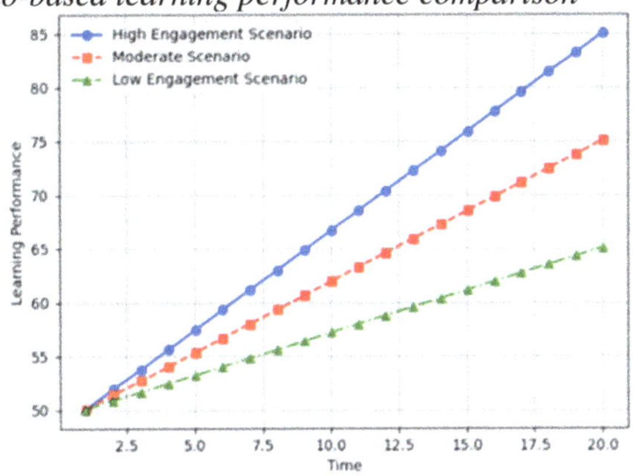

As can be seen, in the high engagement scenario, performance growth is accompanied by a steeper slope and the learner achieves a higher level of proficiency in a shorter time. In the balanced scenario, the steady progress trend continues but with a moderate slope. In contrast, in the low engagement scenario, performance growth is slower and a significant gap is created with other scenarios. These differences indicate that the proposed model is well able to reflect the behavioral conditions of the learner in the decision-making process. To provide a quantitative assessment of the results of the scenarios, Table 4 is presented below.

Table 4. Performance comparison across different learning scenarios

Scenario	Final Performance	Average Growth Rate	Cognitive Load	Completion Time
High Engagement	85.2	1.85	0.78	14
Moderate	75.1	1.32	0.65	17
Low Engagement	64.8	0.92	0.51	20

The values in Table (4) show that the high-involvement scenario brings the highest final performance level and growth rate, but on the other hand, it also imposes a greater cognitive load on the learner. The balanced scenario establishes a balance between performance and cognitive cost and is considered a more suitable option in many situations from a practical point of view. In contrast, the low-involvement scenario, although it creates the least cognitive pressure, comes at the cost of a significant decrease in the level of performance and an increase in the time to achieve educational goals.

The analysis of the results shows that the use of digital twins, along with multi-objective optimization, can provide a powerful tool for decision-making in learning systems. From a management perspective, this framework allows educational decisions to be made not based on guesswork or limited experience, but on real data and reliable predictions. Educational managers and learning system designers can use the model outputs to define personalized learning paths that are both optimal in terms of time efficiency and balanced in terms of learning quality and cognitive load. This approach is especially important in online learning environments and smart learning platforms, where the diversity of users and resource constraints increase the need for accurate and adaptive decision-making.

On the other hand, the analysis of scenarios and parameter sensitivity shows that effective management of the learning process requires a detailed understanding of the individual and environmental conditions of learners. The results indicate that the same policies do not work well for all users and that adopting adaptive approaches can lead to significant performance improvements. In this regard, managers can establish a proper balance between different goals by adjusting parameters such as activity intensity, time distribution, and content difficulty level. Also, choosing the right algorithm to solve the model is of practical importance, because the quality of the generated responses directly affects executive decisions. Overall, the proposed framework enables learning management to transform from a static and generic process to an intelligent, dynamic, and data-driven system.

9- CONCLUSION

The results of this study showed that the combination of digital twin with fuzzy multi-objective optimization can provide a coherent, dynamic, and data-driven framework for designing learning paths. In this approach, learning was modeled as a time-dependent and adaptive process in which the learner's state is continuously updated and educational decisions are made based on accurate predictions and multi-objective analyses. The use of digital twin enabled the system to provide a close-to-real picture of the learner's behavior, performance, and progress and directly feed this information into the decision-making process. As a result, the gap between real data and proposed decisions was significantly reduced.

On the other hand, the use of fuzzy multi-objective optimization enabled the inherent conflicts in the learning process, such as the balance between learning quality, time, and cognitive load, to be managed systematically. The results of the Pareto front analysis showed that the model is able to produce a set of diverse and efficient solutions, each of which represents a different level of compromise between objectives. This feature allows decision makers to choose the appropriate path based on the conditions and preferences. Also, the dynamic analysis of learning paths showed that decisions made at each time period have long-term effects on the learning process and that choosing balanced policies in many cases leads to more stable performance.

The evaluation of the digital twin performance also indicated that this component plays a key role in improving the quality of decisions. The significant reduction in prediction error and increased accuracy in choosing optimal paths showed that the use of predictive models along with optimization can lead to more informed and efficient decision-making. In addition, the sensitivity analysis of parameters showed that the proposed model behaves logically and stably with respect to changes in inputs and shows predictable reactions in different intervals. This feature is of great importance for application in real environments that are associated with uncertainty.

Comparison of optimization algorithms also showed that the choice of solution method has a direct impact on the quality of the results. Among the algorithms studied, NSGA-II was able to provide better performance in terms of convergence, Pareto front quality, and stability of responses, while other algorithms also performed acceptable in some indicators. These findings indicate that the use of appropriate meta-heuristic methods plays an important role in extracting high-quality responses from complex models.

Despite the achievements, this research is also accompanied by some limitations. First, part of the data used was generated in a simulated form, which, although adjusted based on real patterns, may not reflect all the complexities of real environments. Second, the presented model has considered some human factors such as deep motivation or psychological characteristics in a simplified manner. Also, the practical implementation of the system on a large scale and in real environments requires further infrastructural and computational studies.

In the following, several research directions can be proposed. The use of completely real and online data in real time can increase the accuracy and applicability of the model. The development of self-learning digital twins using reinforcement learning methods can also lead to continuous improvement of the system's performance. In addition, the integration of the model with emerging technologies such as deep learning or metaverse environments can open new horizons for personalized learning. The simultaneous study of multiple learners in the form of an interactive and networked system will also be another valuable direction for future research.

REFERENCES

Chen, Z., Zou, J., & Wang, W. (2023). Digital twin-oriented collaborative optimization of fuzzy flexible job shop scheduling under multiple uncertainties. *Sadhana, 48*(2), 78. DOI: 10.1007/s12046-023-02133-z

Feng, J., & Kan, J. (2025). A novel multi-objective fuzzy deep learning framework for predictive maintenance in Industrial Internet of Things. *IEEE Access : Practical Innovations, Open Solutions, 13*, 41955–41973. DOI: 10.1109/ACCESS.2025.3547863

Galuzin, V., Galitskaya, A., Grachev, S., Larukhin, V., Novichkov, D., Skobelev, P., & Zhilyaev, A. (2022). Autonomous digital twin of enterprise: Method and toolset for knowledge-based multi-agent adaptive management of tasks and resources in real time. *Mathematics, 10*(10), 1662. DOI: 10.3390/math10101662

Kabashkin, I. (2025). AI-based digital twins of students: A new paradigm for competency-oriented learning transformation. *Information (Basel), 16*(10), 846. DOI: 10.3390/info16100846

Li, L., You, J., & Xu, T. (2025). Risk Analysis of Digital Twin Project Operation Based on Improved FMEA Method. *Systems, 13*(1), 48. DOI: 10.3390/systems13010048

Llopis-Albert, C., Rubio, F., Devece, C., & García-Hurtado, D. (2024). Digital twin-based approach for a multi-objective optimal design of wind turbine gearboxes. *Mathematics, 12*(9), 1383. DOI: 10.3390/math12091383

Mo, F., Rehman, H. U., Chaplin, J. C., Sanderson, D., & Ratchev, S. (2025). Digital twin-based self-learning decision-making framework for industrial robots in manufacturing. *International Journal of Advanced Manufacturing Technology, 139*(1), 221–240. DOI: 10.1007/s00170-025-15844-w

Nozari, H. (2025). Optimizing transmedia storytelling strategies across platforms for Maximum audience engagement. *Entertainment Computing*, •••, 101061.

Nozari, H. (2026). AI-Augmented Creative Assessment: From Static Tests to Dynamic Insight Generation. In AI-Augmented Creativity in Learning Analytics (pp. 25-42). IGI Global Scientific Publishing.

Nozari, H. (2026). Digital twin-based predictive maintenance in cold chain logistics. *Operations Research, 60*(1), 481–499. DOI: 10.1051/ro/2025167

Nozari, H. (2026). Self-Evolving Neuromorphic Systems for Predictive Learning Interventions. In AI-Augmented Creativity in Learning Analytics (pp. 105-122). IGI Global Scientific Publishing.

Nozari, H., & Yordanova, Z. (2025). An intelligent digital twin approach for optimizing multi-channel supply chains in uncertain environments. Green Technologies and Sustainability, 100309.

Rahmani-Sane, G., Azad, S., Ameli, M. T., & Haghani, S. (2025). The applications of artificial intelligence and digital twin in power systems: An in-depth review. *IEEE Access : Practical Innovations, Open Solutions*, *13*, 108573–108608. DOI: 10.1109/ACCESS.2025.3580340

Shoaib, M., Zhang, S., Ali, H., Ahmad, M. S., & Khan, M. A. (2026). Integrating circular economy while adopting digital twin for enhancing logistics efficiency: A hybrid Fuzzy Delphi-FUCOM based approach. *International Journal of Logistics*, *29*(3), 300–342. DOI: 10.1080/13675567.2025.2451750

Xu, Q., Ali, S., Yue, T., & Arratibel, M. (2022, November). Uncertainty-aware transfer learning to evolve digital twins for industrial elevators. In *Proceedings of the 30th ACM Joint European Software Engineering Conference and Symposium on the Foundations of Software Engineering* (pp. 1257-1268). DOI: 10.1145/3540250.3558957

Yordanova, Z., & Nozari, H. (2026). Seamless Data Integration for Predictive Learning Environments. In AI-Augmented Creativity in Learning Analytics (pp. 293-318). IGI Global Scientific Publishing.

Chapter 13
IoT-Integrated Digital Twin Systems for Real-Time Monitoring of Learning Behaviors

Hossein Abdi
http://orcid.org/0009-0003-6528-3662
Bio10, Australia

Naser Heidari
Bio10, Dubai, UAE

ABSTRACT

This research presents a conceptual framework for smart education systems based on digital twins and the Internet of Things, which aims to monitor and interpret learner behavior in real time. Unlike common approaches that limit learning to discrete indicators such as grades, clicks, or attendance time, this framework considers the learner as a dynamic and evolving system. Multi-source data is transformed into behavioral signals and analyzed in the form of a time-based learning trajectory. This approach can pave the way for adaptive educational interventions, deeper personalization, and more responsible design of smart learning environments.

1- INTRODUCTION

In recent years, the expansion of digital learning environments has led to the generation and storage of a significant amount of data related to learners' activities. However, a large part of this data is still used in a static, scattered and uninterpret-

DOI: 10.4018/979-8-2600-1674-9.ch013

ed form. What is observed in many common educational systems is merely the recording of events such as login, duration of attendance or test results; while these indicators alone are not able to truly represent the learning process. Learning is a dynamic, multi-layered and context-dependent phenomenon that is formed and changes over time. Therefore, the main challenge lies not in "data collection", but in "understanding learning behavior" (Kalogeras et al., 2025).

In such a context, the concept of real-time monitoring of learner behavior becomes particularly important. However, obtaining an accurate and vivid picture of learning behavior requires going beyond the traditional boundaries of data analysis. Traditional learning management systems, while providing the ability to store and retrieve information, are unable to identify hidden behavioral patterns, gradual changes, and complex interactions between different learning factors. On the other hand, traditional learning analytics approaches often rely on historical data and are less able to provide immediate and actionable insights (Amaresh et al., 2026). This gap highlights the need for frameworks that can model learner behavior not as a set of data points, but as an evolving process.

Meanwhile, the emergence of IoT technologies has opened up new horizons in recording and analyzing learning behavior. Sensors, wearables, and smart environments can provide data beyond explicit interactions with educational systems; data that reflects the temporal, environmental, and even physiological dimensions of learner behavior. This data, if processed correctly, can reveal signs of focus, engagement, fatigue, or participation patterns. However, the diversity, volume, and heterogeneity of this data pose significant challenges in their interpretation and integration. Without an appropriate conceptual structure, such data are not only not useful, but may also lead to misinterpretations (Goyal et al., 2026).

In response to these challenges, the concept of the digital twin has emerged as a novel approach to dynamically and real-timely representing complex systems. In the field of education, the digital twin can act as a living representation of the learner, which is continuously updated based on the received data. Unlike static models or traditional profiles, this twin not only reflects the current state of the learner, but also follows his or her evolution path over time. Such an approach allows for the observation of behavioral patterns, prediction of changes, and a deeper understanding of the learning process. However, effective implementation of digital twins in educational environments requires intelligent integration of multi-source data and designing appropriate mechanisms for their interpretation.

The combination of the Internet of Things and digital twins provides a context in which raw behavioral data is transformed into meaningful signals and aggregated into a dynamic model of the learner. This integration enables real-time monitoring of learning behavior with greater accuracy and depth, paving the way for adaptive responses. In such a framework, the focus shifts from simply "recording data" to "understanding behavior," a shift that can fundamentally transform the way educational processes are designed and managed. However, this transformation requires a rethinking of how learning data is defined, collected, and interpreted (Rajaram & Almalki, 2026).

The present study aims to provide a conceptual framework for digital twin systems integrated with the Internet of Things, and examines how learning behaviors are monitored in real-time. The main focus of this study is to explain how to transform multi-source data into dynamic representations of the learner and extract meaningful insights from these representations. In this direction, an attempt has been made to provide a process-oriented and interpretation-oriented view of learning behavior by moving beyond static and descriptive approaches. The innovation of this work lies in combining technological and conceptual perspectives in order to create a bridge between data and understanding; a bridge that can pave the way for a new generation of intelligent learning systems.

Ultimately, this research emphasizes the idea that the future of intelligent learning lies not in the accumulation of more data, but in the ability to interpret live and meaningfully the behavior of learners. The digital twin, interacting with data from the Internet of Things, makes it possible to observe and understand learning as an evolving process, not simply a set of measurable outcomes. Such a view could pave a new path for designing educational systems in which a deep understanding of learner behavior is the basis for decision-making and continuous improvement.

2- WHEN LEARNING BECOMES OBSERVABLE

Despite the vast advances in digital learning infrastructure, making learning "visible" remains a fundamental challenge in the field. What is recorded in many educational systems today is more a reflection of users' superficial activities than an indication of the actual learning process. For example, the number of times a system is logged, the length of time spent on a page, or even test scores, only reveal a small part of what is happening in the learner's mind. While this data is valuable, it alone cannot answer the question of "how learning is taking place."

The key issue here is the difference between "data" and "behavior." Data is often stored as discrete, uncontextualized points, whereas learning behavior is a continuous, temporal, and contextual phenomenon. When a learner pauses a video, rewinds, or takes a break from the system for a while, these events only make sense if they are interpreted in the appropriate temporal and cognitive context. Otherwise, what we have is simply a collection of scattered events that lack analytical coherence (Eiaseb et al., 2026).

In recent years, there have been efforts to enrich the analysis of learning behavior through learning analytics and educational data mining approaches. These approaches have been able to identify patterns in historical data and, to some extent, help predict future performance. However, most of these methods rely on retrospective data and are less able to provide a live, evolving picture of learner behavior. In other words, what is offered is more of a "reconstruction of the past" than an "understanding of the present moment."

Making learning truly visible requires moving beyond these limitations and moving towards capturing and interpreting data that was previously unavailable. This is where the role of connected environments and new technologies comes into play. The proliferation of smart devices, sensors, and interactive tools has made it possible to collect data that covers new dimensions of learner behavior. This data can include movement patterns, changes in the level of engagement, behavioral interruptions, and even environmental conditions that affect the learning process. Such information, if interpreted correctly, can reveal signs of cognitive engagement, fatigue, or even confusion (Yordanova & Nozari, 2026).

However, the increase in the volume and variety of data does not automatically mean that our understanding of learning will increase. In fact, without a framework that can organize this data into a coherent structure, we risk getting lost in the mass of information. One of the major challenges in this area is the distinction between "signal" and "noise." Much of the recorded data may lack analytical value or only become meaningful when combined with other data. Therefore, making learning observable depends not only on collecting more data, but also on the ability to extract meaningful signals from this data (Pham et al., 2026).

Another important point is the role of context in interpreting learning behavior. The same behavior can have completely different meanings in different situations. For example, pausing for a long time on a piece of content can be a sign of deep concentration or, conversely, a sign of lack of understanding and confusion. Interpreting these behaviors can be misleading without taking into account contextual factors such as the type of content, the level of difficulty, or even environmental conditions. Therefore, any effort to make learning observable must seriously consider the issue of contextuality (Muhudin et al., 2026).

In the meantime, the concept of temporal continuity is also of particular importance. Learning is not an instantaneous process, but rather occurs over time and through repeated interactions. Therefore, truly observing learning requires following the process over time and identifying trends and changes in it. Focusing solely on single data points deprives us of understanding this dynamic. In contrast, viewing learning as a trajectory allows us to identify patterns of growth, decline, or change in direction.

Ultimately, making learning observable is a conceptual shift that requires a re-thinking of how we view, treat, and interpret data. This shift moves us from passively recording events to actively understanding processes. In such a framework, data is no longer the end goal, but a means to deeper insight into how people learn. This shift in perspective paves the way for the development of approaches in which learning behavior is not only observed, but also meaningfully understood and interpreted, a necessary step for designing a new generation of intelligent learning systems.

3- THE LEARNER BEYOND DATA POINTS

In many educational systems, the representation of the learner is implicitly limited to a set of measurable indicators, such as grades, number of interactions, or time spent on content. While useful for initial analysis and reporting, this type of representation seems inadequate for understanding the true nature of learning. Learning is not simply the result of a series of recordable events, but rather a dynamic, continuous, and context-dependent process that takes shape and evolves over time. Thus, reducing the learner to "data points" not only provides an incomplete picture of reality, but can also lead to inaccurate perceptions of learning behavior (Nozari, 2025).

The main issue here is how we look at the data. In traditional approaches, each data point is treated as an independent observation; in other words, the learner's behavior is reduced to a set of discrete points that lack meaningful connections to each other. However, many key features of learning (such as gradual progress, sudden decline, or recurring patterns) can only be understood in the context of time and in terms of the relationships between these points. So, what matters is not the data itself, but how it is organized and interpreted within a temporal and conceptual framework (Mishra et al., 2026).

To make this distinction clearer, Figure 1 is presented as a conceptual representation in this section. It illustrates the transition from a data point-based view to a learning trajectory-based view. On the left side of the figure, the learner is represented as a set of discrete data points; each point represents a specific event or measurement, with no explicit relationship to the other points. On the right, the same data are organized as a continuous, time-based trajectory that shows behavioral changes over time. This trajectory emphasizes trends, patterns, and overall direction of behavior rather than focusing on individual values.

Figure 1. The transition from data point-based to learning path-based representations

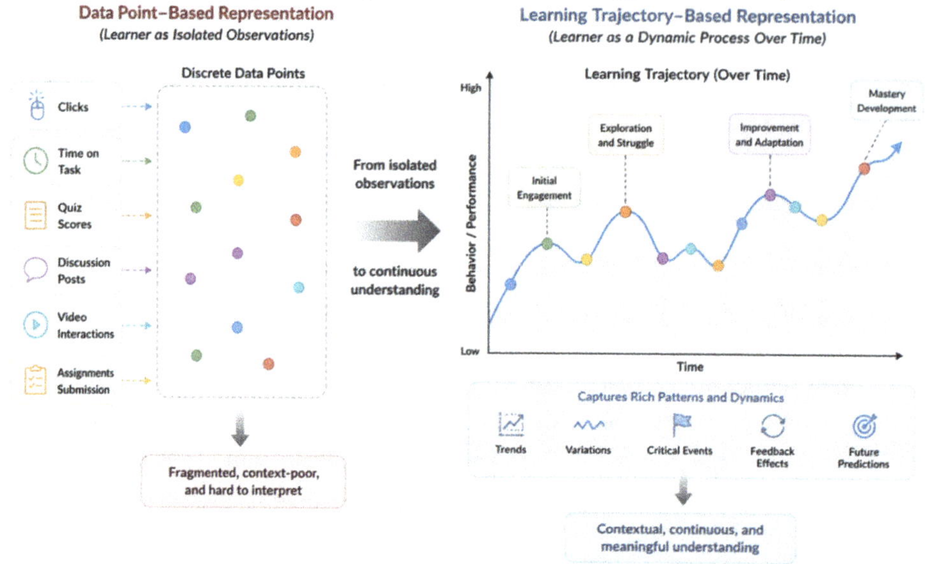

As can be seen in Figure 1, the main difference between these two approaches lies at the level of interpretation. In data point-based representations, analyses are often limited to comparing values or identifying simple correlations. In contrast, path-based representations allow for the understanding of hidden trends, identifying turning points, and analyzing behavioral changes. For example, a gradual increase in the level of engagement or a sudden decrease in participation can only be detected if the data is examined within a coherent time frame. This type of analysis is directly related to a deeper understanding of the learning process.

Another important aspect of this evolution is the role of context in interpreting learner behavior. In data point-based approaches, it is often assumed that each data point has a fixed meaning, while in reality, the meaning of each behavior is highly dependent on its surrounding conditions. For example, spending a lot of time on an activity can be a sign of high concentration or a sign of confusion; it is not possible to distinguish the two without considering the position of that behavior in the overall learning trajectory. In a trajectory-based representation, each point is seen as part of a larger narrative that must be interpreted in relation to other points and environmental conditions (Manimegalai et al., 2026).

Furthermore, viewing the learner as a trajectory allows for the identification of more complex patterns that are not visible in static analyses. These patterns can include learning cycles, changes in interaction style, or even different responses to different types of content. Such insights provide a basis for designing more precise and targeted educational interventions. In other words, when the learner is considered as a dynamic system, it is possible to understand his behavior at a level beyond surface indicators (AbdelRaouf et al., 2026).

In the meantime, the concept of the digital twin is proposed as a suitable framework for realizing this type of representation. A digital twin can dynamically model this learning trajectory and update it as new data is received. Unlike static models that only provide a snapshot of the learner, a twin can seamlessly capture history, trends, and behavioral patterns. This allows for predictive analytics and adaptive responses without the need to constantly redefine the model (Nozari, 2026a).

Ultimately, the shift from a data-point-based view to a learning trajectory-based view represents a paradigm shift in the analysis of learner behavior. It moves us from focusing on "what happened" to understanding "how and why it happened." In such a framework, data is viewed not as an end goal, but as a tool for discovering patterns and understanding hidden processes. This approach paves the way for the development of systems that can not only record learning, but also interpret and guide it in a meaningful way, a fundamental step towards realizing truly intelligent education.

4- A TWIN THAT EVOLVES, NOT JUST REFLECTS

In many early applications of digital twins, the focus has been on creating an accurate representation of the current state of a system; one that can reflect the current situation and allow for monitoring. However, in the context of education, such an approach alone is not enough. Learning is not a static phenomenon that can be "recorded" at a specific moment, but rather a dynamic and changing process that takes shape over time. Therefore, a digital twin in this context cannot simply be a mirror; it must become a living entity that grows, changes, and evolves along with the learner (Li et al., 2026).

The key distinction here is between "reflection" and "evolution." A reflective twin receives input data and displays the current state, without having a deep understanding of the process of change. In contrast, an evolutionary twin not only receives data but also interprets it in a temporal context and shapes behavioral patterns over time. The twin is able to store the past, interpret the present, and provide clues to the future. This capability transforms it from a simple monitoring tool to a system of understanding and analysis.

To illustrate this difference, Figure 2 shows a conceptual view of the architecture of an evolutionary digital twin in learning environments. In this figure, data flows from various sources (including user interactions, environmental data, and behavioral signals) to an analytics core. This core processes the data not in isolation, but in a temporal structure. The twin's modeling layer then uses this data to create a dynamic representation of the learner's state and trajectory that is continuously updated. Finally, this representation is passed to the decision layer to generate appropriate adaptive responses.

Figure 2. Conceptual architecture of an evolutionary digital twin in learning behavior monitoring

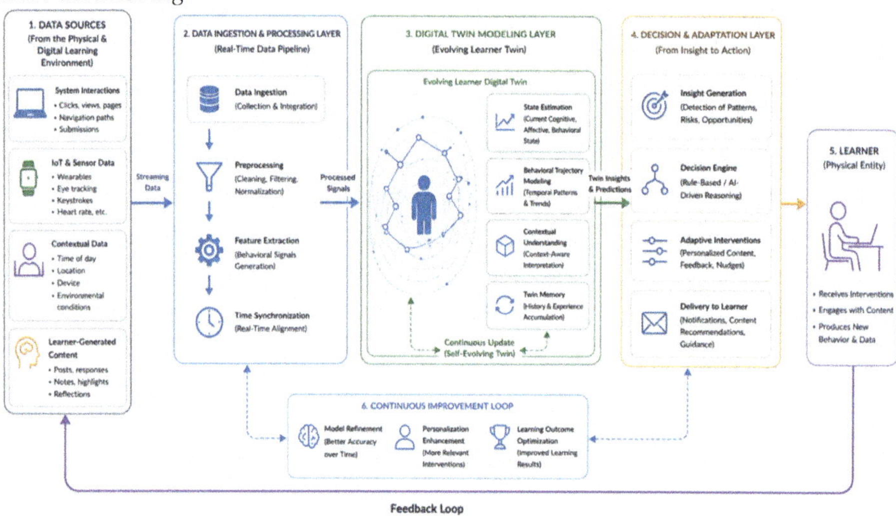

As can be seen in Figure 2, the key feature of this architecture is the existence of a continuous feedback loop between the learner and the twin. Data is continuously input into the system, updating the twin model, and the resulting outputs again influence the learner's behavior. This cycle creates a live, two-way interaction in which the twin not only reflects the behavior, but also plays a role in shaping it.

Another important aspect of this structure is the concept of real-time synchronization. The evolutionary twin should be able to detect changes in the learner's behavior with minimal delay and reflect them in its model. This synchronization is crucial, especially in dynamic environments, as any delay can lead to inconsistent or even misleading decisions. However, real-time synchronization is not limited to processing speed alone, but also depends on the ability to correctly interpret data in real time.

Here, the twin modeling layer plays a pivotal role. This layer must be able to integrate heterogeneous and multi-source data into a coherent structure and use it to create a meaningful representation. Unlike static models that only provide a snapshot, the evolutionary twin model must be able to track changes over time and extract behavioral patterns. This feature allows for more advanced analytics such as identifying hidden trends, predicting future changes, and detecting anomalies.

In addition, the evolutionary twin must have some degree of "memory." This memory allows the system to consider not only the current state but also the history of the learner's behavior. Without such a capability, each analysis is performed independently, and the connection between events is lost. In contrast, with a structured memory, the twin can identify long-term patterns and make more accurate decisions.

Ultimately, the digital twin in this context becomes a dynamic entity that functions beyond a display device. By combining data, time, and context, the twin is able to provide a living picture of the learner and enhance our understanding of the learning process to a deeper level. Such an approach paves the way for the development of systems that not only monitor behavior, but also understand it, predict it, and, if necessary, intelligently intervene in it.

5- SIGNALS FROM THE PHYSICAL-DIGITAL BOUNDARY

The boundary between the physical and digital worlds has become one of the most dynamic points of evolution in intelligent systems in recent years. In the field of education, this boundary is also where the actual behavior of the learner (as it occurs in interactions with the environment, tools, and even biological conditions) is transformed into data that can be recorded and analyzed. However, what is important here is not simply "data" but "signals"; a distinction that is crucial to understanding for the development of digital twin-based systems. At first glance, any type of data extracted from learner interactions may be considered valuable input. But the reality is that not all data is equally meaningful. Much raw data is a reflection of noise, random behavior, or unrelated factors. Signals, in contrast, are meaningful patterns extracted from data that can be indicative of the cognitive, behavioral, or emotional state of the learner. Therefore, the main challenge at this boundary is to transform scattered and heterogeneous data into interpretable signals (Nozari, 2026b).

A key characteristic of data coming from the physical-digital boundary is its multidimensionality. This data can come from a variety of sources, including direct interactions with learning systems, environmental data, and even biological signals. For example, click and navigation patterns on an educational platform provide information about how a learner interacts with content. In addition, data such as time of day, light levels, or ambient noise levels can provide the context in which these interactions occur. In some cases, data from wearable devices can also reflect physiological state cues such as heart rate or activity level. Each of these sources provides only part of the picture; but when combined, they can lead to a more comprehensive understanding of learner behavior (Mohandes et al., 2026).

However, integrating these diverse data sources comes with serious challenges. First, there is the structural heterogeneity of the data. Interactional, environmental, and biological data are each recorded in different formats and require their own specific processing. Second, there is the issue of temporal synchronization. In order to establish relationships between different data, these data need to be placed in a common time frame. Without such temporal alignment, accurate behavioral analysis would not be possible. Third, there is the issue of data quality. Data collected from real environments are often accompanied by noise, missing data, or measurement errors that can affect the accuracy of the analyses. Among these, the signal extraction process is considered a key step. This process involves several basic steps: data cleaning, normalization, feature extraction, and finally, the identification of meaningful patterns. For example, from a simple sequence of clicks, features such as the speed of interaction, patterns of return to content, or the degree of dispersion of attention can be extracted. Similarly, from temporal data, unusual rhythms of activity or interruptions can be identified. These features, if analyzed together and in the right context, can be transformed into signals that reflect the real state of the learner (Nozari & Yordanova, 2026).

One of the important points in this process is to pay attention to the context. As mentioned earlier, the same behavior can have different meanings in different situations. Therefore, extracting a signal without taking into account the context can lead to misinterpretations. For example, a sudden decrease in the level of interaction may be a sign of fatigue in one scenario, and in another scenario the result of an external interruption. Only by considering environmental and temporal data can this difference be recognized. Consequently, signals must always be defined and interpreted in a contextual manner (Shende & Pandey, 2026).

Furthermore, signals are often not directly observable, but rather are derived from a combination of several indicators. For example, "cognitive engagement" may be inferred from a combination of time spent, patterns of re-entry, and changes in the speed of interaction. This suggests that signals are inferential in nature and require models that can reliably make this inference. Here, the role of the digital twin is highlighted, as it can aggregate these signals into a coherent structure and track them over time. On the other hand, the issue of sensitivity and privacy is also of particular importance at this frontier. Data collected from the physical and biological environment can be very sensitive and require careful management. Therefore, designing systems that can extract meaningful signals without violating the learner's privacy is a major challenge. This requires the use of approaches in which data is collected and processed in a minimal and targeted manner (Nozari, 2026c).

Ultimately, the physical-digital boundary can be thought of as the point at which "behavior" is transformed into "data" and then into "signals." This transformation, if done properly, can provide a foundation for a deeper understanding of the learning process. Otherwise, one is left with a mass of unstructured and uninterpretable data that is not only unhelpful but can also be misleading. The success of digital twin-based systems in education, therefore, depends largely on their ability to manage this boundary and extract meaningful signals from multi-source data. This perspective moves us from focusing on collecting more data to designing systems that can intelligently interpret the data that is available. In such a framework, signals are considered the basic units of meaning. Units that can represent learner behavior in a more accurate, deeper, and actionable way.

6- HOW THE TWIN MAKES SENSE OF BEHAVIOR

At the point where data is transformed into signals, the main question is how these signals lead to "understanding." Many analytical systems are capable of extracting patterns, but pattern extraction does not necessarily mean understanding behavior. The difference between the two lies in how the information is interpreted, organized, and linked into a meaningful framework. The digital twin here plays a role beyond a processing tool; it is designed to interpret the learner's behavior in the context of time, context, and multi-layered interactions. To achieve this level of understanding, the twin must have a multi-layered structure, in which each layer performs a specific task in transforming data into meaning. At the first level, input signals from different sources are aligned in a common space. This alignment involves not only temporal coordination but also conceptual integration; This means that data of different natures are redefined in terms of comparable and combinable features. This step provides a basis for subsequent analysis, because without a common language, there will be no coherent interpretation of the data (Parmar et al., 2026).

Next, the twin moves on to identify patterns. These patterns can appear in the form of time trends, behavioral fluctuations, or recurring sequences. But the important thing is that these patterns do not have meaning on their own; what matters is placing them in an interpretive context. For example, a gradual increase in interaction may be a sign of progress, but if it is accompanied by an increase in errors, it could indicate an effort without sufficient understanding. Therefore, the twin must be able to identify relationships between patterns and place them in a broader analytical framework (Som & Jamader, 2026).

One key tool in this process is the concept of "state." By defining a set of interpretable states (such as high cognitive engagement, low engagement, or behavioral instability), a digital twin can map input signals into meaningful states. These states are not statically defined, but are updated over time based on incoming data. In other words, each learner is in a specific state at any given moment, the result of past interactions and their current circumstances. This state is a point on a continuous path and only makes sense in relation to the overall path (Tadj, 2026).

In the meantime, the role of memory in a digital twin is crucial. Unlike systems that only pay attention to current data, a twin has a structured memory that stores the history of the learner's behavior. This memory allows the system to identify long-term patterns and understand gradual changes. For example, a slow decline in engagement may not be noticeable in the short term, but over a longer period of time, it will appear as a meaningful trend. Without such a memory, many of these patterns will remain hidden from the system.

In addition, the digital twin must be able to interpret behavior in context. As discussed in the previous sections, behavior without context is meaningless. Therefore, the twin pays attention not only to behavioral signals but also to contextual information. This information can include the type of content, the time of day, environmental conditions, or even the individual characteristics of the learner. By combining these factors, the system can provide a more accurate interpretation of behavior. For example, decreased attention at the end of the day may be considered normal, while the same behavior at the beginning of the day could be a sign of difficulty in understanding the content.

Another important aspect of understanding behavior is the ability to detect anomalies. By comparing current behavior with past patterns, a digital twin can identify unexpected changes. These anomalies can be signs of learning difficulties, changes in motivation, or even external factors. Recognizing these changes early allows for a quick and effective response. However, this process requires high sensitivity and accuracy, because not every unexpected change necessarily means a problem. As a result, the twin must be able to distinguish between normal changes and real anomalies. At a deeper level, a digital twin seeks to create a "coherent interpretation" of behavior. This interpretation is the result of combining states, patterns, context, and history. In other words, the system attempts to answer the question "What does this behavior mean?" rather than simply "What happened?" This shift in question type represents a shift from descriptive to interpretive analysis. In such a framework, the twin can reconstruct the learner's behavior as a dynamic narrative—a narrative in which each event makes sense in relation to other events (Zhang et al., 2026).

Finally, understanding behavior in a digital twin is not a static process, but is constantly being updated. As new data comes in, previous interpretations may be modified or new meanings may be formed. This dynamism is one of the key features of the twin that distinguishes it from traditional models. Here, understanding is not a final result, but an ongoing process that is shaped by interaction with data, context, and time.

Overall, by combining multiple layers of analysis (from data alignment to contextual interpretation), the digital twin is able to understand learner behavior in a way that goes beyond superficial analysis. This ability provides a foundation for designing systems that can not only observe behavior, but also interpret it meaningfully and make decisions based on it.

7- CLOSING THE LOOP WITH THE LEARNER

In smart learning systems, the value of a digital twin is not limited to its ability to capture data, extract signals, and interpret learner behavior. Such a capability, while essential for understanding the learning situation, only becomes truly effective when the insights from the analysis can be translated into appropriate instructional actions. From this perspective, a digital twin is not simply an observation and analysis mechanism, but rather part of an adaptive cycle that connects system perception with instructional intervention. This connection is the closed loop that enables behavioral understanding to be translated into targeted learning responses (Ramamurthy et al., 2026).

At this point, the focus shifts from "understanding behavior" to "influencing behavior." But this influence should not be prescriptive, static, or one-way. Instead, the interaction between the learner and the twin should be structured as a dynamic, adaptive loop, where each action the system takes is based on its current understanding of the learner's state, and the action itself provides new data to update the twin. This loop is what can be referred to as a living feedback loop.

To better understand this interaction, Figure 3 shows a conceptual view of the closed loop between the learner and the digital twin. In this figure, the learner's behavior is taken as the starting point, which is transformed into data through various interactions. This data enters the twin, where it is transformed into signals and then into insights. These insights are then transformed into adaptive decisions and interventions, and then back into the learning environment, where they influence the learner's behavior. This process is repeated continuously, and with each iteration, the system gains a more accurate understanding of the learner.

Figure 3. The closed loop of interaction between the learner and the digital twin in adaptive learning

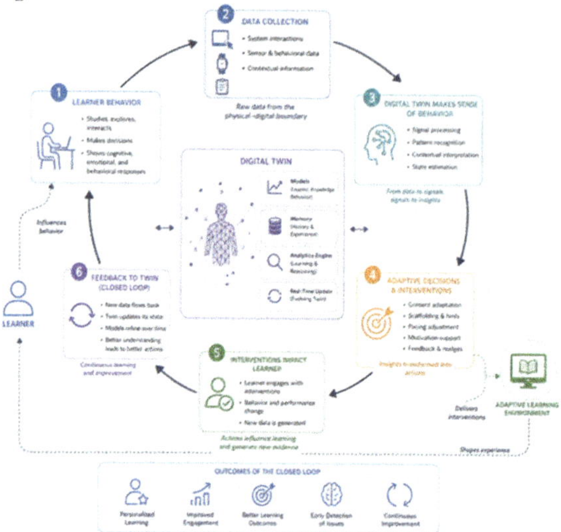

As can be seen in Figure 3, this loop has several key features that distinguish it from traditional approaches. First, it is continuous. Here, decision-making is not a one-off event, but rather part of a continuous process that is updated with each new data. This continuousness allows the system to respond to gradual changes in the learner's behavior and avoid sudden and incoherent reactions.

The second feature is the contextuality of interventions. Decisions made in this loop are not based on predetermined and fixed rules, but on the learner's current state and past trajectory. For example, if the twin detects that the learner is experiencing a drop in cognitive engagement at a particular stage, the intervention can be designed to provide alternative content, reduce complexity, or even provide a purposeful break. Conversely, if the same behavior occurs in a different context, a different response may be more appropriate. This flexibility is one of the main advantages of digital twin-based systems.

Another important point is the role of the learner in this cycle. Unlike some automated systems that consider the learner as a passive element, in this framework the learner is an active part of the feedback loop. His behaviors not only constitute the input to the system, but also how he reacts to interventions is considered as new data. This two-way interaction allows for mutual learning: the system learns from the learner, and at the same time, the learner is guided by the system's interventions.

However, designing such a cycle is not without its challenges. One of the most important challenges is to avoid "overreaction." If the system reacts to every small change in the learner's behavior, it may cause instability in the learning experience.

For example, constantly changing the content path or system settings can confuse or reduce the learner's confidence. Therefore, the twin must be able to distinguish between meaningful changes and natural fluctuations and intervene only when intervention is truly needed.

Another challenge is to maintain a balance between personalization and learner autonomy. While these systems aim to provide an experience tailored to individual needs, excessive intervention can deprive the learner of a sense of control. As a result, interventions should be designed to act more as suggestions, guidance, or opportunities for choice rather than direct guidance. This approach allows the learner to continue to play an active role in their learning process.

Ultimately, closing the loop between the digital twin and the learner is the point at which the system transforms from an analytical tool to an active agent in the learning process. This transformation enables the creation of systems that not only understand behavior, but can also intervene in it intelligently and contextually. Such systems are the foundation for a new generation of intelligent education in which learning is viewed as a living, interactive, and evolving process.

8- WHERE PRECISION MEETS SENSITIVITY

As the precision of monitoring and interpreting learner behavior increases, an important question arises: how far should this precision go? Systems designed based on digital twins and multi-source data have the potential to provide a very detailed and accurate picture of the learner's behavior, cognitive state, and even contextual conditions. However, this same ability can become a major challenge, because as the precision of the system increases, so does its sensitivity to privacy, individual autonomy, and ethical boundaries. At this point, system design no longer becomes a purely technical issue, but a human and social one.

One of the first challenges in this area is defining the boundary between "understanding" and "interference." Digital twin-based systems can identify behaviors that even the learner is not aware of, for example, a gradual decrease in concentration or a change in the pattern of interaction with content. This type of insight, if used correctly, can help improve the learning experience. But if these insights are applied without the user's consent and awareness, they may lead to excessive surveillance or even unwanted interference. Therefore, the main challenge here is to use analytical rigor without crossing the acceptable boundaries of human interaction (Giwa & Kim, 2026).

In this regard, the concept of "transparency" plays a key role. The learner needs to know what kind of data is being collected from him, how this data is processed, and what impact it has on the system's decisions. This transparency not only helps to build trust, but also allows the user to participate consciously in the learning process. In the absence of such transparency, even the most accurate systems may encounter resistance or distrust from users. Therefore, it is of particular importance to design interfaces and mechanisms that can present this information in an understandable and unobtrusive manner.

Another important issue is "data minimalism." While new technologies have made it possible to collect vast amounts of data, this does not mean that all of it should be used. In many cases, sufficient insights can be gained using a limited but targeted set of data. This approach not only helps reduce the complexity of the system, but also reduces the risks associated with privacy violations. Therefore, one of the design principles in this area is to consciously select the data that is truly necessary for analyzing behavior.

Along with these issues, the issue of "bias" must also be considered. The models used in digital twins are trained on past data and may reproduce patterns that are not necessarily fair or accurate. For example, if the initial data indicates poor performance of a particular group, the system may unintentionally suggest interventions that reinforce this situation. Therefore, the system design should be such that it can detect and correct these biases, rather than fix them (Ren et al., 2026).

On the other hand, the sensitivity of the system to behavioral changes also requires fine-tuning. A very sensitive system may react to every small fluctuation, resulting in an unstable experience for the learner. Conversely, a system with low sensitivity may ignore important changes. Therefore, determining the appropriate level of sensitivity, while maintaining both the accuracy of the analysis and ensuring the stability of the user experience, is one of the key challenges in the design of these systems. This becomes especially important in real-world environments where human behavior is inherently variable and nonlinear.

Also, the role of "user control" should be considered. The learner should not be a mere passive recipient of system interventions, but should be able to adjust, limit, or even disable some capabilities. This control helps maintain a sense of ownership and autonomy in the learning process and prevents over-reliance on the system. In fact, the goal is not for the system to replace human decision-making, but rather to act as a support tool that makes decision-making more informed and effective.

On a broader level, the design of digital twin-based systems requires an interdisciplinary approach in which technical, educational, psychological, and ethical considerations are simultaneously taken into account. For example, understanding how a particular intervention can affect a learner's motivation or sense of self-efficacy requires knowledge beyond data analysis. For this reason, the development of these systems should be carried out with the participation of experts from different fields to avoid one-sidedness.

Ultimately, it can be said that the intersection of accuracy and sensitivity is where the true quality of an intelligent system is determined. A system that focuses solely on accuracy may become intrusive and unreliable, while a system that is overly conservative may fail to provide useful insights. Striking a balance between the two requires careful design, ongoing evaluation, and attention to the needs and preferences of users.

In this context, a digital twin must not only understand "right," but also act "right." In a way that both maintains analytical accuracy and respects the dignity and autonomy of the learner. This perspective paves the way for the development of systems that can intervene responsibly and effectively in the learning process, providing a balanced experience between technology and humanity.

9- CONCLUSION

The evolution of smart education systems requires a rethinking of the way learning is understood and represented, rather than simply relying on the development of technological tools. In many common approaches, learning is still analyzed through indicators such as grades, attendance, number of clicks, time spent in the system, or test results. These indicators can show parts of the learner's activity, but they are not sufficient to explain how learning takes place, behavior changes, the gradual growth of understanding, and the complex interaction between the learner and the educational environment. From this perspective, the main problem is not only the lack of data, but also the limitations of the frameworks that transform this data into meaning.

The present study emphasizes the idea that the digital twin, especially when integrated with Internet of Things technologies, can play an important role in overcoming this limitation. In such a framework, the learner is not seen as a collection of scattered data, but as a dynamic, contextual, and evolving system. This view allows learner behavior to be analyzed as a time trajectory; a trajectory in which every interaction, every interruption, every change in participation level, and every instructional response can be part of a larger pattern.

One of the most important values of this approach is the transformation of raw data into meaningful signals. Data obtained from digital interactions, sensors, wearables, environmental conditions, or behaviors recorded in educational systems cannot alone represent the true state of the learner. This data becomes valuable when interpreted in the context of time, context, and behavioral history. By providing a unified structure, the digital twin makes it possible to organize this data, extract behavioral signals, and shape a living representation of the learner.

This live representation is not simply a snapshot of the learner's current state. The digital twin can capture the learner's behavioral past, analyze their current state, and reveal clues about their likely future trajectory. For this reason, its fundamental difference from traditional models of the learner is its dynamism and ability to evolve. In this framework, the learner is not stopped at a fixed moment, but is seen along a learning path that is constantly being redefined as new data enters.

The practical value of this framework becomes more apparent when behavior analysis is linked to educational action. If the digital twin only observes and interprets behavior, its role will be limited to that of an analytical tool. But when the insights from the analysis are translated into educational decisions and interventions, the system enters a true adaptive cycle. In this cycle, the learner's behavior generates data, the data updates the twin, the twin interprets the situation, the system suggests appropriate interventions, and the learner's response is again transformed into new data to refine the model.

Such a cycle can take intelligent learning beyond simple personalization. In many existing systems, personalization is often limited to suggesting content based on past performance or apparent preferences. But in the digital twin framework, personalization can be based on a deeper understanding of the learner's behavioral, cognitive, and contextual state. In this way, the system not only knows what the learner has done, but also tries to understand why a behavior occurred, under what circumstances it was formed, and what kind of response might be more appropriate to continue the learning path.

Despite these capabilities, this research shows that increasing the accuracy of behavior monitoring must be accompanied by human and ethical sensitivity. The more precisely a system can observe and analyze learner behavior, the greater its responsibility in terms of privacy, transparency, user control, and prevention of excessive interference. A smart educational system should not become a tool for constant surveillance and hidden pressure on the learner. On the contrary, it should be designed to use data to support learning, enhance learner autonomy, and improve the educational experience.

Hence, a balance between accuracy and sensitivity is a fundamental principle in the design of educational digital twin systems. Transparency in data collection, minimal and purposeful use of information, contextual interpretation of behavior, user controllability of the system, and avoidance of unexplained decisions are all essential to building trust. Without such principles, even the most advanced technical architecture may encounter user resistance or have unintended consequences.

Overall, digital twins integrated with the Internet of Things can provide a new path to understanding learning in smart environments. This approach moves education from the stage of recording scattered data to the stage of interpreting live behavior. In this view, learning is not a final outcome, but a continuous, observable, interpretable, and supportable process. The importance of this transformation is that it moves technology from the role of a storage and reporting tool to an active part of the process of understanding and improving learning.

Therefore, the future of intelligent education systems depends on the development of frameworks that can responsibly connect data and meaning, observation and interpretation, analysis and intervention, and technology and people. The digital twin, when properly designed, can make such a connection possible and pave the way for learning environments that not only measure learner performance, but also understand, support, and respond to their development path in an intelligent and human way.

REFERENCES

AbdelRaouf, H., Hasnaine, Q. R., Fouda, M. M., Fadlullah, Z. M., & Ibrahem, M. I. (2026). Paradigm Shift Toward Distributed Learning in IoT Intelligence: A Comprehensive Survey of Opportunities and Challenges. *IEEE Internet of Things Journal, 13*(10), 20128–20154. DOI: 10.1109/JIOT.2026.3657733

Amaresh, K., Kumar, J. S. V. S., Mustafa, M., Kumar, N. M. G., & Tabassum, S. (2026). Integrated IoT and digital twin architecture for optimising xEV performance and grid interaction. *International Journal of Mathematical Modelling and Numerical Optimisation, 16*(2-4), 314–336. DOI: 10.1504/IJMMNO.2026.153031

Eiaseb, N. P. I. G., Goagoses, N., Hamukoshi, S. S., & Eiases, R. H. S. (2026). Exploring the Role of Digital Twins in Enhancing Smart City IoT Applications: A Critical Review. IoT-Driven Business Transformation: Strategy, Data, Trust, and Security, 183-218.

Giwa, O., & Kim, S. (2026). A Decade Later: Evolution of Real-Time Embedded Virtual Presence Systems (An HCI Perspective). *ACM Transactions on Embedded Computing Systems, 25*(2), 1–29. DOI: 10.1145/3788875

Goyal, I., Sai, S., Pabbati, M., Chamola, V., & Ranjan, V. (2026). Empowering Digital Twins With Agentic AI: Applications, Case Studies, and Limitations. *IEEE Communications Standards Magazine*, 1–11. DOI: 10.1109/MCOMSTD.2026.3669229

Kalogeras, S., Samadi, S., & Nozari, H. (Eds.). (2025). *AI-Augmented Creativity in Learning Analytics*. IGI Global. DOI: 10.4018/979-8-3373-5117-9

Li, X., Gan, W., Liu, X., & Yang, J. (2026). Rule-Based Digital Twin: An Integrated Parametric-BIM Workflow for Life-Cycle Delivery of Free-Form, Special-Shaped Envelopes in Large-Scale Public Buildings. *Buildings (Basel, Switzerland), 16*(4), 778. DOI: 10.3390/buildings16040778

Manimegalai, S., & Binu Ben Jose, D. R. (2026). Application of Digital Technologies in Renewable Energy Systems. Energy Systems Engineering: Modeling. *Analysis and Applications*, •••, 187–226.

Mishra, S., Aldafas, T. S. M., & Alshammari, N. S. (2026). A zero-trust digital twin framework for privacy-preserving multi-dataset intrusion detection in industrial IoT with lightweight blockchain auditing. *Scientific Reports, 16*(1), 15236. DOI: 10.1038/s41598-026-42041-w PMID: 41917091

Mohandes, S. R., Singh, A. K., Ibrahim, A., Ma, N., Kineber, A. F., & Shakor, P. (2026). Pioneering digital transformation: unveiling the blockchain and digital twin technologies' synergy. Journal of Engineering, Design and Technology, 1-25.

Muhudin, A. A., Shafiullah, M., Al-Ramadan, B., Zami, M. S., Zamani, M. T., & Herzallah, L. (2026). Reframing BIM and Digital Twins for Intelligent Built Environments. *Smart Cities*, *9*(4), 71. DOI: 10.3390/smartcities9040071

Nozari, H. (2025). Optimizing transmedia storytelling strategies across platforms for Maximum audience engagement. *Entertainment Computing*, •••, 101061.

Nozari, H. (2026a). Self-Evolving Neuromorphic Systems for Predictive Learning Interventions. In AI-Augmented Creativity in Learning Analytics (pp. 105-122). IGI Global Scientific Publishing.

Nozari, H. (2026b). Digital twin-based predictive maintenance in cold chain logistics. *Operations Research*, *60*(1), 481–499. DOI: 10.1051/ro/2025167

Nozari, H. (2026c). AI-Augmented Creative Assessment: From Static Tests to Dynamic Insight Generation. In AI-Augmented Creativity in Learning Analytics (pp. 25-42). IGI Global Scientific Publishing.

Nozari, H., & Yordanova, Z. (2026). Digital twin–driven decision support for human capital management under uncertainty. Green Technologies and Sustainability, 100353.

Parmar, H., Murari, U. K., & Singh, S. K. (2026, February). Smart Polymer-Integrated IoT Systems: A Mathematical Framework for Real-Time Sensing and Adaptive Material Behavior. *Macromolecular Symposia*, *415*(1), e70183. DOI: 10.1002/masy.70183

Pham, T. A., Ioannou, P. G., & Likhitruangsilp, V. (2026). Designing a BIM-enhanced digital twin architecture for construction pollution management in building renovation projects. *International Journal of Construction Management*, •••, 1–26. DOI: 10.1080/15623599.2026.2651946

Rajaram, A., & Almalki, F. A. (2026). Energy Efficient Decentralized Digital Twins with IoT and Blockchain for Self-Optimizing Urban Infrastructure and Sustainable Energy Management. *Sustainable Computing : Informatics and Systems*, *50*, 101319. DOI: 10.1016/j.suscom.2026.101319

Ramamurthy, K., Kulanthaivelu, S., & Jenish, S. A. (2026). Future directions and emerging trends of adaptive artificial intelligence in wireless sensor networks, Internet of Things, and Industrial Internet of Things. Adaptive AI in Sensor Informatics, 291-308.

Ren, K., Xu, C., Xiong, C., Bin, J., Zhang, Z., Wang, T., He, C., Shao, Y., Fei, X., Jiang, Y., Chen, Y., & Huang, Y. (2026). Optimization of Thermal Flow Dynamics in Tobacco Leaf Curing via IoT-Integrated Deep Neural Network-Assisted CFD. *IEEE Internet of Things Journal*, *13*(10), 21510–21525. DOI: 10.1109/JIOT.2026.3666820

Shende, S. A., & Pandey, P. M. (2026). Multi-sensor IoT integrated framework for monitoring motion deviation, vibration and surface defect detection in extrusion-based additive manufacturing. *Progress in Additive Manufacturing*, •••, 1–19. DOI: 10.1007/s40964-026-01605-y

Som, S., & Jamader, A. R. (2026). Metaverse Marketing Strategies Using IoT and 5G. In Digital Twins and Simulation Technology (pp. 55-73). Chapman and Hall/CRC.

Tadj, L. (2026). IoT-Enabled Model Predictive Control for Perishable Goods Production With Dynamic Spoilage Mitigation. *IEEE Access : Practical Innovations, Open Solutions*, *14*, 6768–6785. DOI: 10.1109/ACCESS.2026.3651980

Yordanova, Z., & Nozari, H. (2026). Seamless Data Integration for Predictive Learning Environments. In AI-Augmented Creativity in Learning Analytics (pp. 293-318). IGI Global Scientific Publishing.

Zhang, L., Tang, C., Ye, Y., Yang, J., & Xu, F. (2026). Intelligent HBIM Framework for Group-Oriented Preventive Protection: A Case Study of the Suopo Ancient Watchtower Complex in Danba. *Buildings (Basel, Switzerland)*, *16*(5), 995. DOI: 10.3390/buildings16050995

Chapter 14

Designing Digital Twin-Driven Lifelong Learning Ecosystems: A Conceptual Framework for Personalized Education

Ankita Priti Roy
http://orcid.org/0000-0002-8986-984X
Kristu Jayanti University, Bengaluru, India

Arti Singh
Kristu Jayanti University, Bengaluru, India

ABSTRACT

With 44% of workers' core skills facing disruption within five years, lifelong learning has become a critical imperative that traditional educational models cannot meet. This chapter proposes the Digital Twin-Driven Lifelong Learning System (DT-LLS), a novel five-layer framework operationalizing digital twin technology across the full human learning continuum. Grounded in a 2020–2026 literature synthesis, it targets five critical gaps: absent lifelong twin continuity, siloed learning contexts, unvalidated ethical governance, unproven scalability, and underdeveloped affective modeling. Five interoperable layers Learner Data Acquisition, Human Digital Twin Modeling, Adaptive Intelligence Engine, Learning Delivery Interface, and Continuous Evolution Loop integrate xAPI standards, Deep Knowledge Tracing, federated learning, and ontologies aligned to ESCO and Industry 5.0. Six principles govern implementation: learner sovereignty, context agnosticism, progressive fidelity, transparency, equitable design, and human-AI complementarity. A seven-direction research agenda is also provided.

DOI: 10.4018/979-8-2600-1674-9.ch014

1. INTRODUCTION TO LIFELONG LEARNING AND DIGITAL TRANSFORMATION

The twenty-first century knowledge economy is characterised by accelerating technological disruption, volatile labour markets, and rapidly shifting skill demands that outpace the adaptive capacity of traditional educational institutions. Pietrzykowski (2023) projects that 44% of workers' core competencies will be rendered obsolete within five years as a consequence of artificial intelligence, automation, and the reconfiguration of global value chains a trajectory that positions lifelong, continuous learning not as an aspirational ideal but as a structural necessity for individuals, organisations, and societies alike (Weerakkody et al., 2016). Traditional educational systems, however, remain largely designed around fixed curricula, time-bounded instruction, and summative snapshot assessments that are structurally misaligned with the dynamic, iterative nature of contemporary competency development (Henry et al., 2019). These systems process learners as cohorts rather than individuals, foregrounding standardised outcomes over personalised trajectories, and leave learners' experiences across formal education, informal communities, and workplace environments fragmented and analytically disconnected from one another (Poquet et al., 2021).

Industry 5.0 the European Commission's strategic framework for a human-centred, sustainable, and resilient European industry places correspondingly demanding requirements on educational infrastructures (European Commission, 2021). Rather than technical upskilling alone, this paradigm calls for learners who are cognitively adaptable, ethically grounded, and capable of sustained collaboration across human-machine boundaries, while preserving alignment with core human values (Costello et al., 2024). Educational systems responsive to this vision must possess the institutional capacity to map evolving competency demands to individual developmental trajectories, identify emergent skill gaps in real time, and deliver context-sensitive learning support across the full arc of a professional life (Ronja et al., 2025). Digital twin technology, originally developed in aerospace and manufacturing (Grieves & Vickers, 2016), offers a compelling solution to this challenge: by constructing dynamic, data-synchronised virtual representations of complex systems, it enables continuous monitoring, scenario simulation, and proactive optimisation of the entity being modelled.

The scholarly literature on educational digital twins, though expanding rapidly, remains limited to engineering education, higher education, and professional training (Kinsner, 2021). No frameworks yet address lifelong learning across all stages from childhood to retirement integrating formal, informal, and workplace modes in a unified twin architecture. This gap signals a prime opportunity for conceptual advances (Addanki & Corrin, 2023). The chapter makes three principal contributions to the emerging scholarship on digital twin applications in education. First, it synthesises the existing literature on educational digital twin implementations, analyses the scope and methodological foundations of current applications, and identifies five critical structural gaps that constrain both theoretical development and practical deployment. Second, it introduces the Digital Twin-Driven Lifelong Learning System (DT-LLS) a novel five-layer conceptual framework that operationalises digital twin technology across the full continuum of human learning through modular components addressing learner data acquisition, Human Digital Twin modelling, adaptive intelligence, learning delivery, and longitudinal self-improvement. Third, it examines the ethical, technical, and systemic challenges attendant on large-scale implementation, proposes a governance sub-framework for responsible deployment, and establishes seven prioritised directions for future empirical and technical research.

2. FUNDAMENTALS OF DIGITAL TWIN TECHNOLOGY

Understanding the DT-LLS framework requires a grounded appreciation of digital twin technology itself its origins, core architecture, distinguishing properties, and the specific adaptations necessary for application to human learners. This section provides that foundation, drawing on both foundational engineering literature and the emerging educational applications literature.

2.1 Origins and Conceptual Development

The digital twin concept was introduced by (Grieves, 2022) in product lifecycle management as a synchronized digital counterpart to its physical twin. It gained momentum via NASA's spacecraft monitoring and spread to aerospace, automotive, energy, healthcare, and urban systems; Siemens, GE, and others popularized it industrially through demonstrated gains in asset performance, maintenance, and optimization (Yao et al., 2023). Unlike input-output simulations or static models, digital twins enable continuous bidirectional data synchronization—receiving real-world data to update virtual states and feeding back insights to influence the physical entity. This closed-loop (physical → virtual → physical) architecture provides their unique power (Durão et al., 2021; Kuehn, 2018)

2.2 Human Digital Twins: Architecture and Properties

The extension of digital twin technology from engineered systems to human subjects the Human Digital Twin expands the concept's scope and complexity.

Unlike mechanical systems' defined states, humans span biological, psychological, social, and cultural dimensions that are hard to observe and model. Effective HDTs integrate diverse data streams (physiological, cognitive, behavioral, affective, social, environmental) for faithful yet computationally tractable representations (Kabashkin, 2025). Romero et al. (2023) identifies four properties for learning-oriented twins: fidelity (accurate cognitive/affective modeling, improving with data volume/ diversity); adaptivity (responsive updates without retraining) (Moya et al., 2020); interoperability (standardized data exchange with external systems); and intelligibility (interpretable outputs essential for trust and human-AI collaboration).

2.3 A Taxonomy of Educational Digital Twins

Drawing on the functional taxonomy proposed by Kabashkin (2025) and adapting it to educational contexts, four digital twin types are relevant to learning systems. Each type represents an increasing level of analytical sophistication and operational impact, and a mature DT-LLS must ultimately integrate all four within its Adaptive Intelligence Engine.

- **Descriptive Twins:** represent the learner's current state: what knowledge has been demonstrated, which skills have been assessed, what engagement levels have been observed, and which competencies have been credentialed. This type provides the foundational situational awareness from which all subsequent analysis proceeds (Liebowitz, 2021).
- **Diagnostic Twins:** analyze the causes of observed performance patterns, identifying learning style mismatches, prerequisite knowledge deficiencies, attentional disruptions, motivational barriers, or environmental factors that account for deviations from expected trajectories. Diagnostic analysis transforms observation into explanation (Kärner et al., 2020).
- **Predictive Twins:** forecast future learning trajectories, performance on upcoming assessments, dropout risk probability, and competency attainment timelines using statistical and machine learning models trained on historical cohort data. This type transforms explanation into anticipation, enabling proactive rather than reactive intervention (Psyridou et al., 2024).
- **Prescriptive Twins:** generate actionable recommendations: optimal content sequencing, pedagogical modality selection, difficulty calibration, motivational nudges, peer matching, and instructor escalation triggers designed to maximize the probability of favorable learning outcomes given the learner's current twin state. This type closes the loop from anticipation to action (Kővári, 2025).

The sequential relationship among these twin types' descriptive enabling diagnostic, diagnostic enabling predictive, and predictive enabling prescriptive defines a progressive maturity model for DT-LLS implementation. Organizations at early stages of digital twin adoption may feasibly implement descriptive and diagnostic capabilities using existing LMS data infrastructure, while predictive and prescriptive capabilities require more sophisticated AI infrastructure and larger datasets.

3. DIGITAL TWINS IN EDUCATION: CURRENT APPLICATIONS AND RESEARCH GAPS

Scholarly interest in educational digital twins has accelerated markedly since 2020, with a notable concentration of empirical and conceptual work in engineering education, higher education institutions, and professional training contexts(Chamorro-Atalaya et al., 2024; Hazrat et al., 2023). A systematic review of the available literature from 2020 to 2026 reveals both significant achievements and persistent structural gaps that directly motivate the DT-LLS framework proposed in Section 4.

3.1 Digital Twins in Engineering and STEM Education

Engineering education pioneers' educational digital twins, ideal for simulation-based and physical-system modeling. Karanam and Hartman (Karanam & Hartman, 2025) integrated DTs with virtual platforms in manufacturing programs; students gained deeper manufacturing understanding than with static simulations by bridging theory-practice gaps and revealing decision impacts. Hazrat et al. (Hazrat et al., 2023) applied DTs in mechanical engineering to foster multidisciplinary skills and human-centric decisions via dynamic life cycle assessments of smart systems (Madarkar et al., 2024), enabling experiential learning beyond labs. Zhang et al. (2024) developed a DT system for project-based landscaping courses; vocational students showed superior critical thinking, lower cognitive load, better experience, and higher performance vs. controls.

3.2 Institutional-Level Digital Twins in Higher Education

Beyond individual learner modeling, researchers have explored digital twins at the institutional level. Kartashova et al. proposed using digital twin technology to build a digital prototype of an educational institution supporting blended learning continuity and individual learner development trajectories(Семеріков et al., 2021). This macro-level twinning approach complements learner-level twins by situating individual trajectories within the systemic context that shapes and constrains them.

Similarly, Al-Obaidi et al. highlighted the potential of digital twins for optimizing campus infrastructure and resources, including energy management and space utilization, thereby enhancing the overall operational efficiency of higher education institutions (Addanki & Corrin, 2023). The utility of Digital Twins extends beyond infrastructure, encompassing complex decision-making processes through the integration of learning analytics and generative AI, which facilitates data-driven insights for strategic planning and resource allocation within higher education institutions (Vrček et al., 2025). This integration enables the development of high-fidelity institutional digital twins capable of modeling intricate educational ecosystems and supporting advanced research at the doctoral level[REMOVED HYPERLINK FIELD].

3.3 AI-Augmented Learner Digital Twins

Kabashkin's AI-based student digital twins framework employs AI algorithms, semantic ontologies across educational/career domains, and real-time feedback for personalized learning orchestration (Kabashkin, 2025). Though ambitious, it remains prototypical, requiring advances in scalability, privacy, and pedagogical validity. Key gaps include integrating AI, Digital Twins, and Metaverse for Industry 5.0-aligned high-fidelity simulations, adaptive learning, and competence development (Syarifuddin et al., 2025) despite AI's predominance in personalization over comprehensive simulation/predictive analytics (Bond et al., 2024; Tlili et al., 2022) and concentration in high-income countries' fields like language learning, CS, and engineering, neglecting under-resourced areas (Crompton & Burke, 2023). A finding that directly informed the design of the DT-LLS Continuous Evolution Loop described in Section 4.

3.4 Structured Research Gaps Analysis

The five research gaps presented in Table 1 were identified through a two-stage conceptual synthesis process. In the first stage, a structured review of empirical and conceptual literature published between 2020 and 2026 was conducted across Google Scholar, Scopus, and Web of Science, using search strings combining terms such as digital twin, education, adaptive learning, lifelong learning, and human digital twin. Inclusion criteria required that sources address digital twin applications in educational or training contexts; exclusion criteria eliminated engineering-domain twin studies with no pedagogical application. In the second stage, identified studies were thematically coded by research focus, learner population, learning context, and methodological approach. Gaps were defined as areas where fewer than five empirical studies existed, where prior conceptual proposals remained empirically unvalidated, or where no study integrated all relevant constructs for instance, no single study was found that simultaneously modelled formal, informal, and workplace learning within a unified twin architecture. These gap criteria align with established practices in conceptual gap analysis in educational technology (Chamorro-Atalaya et al. 2024).

Table 1. Structured research gaps in educational digital twin literature and implications for the DT-LLS framework

Research Gap	Current State in Literature	Implication for DT-LLS	Priority
Gap 1 Lifelong Continuity	Studies focus on single courses or semesters; no twin persists across the learning lifespan (Yamin et al., 2023)	Persistent, portable twin architecture spanning decades is required; identity management across institutional boundaries is essential	**Critical**
Gap 2 Cross-Context Integration	Formal, informal, and workplace learning data remain siloed; no study integrates all three contexts within a unified twin model (Addanki & Corrin, 2023; Poquet et al., 2021)	DT-LLS must define semantic data bridges and consent protocols across heterogeneous learning contexts and credential registries	**Critical**
Gap 3 Ethical Governance	Ethical analysis is largely theoretical; few empirical studies on learner privacy perceptions or consent effectiveness (Chamorro-Atalaya et al., 2024)	Privacy-by-design, algorithmic fairness auditing, and learner consent management must be core architectural features, not compliance add-ons	**High**
Gap 4 Scalability Evidence	Proof-of-concept deployments dominate (<100 learners); large-scale implementations (>1,000 learners) over extended periods are rare (Zhang et al., 2024)	Framework must specify cloud-native, horizontally scalable infrastructure capable of institutional or national deployment at acceptable latency	**High**
Gap 5 Affective & Social Modelling	Cognitive performance modelling dominates; affective states, motivation, self-efficacy, and socio-collaborative dynamics are substantially undermodelled (Kabashkin, 2025)	Twin architecture must incorporate validated multimodal affective sensing and socio-collaborative data streams to support holistic learner modelling	**Moderate**

Priority legend: Critical - foundational prerequisite for DT-LLS feasibility; **High** - essential for responsible deployment; **Moderate** - important for holistic learner modelling but addressable in later implementation phases.

4. THE DT-LLS CONCEPTUAL FRAMEWORK: ARCHITECTURE AND DESIGN PRINCIPLES

The Digital Twin-Driven Lifelong Learning System (DT-LLS) is a novel conceptual framework that operationalizes digital twin technology across the full continuum of human learning. Unlike prior proposals that apply digital twins episodically within discrete educational contexts, DT-LLS is explicitly designed for persistence in maintaining and enriching the learner's digital twin across decades of learning and professional development and for portability, enabling the twin to travel with the learner across institutional, organizational, and geographic boundaries. The DT-LLS is formally defined as: a persistent, portable, modular software-and-data architecture that constructs and continuously updates a high-fidelity computational model of an individual learner the Human Digital Twin by aggregating multimodal evidence across formal, informal, and workplace learning contexts throughout the learner's lifespan, and that leverages this model to generate adaptive, explainable, and equitable personalised interventions aligned with evolving competency standards.

Three definitional boundaries distinguish DT-LLS from prior frameworks. First, scope: unlike course-level adaptive systems (e.g., intelligent tutoring systems such as Cognitive Tutor or ASSISTments) or institution-level analytics dashboards, DT-LLS is explicitly designed for lifespan continuity spanning decades, not semesters. Second, architecture: unlike Kabashkin's (2025) AI-based student twin prototype, which focuses on a single institution's curriculum ontology, DT-LLS is context-agnostic it treats formal, informal, and workplace evidence as co-equal data streams within a unified twin model. Third, governance: unlike prior adaptive learning platforms that treat learner data as institutional property, DT-LLS embeds learner data sovereignty as a non-negotiable architectural constraint, not a compliance add-on.The framework is organized around five interoperable architectural layers, each contributing a distinct functional capability to the overall system, as depicted in Figure 1.

4.1 Framework Architecture Figure 1

Figure 1 presents the DT-LLS five-layer architecture as a bidirectional, closed-loop system in which data flows upward from the physical learner through four increasingly analytical layers, and in which the fifth layer the Continuous Evolution Loop feeds enriched longitudinal insights back downward through all lower layers, creating the bidirectional physical-to-virtual-to-physical synchronisation that characterises digital twin operation.

Layer 1 (Learner Data Acquisition) serves as the system's observational substrate. Its inputs are raw multimodal signals LMS interaction logs, xAPI event streams, wearable sensor readings, and workplace performance records. Its primary output is a standardised, semantically tagged event record deposited into a Learning Record Store. This layer has no inference capability; it observes, standardises, and routes.

Layer 2 (Human Digital Twin Modeling) receives Layer 1's event records and produces the four continuously updated sub-models (Knowledge Graph, Competency Ontology, Affective State Model, Behavioral Pattern Model) that together constitute the learner's digital twin. The output of this layer is a struc-

tured, queryable learner state representation that is human-readable through the Open Learner Model interface and machine-readable for Layer 3 processing.
Layer 3 (Adaptive Intelligence Engine) queries the twin state from Layer 2 and produces actionable outputs: ranked content recommendations, predicted performance trajectories, dropout risk scores, and natural-language tutoring dialogues. It writes its outputs back to Layer 2 (updating the twin's predictive sub-models) and forwards recommendations to Layer 4.
Layer 4 (Learning Delivery Interface) receives Layer 3 recommendations and translates them into learner-facing experiences sequenced content, adaptive assessments, micro-credential challenges, and collaborative activities. Learner responses to these experiences generate new event records that flow back into Layer 1, closing the within-session feedback loop.
Layer 5 (Continuous Evolution Loop) operates on a longer temporal scale. It aggregates longitudinal twin updates, recalibrates the competency ontology against evolving workforce standards, processes life-event transitions, and exports portable Open Learner Model portfolios. Crucially, it also re-initiates Layer 2 retraining cycles when accumulated evidence triggers model drift detection, ensuring the twin remains valid across years rather than sessions. The bidirectional arrows in Figure 1 represent both the upward flow of raw evidence and the downward propagation of refined models and recalibrated parameters making the DT-LLS a genuinely self-improving system over the learner's lifespan.

Figure 1. DT-LLS five-layer architecture for digital twin-driven lifelong learning systems

LAYER 5 — CONTINUOUS EVOLUTION LOOP Longitudinal twin updates | Open Learner Model portfolio | Life-event recalibration | Cross-system credential export
LAYER 4 — LEARNING DELIVERY INTERFACE Adaptive multi-modal content | Micro-credential pathways | Social & collaborative learning spaces | XR/immersive environments
LAYER 3 — ADAPTIVE INTELLIGENCE ENGINE Deep Knowledge Tracing | RL-based recommendation | LLM natural language tutoring | Federated learning models
LAYER 2 — HUMAN DIGITAL TWIN (HDT) MODEL Knowledge graph | Affective state model | Behavioral pattern model | Competency ontology (EQF/ESCO)
LAYER 1 — LEARNER DATA ACQUISITION LMS logs | Assessment data | Wearable/physiological sensors | Workplace performance | xAPI / LRS
↕ PHYSICAL LEARNER — Real-World Entity ↕ Individual across formal education, informal learning, and workplace — full life course

The architecture depicts a bidirectional, closed-loop system in which learning evidence flows upward from the physical learner through five progressively analytical layers, while refined model parameters and recalibrated outputs propagate downward to inform all lower layers. Layer 1 (Learner Data Acquisition) serves as the observational substrate, capturing multimodal signals from formal LMS environments, informal digital platforms, workplace performance systems, and physiological devices; its output is a standardised, semantically tagged event record deposited into a Learning Record Store via the xAPI protocol. Layer 2 (Human Digital Twin Modelling) transforms these records into four continuously updated sub-models the Knowledge Graph, Competency Ontology, Affective State Model, and Behavioural Pattern Model that together constitute the learner's computational representation; its output is a structured, queryable twin state exposed through both a machine-readable API (for Layer 3) and a human-readable Open Learner Model interface (for the learner). Layer 3 (Adaptive Intelligence Engine) queries the twin state and produces actionable outputs: ranked content recommendations, performance trajectory predictions, dropout-risk probability scores, and natural-language tutoring dialogues; it writes prediction updates back to Layer 2 and forwards intervention recommendations to Layer 4. Layer 4 (Learning Delivery Interface) translates Layer 3 recommendations into sequenced learning experiences; learner responses to these experiences generate new event records that re-enter Layer 1, closing the within-session feedback loop. Layer 5 (Continuous Evolution Loop) operates on an extended temporal scale, aggregating longitudinal twin updates, recalibrating the competency ontology against evolving workforce standards, processing life-event transitions, and triggering Layer 2 retraining cycles when accumulated evidence activates model-drift detection thresholds. Upward arrows represent the flow of raw observational evidence from the physical learner; downward arrows represent the propagation of refined model parameters and recalibrated recommendations. The horizontal bidirectional arrow between Layer 3 and Layer 2 represents the within-session update cycle by which new predictions continuously enrich the twin state.

4.2 Design Principles

Six overarching design principles govern the DT-LLS framework, each derived from the research gap analysis in Section 3 and the Industry 5.0 values of human-centricity, sustainability, and resilience(Borchardt et al., 2022).

Table 2. DT-LLS design principles with operational requirements

Design Principle	Definition	Measurable Operational Requirements
Learner Sovereignty	The learner owns their digital twin. All data collection, sharing, and processing occurs with explicit, granular, and revisable consent. The learner can inspect, correct, export, and delete their twin at any time without loss of independently earned credentials.	• Consent interface provides ≥8 distinct data-type categories for granular opt-in/opt-out. • Deletion requests fulfilled within 72 hours (GDPR Art. 17 standard). • Learner-visible audit log updated within 24 hours of any data processing event. • Full twin export in W3C Verifiable Credential format available within 5 business days. • Compliance verified via annual consent audit with results reported to governance committee.
Context Agnosticism	The DT-LLS treats learning evidence equivalently regardless of its origin. Formal education, informal communities, workplace projects, and self-directed learning are integrated as co-equal data streams within the twin's knowledge architecture.	• System ingests from ≥3 distinct context types (formal LMS, informal platform, workplace system). • Convergent validity: cross-context correlation between twin-state mastery estimate and independently verified competency ≥0.70 (Pearson r). • No statistically significant difference in recommendation quality across context types (ANOVA $p > 0.05$ in annual fairness audit). • Semantic data bridges map each non-formal evidence type to ≥1 competency ontology node.
Progressive Fidelity	The digital twin begins with low fidelity using minimal data and progressively increases in representational richness as evidence accumulates. Effective personalisation is achievable at all stages.	• Minimum viable twin operational with ≤30 LMS interaction events (Baseline tier). • Prediction accuracy (AUC) ≥0.60 at Baseline tier, ≥0.75 at Enhanced tier (50–500 events), ≥0.85 at Advanced tier (>500 events). • Current fidelity tier (Baseline/Enhanced/Advanced) explicitly displayed to learner in Open Learner Model interface. • Fidelity progression benchmarks validated against cohort holdout sets annually.
Intelligible Transparency	All representations and recommendations generated by the twin are explainable in natural language accessible to learners. Black-box decision-making is prohibited; all reasoning is inspectable and contestable.	• ≥90% of learners in annual usability testing correctly identify the stated reason for a given recommendation using the natural-language explanation. • Recommendation explanations achieve ≤Grade 10 Flesch–Kincaid reading level. • Every recommendation accompanied by a 'Contest this' link triggering human review within 5 business days. • Zero high-stakes decisions (credential awarding, dropout flagging, career pathway assignment) issued without an auditable explanation log.

continued on following page

Table 2. Continued

Design Principle	Definition	Measurable Operational Requirements
Equitable Design	The framework actively monitors and mitigates demographic disparities in recommendations. Mechanisms detect and correct algorithmic bias to ensure fair and inclusive personalisation across diverse learner populations.	• Fairness audit conducted at minimum annually across gender, first-generation status, and socioeconomic quartile. • Demographic parity difference $\leq$0.05 for high-stakes recommendations (dropout flagging, content difficulty assignment). • Corrective retraining triggered automatically if disparity exceeds 0.05 threshold. • Audit results published in an accessible summary report available to all institutional stakeholders. • Underrepresented learners included in participatory design cycles for ontology and interface updates.
Human-AI Complementarity	The DT-LLS is designed to augment rather than replace human educators. AI handles large-scale data analysis and personalisation; educators contribute mentorship, motivation, and contextual judgment.	• $\geq$20% of high-stakes AI-generated interventions (at-risk flags, major pathway recommendations) reviewed and acted upon by a human educator within 5 business days. • Educator dashboard provides override capability for all AI recommendations; override rate tracked as a system health metric. • Credentialling, enrolment, and exclusion decisions are human-authorised; AI provides evidence but cannot execute these actions autonomously. • Educator engagement with twin-generated insights measured quarterly; minimum engagement threshold defined per institutional deployment.

Figure 2 presents the six DT-LLS design principles as a governance guardrail layer that overlays and constrains the five-layer architecture depicted in Figure 1. Unlike Table 2, which specifies each principle's definition and operational requirements in tabular form, Figure 2 illustrates the principles' positional relationship to the framework architecture, showing that they operate as system-wide constraints rather than layer-specific features.

Figure 2. DT-LLS design principles

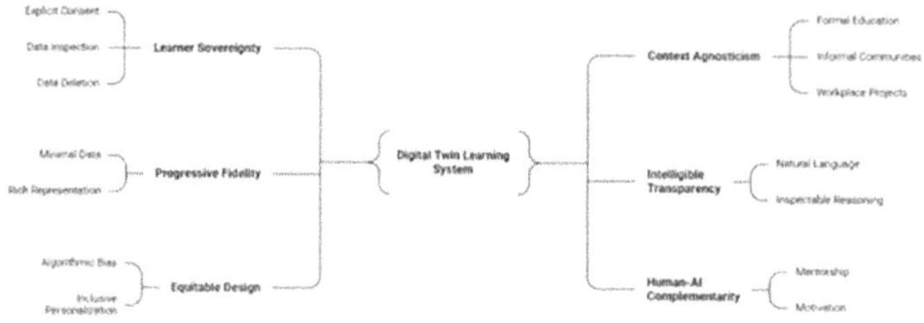

4.3 Layer 1: Learner Data Acquisition

The Learner Data Acquisition layer forms the DT-LLS observational foundation, capturing heterogeneous data streams from all learning contexts. Effective twin construction requires diverse, granular, continuous, and standardized data for cross-system aggregation (Bond et al. 2024). It operates as context-agnostic infrastructure, ingesting from formal LMS, informal platforms, workplace systems, and physiological devices. Structured LMS data assessment scores, time-on-task, interaction logs, forum participation, submissions provides the baseline, with xAPI enabling semantic interoperability via Learning Record Stores. Unstructured streams (free-text, peer comments, portfolios, video traces) are transformed using NLP and computer vision. Physiological/behavioral sensors (wearables for HRV/EDA/accelerometry; eye-tracking; ambient classroom sensors) enable high-fidelity affective/cognitive load modeling(Kabashkin, 2025), despite integration challenges. A tiered architecture behavioral logs (baseline), voluntary wearables (enhancement), lab-grade sensing (advanced supports progressive adoption.

4.4 Layer 2: Human Digital Twin (HDT) Modeling

Layer 2 transforms Layer 1's diverse raw data into structured models of the learner's cognitive, affective, behavioral, and developmental states. It comprises four interconnected sub-models that form the continuously updating digital twin. The Knowledge Graph probabilistically tracks mastery, prerequisites, and forgetting curves using Bayesian Knowledge Tracing (Pinto & Paquette, 2024) and deep learning extensions (Pinto & Paquette, 2024), feeding Layer 3 content sequencing. The Competency Ontology aligns skills and knowledge to standards like the European Qualifications Framework(Fouquet, 2023), ESCO (Opik et al., 2017), O*NET(Burrus et al., 2013), and Industry 5.0 capabilities (Oeij et al., 2024) for precise assessments. The Affective State Model infers motivation, self-efficacy, engagement, and load from multimodal signals across real-time, daily, and longitudinal scales. The Behavioral Pattern Model profiles persistence, help-seeking, collaboration, and metacognition.

4.4.1 Knowledge Graph Sub-Model

The Knowledge Graph probabilistically tracks a learner's mastery of concepts, their prerequisite relationships, and temporal decay using Bayesian Knowledge Tracing (BKT) and deep learning extensions. For example, a learner studying data science might have the node "Python list comprehension" carrying a mastery probability of 0.73 (±0.08 SE) derived from 12 assessed interactions. A directed edge to the prerequisite node "Python loops" carries a weight of 0.84, estimated from cohort-level co-occurrence analysis across 1,200 learners. The node's forgetting-curve spacing parameter (d = 0.25) is calibrated from response-latency data across four spaced-repetition sessions, enabling the system to schedule review recommendations before mastery drops below a threshold of 0.65.

Data types ingested: xAPI verb-sequence logs ('answered', 'completed', 'failed') with ISO 8601 timestamps; binary correctness signals (0/1); response latency in milliseconds; LMS rubric scores on a 0–100 scale; peer-assessment ratings in JSON-LD.

Measurement method: BKT parameters (p(L0), p(T), p(G), p(S)) estimated via expectation-maximisation on response sequences; DKT using LSTM/transformer architectures on sequential response data for complex dependency capture. Cold-start problem addressed by initialising mastery at prior mean from cohort distribution.

Validation metrics: AUC ≥0.80 for next-response prediction on held-out test sets; calibration error ≤5% using Platt scaling; test–retest reliability of mastery estimates r ≥0.85 over a 72-hour interval without new interactions; RMSE ≤0.10 on held-out response prediction as deployment quality threshold.

4.4.2 Competency Ontology Sub-Model

The Competency Ontology aligns demonstrated skills to internationally recognised workforce frameworks. As a concrete illustration, a node representing "data wrangling with pandas" is linked to ESCO skill URI esco/skill/S4.1.2, mapped to EQF Level 4, and augmented with three employer-defined observable performance indicators co-designed with a partner technology firm: (1) the learner independently produces a clean dataset from raw CSV input within 30 minutes; (2) handles missing values using at least two validated imputation strategies; (3) documents transformation decisions in reproducible code with inline commentary. This tri-level structure international standard, qualification level, observable workplace behaviour operationalises 'competency' beyond simple knowledge-recall.

Data types ingested: OWL ontology nodes in RDF/Turtle format; ESCO URI references; EQF level mappings; employer-provided JSON rubrics with performance descriptors; Open Badge 3.0 assertions for formally credentialled competencies.

Measurement method: Competency attainment determined via multi-evidence triangulation weighted as follows: formal assessment scores (0.40), portfolio artefact evaluation against rubric (0.30), peer and supervisor evaluations (0.30). Inter-rater reliability of human assessors required at $\kappa \geq 0.75$ before scores are integrated.

Validation metrics: Convergent validity assessed by comparing DT-LLS competency estimates against independent workplace performance ratings from supervisors (Pearson $r \geq 0.65$ required); quarterly alignment audits against ESCO, O*NET, and Industry 5.0 competency updates to detect ontology drift.

4.4.3 Affective State Model

The Affective State Model infers motivational, emotional, and cognitive-load states by integrating multimodal behavioural signals. As a concrete example: during a challenging programming exercise, the system integrates three simultaneously available signals. First, elevated response latency (mean 8.2 s versus a learner baseline of 3.1 s, $z = +2.4$) indicates increased cognitive load. Second, a sharp decline in interaction frequency (0.3 events/min versus baseline 1.1 events/min, $z = -2.1$) suggests disengagement. Third, a voluntary self-report of 'confused' on an embedded 5-point scale confirms the inference. The model updates the engagement score from 0.68 to 0.41 and the frustration probability from 0.12 to 0.61, triggering a Layer 3 recommendation for an explanatory micro-content item and an optional human-tutor check-in.

Data types ingested: Mouse-movement velocity (pixels/second); keystroke inter-event latency (ms); voluntary self-report via embedded 5-item affect scale administered at session midpoint; eye-tracking fixation duration (ms) when available; electrodermal activity (μS) from connected wearables in Advanced-tier deployments; xAPI 'experienced' and 'interacted' verbs with timestamp.

Measurement method: Multimodal fusion using a trained stacked ensemble (gradient-boosted trees over standardised behavioural features, with optional physiological channels added at Enhanced and Advanced tiers). Calibrated against self-report ground truth. Real-time inference latency target ≤ 2 seconds.

Validation metrics: Affect prediction accuracy compared against validated self-report instruments (PANAS-SF; Academic Emotions Questionnaire) achieving Spearman $\rho \geq 0.60$ in controlled studies; ecological validity assessed through experience-sampling method (ESM) studies in naturalistic learning settings; false-positive rate for distress flags ≤0.10 to avoid unnecessary interruptions.

4.4.4 Behavioural Pattern Model

The Behavioural Pattern Model identifies metacognitive and strategic patterns from observable learning behaviours. For example, the system identifies that a specific learner initiates 68% of sessions in late-evening slots (22:00–00:00), skips worked examples at a rate of 0.84 (mean skip proportion), and seeks help only after three or more consecutive failed attempts. Cohort-level clustering maps this profile to a 'self-directed late-night practitioner' cluster a group associated in longitudinal data with above-average persistence in weeks one through five but significantly elevated burnout risk from week six onward. Layer 3 is notified at week five to deploy a proactive wellbeing check-in and reduce session length recommendations.

Data types ingested: Session start/end timestamps; full LMS clickstream logs; help-request event counts per session; peer-forum post frequency and sentiment score (VADER); submission-attempt counts per assignment; content skip events.

Measurement method: Unsupervised clustering using k-means with silhouette coefficient optimisation (k = 3–8 evaluated) on normalised behavioural feature vectors, updated weekly using a 21-day sliding window. Cluster labels assigned through expert qualitative interpretation of centroid feature profiles.

Validation metrics: Cluster stability assessed via Jaccard coefficient across bootstrapped cohort resamples ≥0.70; predictive utility validated by association with independently measured learning outcomes (grade, completion) using logistic regression AUC ≥0.72 on held-out cohorts; annual revalidation required as learner population characteristics shift.

4.5 Layer 3: Adaptive Intelligence Engine

The Adaptive Intelligence Engine (Layer 3) operates as a hierarchical stack of AI sub-components, each fulfilling a distinct functional role within the recommendation pipeline. Rather than acting as a single monolithic model, Layer 3 assembles specialised techniques whose outputs are combined and passed to Layer 4. Table 3 maps each technique to its functional role, data source, output target, and principal limitation; the prose below elaborates the key design choices.

Table 3. Adaptive intelligence engine: AI sub-components, functional roles, and limitations within Layer 3

Technique	Functional role in Layer 3	Input source	Output target	Key limitation
Deep Knowledge Tracing (DKT)	Real-time mastery estimation from response sequences	Knowledge Graph (Layer 2)	Updated mastery probabilities → Layer 2; content difficulty set → Layer 4	Requires ≥50 interaction events for reliable estimates; cold-start problem for new learners mitigated by cohort-prior initialisation.
Reinforcement Learning (RL)	Content, modality, and difficulty optimisation in real time	Full twin state (Layer 2), learner response feedback (Layer 1)	Optimal content sequence and modality selection → Layer 4	Multi-objective reward functions require careful tuning; exploration phase may temporarily reduce individual-learner performance before optimal policy converges.
Large Language Models (LLMs)	Natural-language tutoring, misconception detection, and Socratic feedback generation	Free-text learner responses (Layer 1 NLP pipeline), Knowledge Graph context (Layer 2)	Corrective explanations, Socratic questions, knowledge-aligned feedback → Layer 4 dialogue interface	Hallucination risk mitigated by grounding all generated outputs against verified Knowledge Graph nodes; computationally intensive inference batching required at scale.
Federated Learning	Privacy-preserving model training across distributed institutions	On-device gradient updates from distributed learner nodes (no raw data transmitted)	Aggregated global model updates → DKT, RL, and LLM sub-components	Convergence slower than centralised training; non-IID data distributions across institutions may degrade model quality; requires each participating institution to maintain sufficient local compute.
Graph Neural Networks (GNNs)	Concept-dependency reasoning over the competency ontology graph	Competency Ontology graph structure (Layer 2)	Enhanced prerequisite relationship scores → DKT and RL sub-components	Computationally expensive for ontologies exceeding 10,000 nodes; ontology quality directly constrains recommendation quality errors in the graph propagate into recommendations.
Transformer attention models	Longitudinal competency trajectory prediction and dropout-risk scoring	Full event sequence from LRS (Layer 1), extended temporal window	Dropout-risk scores and trajectory forecasts → educator dashboard (Layer 4)	Attention windows must be calibrated per learning context; risk of encoding historical cohort biases into individual forecasts if training data reflects structural inequities.

These sub-components are not independent pipelines but form a cascading inference chain: GNNs refine the ontology structure consumed by DKT; DKT mastery estimates seed the reward signal for RL; RL-selected content is handed to the LLM for natural-language presentation; and federated learning keeps all models current without centralising raw learner data. This architecture allows the system to remain modular an institution without wearable infrastructure can operate at Baseline tier using only the DKT and RL components, while a well-resourced deployment activates the full stack.

4.6 Layer 4: Learning Delivery Interface

The Learning Delivery Interface transforms Adaptive Intelligence Engine recommendations into personalized, multimodal experiences with dynamic difficulty adjustment, micro-credentials, and social learning. Following Universal Design for Learning principles, it selects optimal formats (videos, simulations, examples, case studies, discussions, journaling) based on the digital twin's profile of learner preferences, comprehension, and affective state (Addanki & Corrin, 2023). Micro-credential pathways provide stackable digital badges (Francia et al., 2023) linked to the competency ontology for lifelong portfolios; social features enable peer matching, diverse teams, and mentor links.

4.7 Layer 5: Continuous Evolution Loop

The Continuous Evolution Loop distinguishes DT-LLS from prior adaptive systems, which update models only within courses or sessions. It persistently enriches the learner's digital twin across lifelong contexts (Kabashkin, 2025).

Three core processes drive the loop:

- **Longitudinal updating** continuously refines the HDT with new evidence including knowledge decay (via spaced repetition models), schema integration, and practice consolidation triggering timely reviews for sustained competency (Richter et al., 2019).
- **Competency portfolio management** builds a learner-owned **Open Learner Model**: a portable, privacy-controlled record of assessments, credentials, work samples, evaluations, and attestations, shareable with employers and institutions (Hoffman & Olmsted, 2016).
- **Life-event recalibration** adapts pathways for transitions like career changes, relocations, parental leave, health issues, or retirement, preserving prior evidence (Poquet et al., 2021).

5. INTEGRATION WITH AI, LEARNING ANALYTICS, AND SMART ENVIRONMENTS

The DT-LLS framework does not exist in technological isolation; it is embedded within and mutually enabling with a broader ecosystem of complementary technologies and standards. This section examines three critical integration domains artificial intelligence and machine learning, learning analytics infrastructure, and smart learning environments and explicitly addresses the DT-LLS's alignment with Industry 5.0 workforce development imperatives.

5.1 AI and Machine Learning Integration

The DT-LLS Adaptive Intelligence Engine leverages a layered AI stack supervised, unsupervised, and reinforcement learning for precise personalization. Supervised models, trained on historical cohort data, deliver domain- and demographic-specific performance baselines, with continuous drift monitoring to ensure accuracy. Unsupervised clustering uncovers learner typologies, exposing intervention responses that surpass simplistic learning styles and sharpen recommendations (Kabashkin, 2025). Graph neural networks on knowledge graphs drive advanced concept dependency reasoning (Zhu et al. 2019) Unlike recurrent models that lose structural fidelity (Velickovic, P. et al. 2018) transformer attention prioritizes recent, high-quality data over outdated evidence for robust competency predictions (Choi et al., 2020).

5.2 Learning Analytics Infrastructure and Standards

Learning analytics underpins DT-LLS by converting raw interaction data into actionable insights at individual, cohort, and system levels (Cohen, 2018; Šereš et al., 2022) xAPI with Learning Record Stores enables granular, cross-platform aggregation for precise twin modeling (Gelan et al., 2018; Sadallah, 2019)IMS Caliper adds semantic context (Costa et al., 2020; Samuelsen et al., 2021).(Costa et al., 2020; Samuelsen et al., 2021)ogether, they ensure interoperable data for portable twins across boundaries (Gelan et al., 2018; Samuelsen et al., 2021).

Table 4. Role-based analytics outputs in DT-LLS framework

Stakeholder Role	Key Analytics Outputs
Learners *via Open Learner Model*	Interpretable views of competencies, personalized learning pathways, optimal next-step recommendations, and continuous goal-tracking mechanisms to support self-regulated learning.
Educators	Early identification of at-risk learners, analysis of cohort-level learning gaps, and data-driven instructional adaptations informed by digital twin insights.
Administrators	System-level performance monitoring, resource allocation optimization, and evidence-based curriculum redesign aligned with emerging learning needs.

The DT-LLS enables multi-level analytics tailored to different stakeholders, ensuring that insights generated from digital twins translate into actionable decisions across the educational ecosystem.

5.3 Smart Learning Environments and IoT Integration

The physical learning environment becomes a data source within the DT-LLS through IoT sensor integration in smart classroom and workspace deployments. Ambient sensing including occupancy detection, noise and air quality monitoring, thermal comfort measurement, and camera-based posture and attention tracking contributes environmental context data that enriches the HDT's situational model (Zhao et al., 2020). This environmental layer enables the system to account for physical conditions in performance predictions: identifying, for instance, that a learner's characteristically reduced engagement in afternoon sessions correlates with consistently elevated classroom CO2 concentrations rather than with content difficulty, generating a different and more appropriate intervention recommendation than purely cognitive modeling would produce.

5.4 Industry 5.0 Alignment and Workplace Learning Integration

Industry 5.0 envisions a productive complementarity between human capabilities and artificial intelligence: AI systems handle routine pattern recognition and data-intensive optimisation, while humans provide judgment, creativity, ethical reasoning, and relational intelligence (European Commission, 2021). Within the DT-LLS framework, this division of labour is not merely aspirational framing but is architecturally instantiated at three specific layers. At Layer 3, the Adaptive Intelligence Engine handles computationally intensive mastery estimation, trajectory prediction, and content optimisation, but explicitly delegates high-stakes decisions credentialling, career-pathway endorsement, and wellbeing escalations to human educators via the Layer 4 educator dashboard, embodying the human-AI complementarity principle in system design. At Layer 5, the Continuous Evolution Loop co-updates its competency ontology with industry partners through participatory revision cycles, ensuring that the skills tracked by the twin remain genuinely current with evolving workforce demands rather than drifting toward institutional inertia.

Industry 5.0 additionally identifies three meta-categories of workforce competency that distinguish its demands from those of earlier automation paradigms: human-AI collaboration skills (the capacity to work effectively alongside intelligent systems); sustainability-oriented competencies (systems thinking, circular economy literacy, responsible innovation); and resilience skills (adaptive capacity, ambiguity tolerance, and self-directed continuous learning) (Oeij et al., 2024). These three meta-categories are represented as top-level structural divisions within the DT-LLS Competency Ontology, and the Layer 3 RL module's reward function is parameterised to develop these alongside domain-specific technical skills. The practical consequence is that a DT-LLS-equipped learner pursuing a data engineering career receives not only targeted Python and SQL learning pathways but also adaptive content developing human-AI collaboration literacy and ethical data stewardship competencies that generic adaptive learning platforms, focused solely on technical skill mastery, do not currently model.

At the institutional level, DT-LLS integrates bidirectionally with enterprise HR management systems, performance management platforms, and employer-designed competency rubrics via the Layer 5 portability interface. Workplace evidence project deliverables, 360-degree evaluations, professional certifications, and job-shadowing records is ingested via the xAPI workplace extension profile and mapped to the competency ontology, crediting experiential learning on an equal footing with formal credentials. This dissolution of the boundary between educational completion and professional development enables the twin to function simultaneously as a learning support tool, a competency portfolio, and a workforce-readiness indicator across a full career arc. The empirical question of how frequently industry-partner ontology revisions are required and what governance mechanisms ensure their quality and representativeness is identified as a priority research direction in Section 7 (Direction 7: Industry 5.0 Competency Co-Design).

6. ETHICAL GOVERNANCE FRAMEWORK FOR DT-LLS

The transformative potential of the DT-LLS framework does not diminish and in several respects amplifies the ethical challenges inherent in large-scale learner data systems. Responsible implementation requires more than awareness of these challenges; it demands a structured governance architecture that specifies accountabilities, oversight mechanisms, and enforceable learner rights. This section presents the DT-LLS Ethical Governance Sub-Framework (EGS), which organises ethical requirements across three governance tiers: architectural (embedded in the system's data and AI design), institutional (implemented by deploying organisations), and regulatory (aligned with external legal and policy standards). Table 5 presents the EGS governance matrix; the subsections that follow provide detailed treatment of each challenge domain.

Table 5. DT-LLS Ethical Governance Sub-Framework (EGS): Responsibilities, mechanisms, learner rights, and oversight by governance tier

Tier	Challenge domain	Responsible party	Mechanism	Learner rights	Oversight body	Cycle
Architectural	Data privacy & regulatory compliance	System architect / data engineer	Privacy-by-design; purpose limitation; auto-deletion timers; data minimisation by tier	Right to inspect; right to delete; right to export in portable format	Internal Data Protection Officer; GDPR / FERPA authority	Continuous
Architectural	Algorithmic bias & fairness	AI engineer; framework developer	Fairness-constrained model training (demographic parity ≤ 0.05); bias audit pipeline in CI/CD	Right to explanation; right to contest recommendation	Independent Algorithmic Audit Panel	Annual
Institutional	Informed consent	Deploying institution; instructional designer	Granular layered consent interface; consent revision portal active throughout enrolment	Right to withdraw consent at any tier without academic penalty	Institutional Ethics Review Board	Per deployment
Institutional	Accountability & high-stakes decisions	Deploying institution; AI developer (joint)	Responsibility matrix; human-in-the-loop mandatory for credentialling, exclusion, and escalation decisions	Right to human review of AI recommendations within 5 business days; right to written justification	Institutional Governance Committee; external ombudsperson	Per decision

continued on following page

Table 5. Continued

Tier	Challenge domain	Responsible party	Mechanism	Learner rights	Oversight body	Cycle
Institutional	Scalability & equity of access	Infrastructure team; policy maker	Tiered architecture (Baseline operable on low-resource infrastructure); open-source tooling for under-resourced contexts	Right to equivalent core functionality regardless of institutional wealth	Equity Impact Assessment body (biennial)	Biennial
Regulatory	Data sovereignty & power asymmetries	National / regional regulator; standards body	Alignment with GDPR, FERPA, UNESCO AI Ethics in Education principles; contractual data-sharing agreements with liability clauses	Right to lodge formal complaint; right to seek independent legal remedy; right to data portability under open standards	External regulatory body; UNESCO / OECD AI policy alignment	Per jurisdiction

6.1 Data Privacy and Regulatory Compliance

The DT-LLS creates highly sensitive lifelong profiles of learners' physiological, cognitive, behavioral, and emotional states. Strict regulations GDPR, FERPA, emerging AI laws demand rigorous data handling. Privacy-by-design is imperative across layers: minimize to educational needs; limit purposes; enforce retention with auto-deletion; enable twin erasure while preserving credentials (Chamorro-Atalaya et al. 2024). Biometrics from wearables (heart rate variability, electrodermal activity) severely threaten bodily integrity and health privacy. Mandate tiered consents, granular agreements, and robust anonymization as core requirements.

6.2 Algorithmic Bias and Equity

AI models trained on biased historical data inherit and amplify inequities. They encode structural disadvantages in underserved groups as inherent traits Gándara et al., (2024) ; Madaio et al., (2021) overestimating dropout risk for first-generation learners (Yu et al., 2021), directing harder content to high-SES students Marras et al., (2021); Shi & Li, (2024),and enabling self-fulfilling prophecies through inferior interventions for “low-potential” cases. DT-LLS counters this with a multi-layered strategy: fairness-aware training using demographic parity, equalized odds, or individual fairness constraints (Raftopoulos et al., 2025; Shen et al., 2022). Continuous audits tracking recommendations, content difficulty, and interventions by demographics Funda, (2025); Morales-Navarro et al., (2024) participatory design embedding equity via underrepresented learner involvement.

6.3 Interoperability and Technical Standardization

The DT-LLS vision of a persistent, portable lifelong twin requires data interoperability across an extraordinary diversity of technical systems that currently operate with incompatible data models, authentication frameworks, and API architectures (Nahhas et al., 2018; OECD, 2023). Achieving cross-institutional twin portability requires convergence on open standards for learner data (xAPI, IMS Caliper), verifiable credentials (W3C Verifiable Credentials, Open Badges 3.0), competency description (CASE, ESCO), and learner identity management (LTI Advantage, SAML federations)(Grech et al., 2021; Redmond & Macfadyen, 2020). Governance agreements between institutions defining data sharing obligations, liability frameworks, and dispute resolution mechanisms must accompany technical standards to create the trusted ecosystem within which twin portability can function in practice(Grech et al., 2021; Page et al., 2023).

6.4 Scalability and Infrastructure Economics

Real-time DT-LLS twin synchronization at scale demands massive compute resources (Liu et al., 2024). Continuous multimodal data processing for thousands of learners requires cloud-native, scalable architectures with low-latency pipelines and efficient inference. High deployment costs threaten equity in resource-poor settings(Odabaşı & Özkan, 2025); counter with open-source tools, national shared infrastructure, and tiered features(Infante et al., 2024)

6.5 Learner Autonomy and the Calibration of Directiveness

Powerful personalization creates a tension: precise guidance hinders self-directed skills goal-setting, self-assessment, strategy selection, help-seeking essential for lifelong learning (Verghis et al., 2025). Constant algorithmic direction yields system-optimized but independent-learning-deficient learners, undermining the mission (Özer et al., 2025). DT-LLS must calibrate directiveness by developmental stage, fading scaffolding and shifting metacognitive control per Vygotsky's zone of proximal development and self-determination theory (Yan et al., 2025).

6.6 Ethical Governance, Accountability, and Power Asymmetries

DT-LLS's vast lifelong learner data concentration demands unprecedented accountability beyond prior systems. Governance must clearly assign responsibility for harmful recommendations; provide learner mechanisms to contest, correct, or supplement twin inaccuracies; empower oversight audits; and ban commercial data exploitation (Addanki & Corrin, 2023). Address power asymmetries through learner governance seats, independent audits, and enforceable data agreements with real penalties. Map structures explicitly to UNESCO's AI Ethics in Education principles.

7. FUTURE RESEARCH DIRECTIONS

The DT-LLS framework is explicitly conceptual in its current form: its empirical validation, technical specification, and equity assessment require sustained interdisciplinary research investment. Table 6 presents a structured future research agenda identifying seven priority directions, each with specific research questions, methodological approaches, contributing disciplines, and indicative research horizon.

Table 6. Structured future research agenda for digital twin-driven lifelong learning systems

#	Research direction	Key questions & methods	Disciplines	Horizon	Priority	Type	Rationale
7	Industry 5.0 competency co-design	How should competency ontologies be co-designed with industry partners to remain dynamically current? Participatory action research with employers.	Workforce Dev.; HRD; OB	Short-term (1–3 yrs)	HIGH	Governance	Immediate need to validate the industry 5.0 ontology parameterisation before large-scale deployment. Employer partnerships are realisable within current research infrastructure.
2	Privacy-preserving federated twin learning	Can federated architectures match centralised accuracy at GDPR-compliant privacy budgets? Differential privacy benchmarks across simulated institutional networks.	ML; Privacy Engineering; Law	Short–medium (2–4 yrs)	HIGH	Technical	Privacy architecture is a foundational prerequisite for any real deployment; technically mature field ready for application-specific benchmarking.
5	Equity and bias auditing methods	How do DT-LLS recommendations vary across race, gender, and SES? Systematic fairness audit frameworks with participatory learner evaluation.	Ed. Equity; AI Ethics; Sociology	Short–medium (2–4 yrs)	HIGH	Ethical	Ethical prerequisite for any pilot deployment. Methodologically achievable with existing datasets; urgency elevated by documented bias risks in learning analytics.
6	Human-AI tutoring synergy	What optimal balance of LLM tutoring and human instructor interaction maximises learning outcomes for different learner types? Randomised controlled trials.	Instructional Design; HCI; Ed. Psych.	Medium (2–5 yrs)	MEDIUM	Technical + Empirical	Critical for Layer 4 design but requires LLM tutoring tools at sufficient maturity for controlled experimentation; achievable within a 3–5-year window.

continued on following page

Table 6. Continued

#	Research direction	Key questions & methods	Disciplines	Horizon	Priority	Type	Rationale
4	Cross-institutional twin portability	What standards and governance agreements enable twin portability without semantic data loss? Design science research; institutional case studies.	Info. Systems; Ed. Policy; Law	Medium (3–5 yrs)	MEDIUM	Technical + Governance	Depends on standards bodies (IMS Global, W3C) reaching consensus; achievable within medium term given current momentum but requires policy-level coordination.
3	Multimodal affective modelling precision	Which sensor combinations optimally predict engagement and cognitive load? Controlled within-subject physiological and behavioural studies.	Cognitive Neuroscience; Ed. Psych.; HCI	Medium–long (3–6 yrs)	MEDIUM	Empirical	Technically achievable but requires longitudinal controlled studies across diverse learner populations; ethical constraints on physiological sensing require careful governance design.
1	Longitudinal twin validity	Do HDT representations accurately track real-world competency development over 5–10-year horizons? Longitudinal cohort studies with employer-verified competency validation.	EdTech; Psychometrics; CS	Long-term (5–10 yrs)	MEDIUM	Empirical	Most transformative research question for the field but requires longitudinal data infrastructure not yet in existence; foundational work on twin validity (Directions 2, 3, 4) must precede full lifespan studies.

High-priority short-term directions address foundational governance and technical prerequisites; medium and long-term directions require mature deployment infrastructure or longitudinal data availability. Type classifications: Empirical (primary data studies); Technical (system/algorithm development); Ethical (bias, equity, governance); Governance (policy, standards, co-design). Beyond Table 6, three emerging technologies demand urgent DT-LLS research.

1. **XR Integration.** XR environments enrich the Learning Delivery Interface with spatial navigation, gaze, and manipulation data, enabling precise psychomotor modeling for vocational training (Karanam & Hartman, 2025). Prioritize as a near-term opportunity.
2. **Brain-Computer Interfaces.** Direct neural signals via BCI will boost affective/cognitive modeling fidelity but require safeguards for neural privacy and surveillance ethics. Early EEG studies confirm correlations with attention and overload.
3. **Blockchain Credentials.** Link Verifiable Credentials to DT-LLS ontologies for decentralized, tamper-proof portability empowering learner control and equity without intermediaries.

8. CONCLUSION

This chapter argues that digital twins revolutionize lifelong learning not mere adaptation, but a paradigm shift reconceptualizing education's knowledge and support across human development (Yamin et al. 2023). The proposed DT-LLS framework delivers an ambitious yet modular architecture, enabling phased implementation toward full lifelong twins. Its five layers (data acquisition, HDT modeling, adaptive intelligence, delivery, evolution) directly address literature gaps: absent lifelong continuity, siloed contexts, inadequate ethics (Addanki & Corrin, 2023), unproven scalability (Liu et al., 2024; Odabaşı & Özkan, 2025) and underdeveloped affective/social modeling (Verghis et al., 2025). Six principles learner sovereignty, context agnosticism, progressive fidelity, intelligible transparency, equitable design, human-AI complementarity—guide implementation (Yan et al., 2025). DT-LLS aligns explicitly with Industry 5.0 human-centric values prioritizing flourishing, sustainability, and resilience over narrow metrics empowering learners via sovereignty, Open Learner Models, and calibrated directiveness to build self-directed skills $(Verghis et al., 2025; Yan et al., 2025). Section 6 challenges privacy Addanki & Corrin, (2023); Infante et al., (2024); Odabaşı & Özkan, (2025), autonomy, governance are demanding yet surmountable through federated learning, open standards, fairness training, and AI policies; DT-LLS enables phased adoption without full precondition resolution. For educators and instructional designers, the DT-LLS offers a vision of personalized support freed from the constraints of human attention and institutional memory: every learner receiving, in every moment, the intervention most likely to advance their growth toward their own goals. For policymakers, it offers a framework for lifelong learning infrastructure as public good a persistent, portable, learner-owned resource that accumulates value across a lifetime and travels across institutional, national, and sectoral boundaries without loss. For researchers, it provides a structured agenda of empirical, design, and ethical questions whose answers will determine whether this vision can be realized equitably, sustainably, and in alignment with the human values that must remain at the center of any system that claims to serve education. The convergence of digital twin technology, artificial intelligence, learning analytics, and Industry 5.0 human-centric philosophy creates a historic opportunity to redesign the infrastructure of human learning for the century ahead. Realizing that opportunity demands not merely technical innovation but sustained interdisciplinary collaboration among computer scientists, educational researchers, cognitive scientists, ethicists, policymakers, and above all the learners whose lives the system is designed to serve. This chapter is offered as a conceptual foundation and research catalyst for that collaborative endeavor. For educators, DT-LLS delivers boundless personalized support tailored interventions advancing learner goals anytime (Addanki & Corrin, 2023). Policymakers gain portable, lifelong infrastructure as a public good, crossing boundaries seamlessly (Infante et al., 2024; to Yamin et al. 2023) Researchers receive a rigorous agenda for equitable, sustainable realization aligned with human values (Addanki & Corrin, 2023). Digital twins, AI, analytics, and Industry 5.0 converge to redesign learning infrastructure (Odabaşı & Özkan, 2025). Success requires interdisciplinary collaboration among experts and learners. This chapter provides the conceptual foundation (Yan et al., 2025). Ultimately, the aim is to leverage these advancements to create adaptive, personalized learning experiences that cater to the unique needs of each student, bridging the gap between educational theory and practical application (Adel, 2024; Xu & Zhang, 2023).

REFERENCES

Addanki, K., & Corrin, L. (2023). Unveiling the potential of Digital Twin technology for Higher Education. *ASCILITE Publications*, 12–21. DOI: 10.14742/apubs.2023.635

Adel, A. (2024). The Convergence of Intelligent Tutoring, Robotics, and IoT in Smart Education for the Transition from Industry 4.0 to 5.0. *Smart Cities*, *7*(1), 325–369. DOI: 10.3390/smartcities7010014

Bond, M., Khosravi, H., de Laat, M., Bergdahl, N., Negrea, V., Oxley, E., Pham, P., Chong, S. W., & Siemens, G. (2024). A meta systematic review of artificial intelligence in higher education: A call for increased ethics, collaboration, and rigour. *International Journal of Educational Technology in Higher Education*, *21*(1), 4. Advance online publication. DOI: 10.1186/s41239-023-00436-z

Borchardt, M., Pereira, G. M., Milan, G. S., Scavarda, A., Nogueira, E. O., & Poltosi, L. C. (2022). Industry 5.0 Beyond Technology: An Analysis Through the Lens of Business and Operations Management Literature. *Organizacija*, *55*(4), 305–321. DOI: 10.2478/orga-2022-0020

Burrus, J., Jackson, T., Xi, N., & Steinberg, J. (2013). IDENTIFYING THE MOST IMPORTANT 21ST CENTURY WORKFORCE COMPETENCIES: AN ANALYSIS OF THE OCCUPATIONAL INFORMATION NETWORK (O*NET). *ETS Research Report Series, 2013*(2). DOI: 10.1002/j.2333-8504.2013.tb02328.x

Chamorro-Atalaya, O., Flores-Velásquez, C. H., Flores-Cáceres, R., Arévalo-Tuesta, J. A., Zevallos-Castañeda, M., Quispe, G. E. T., Aranda-Dextre, C. C., Cruz-Telada, Y., Caller-Luna, J., & Alarcón-Anco, R. (2024). Use of Digital Twin Technology in the Teaching-Learning Process, in the field of University Education: A Bibliometric Review. *International Journal of Learning Teaching and Educational Research*, *23*(2), 313–329. DOI: 10.26803/ijlter.23.2.15

Choi, Y., Lee, Y., Cho, J., Baek, J., Kim, B., Cha, Y., Shin, D., Bae, C., & Heo, J. (2020). *Towards an Appropriate Query*. Key, and Value Computation for Knowledge Tracing., DOI: 10.1145/3386527.3405945

Cohen, J. (2018). Evidence based learning design – the opportunities afforded by learning analytics. *Development and Learning in Organizations*, *32*(4), 10–13. DOI: 10.1108/DLO-10-2017-0084

Costa, L., Sanches, L., Amorim, R. J. R., Salvador, L. do N., & Souza, M. (2020). Monitoring Academic Performance Based on Learning Analytics and Ontology: A Systematic Review [Review of *Monitoring Academic Performance Based on Learning Analytics and Ontology: A Systematic Review*]. *Informatics in Education*, 361–397. Vilnius University. DOI: 10.15388/infedu.2020.17

Costello, E., Brunton, J., Otrel-Cass, K., Lyngdorf, N. E. R., & Brown, M. (2024). Hacking Happier Futures : An AI-augmented student hackathon to address affective and ethical digital learning challenges. *Research Portal Denmark*, 9. https://local.forskningsportal.dk/local/dki-cgi/ws/cris-link?src=aau&id=aau-40fe5df2-680d-4e0a-8285-69066ff15b33&ti=Hacking%20Happier%20Futures%20%3A%20An%20AI-augmented%20student%20hackathon%20to%20address%20affective%20and%20ethical%20digital%20learning%20challenges

Crompton, H., & Burke, D. (2023). Artificial intelligence in higher education: The state of the field. *International Journal of Educational Technology in Higher Education, 20*(1), 22. Advance online publication. DOI: 10.1186/s41239-023-00392-8

Durão, L. F. C. S., Zancul, E., & Schützer, K. (2021). Closed-Loop Digital Twin for the Product Lifecycle. *Research Square (Research Square).* DOI: 10.21203/rs.3.rs-186777/v1

European Commission. (2021). *Industry 5.0: Towards a sustainable, human-centric and resilient European industry*. Publications Office of the European Union., DOI: 10.2777/308407

Fouquet, F. (2023). Overeducation and labour market trajectories. *HAL (Le Centre Pour La Communication Scientifique Directe).* https://theses.hal.science/tel-04373668

Francia, A., Mariani, S., Adduce, G., Vecchiarelli, S., & Zambonelli, F. (2023). Digital Management of Competencies in Web 3.0: The C-Box® Approach. *Future Internet, 15*(11), 350–350. DOI: 10.3390/fi15110350

Funda, V. (2025). A systematic review of algorithm auditing processes to assess bias and risks in AI systems. *Journal of Infrastructure Policy and Development, 9*(2), 11489–11489. DOI: 10.24294/jipd11489

Gándara, D., Anahideh, H., Ison, M. P., & Picchiarini, L. (2024). Inside the Black Box: Detecting and Mitigating Algorithmic Bias Across Racialized Groups in College Student-Success Prediction. *AERA Open, 10*, 23328584241258741. Advance online publication. DOI: 10.1177/23328584241258741

Gelan, A., Fastré, G., Verjans, M., Martin, N., Janssenswillen, G., Creemers, M., Lieben, J., Depaire, B., & Thomas, M. (2018). Affordances and limitations of learning analytics for computer-assisted language learning: A case study of the VITAL project. *Computer Assisted Language Learning, 31*(3), 294–319. DOI: 10.1080/09588221.2017.1418382

Grech, A., Sood, I., & Ariño, L. (2021). Blockchain, Self-Sovereign Identity and Digital Credentials: Promise Versus Praxis in Education. *Frontiers in Blockchain, 4*, 616779. Advance online publication. DOI: 10.3389/fbloc.2021.616779

Grieves, M. (2022). Intelligent digital twins and the development and management of complex systems. *Digital Twin, 1*(1), 8. Advance online publication. DOI: 10.12688/digitaltwin.17574.1

Grieves, M., & Vickers, J. (2016). *Digital Twin: Mitigating Unpredictable*. Undesirable Emergent Behavior in Complex Systems., DOI: 10.1007/978-3-319-38756-7_4

Hazrat, M. A., Hassan, N. M. S., Chowdhury, A. A., Rasul, M. G., & Taylor, B. (2023). Developing a Skilled Workforce for Future Industry Demand: The Potential of Digital Twin-Based Teaching and Learning Practices in Engineering Education. *Sustainability (Basel), 15*(23), 16433–16433. DOI: 10.3390/su152316433

Henry, M., Gibson, D., Flodin, C., & Ifenthaler, D. (2019). Learning Innovations for Identifying and Developing Talent for University. In *IntechOpen eBooks*. IntechOpen., DOI: 10.5772/intechopen.81380

Hoffman, M., & Olmsted, R. (2016). 15. Credentials for Open Learning: Scalability and Validity. In *Open Education* (pp. 301–320). Plekhanov Russian Economic University. DOI: 10.11647/OBP.0103.15

Infante, S. Q., Robles, J., Martín, C., Rubio, B., & Díáz, M. (2024). Distributed digital twins on the open-source OpenTwins framework. *Advanced Engineering Informatics, 64*, 102970–102970. DOI: 10.1016/j.aei.2024.102970

Kabashkin, I. (2025). AI-Based Digital Twins of Students: A New Paradigm for Competency-Oriented Learning Transformation. *Information (Basel), 16*(10), 846–846. DOI: 10.3390/info16100846

Karanam, S. A. K., & Hartman, N. (2025a). A systematic review of Digital Twin (DT) and virtual learning environments (VLE) for smart manufacturing education. *Manufacturing Letters, 44*, 1597–1608. DOI: 10.1016/j.mfglet.2025.06.179

Karanam, S. A. K., & Hartman, N. W. (2025b). Digital twin and virtual learning environments for advanced manufacturing education. *Manufacturing Letters*. Advance online publication. DOI: 10.1016/j.mfglet.2025.02.001

Kärner, T., Warwas, J., & Schumann, S. (2020). A Learning Analytics Approach to Address Heterogeneity in the Classroom: The Teachers' Diagnostic Support System. *Technology Knowledge and Learning*, *26*(1), 31–52. DOI: 10.1007/s10758-020-09448-4

Kinsner, W. (2021a, June 16). TOWARDS EVOLVING ENGINEERING EDUCATION BASED ON SYMBIOTIC COGNITIVE DIGITAL TWINS. *Proceedings of the Canadian Engineering Education Association (CEEA)*. DOI: 10.24908/pceea.vi0.14865

Kinsner, W. (2021b). *Digital Twins for Personalized Education and Lifelong Learning*. 1–6. DOI: 10.1109/CCECE53047.2021.9569178

Kővári, A. (2025). AI Gem: Context-Aware Transformer Agents as Digital Twin Tutors for Adaptive Learning. *Computers*, *14*(9), 367–367. DOI: 10.3390/computers14090367

Kuehn, W. (2018). Digital twins for decision making in complex production and logistic enterprises. *International Journal of Design & Nature and Ecodynamics*, *13*(3), 260–271. DOI: 10.2495/DNE-V13-N3-260-271

Liebowitz, J. (2021). Online Learning Analytics. In *Auerbach Publications eBooks*. DOI: 10.1201/9781003194620

Liu, W., Fu, Y., Guo, Y., Wang, F. L., Sun, W., & Zhang, Y. (2024). Two-Timescale Synchronization and Migration for Digital Twin Networks: A Multi-Agent Deep Reinforcement Learning Approach. *arXiv (Cornell University)*. /arxiv.2409.01092DOI: 10.48550

Madaio, M., Blodgett, S. L., Mayfield, E., & Dixon-Román, E. (2021). Confronting Structural Inequities in AI for Education. *arXiv (Cornell University)*. https://arxiv.org/pdf/2105.08847v1

Madarkar, R., Luo, X., Walker, C., Madathil, A. P., & Liu, Q. (2024). Prospects of Digital Twin for Dynamic Life Cycle Assessment of Smart Manufacturing Systems. *MATEC Web of Conferences, 401*, 13006–13006. DOI: 10.1051/matecconf/202440113006

Marras, M., Boratto, L., Ramos, G., & Fenu, G. (2021). Equality of Learning Opportunity via Individual Fairness in Personalized Recommendations. *International Journal of Artificial Intelligence in Education*, *32*(3), 636–684. DOI: 10.1007/s40593-021-00271-1

Morales-Navarro, L., Kafai, Y. B., Nguyen, H., DesPortes, K., Vacca, R., Matuk, C., Silander, M., Amato, A., Woods, P., Castro, F. B. D., Shaw, M. S., Akgün, S., Greenhow, C., & Garcia, A. (2024). Learning about Data, Algorithms, and Algorithmic Justice on TikTok in Personally Meaningful Ways. *arXiv (Cornell University).* /arxiv.2405.15437DOI: 10.22318/icls2024.704174

Moya, B., Badías, A., Alfaro, I., Chinesta, F., & Cueto, E. (2020). Digital twins that learn and correct themselves. *International Journal for Numerical Methods in Engineering*, *123*(13), 3034–3044. DOI: 10.1002/nme.6535

Nahhas, S., Bamasag, O., Khemakhem, M., & Bajnaid, N. (2018). Added Values of Linked Data in Education: A Survey and Roadmap. *Computers*, *7*(3), 45–45. DOI: 10.3390/computers7030045

Odabaşı, M., & Özkan, E. B. (2025). Simulation of Physiological Parameters for Homeostatic Maintenance: The Role of Digital Twin Technology. *DergiPark (Istanbul University).* https://dergipark.org.tr/en/pub/abmyoder/issue/93995/1747252

OECD. (2023). Interoperability: unifying and maximising data reuse within digital education ecosystems. In *Digital education outlook.* Organization for Economic Cooperation and Development., DOI: 10.1787/12f8ebe3-

Oeij, P. R. A., Lenaerts, K., Dhondt, S., van Dijk, W., Schartinger, D., Sabrina, S., & Warhurst, C. (2024). A Conceptual Framework for Workforce Skills for Industry 5.0: Implications for Research, Policy and Practice. *Journal of Innovation Management*, *12*(1), 205–233. DOI: 10.24840/2183-0606_012.001_0010

Opik, R., Kirt, T., & Liiv, I. (2017). Megatrend and Intervention Impact Analyser for Jobs: A European Big Data\n Hackathon Entry. *arXiv (Cornell University).* / arxiv.1708.08262DOI: 10.48550

Özer, M., Tanberkan, H., & Perc, M. (2025). Artificial Intelligence Threatens Critical Thinking in Education Systems. *Journal of Higher Education and Science*, *15*(2), 157–164. DOI: 10.5961/higheredusci.1747885

Page, P., Knowles, P., & Mitwicki, R. (2023). Distributed Governance: a Principal-Agent Approach to Data Governance — Part 1 Background & Core Definitions. *arXiv (Cornell University).* /arxiv.2308.07280DOI: 10.48550

Pietrzykowski, M. (2023). Transdisciplinary Curricula as a Key Strategy for Education of Digital Innovators and Entrepreneurial Leaders in the Era of Digital Transformation. In *Bogucki Wydawnictwo Naukowe eBooks* (pp. 46–85). Bogucki Wydawnictwo Naukowe., DOI: 10.12657/9788379863761-4

Pinto, J. D., & Paquette, L. (2024). Deep Learning for Educational Data Science. *arXiv (Cornell University)*. /arxiv.2404.19675DOI: 10.1007/978-3-031-64487-0_6

Poquet, O., Kitto, K., Jovanović, J., Dawson, S., Siemens, G., & Markauskaitė, L. (2021). Transitions through lifelong learning: Implications for learning analytics. *Computers and Education Artificial Intelligence*, *2*, 100039–100039. DOI: 10.1016/j.caeai.2021.100039

Psyridou, M., Prezja, F., Torppa, M., Lerkkanen, M., Poikkeus, A., & Vasalampi, K. (2024). Machine learning predicts upper secondary education dropout as early as the end of primary school. *Scientific Reports*, *14*(1), 12956–12956. DOI: 10.1038/s41598-024-63629-0 PMID: 38839872

Raftopoulos, G., Fazakis, N., Davrazos, G., & Kotsiantis, S. (2025). A Comprehensive Review and Benchmarking of Fairness-Aware Variants of Machine Learning Models. *Algorithms*, *18*(7), 435–435. DOI: 10.3390/a18070435

Redmond, W. D., & Macfadyen, L. P. (2020). A Framework to Leverage and Mature Learning Ecosystems. [iJET]. *International Journal of Emerging Technologies in Learning*, *15*(5), 75–75. DOI: 10.3991/ijet.v15i05.11898

Richter, F. R., Bays, P. M., Jeyarathnarajah, P., & Simons, J. S. (2019). Flexible updating of dynamic knowledge structures. *Scientific Reports*, *9*(1), 2272–2272. DOI: 10.1038/s41598-019-39468-9 PMID: 30783199

Romero, P., Fitz, S., & Nakatsuma, T. (2023). Do GPT Language Models Suffer From Split Personality Disorder? The Advent Of Substrate-Free Psychometrics. *Research Square (Research Square)*. DOI: 10.21203/rs.3.rs-2717108/v1

Ronja, M., Claudia, H., Quintus, S., & Kristina, S. (2025). Personalized Knowledge Transfer Through Generative AI: Contextualizing Learning to Individual Career Goals. *arXiv (Cornell University)*. /arxiv.2508.04070DOI: 10.48550

Sadallah, M. (2019). Models and Tools for Usage-based e-Learning Documents Reengineering. *HAL (Le Centre Pour La Communication Scientifique Directe)*. https://theses.hal.science/tel-02911978

Samuelsen, J., Chen, W., & Wasson, B. (2021). Enriching context descriptions for enhanced LA scalability: A case study. *Research and Practice in Technology Enhanced Learning*, *16*(1), 6. Advance online publication. DOI: 10.1186/s41039-021-00150-2

Šereš, L., Pavlićević, V., Petrović, G., Horvat, D., & Ivanišević, R. (2022). Learning analytics: Prospects and challenges. *Strategic Management*, *27*(3), 48–55. DOI: 10.5937/StraMan2200020S

Shen, A., Han, X., Cohn, T., Baldwin, T., & Frermann, L. (2022). Optimising Equal Opportunity Fairness in Model Training. *arXiv (Cornell University)*. /arxiv.2205.02393DOI: 10.18653/v1/2022.naacl-main.299

Shi, W., & Li, J. (2024). New Digital Divide Shaped by Algorithm? Evidence from Agent-Based Testing on Douyin's Health-Related Video Recommendation. *Communication Research, 51*(7), 867–890. DOI: 10.1177/00936502241262056

Syarifuddin, S., Kurra, T., Susanto, A., Saputra, H. D., Lumbantobing, M. A., Pancawati, R., Lieung, K. W., & Mara, A. A. P. T. (2025). Artificial Intelligence-Based Digital Twins Metaverse to Improve STEM Work Skills and Adaptive Expertise in Higher Education: A Conceptual Framework. *F1000 Research, 14*, 1376–1376. DOI: 10.12688/f1000research.174205.1

Tlili, A., Huang, R., Shehata, B., Liu, D., Zhao, J., Metwally, A. H. S., Wang, H., Denden, M., Bozkurt, A., Lee, L., Beyoğlu, D., Altınay, F., Sharma, R. C., Altınay, Z., Li, Z., Liu, J., Ahmad, F., Hu, Y., Salha, S., & Burgos, D. (2022). Is Metaverse in education a blessing or a curse: A combined content and bibliometric analysis. *Smart Learning Environments, 9*(1), 24. Advance online publication. DOI: 10.1186/s40561-022-00205-x

Verghis, A. M., Jose, B., Sheeja, P. R., Varghese, S., Mumthas, S., & Shaiju, K. S. (2025). Beyond personalization: Autonomy and agency in intelligent systems education. *Frontiers in Education, 10*, 1610239. Advance online publication. DOI: 10.3389/feduc.2025.1610239

. Vrček, N.,Ređep, N. B., Šlibar, B., & Grabar, D. (2025). Smart Decision-Making: The Role of Digital Twins, Retrieval-Augmented Generation-Enhanced AI, and Learning Analytics. *Ubiquity Proceedings*, 2–2. DOI: 10.5334/uproc.170

Weerakkody, V., Osmani, M., Waller, P., Hindi, N., & Al-Esmail, R. (2016). Situating Continuing Professional Development in Life Long Learning in Qatar. *International Journal of Business and Management, 11*(11), 81–81. DOI: 10.5539/ijbm.v11n11p81

Xu, S., & Zhang, X. (2023). Leveraging generative artificial intelligence to simulate student learning behavior. *arXiv (Cornell University)*. /arxiv.2310.19206DOI: 10.48550

Yamin, M. M., Imran, A. S., & Katt, B. (2023). Towards a digital twin framework for lifelong learning. *2023 IEEE Global Engineering Education Conference (EDUCON)*. DOI: 10.1109/EDUCON54358.2023.10099333

Yan, H., Lin, F., & Kinshuk, K. (2025). Adaptive Practicing Design to Facilitate Self-Regulated Learning. *Canadian Journal of Learning and Technology*, *50*(3), 1–22. DOI: 10.21432/cjlt28768

Yao, J., Yang, Y., Wang, X., & Zhang, X. (2023). Systematic review of digital twin technology and applications. *Visual Computing for Industry, Biomedicine, and Art*, *6*(1), 10–10. DOI: 10.1186/s42492-023-00137-4 PMID: 37249731

Yu, R., Lee, H., & Kizilcec, R. F. (2021). Should College Dropout Prediction Models Include Protected Attributes? *arXiv (Cornell University)*. /arxiv.2103.15237DOI: 10.1145/3430895.3460139

Zhang, J., Zhu, J., Tu, W., Wang, M., Yang, Y., Qian, F., & Xu, Y. (2024). The Effectiveness of a Digital Twin Learning System in Assisting Engineering Education Courses: A Case of Landscape Architecture. *Applied Sciences (Basel, Switzerland)*, *14*(15), 6484–6484. DOI: 10.3390/app14156484

Zhao, N., Seitinger, S., Richer, R., & Paradiso, J. A. (2020). Real-time work environment optimization using multimodal media and body sensor network. *Smart Health (Amsterdam, Netherlands)*, *19*, 100164–100164. DOI: 10.1016/j.smhl.2020.100164

. Zhu, H., Lin, Y., Liu, Z., Fu, J., Chua, T., & Sun, M. (2019). *Graph Neural Networks with Generated Parameters for Relation Extraction*. DOI: 10.18653/v1/P19-1128

Compilation of References

Abdelrahman, G., Wang, Q., & Nunes, B. (2023). Knowledge tracing: A survey. *ACM Computing Surveys*, *55*(11), 224. Advance online publication. DOI: 10.1145/3569576

AbdelRaouf, H., Hasnaine, Q. R., Fouda, M. M., Fadlullah, Z. M., & Ibrahem, M. I. (2026). Paradigm Shift Toward Distributed Learning in IoT Intelligence: A Comprehensive Survey of Opportunities and Challenges. *IEEE Internet of Things Journal*, *13*(10), 20128–20154. DOI: 10.1109/JIOT.2026.3657733

Aboulsafa, E. I., Elkhayat, G. A., Abdul-kader, H. M., & Almorsy, S. A. (2025, May). Proposed Student Digital Twin Data Model and System Architecture for Personalized Learning. In *2025 International Conference on Machine Intelligence and Smart Innovation (ICMISI)* (pp. 341-346). IEEE. DOI: 10.1109/ICMISI65108.2025.11115606

Abraham, R., Schneider, J., & vom Brocke, J. (2019). Data governance: A conceptual framework, structured review, and research agenda. *International Journal of Information Management*, *49*, 424–438. DOI: 10.1016/j.ijinfomgt.2019.07.008

Adams, C., Pente, P., Lemermeyer, G., & Rockwell, G. (2023). Ethical principles for artificial intelligence in K-12 education. *Computers and Education: Artificial Intelligence*, *4*, 100131. DOI: 10.1016/j.caeai.2023.100131

Addanki, K., & Corrin, L. (2023). Unveiling the potential of Digital Twin technology for Higher Education. *ASCILITE Publications*, 12–21. DOI: 10.14742/apubs.2023.635

Adel, A. (2024). The Convergence of Intelligent Tutoring, Robotics, and IoT in Smart Education for the Transition from Industry 4.0 to 5.0. *Smart Cities*, *7*(1), 325–369. DOI: 10.3390/smartcities7010014

Adhya, D. H., & Panda, S. (2026). An integrative systematic review analysis of research on technology-enabled personalized learning and self-regulated learning. *Smart Learning Environments*, *13*(1), 3. DOI: 10.1186/s40561-025-00428-8

Agarwal, B., Urlings, C., van Lankveld, G., & Klemke, R. (2026). Identifying the ethical values and norms for artificial intelligence in education: A systematic literature review. *International Journal of Artificial Intelligence in Education, 36*(1–2), 100004. DOI: 10.1016/j.ijaied.2026.100004

Agarwal, V., Verma, P., & Ferrigno, G. (2025). Education 5.0 challenges and sustainable development goals in emerging economies: A mixed-method approach. *Technology in Society, 81*, 102814. DOI: 10.1016/j.techsoc.2025.102814

Agbo, F. J., Olaleye, S. A., Bower, M., & Oyelere, S. S. (2023). Examining the relationships between students' perceptions of technology, pedagogy, and cognition: The case of immersive virtual reality mini games to foster computational thinking in higher education. *Smart Learning Environments, 10*(1), 16. DOI: 10.1186/s40561-023-00233-1

Agrawal, A., Nagaraj, S., Imambi, S. S., Borse, K. T., Dhange, P. G., Goud, V. S., & Gupta, D. (2026). Barriers and limitations in artificial intelligence for decoding non-human signals. In Ameur, W., & Arbi, A. (Eds.), *Harnessing AI for human-animal communication* (pp. 85–116). IGI Global Scientific Publishing., DOI: 10.4018/979-8-3373-5483-5.ch004

Alghamdi, S., Yoon, H. Y., & Song, Y. T. (2025, May). Digital Twins in Education Applications, Challenges, and Future Directions. In 2025 IEEE/ACIS 23rd International Conference on Software Engineering Research, Management and Applications (SERA) (pp. 225-232). IEEE.

Alshahrani, S., Adenle, Y. A., & Alshuwaikhat, H. M. (2026). The development of a 3D model based on digital twin for campus master plan optimization. *Discover Cities, 3*(1), 52. DOI: 10.1007/s44327-026-00236-w

Amaresh, K., Kumar, J. S. V. S., Mustafa, M., Kumar, N. M. G., & Tabassum, S. (2026). Integrated IoT and digital twin architecture for optimising xEV performance and grid interaction. *International Journal of Mathematical Modelling and Numerical Optimisation, 16*(2-4), 314–336. DOI: 10.1504/IJMMNO.2026.153031

Ammer, M. A., & Mamadjanova, T. (2025b). Impact of educational quality, educational resource, and educational climate on educational engagement and student intention to attend lectures. Espacio, Tiempo y Educación. Advance online publication. DOI: 10.14516/ete.12208

Ammer, M. A., & Mamadjanova, T. (2025). Effects of educational digital literacy, educational aspirations, self-directed learning on e-learning motivation and effectiveness. *Educational Sciences: Theory & Practice*. Advance online publication. DOI: 10.12738/jestp.2025.1.18

Amo-Filva, D., Fonseca, D., García-Peñalvo, F. J., Alier Forment, M., Casany Guerrero, M. J., & Godoy, G. (2024). Exploring the landscape of learning analytics privacy in fog and edge computing: A systematic literature review. *Computers in Human Behavior, 158*, 108303. DOI: 10.1016/j.chb.2024.108303

Anas, A., Mouna, E., Abdellatif, K., Hamidou, T., Anis, L., & Cédric, A. (2026). Adaptive Control in Multi-Agent Digital Twins for Sustainable Smart Farming: Game Theory-Driven Optimization. *IEEE Internet of Things Journal*, 1. DOI: 10.1109/JIOT.2026.3689694

Anders, G. (2013). *Die Antiquiertheit des Menschen* (Vol. 1). C.H. Beck. (Original work published 1956)

Arantes, J. (2024). Digital twins and the terminology of 'personalization' or 'personalized learning' in educational policy: A discussion paper. *Policy Futures in Education, 22*(2), 210–226. DOI: 10.1177/14782103231176357

Arendt, H. (1973). *The origins of totalitarianism*. Harcourt Brace Jovanovich. (Original work published 1951)

Aria, M., & Cuccurullo, C. (2017). Bibliometrix: An R-tool for comprehensive science mapping analysis. *Journal of Informetrics, 11*(4), 959–975. DOI: 10.1016/j.joi.2017.08.007

Arrieta, A. B., Díaz-Rodríguez, N., Del Ser, J., Bennetot, A., Tabik, S., Barbado, A., García, S., Gil-López, S., Molina, D., Benjamins, R., Chatila, R., & Herrera, F. (2020). Explainable Artificial Intelligence (XAI): Concepts, taxonomies, opportunities and challenges toward responsible AI. *Information Fusion, 58*, 82–115. DOI: 10.1016/j.inffus.2019.12.012

Asare, K. A., Liu, R., Anumba, C. J., & Issa, R. R. (2024). Real-world prototyping and evaluation of digital twins for predictive facility maintenance. *Journal of Building Engineering, 97*, 110890. DOI: 10.1016/j.jobe.2024.110890

Ashmel, M., Tlemsani, I., Mason-Jones, R., Matthews, R., & Ndrecaj, V. (2024). Higher education via the lens of Industry 5.0: Strategy and perspective. *Social Sciences & Humanities Open, 9*, 100828. DOI: 10.1016/j.ssaho.2024.100828

Attaran, M., & Celik, B. G. (2023). Digital twin: Benefits, use cases, challenges, and opportunities. *Decision Analytics Journal, 6*, 100165. DOI: 10.1016/j.dajour.2023.100165

Autili, M., Corsi, R., De Sanctis, M., Inverardi, P., & Pelliccione, P. (2026). Ethics label for digital systems to promote transparency and user awareness. *Journal of Systems and Software, 235*, 112752. DOI: 10.1016/j.jss.2025.112752

Azevedo, R., Bouchet, F., Duffy, M., Harley, J., Taub, M., Trevors, G., Cloude, E., Dever, D., Wiedbusch, M., Wortha, F., & Cerezo, R. (2022). Lessons learned and future directions of MetaTutor: Leveraging multichannel data to scaffold self-regulated learning with an intelligent tutoring system. *Frontiers in Psychology*, *13*, 813632. Advance online publication. DOI: 10.3389/fpsyg.2022.813632 PMID: 35774935

Baaj, I., Bouraoui, Z., Cornuéjols, A., Denœux, T., Destercke, S., Dubois, D., Lesot, M.-J., Marques-Silva, J., Mengin, J., Prade, H., Schockaert, S., Serrurier, M., Strauss, O., & Vrain, C. (2024). Synergies between machine learning and reasoning: An introduction by the Kay R. Amel group. *International Journal of Approximate Reasoning*, *171*, 109206. DOI: 10.1016/j.ijar.2024.109206

Baas, J., Schotten, M., Plume, A., Côté, G., & Karimi, R. (2020). Scopus as a curated, high-quality bibliometric data source for academic research. *Quantitative Science Studies*, *1*(1), 377–386. DOI: 10.1162/qss_a_00019

Babu, C. S., Afreed, M. N., Sree, V. S., & Arshath, J. M. (2026). The Role of Digital Twins in AI-Driven Industry 4.0 and 5.0: Enhancing Sustainability and Innovation. AI-Driven Smart Industrial Technologies, 243-284.

Bäcklund, K., Lundqvist, P., & Molinari, M. (2024). Showcasing a digital twin for higher educational buildings: Developing the concept toward human centricity. *Frontiers in Built Environment*, *10*, 1347451. DOI: 10.3389/fbuil.2024.1347451

Baker, R. S., & Hawn, A. (2022). Algorithmic bias in education. *International Journal of Artificial Intelligence in Education*, *32*(4), 1052–1092. DOI: 10.1007/s40593-021-00285-9

Bankins, S., Formosa, P., Montefiore, T., Richards, D., Cenacchi, F., & McEwan, M. (2025). Virtual reality and work: Ethical and inclusion implications of facial representation in VR. *The Journal of Strategic Information Systems*, *34*(4), 101937. DOI: 10.1016/j.jsis.2025.101937

Bao, Z., Siraj, S. B., & Halili, S. H. (2025, April). The Convergence of Digital Twins and Eye-Tracking: Toward Zero UI in Wearable Human-Robot Interaction. In 2025 3rd International Conference on Control and Robot Technology (ICCRT) (pp. 123-129). IEEE.

Baofu, P. (2009). *The future of post-human mass media: A preface to a new theory of communication*. Cambridge Scholars Publishing.

Barricelli, B. R., Casiraghi, E., & Fogli, D. (2019). A survey on digital twin: Definitions, characteristics, applications, and design implications. *IEEE Access : Practical Innovations, Open Solutions, 7*, 167653–167671. DOI: 10.1109/ACCESS.2019.2953499

Bayly-Castaneda, K., Ramirez-Montoya, M.-S., & Morita-Alexander, A. (2024). Crafting personalized learning paths with AI for lifelong learning: A systematic literature review. *Frontiers in Education, 9*, 1424386. Advance online publication. DOI: 10.3389/feduc.2024.1424386

Bellini, E., Bagnoli, F., Caporuscio, M., Damiani, E., Flammini, F., Linkov, I., & Marrone, S. (2021, July). Resilience learning through self adaptation in digital twins of human-cyber-physical systems. In *2021 IEEE International Conference on Cyber Security and Resilience (CSR)* (pp. 168-173). IEEE. DOI: 10.1109/CSR51186.2021.9527913

Berendt, B., Littlejohn, A., & Blakemore, M. (2020). AI in education: Learner choice and fundamental rights. *Learning, Media and Technology, 45*(3), 312–324. DOI: 10.1080/17439884.2020.1786399

Bernacki, M. L., Greene, M. J., & Lobczowski, N. G. (2021). A systematic review of research on personalized learning: Personalized by whom, to what, how, and for what purpose(s)? *Educational Psychology Review, 33*(4), 1675–1715. DOI: 10.1007/s10648-021-09615-8

Bhatti, M. A., & Pardaev, J. (2025). *Exploring accreditation's role in fostering inclusive education via educational equity and technology*. Revista Electrónica de LEEME., DOI: 10.58262/LEEME.56.05

Bhatti, M. A., & Sattarov, A. (2025). *Impact of religious tourism on spiritual belief: Role of visit motivation, cultural contact, and cultural attachment*. European Journal for Philosophy of Religion., DOI: 10.24204/ejpr.2025.4814

Bhatt, P., Sethi, A., Tasgaonkar, V., Shroff, J., Pendharkar, I., Desai, A., Sinha, P., Deshpande, A., Joshi, G., Rahate, A., Jain, P., Walambe, R., Kotecha, K., & Jain, N. K. (2023). Machine learning for cognitive behavioral analysis: Datasets, methods, paradigms, and research directions. *Brain Informatics, 10*(1), 22. Advance online publication. DOI: 10.1186/s40708-023-00196-6 PMID: 37524933

Biesta, G. (2006). *Beyond learning: Democratic education for a human future*. Paradigm Publishers.

Bloom, B. S. (1984). The 2 sigma problem: The search for methods of group instruction as effective as one-to-one tutoring. *Educational Researcher*, *13*(6), 4–16. DOI: 10.3102/0013189X013006004

Boje, C., Guerriero, A., Kubicki, S., & Rezgui, Y. (2020). Towards a semantic Construction Digital Twin: Directions for future research. *Automation in Construction*, *114*, 103179. DOI: 10.1016/j.autcon.2020.103179

Boltsi, A., Kosmanos, D., Xenakis, A., Chatzimisios, P., & Chaikalis, C. (2025). Towards a Novel Digital Twin Framework Proposal Within the Engineering Design Process for Future Engineers: An IoT Smart Building Use Case. *Sensors (Basel)*, *25*(11), 3504. DOI: 10.3390/s25113504 PMID: 40969060

Bond, M., Khosravi, H., de Laat, M., Bergdahl, N., Negrea, V., Oxley, E., Pham, P., Chong, S. W., & Siemens, G. (2024). A meta systematic review of artificial intelligence in higher education: A call for increased ethics, collaboration, and rigour. *International Journal of Educational Technology in Higher Education*, *21*(1), 4. Advance online publication. DOI: 10.1186/s41239-023-00436-z

Borchardt, M., Pereira, G. M., Milan, G. S., Scavarda, A., Nogueira, E. O., & Poltosi, L. C. (2022). Industry 5.0 Beyond Technology: An Analysis Through the Lens of Business and Operations Management Literature. *Organizacija*, *55*(4), 305–321. DOI: 10.2478/orga-2022-0020

Borchers, C., Zhang, J., Baker, R. S., & Aleven, V. (2024). Using think-aloud data to understand relations between self-regulation cycle characteristics and student performance in intelligent tutoring systems. In *Proceedings of the 14th Learning Analytics and Knowledge Conference (LAK '24)* (pp. 529–539). ACM. DOI: 10.1145/3636555.3636911

Brown, J. S., Collins, A., & Duguid, P. (1989). Situated cognition and the culture of learning. *Educational Researcher*, *18*(1), 32–42. DOI: 10.3102/0013189X018001032

Burrus, J., Jackson, T., Xi, N., & Steinberg, J. (2013). IDENTIFYING THE MOST IMPORTANT 21ST CENTURY WORKFORCE COMPETENCIES: AN ANALYSIS OF THE OCCUPATIONAL INFORMATION NETWORK (O*NET). *ETS Research Report Series, 2013*(2). DOI: 10.1002/j.2333-8504.2013.tb02328.x

Canal, F. Z., Müller, T. R., Matias, J. C., Scotton, G. G., de Sá, A. R.Junior, Pozzebon, E., & Sobieranski, A. C. (2022). A survey on facial emotion recognition techniques: A state-of-the-art literature review. *Information Sciences*, *582*, 593–617. DOI: 10.1016/j.ins.2021.10.005

Chamorro-Atalaya, O., Flores-Velásquez, C. H., Flores-Cáceres, R., Arévalo-Tuesta, J. A., Zevallos-Castañeda, M., Quispe, G. E. T., Aranda-Dextre, C. C., Cruz-Telada, Y., Caller-Luna, J., & Alarcón-Anco, R. (2024). Use of Digital Twin Technology in the Teaching-Learning Process, in the field of University Education: A Bibliometric Review. *International Journal of Learning Teaching and Educational Research, 23*(2), 313–329. DOI: 10.26803/ijlter.23.2.15

Chen, X. (2025). Innovation in curriculum system for communication majors based on new media technology and big data analytics. *International Journal of Information System Modeling and Design, 16*(1), 1–26. Advance online publication. DOI: 10.4018/IJISMD.391367

Chen, Z., Zou, J., & Wang, W. (2023). Digital twin-oriented collaborative optimization of fuzzy flexible job shop scheduling under multiple uncertainties. *Sadhana, 48*(2), 78. DOI: 10.1007/s12046-023-02133-z

Chiu, T. K. F., Xia, Q., Zhou, X., Chai, C. S., & Cheng, M. (2023). Systematic literature review on opportunities, challenges, and future research recommendations of artificial intelligence in education. *Computers and Education: Artificial Intelligence, 4*, 100118. Advance online publication. DOI: 10.1016/j.caeai.2022.100118

Choi, Y., Lee, Y., Cho, J., Baek, J., Kim, B., Cha, Y., Shin, D., Bae, C., & Heo, J. (2020). *Towards an Appropriate Query*. Key, and Value Computation for Knowledge Tracing., DOI: 10.1145/3386527.3405945

Cobo, M. J., López-Herrera, A. G., Herrera-Viedma, E., & Herrera, F. (2011). Science mapping software tools: Review, analysis, and cooperative study. *Journal of the American Society for Information Science and Technology, 62*(7), 1382–1402. DOI: 10.1002/asi.21525

Cohen, J. (2018). Evidence based learning design – the opportunities afforded by learning analytics. *Development and Learning in Organizations, 32*(4), 10–13. DOI: 10.1108/DLO-10-2017-0084

Conati, C., Barral, O., Putnam, V., & Rieger, L. (2021). Toward personalized XAI: A case study in intelligent tutoring systems. *Artificial Intelligence, 298*, 103503. Advance online publication. DOI: 10.1016/j.artint.2021.103503

Cong, W., Tao, W., & Jinsong, B. (2026). Agentic digital twin-embedded maintenance methodology for energy equipment: A self-evolving operational paradigm. *Journal of Manufacturing Systems, 84*, 100–116. DOI: 10.1016/j.jmsy.2025.11.020

Costa, L., Sanches, L., Amorim, R. J. R., Salvador, L. do N., & Souza, M. (2020). Monitoring Academic Performance Based on Learning Analytics and Ontology: A Systematic Review [Review of *Monitoring Academic Performance Based on Learning Analytics and Ontology: A Systematic Review*]. *Informatics in Education*, 361–397. Vilnius University. DOI: 10.15388/infedu.2020.17

Costello, E., Brunton, J., Otrel-Cass, K., Lyngdorf, N. E. R., & Brown, M. (2024). Hacking Happier Futures : An AI-augmented student hackathon to address affective and ethical digital learning challenges. *Research Portal Denmark*, 9. https://local.forskningsportal.dk/local/dki-cgi/ws/cris-link?src=aau&id=aau-40fe5df2-680d-4e0a-8285-69066ff15b33&ti=Hacking%20Happier%20Futures%20%3A%20An%20AI-augmented%20student%20hackathon%20to%20address%20affective%20and%20ethical%20digital%20learning%20challenges

Crawford, K. (2021). *Atlas of AI: Power, politics, and the planetary costs of artificial intelligence*. Yale University Press.

Cremonini, C. E., Capela, C., da Silva, A., Gaspar, M. C., & Vasco, J. C. (2025). Digital twin integration for workforce training: Transforming SMES in the ornamental stone industry. *Systems*, *13*(2), 120. DOI: 10.3390/systems13020120

Crnjac Zizic, M., Gjeldum, N., Mladineo, M., Bilic, B., & Aljinovic Mestrovic, A. (2025). Towards Sustainable Personalized Assembly Through Human-Centric Digital Twins. *Sensors (Basel)*, *25*(18), 5662. DOI: 10.3390/s25185662 PMID: 41012901

Crompton, H., & Burke, D. (2023). Artificial intelligence in higher education: The state of the field. *International Journal of Educational Technology in Higher Education*, *20*(1), 22. Advance online publication. DOI: 10.1186/s41239-023-00392-8

Davila-Gonzalez, S., & Martin, S. (2024). Human digital twin in industry 5.0: A holistic approach to worker safety and well-being through advanced ai and emotional analytics. *Sensors (Basel)*, *24*(2), 655. DOI: 10.3390/s24020655

Declerck, R., Reed, S., & Bert, C. (2006). *The grammar of the English tense system: A comprehensive analysis*. Walter de Gruyter. DOI: 10.1515/9783110199888

Dewey, J. (1938). *Experience and education*. Macmillan.

Dobaj, J., Riel, A., Macher, G., & Egretzberger, M. (2023). Towards devops for cyber-physical systems (cpss): Resilient self-adaptive software for sustainable human-centric smart cps facilitated by digital twins. *Machines (Basel)*, *11*(10), 973. DOI: 10.3390/machines11100973

Doskenov, B., Adaji, O., & Dosumu, R. (2025). Improving Manufacturing with Adaptive Learning in Industry 4.0: Challenges, and Policy Implications. *Current Journal of Applied Science and Technology*, *44*(4), 111–132. DOI: 10.9734/cjast/2025/v44i44518

Du Plooy, E., Casteleijn, D., & Franzsen, D. (2024). Personalized adaptive learning in higher education: A scoping review of key characteristics and impact on academic performance and engagement. *Heliyon*, *10*(22), e39630. Advance online publication. DOI: 10.1016/j.heliyon.2024.e39630 PMID: 39524879

Durão, L. F. C. S., Zancul, E., & Schützer, K. (2021). Closed-Loop Digital Twin for the Product Lifecycle. *Research Square (Research Square)*. DOI: 10.21203/rs.3.rs-186777/v1

Eco, U. (1986). *Travels in hyperreality*. Harcourt.

Eiaseb, N. P. I. G., Goagoses, N., Hamukoshi, S. S., & Eiases, R. H. S. (2026). Exploring the Role of Digital Twins in Enhancing Smart City IoT Applications: A Critical Review. IoT-Driven Business Transformation: Strategy, Data, Trust, and Security, 183-218.

Elsokkary, N., Khan, W., Shurrab, M., Mizouni, R., Singh, S., Bentahar, J., Mourad, A., & Otrok, H. (2026). Reinforcement learning and the Metaverse: A symbiotic collaboration. *Artificial Intelligence Review*, *59*(1), 34. DOI: 10.1007/s10462-025-11433-1

Escalante, J., Pack, A., & Barrett, A. (2023). AI-generated feedback on writing: Insights into efficacy and ENL student preference. *International Journal of Educational Technology in Higher Education*, *20*(1), 57. Advance online publication. DOI: 10.1186/s41239-023-00425-2

European Commission. (2021). *Industry 5.0: Towards a sustainable, human-centric and resilient European industry*. Publications Office of the European Union., DOI: 10.2777/308407

European Parliament & Council of the European Union. (2016). *Regulation (EU) 2016/679 of the European Parliament and of the Council of 27 April 2016 on the protection of natural persons with regard to the processing of personal data (General Data Protection Regulation)*. Official Journal of the European Union.

European Parliament & Council of the European Union. (2024). *Regulation (EU) 2024/1689 of the European Parliament and of the Council of 13 June 2024 laying down harmonised rules on artificial intelligence (Artificial Intelligence Act)*. Official Journal of the European Union.

Ezeoguine, P. E., & Kasumu, R. Y. (2024). Undergraduate students' perception of digital twins technology in education: Uses and challenges. *Int. J. Educ. Eval, 10*(2), 381–396. DOI: 10.56201/ijee.v10.no2.2024.pg381.396

Farrow, R. (2023). The possibilities and limits of XAI in education: A socio-technical perspective. *Learning, Media and Technology, 48*(2), 266–279. DOI: 10.1080/17439884.2023.2185630

Feng, J., & Kan, J. (2025). A novel multi-objective fuzzy deep learning framework for predictive maintenance in Industrial Internet of Things. *IEEE Access : Practical Innovations, Open Solutions, 13*, 41955–41973. DOI: 10.1109/ACCESS.2025.3547863

Fischer, B., & Frennert, S. (2025). Towards an experiential ethics of AI and robots: A review of empirical research on human encounters. *Technological Forecasting and Social Change, 219*, 124264. DOI: 10.1016/j.techfore.2025.124264

Fisk, P. (2017). *Education 4.0: The future of learning will be dramatically different, in school and throughout life*. Retrieved from Peter Fisk Official Website.

Floridi, L., Cowls, J., Beltrametti, M., Chatila, R., Chazerand, P., Dignum, V., Luetge, C., Madelin, R., Pagallo, U., Rossi, F., Schafer, B., Valcke, P., & Vayena, E. (2018). AI4People—An ethical framework for a good AI society: Opportunities, risks, principles, and recommendations. *Minds and Machines, 28*(4), 689–707. DOI: 10.1007/s11023-018-9482-5 PMID: 30930541

Fouquet, F. (2023). Overeducation and labour market trajectories. *HAL (Le Centre Pour La Communication Scientifique Directe)*. https://theses.hal.science/tel-04373668

Francia, A., Mariani, S., Adduce, G., Vecchiarelli, S., & Zambonelli, F. (2023). Digital Management of Competencies in Web 3.0: The C-Box® Approach. *Future Internet, 15*(11), 350–350. DOI: 10.3390/fi15110350

Freccero, A., Onwunle, M., Elliott, J., Podder, N., De Oliveira, J. P., & Dewa, L. H. (2025). Students' perceptions of learning analytics for mental health support: Qualitative study. *JMIR Formative Research, 9*, v9i1e70327. Advance online publication. DOI: 10.2196/70327 PMID: 40749729

Fuller, A., Fan, Z., Day, C., & Barlow, C. (2020). Digital twin: Enabling technologies, challenges and open research. *IEEE Access : Practical Innovations, Open Solutions, 8*, 108952–108971. DOI: 10.1109/ACCESS.2020.2998358

Funda, V. (2025). A systematic review of algorithm auditing processes to assess bias and risks in AI systems. *Journal of Infrastructure Policy and Development, 9*(2), 11489–11489. DOI: 10.24294/jipd11489

Galuzin, V., Galitskaya, A., Grachev, S., Larukhin, V., Novichkov, D., Skobelev, P., & Zhilyaev, A. (2022). Autonomous digital twin of enterprise: Method and toolset for knowledge-based multi-agent adaptive management of tasks and resources in real time. *Mathematics*, *10*(10), 1662. DOI: 10.3390/math10101662

Gándara, D., Anahideh, H., Ison, M. P., & Picchiarini, L. (2024). Inside the Black Box: Detecting and Mitigating Algorithmic Bias Across Racialized Groups in College Student-Success Prediction. *AERA Open*, *10*, 23328584241258741. Advance online publication. DOI: 10.1177/23328584241258741

García, Á., Bregon, A., & Martínez-Prieto, M. A. (2022). Towards a connected digital twin learning ecosystem in manufacturing: Enablers and challenges. *Computers & Industrial Engineering*, *171*, 108463. DOI: 10.1016/j.cie.2022.108463

García, Á., Bregon, A., & Martínez-Prieto, M. A. (2024). Digital twin learning ecosystem: A cyber–physical framework to integrate human-machine knowledge in traditional manufacturing. *Internet of Things : Engineering Cyber Physical Human Systems*, *25*, 101094. DOI: 10.1016/j.iot.2024.101094

García-Aranda, C., Martínez-Cuevas, S., Torres, Y., & Pedrote Sanz, M. (2024). A digital twin of a university campus from an urban sustainability approach: Case study in Madrid (Spain). *Urban Science (Basel, Switzerland)*, *8*(4), 167. DOI: 10.3390/urbansci8040167

Garrison, R. (2022). Shared metacognition in a community of inquiry. *Online Learning : the Official Journal of the Online Learning Consortium*, *26*(1), 6–18. DOI: 10.24059/olj.v26i1.3023

Gašević, D., Siemens, G., & Sadiq, S. (2023). Empowering learners for the age of artificial intelligence. *Computers and Education: Artificial Intelligence*, *4*, 100130. Advance online publication. DOI: 10.1016/j.caeai.2023.100130

Gašević, D., Tsai, Y.-S., & Drachsler, H. (2022). Learning analytics in higher education: Stakeholders, strategy, and scale. *The Internet and Higher Education*, *52*, 100833. DOI: 10.1016/j.iheduc.2021.100833

Gelan, A., Fastré, G., Verjans, M., Martin, N., Janssenswillen, G., Creemers, M., Lieben, J., Depaire, B., & Thomas, M. (2018). Affordances and limitations of learning analytics for computer-assisted language learning: A case study of the VITAL project. *Computer Assisted Language Learning*, *31*(3), 294–319. DOI: 10.1080/09588221.2017.1418382

Ghaleb, M. M. S., & Pardaev, J. (2025a). Effects of advertisement language, communication style, information seeking behavior and information source credibility on customers' intentions towards international products via brand trust. *El Profesional de la Información, 34*(2). Advance online publication. DOI: 10.3145/epi.2025.ene.34203

Ghaleb, M. M. S., & Pardaev, J. (2025b). Literature reading self-efficacy and academic achievement. *Educational Sciences: Theory & Practice, 25*(2), 77–92. DOI: 10.12738/jestp.2025.2.06

Ghaleb, M. M. S., & Sattarov, A. (2025). *Use of ChatGPT in education and quality of education: Role of student course engagement and regulator support.* Revista Electrónica de LEEME., DOI: 10.58262/LEEME.55.0020

Ghallab, M. (2019). Responsible AI: Requirements and challenges. *AI Perspectives, 1*(1), 3. DOI: 10.1186/s42467-019-0003-z

Ghosh, S., Hughes, M., Hughes, P., & Hodgkinson, I. (2025). Digital twin, digital thread, and digital mindset in enabling digital transformation: A socio-technical systems perspective. *Technovation, 144*, 103240. DOI: 10.1016/j.technovation.2025.103240

Giwa, O., & Kim, S. (2026). A Decade Later: Evolution of Real-Time Embedded Virtual Presence Systems (An HCI Perspective). *ACM Transactions on Embedded Computing Systems, 25*(2), 1–29. DOI: 10.1145/3788875

Gligorea, I., Cioca, M., Oancea, R., Gorski, A.-T., Gorski, H., & Tudorache, P. (2023). Adaptive learning using artificial intelligence in e-learning: A literature review. *Education Sciences, 13*(12), 1216. Advance online publication. DOI: 10.3390/educsci13121216

Goyal, I., Sai, S., Pabbati, M., Chamola, V., & Ranjan, V. (2026). Empowering Digital Twins With Agentic AI: Applications, Case Studies, and Limitations. *IEEE Communications Standards Magazine*, 1–11. DOI: 10.1109/MCOMSTD.2026.3669229

Grech, A., Sood, I., & Ariño, L. (2021). Blockchain, Self-Sovereign Identity and Digital Credentials: Promise Versus Praxis in Education. *Frontiers in Blockchain, 4*, 616779. Advance online publication. DOI: 10.3389/fbloc.2021.616779

Grieves, M., & Vickers, J. (2017). Digital twin: Mitigating unpredictable, undesirable emergent behavior in complex systems. In *Transdisciplinary Perspectives on Complex Systems*. https://doi.org/DOI: 10.1007/978-3-319-38756-7_4

Grieves, M. (2022). Intelligent digital twins and the development and management of complex systems. *Digital Twin, 1*(1), 8. Advance online publication. DOI: 10.12688/digitaltwin.17574.1

Gupta, D., Kumar, A., Talla, T., Joshi, M., Mehrotra, S., Brar, V., & Agrawal, A. (2026b). Library Contributions to Interdisciplinary Learning: Libraries as Facilitators of Interdisciplinary Research. In Shaik, M., Srivastav, A., Hussain, S., Hakro, A., & Bhasha, S. (Eds.), *Role of Library Resources for Higher Education in the Digital Era* (pp. 151–190). IGI Global Scientific Publishing., DOI: 10.4018/979-8-3373-3005-1.ch007

Gupta, D., Reddy, K. B., Neelima, K., Pathan, S. S., Gupta, B. R., Rajeshwari, P., & Gupta, P. P. (2026a). Integrating AI and Digital Twins for Real-Time Fault Identification in Wind Turbines. In Justo, J., Demidova, G., Mwasilu, F., Lukichev, D., & Bansal, R. (Eds.), *AI-Powered Analysis, Modeling, and Monitoring of Wind Energy Systems* (pp. 43–72). IGI Global Scientific Publishing., DOI: 10.4018/979-8-3373-4159-0.ch002

Gupta, R., Tian, B., Wang, Y., & Nahrstedt, K. (2024). TWIN-ADAPT: Continuous learning for digital twin-enabled online anomaly classification in iot-driven smart labs. *Future Internet, 16*(7), 239. DOI: 10.3390/fi16070239

Hamilton, D., McKechnie, J., Edgerton, E., & Wilson, C. (2021). Immersive virtual reality as a pedagogical tool in education: A systematic literature review of quantitative learning outcomes and experimental design. *Journal of Computers in Education, 8*(1), 1–32. DOI: 10.1007/s40692-020-00169-2

Hariyanto, K., Kristianingsih, F. X. D., & Maharani, R. (2025). Artificial intelligence in adaptive education: A systematic review of techniques for personalized learning. *Discover Education, 4*(1), 458. DOI: 10.1007/s44217-025-00908-6

Hasan, A., & Nguyen, D. T. (2026). Integrating agentic AI and digital twins for intelligent decision-making systems. *Array (New York, N.Y.), 29*, 100721. DOI: 10.1016/j.array.2026.100721

Hawkinson, E. (2022). Automation in education with digital twins: Trends and issues. *International Journal on Open and Distance e-Learning, 8*(2). https://doi.org/DOI: 10.58887/ijodel.v8i2.229

Hazrat, M. A., Hassan, N. M. S., Chowdhury, A. A., Rasul, M. G., & Taylor, B. (2023). Developing a Skilled Workforce for Future Industry Demand: The Potential of Digital Twin-Based Teaching and Learning Practices in Engineering Education. *Sustainability (Basel), 15*(23), 16433–16433. DOI: 10.3390/su152316433

He, C., Huang, Y., Lan, H., He, J., Fan, X., Zhang, D., Lin, J., Liao, M., & Wang, C. (2026). AI-assisted assessment of higher education quality: A visual analytical approach. *Visual Informatics, 100306*, 100306. Advance online publication. DOI: 10.1016/j.visinf.2026.100306

Henry, M., Gibson, D., Flodin, C., & Ifenthaler, D. (2019). Learning Innovations for Identifying and Developing Talent for University. In *IntechOpen eBooks*. IntechOpen., DOI: 10.5772/intechopen.81380

Hernández-Campos, M., Gonzalez-Torres, A., & García-Peñalvo, F. J. (2025). Learning outcomes evaluation through learning analytics systems in higher education: A systematic literature review. *SAGE Open, 15*(3), 21582440251347374. Advance online publication. DOI: 10.1177/21582440251347374

Hoel, T., & Chen, W. (2018). Privacy and data protection in learning analytics should be motivated by an educational maxim—Towards a proposal. *Research and Practice in Technology Enhanced Learning, 13*(1), 20. DOI: 10.1186/s41039-018-0086-8 PMID: 30595748

Hoffman, M., & Olmsted, R. (2016). 15. Credentials for Open Learning: Scalability and Validity. In *Open Education* (pp. 301–320). Plekhanov Russian Economic University. DOI: 10.11647/OBP.0103.15

Holmes, W., Bialik, M., & Fadel, C. (2019). *Artificial intelligence in education: Promises and implications for teaching and learning*. Center for Curriculum Redesign.

Holmes, W., Porayska-Pomsta, K., Holstein, K., Sutherland, E., Baker, T., Shum, S. B., Santos, O. C., Rodrigo, M. T., Cukurova, M., Bittencourt, I. I., & Koedinger, K. R. (2022). Ethics of AI in education: Towards a community-wide framework. *International Journal of Artificial Intelligence in Education, 32*(3), 504–526. DOI: 10.1007/s40593-021-00239-1

Holmes, W., & Tuomi, I. (2022). State of the art and practice in AI in education. *European Journal of Education, 57*(4), 542–570. DOI: 10.1111/ejed.12533

Hooshyar, D., Pedaste, M., Saks, K., Leijen, A., Bardone, E., & Wang, M. (2021). Open learner models in supporting self-regulated learning in higher education: A systematic literature review. *Computers & Education, 154*, 103878. Advance online publication. DOI: 10.1016/j.compedu.2020.103878

Horváth, I., & Tavčar, J. (2022). Designing Cyber-Physical Systems for Runtime Self-Adaptation: Knowing More about What We Miss.... *Journal of Integrated Design & Process Science, 25*(2), 1–26. DOI: 10.3233/JID210030

Huang, L., Dias, L., Nelson, E., Liang, L., Lajoie, S. P., & Poitras, E. G. (2022). The role of self-improving tutoring systems in fostering pre-service teacher self-regulated learning. *Frontiers in Artificial Intelligence*, *4*, 769455. Advance online publication. DOI: 10.3389/frai.2021.769455 PMID: 35047767

Hu, P. (2023). Investigation on smart campus management platform based on digital twin. *Procedia Computer Science*, *228*, 937–945. DOI: 10.1016/j.procs.2023.11.123

Hussaini, A., Qian, C., Guo, Y., Lu, C., & Yu, W. (2023, May). Digital twins of smart campus: Performance evaluation using machine learning analysis. In *2023 IEEE/ACIS 21st International Conference on Software Engineering Research, Management and Applications (SERA)* (pp. 132-137). IEEE. DOI: DOI: 10.1109/SERA57763.2023.10197806

Ifenthaler, D., Hofhues, S., Egloffstein, M., & Helbig, C. (2021). *Digital transformation of learning organizations*. Springer Cham., DOI: 10.1007/978-3-030-55878-9

Infante, S. Q., Robles, J., Martín, C., Rubio, B., & Díáz, M. (2024). Distributed digital twins on the open-source OpenTwins framework. *Advanced Engineering Informatics*, *64*, 102970–102970. DOI: 10.1016/j.aei.2024.102970

Ingason, H. T., Aaltonen, K., Asmundarson, A. S., Fridgeirsson, T. V., Huemann, D., Huemann, M., Kujala, J., Lampela, H., Mancini, M., Mariani, C., & Ringhofer, C. (2025). Personalised learning in project management education: Insights from an artificial intelligence-driven chatbot. *Project Leadership and Society*, *6*, 100193. DOI: 10.1016/j.plas.2025.100193

Islam, M. R., Ahmed, M. U., Barua, S., & Begum, S. (2022). A systematic review of explainable artificial intelligence in terms of different application domains and tasks. *Applied Sciences (Basel, Switzerland)*, *12*(3), 1353. Advance online publication. DOI: 10.3390/app12031353

Ivanov, D. (2026). Agentic digital twins: Bridging model-based and AI-driven decision-making support for a new era of supply chain and operations management. *International Journal of Production Research*, •••, 1–17. DOI: 10.1080/00207543.2026.2630277

Jankovskis, D., Cirule, I., & Carbone, A. (2024). Digital twins and e-learning: Navigating challenges and opportunities. In Casalino, G. (Eds.), *Higher education learning methodologies and technologies online. HELMeTO 2023. Communications in Computer and Information Science* (Vol. 2076). Springer., DOI: 10.1007/978-3-031-67351-1_12

Javed, A., Ashraf, J., & Yong, L. (2026). Synergistic effects of digital capability and human capital development on the twin green and digital transition: Evidence from carbon emissions and renewable energy adoption. *Journal of Environmental Management*, *397*, 128313. DOI: 10.1016/j.jenvman.2025.128313

Jeddoub, I., Nys, G. A., Hajji, R., & Billen, R. (2025). Data integration across urban digital twin lifecycle: A comprehensive review of current initiatives. *Annals of GIS*, *31*(3), 367–386. DOI: 10.1080/19475683.2024.2416135

Jobin, A., Ienca, M., & Vayena, E. (2019). The global landscape of AI ethics guidelines. *Nature Machine Intelligence*, *1*(9), 389–399. DOI: 10.1038/s42256-019-0088-2

Joksimovic, S., Siemens, G., Wang, Y. E., San Pedro, M. O. Z., & Way, J. (2020). Editorial: Beyond cognitive ability. *Journal of Learning Analytics*, *7*(1), 1–4. DOI: 10.18608/jla.2020.71.1

Jonas, H. (1984). *The imperative of responsibility: In search of an ethics for the technological age*. University of Chicago Press. DOI: 10.7208/chicago/9780226850337.001.0001

Jones, D., Snider, C., Nassehi, A., Yon, J., & Hicks, B. (2020). Characterising the Digital Twin: A systematic literature review. *CIRP Journal of Manufacturing Science and Technology*, *29*, 36–52. DOI: 10.1016/j.cirpj.2020.02.002

Kabashkin, I. (2025). AI-based digital twins of students: A new paradigm for competency-oriented learning transformation. *Information (Basel)*, *16*(10), 846. DOI: 10.3390/info16100846

Kabashkin, I. (2026). Cognitive Digital Twin Generations: From Foundational Instruments to Meta-Cognitive Ecosystems. *Information (Basel)*, *17*(3), 285. DOI: 10.3390/info17030285

Kalogeras, S., Samadi, S., & Nozari, H. (Eds.). (2025). *AI-Augmented Creativity in Learning Analytics*. IGI Global. DOI: 10.4018/979-8-3373-5117-9

Karanam, S. A. K., & Hartman, N. W. (2025). A systematic review of digital twin (DT) and virtual learning environments (VLE) for smart manufacturing education. *Manufacturing Letters*, *44*, 1597–1608. DOI: 10.1016/j.mfglet.2025.06.179

Karanam, S. A. K., & Hartman, N. W. (2025b). Digital twin and virtual learning environments for advanced manufacturing education. *Manufacturing Letters*. Advance online publication. DOI: 10.1016/j.mfglet.2025.02.001

Kärner, T., Warwas, J., & Schumann, S. (2020). A Learning Analytics Approach to Address Heterogeneity in the Classroom: The Teachers' Diagnostic Support System. *Technology Knowledge and Learning*, *26*(1), 31–52. DOI: 10.1007/s10758-020-09448-4

Karunaratne, T., Ajiero, I. R., Joseph, R., Farr, E., & Piroozfar, P. (2025). Evaluating the economic impact of digital twinning in the AEC industry: A systematic review. *Buildings (Basel, Switzerland)*, *15*(14), 2583. DOI: 10.3390/buildings15142583

Kasneci, E., Sessler, K., Kuchemann, S., Bannert, M., Dementieva, D., Fischer, F., & Kasneci, G. (2023). ChatGPT for good? On opportunities and challenges of large language models for education. *Learning and Individual Differences*, *103*, 102274. Advance online publication. DOI: 10.1016/j.lindif.2023.102274

Khalifeh, F., Santiago, R., & Palau, R. (2026). Redefining personalized learning in the artificial intelligence era: An updated systematic review from 2019 to 2025. *Smart Learning Environments*, *13*(1), 19. DOI: 10.1186/s40561-026-00440-6

Khatoon, U. T. (2025). Exploring Industry 5.0 in Digital Education: Concepts, Applications, Challenges, Opportunities, and Future Directions–Exploring Europe as an Education Hub. Digital Mentorship: Bridging AI-Human Divide in the Era of Industry 5.0, 165.

Khatri, V., & Brown, C. V. (2010). Designing data governance. *Communications of the ACM*, *53*(1), 148–152. DOI: 10.1145/1629175.1629210

Kinsner, W. (2021, September). Digital twins for personalized education and lifelong learning. In 2021 IEEE Canadian conference on electrical and computer engineering (CCECE) (pp. 1-6). IEEE. DOI: 10.1109/CCECE53047.2021.9569178

Kinsner, W. (2021a, June 16). TOWARDS EVOLVING ENGINEERING EDUCATION BASED ON SYMBIOTIC COGNITIVE DIGITAL TWINS. *Proceedings of the Canadian Engineering Education Association (CEEA)*. DOI: 10.24908/pceea.vi0.14865

Kizilcec, R. F., & Lee, H. (2022). Algorithmic fairness in education. In Holmes, W., & Porayska-Pomsta, K. (Eds.), *The ethics of artificial intelligence in education* (pp. 174–202). Routledge., DOI: 10.4324/9780429329067-10

Kovari, A. (2025). AI Gem: Context-Aware Transformer Agents as Digital Twin Tutors for Adaptive Learning. *Computers*, *14*(9), 367. DOI: 10.3390/computers14090367

Krishna, S. M. (2025). Smart campus ecosystems: Designing digital twins for educational infrastructure and strategic management. *Eksplorium-Buletin Pusat Teknologi Bahan Galian Nuklir, 46*(1), 1279-1293. Retrieved from: https://eksplorium.com/index.php/journal/article/view/148

Kuehn, W. (2018). Digital twins for decision making in complex production and logistic enterprises. *International Journal of Design & Nature and Ecodynamics, 13*(3), 260–271. DOI: 10.2495/DNE-V13-N3-260-271

Kuleto, V., Ilic, M., Dumangiu, M., Rankovic, M., Martins, O. M. D., Paun, D., & Mihoreanu, L. (2021). Exploring opportunities and challenges of artificial intelligence and machine learning in higher education institutions. *Sustainability (Basel), 13*(18), 10424. Advance online publication. DOI: 10.3390/su131810424

Kulik, J. A., & Fletcher, J. D. (2016). Effectiveness of intelligent tutoring systems: A meta-analytic review. *Review of Educational Research, 86*(1), 42–78. DOI: 10.3102/0034654315581420

Lave, J., & Wenger, E. (1991). *Situated learning: Legitimate peripheral participation.* Cambridge university press. Retrieved from: https://bibliotecadigital.mineduc.cl/bitstream/handle/20.500.12365/17387/cb419d882cd5%20bb5286069675b449da38.pdf?sequence=1&isAllowed=y

Lave, J., & Wenger, E. (1991). *Situated learning: Legitimate peripheral participation.* Cambridge University Press. DOI: 10.1017/CBO9780511815355

Lee, D., Kang, Y. S., & Noh, S. D. (2026). Digital twin-driven deep reinforcement learning for real-time optimisation in dynamic AGV systems. *International Journal of Production Research, 64*(1), 106–124. DOI: 10.1080/00207543.2025.2543491

Lee, S. J., & Kwon, K. (2024). A systematic review of AI education in K-12 classrooms from 2018 to 2023: Topics, strategies, and learning outcomes. *Computers and Education: Artificial Intelligence, 6*, 100211. DOI: 10.1016/j.caeai.2024.100211

Lei, M., He, G., Ouyang, Y., Shan, P., & Wang, M. (2026). Cloud-Edge Fusion for Advanced Dynamic Digital Twin Models in Intelligent Distribution Networks. *Journal of Electrical Engineering & Technology, 21*(1), 1037–1044. DOI: 10.1007/s42835-025-02447-4

Lei, Z., Zhou, H., Hu, W., Liu, G. P., & Guan, S. (2023). Web-based digital twin communication system of power systems for training and education. *IEEE Transactions on Power Systems, 39*(2), 3592–3602. DOI: 10.1109/TPWRS.2023.3308510

Lessig, L. (1999). *Code and other laws of cyberspace*. Basic Books.

Leung, Y. (2026). Multiagent Approach to Building Digital Twins of Cities. In *Digital Twins of Cities: Modeling Urban Dynamics and Complexity* (pp. 117–131). Springer Nature Switzerland. DOI: 10.1007/978-3-032-07966-4_7

Li, H., & Hong, T. (2025, June). A digital twin platform for building performance monitoring and optimization: Performance simulation and case studies. In *Building Simulation (Vol. 18*, No. 6, pp. 1561-1579). Beijing: Tsinghua University Press. https://doi.org/DOI: 10.1007/s12273-025-1290-2

Li, Y., Zhang, C., Guo, Z., Yang, N., Yuan, D., & Ding, W. (2026). SafeTwinNet: Secure and Adaptive Learning Ecosystems for Digital Twins. IEEE Communications Standards Magazine.

Liebowitz, J. (2021). Online Learning Analytics. In *Auerbach Publications eBooks*. DOI: 10.1201/9781003194620

Li, L., You, J., & Xu, T. (2025). Risk Analysis of Digital Twin Project Operation Based on Improved FMEA Method. *Systems*, *13*(1), 48. DOI: 10.3390/systems13010048

Lin, T. C., Chiu, C. N., Wang, P. T., & Fang, L. D. (2025, August). VisFactory: Adaptive Multimodal Digital Twin with Integrated Visual-Haptic-Auditory Analytics for Industry 4.0 Engineering Education. In Multimedia (Vol. 1, No. 1, p. 3). MDPI.

Lin, Y. Z., Petal, K., Alhamadah, A. H., Ghimire, S., Redondo, M. W., Corona, D. R. V., . . . Satam, P. (2025). Personalized education with generative ai and digital twins: Vr, rag, and zero-shot sentiment analysis for industry 4.0 workforce development. *arXiv preprint arXiv:2502.14080.* https://doi.org//arXiv.2502.14080DOI: 10.18260/1-2--57038

Lin, C.-C., Huang, A. Y. Q., & Lu, O. H. T. (2023). Artificial intelligence in intelligent tutoring systems toward sustainable education: A systematic review. *Smart Learning Environments*, *10*(1), 41. Advance online publication. DOI: 10.1186/s40561-023-00260-y

Lin, Y., Chen, L., Ali, A., Nugent, C., Cleland, I., Li, R., Ding, J., & Ning, H. (2024). Human digital twin: A survey. *Journal of Cloud Computing (Heidelberg, Germany)*, *13*(1), 131. DOI: 10.1186/s13677-024-00691-z

Lin, Z., & Liu, Y. (2026, January). A "Coach-Assistant" Human-AI Collaborative Paradigm for AI-Empowered Integrated Circuit Design Education. In *Proceedings of the 2026 3rd International Conference on Informatics Education and Computer Technology Applications* (pp. 761-766). DOI: 10.1145/3802133.3802257

Liu, L., & Wan, L. (2024). Innovative models for enhanced student adaptability and performance in educational environments. *PLoS One*, *19*(9), e0307221. Advance online publication. DOI: 10.1371/journal.pone.0307221 PMID: 39240797

Liu, X., Jiang, D., Tao, B., Xiang, F., Jiang, G., Sun, Y., Kong, J., & Li, G. (2023). A systematic review of digital twin about physical entities, virtual models, twin data, and applications. *Advanced Engineering Informatics*, *55*, 101876. DOI: 10.1016/j.aei.2023.101876

Liu, Z., Liu, Q., Chen, J., Huang, S., Gao, B., Luo, W., & Weng, J. (2023). Enhancing deep knowledge tracing with auxiliary tasks. In *Proceedings of the ACM Web Conference 2023* (pp. 4178–4187). ACM. DOI: 10.1145/3543507.3583866

Li, X., Gan, W., Liu, X., & Yang, J. (2026). Rule-Based Digital Twin: An Integrated Parametric-BIM Workflow for Life-Cycle Delivery of Free-Form, Special-Shaped Envelopes in Large-Scale Public Buildings. *Buildings (Basel, Switzerland)*, *16*(4), 778. DOI: 10.3390/buildings16040778

Li, Y., Chen, S., Hwang, K., Ji, X., Lei, Z., Zhu, Y., Ye, F., & Liu, M. (2025). Spatio-temporal data fusion techniques for modeling digital twin City. *Geo-Spatial Information Science*, *28*(2), 541–564. DOI: 10.1080/10095020.2024.2350175

Li, Y., & Lu, B. (2025). Intelligent educational systems based on adaptive learning algorithms and multimodal behavior modeling. *PeerJ. Computer Science*, *11*, e3157. Advance online publication. DOI: 10.7717/peerj-cs.3157 PMID: 40989423

Li, Y., & Zhong, R. Y. (2026). Spatial-temporal traceability and coordination in modular integrated construction: A future framework with hybrid digital twin and reinforcement learning. *International Journal of Construction Management*, *26*(5), 875–904. DOI: 10.1080/15623599.2025.2537727

Llopis-Albert, C., Rubio, F., Devece, C., & García-Hurtado, D. (2024). Digital twin-based approach for a multi-objective optimal design of wind turbine gearboxes. *Mathematics*, *12*(9), 1383. DOI: 10.3390/math12091383

Lodge, J. M., de Barba, P., & Broadbent, J. (2023). Learning with generative artificial intelligence within a network of co-regulation. *Journal of University Teaching & Learning Practice*, *20*(7), 02. Advance online publication. DOI: 10.53761/1.20.7.02

Long, D., & Magerko, B. (2020). What is AI literacy? Competencies and design considerations. In *Proceedings of the 2020 CHI Conference on Human Factors in Computing Systems* (pp. 1–16). ACM. DOI: 10.1145/3313831.3376727

Luckin, R., & Cukurova, M. (2019). Designing educational technologies in the age of AI: A learning sciences-driven approach. *British Journal of Educational Technology*, *50*(6), 2824–2838. DOI: 10.1111/bjet.12861

Luckin, R., Cukurova, M., Kent, C., & du Boulay, B. (2022). Empowering educators to be AI-ready. *Computers and Education: Artificial Intelligence*, *3*, 100076. Advance online publication. DOI: 10.1016/j.cacai.2022.100076

Lu, M., & Hu, Z. (2025). Digital twin-enhanced programming education: An empirical study on learning engagement and skill acquisition. *Computers*, *14*(8), 322. DOI: 10.3390/computers14080322

Lutters, E., & Damgrave, R. (2023). Digital twinning as the basis for integration of education and research in a learning factory. *Procedia CIRP*, *120*, 1463–1468. DOI: 10.1016/j.procir.2023.09.194

Lv, Z., Li, Y., Feng, H., & Lv, H. (2021). Deep learning for security in digital twins of cooperative intelligent transportation systems. *IEEE Transactions on Intelligent Transportation Systems*, *23*(9), 16666–16675. DOI: 10.1109/TITS.2021.3113779

Madaio, M., Blodgett, S. L., Mayfield, E., & Dixon-Román, E. (2021). Confronting Structural Inequities in AI for Education. *arXiv (Cornell University)*. https://arxiv.org/pdf/2105.08847v1

Madarkar, R., Luo, X., Walker, C., Madathil, A. P., & Liu, Q. (2024). Prospects of Digital Twin for Dynamic Life Cycle Assessment of Smart Manufacturing Systems. *MATEC Web of Conferences, 401*, 13006–13006. DOI: 10.1051/matecconf/202440113006

Manimegalai, S., & Binu Ben Jose, D. R. (2026). Application of Digital Technologies in Renewable Energy Systems. Energy Systems Engineering: Modeling. *Analysis and Applications*, •••, 187–226.

Manokeaw, S., Khuwuthyakorn, P., Chan, Y.-C., Tengtrairat, N., Jintapitak, M., Thinnukool, O., Buachart, C., Sinthamrongruk, T., Kridakorn Na Ayutthaya, T., Suriyanon, N., Kanangkaew, S., & Rinchumphu, D. (2025). A dynamic digital twin framework for sustainable facility management in a smart campus: A case study of Chiang Mai university. *Technologies*, *13*(10), 439. DOI: 10.3390/technologies13100439

Marengo, A. (2024). Navigating the nexus of AI and IoT: A comprehensive review of data analytics and privacy paradigms. *Internet of Things : Engineering Cyber Physical Human Systems*, *27*, 101318. DOI: 10.1016/j.iot.2024.101318

Márquez, A. C., & Fernández, J. F. G. (2026). Agentic AI for autonomous preventive maintenance policy governance: A multi-agent framework for dynamic industrial environments. *Expert Systems with Applications*, *314*, 131767. DOI: 10.1016/j.eswa.2026.131767

Marras, M., Boratto, L., Ramos, G., & Fenu, G. (2021). Equality of Learning Opportunity via Individual Fairness in Personalized Recommendations. *International Journal of Artificial Intelligence in Education*, *32*(3), 636–684. DOI: 10.1007/s40593-021-00271-1

Martin, F., Zhuang, M., & Schaefer, D. (2024). Systematic review of research on artificial intelligence in K–12 education. *Computers and Education: Artificial Intelligence*, *6*, 100195. DOI: 10.1016/j.caeai.2023.100195

Matos, T., Santos, W., Zdravevski, E., Coelho, P. J., Pires, I. M., & Madeira, F. (2025). A systematic review of artificial intelligence applications in education: Emerging trends and challenges. *Decision Analytics Journal*, *15*, 100571. DOI: 10.1016/j.dajour.2025.100571

Mayer, R. E. (2024). The past, present, and future of the cognitive theory of multimedia learning. *Educational Psychology Review*, *36*(1), 8. Advance online publication. DOI: 10.1007/s10648-023-09842-1

Mehrabi, N., Morstatter, F., Saxena, N., Lerman, K., & Galstyan, A. (2021). A survey on bias and fairness in machine learning. *ACM Computing Surveys*, *54*(6), 1–35. DOI: 10.1145/3457607

Mei, L., Feng, X., & Cavallaro, F. (2023). Evaluate and identify the competencies of the future workforce for digital technologies implementation in higher education. *Journal of Innovation & Knowledge*, *8*(4), 100445. DOI: 10.1016/j.jik.2023.100445

Mei, S., Xie, Y., Liu, J., Wu, J., & Zhang, C. (2025). Physics-based modeling and intelligent optimal decision method for digital twin system towards sustainable CNC equipment. *Robotics and Computer-integrated Manufacturing*, *95*, 103028. DOI: 10.1016/j.rcim.2025.103028

Mena Guacas, A. F., Mellado-Moreno, P.-C., Calderón-Cisneros, J.-T., & Pelicano Piris, N. (2026). Mapping artificial-intelligence-driven innovation in higher education: A bibliometric review. *Social Sciences & Humanities Open*, *13*, 102561. DOI: 10.1016/j.ssaho.2026.102561

Mendonça, L., Barbosa, J., & Leitao, P. (2026, March). A Human-Centred Architecture Integrating Digital Twin and Agentic AI for Predictive Maintenance. In *2026 IEEE International Conference on Industrial Technology (ICIT)* (pp. 1-6). IEEE. DOI: 10.1109/ICIT64854.2026.11491044

Miadowicz, I., Kuhl, M., Maldonado Quinto, D., Pitz-Paal, R., & Felderer, M. (2026). From Automation to Autonomy: A Digital Twin Framework for Transparent Agent and Human Collaboration in Industrial Multi-Agent Systems. *Systems*, *14*(1), 76. DOI: 10.3390/systems14010076

Miao, F., Holmes, W., Huang, R., & Zhang, H. (2021). *AI and education: Guidance for policy-makers*. UNESCO.

Mishra, L., Gupta, T., & Shree, A. (2020). Online teaching-learning in higher education during lockdown. *International Journal of Educational Research Open*, *1*, 100012. DOI: 10.1016/j.ijedro.2020.100012 PMID: 35059663

Mishra, S., Aldafas, T. S. M., & Alshammari, N. S. (2026). A zero-trust digital twin framework for privacy-preserving multi-dataset intrusion detection in industrial IoT with lightweight blockchain auditing. *Scientific Reports*, *16*(1), 15236. DOI: 10.1038/s41598-026-42041-w PMID: 41917091

Mittelstadt, B. D. (2019). Principles alone cannot guarantee ethical AI. *Nature Machine Intelligence*, *1*(11), 501–507. DOI: 10.1038/s42256-019-0114-4

Mittelstadt, B. D., Allo, P., Taddeo, M., Wachter, S., & Floridi, L. (2016). The ethics of algorithms: Mapping the debate. *Big Data & Society*, *3*(2), 2053951716679679. Advance online publication. DOI: 10.1177/2053951716679679

Mo, F., Rehman, H. U., Chaplin, J. C., Sanderson, D., & Ratchev, S. (2025). Digital twin-based self-learning decision-making framework for industrial robots in manufacturing. *International Journal of Advanced Manufacturing Technology*, *139*(1), 221–240. DOI: 10.1007/s00170-025-15844-w

Mohammed, S. K., Singh, S., Mizouni, R., Otrok, H., & Damiani, E. (2026). Digital Twins Paradigm: A Systematic Review from the Reinforcement Learning Perspective. *ACM Computing Surveys*, *58*(7), 1–33. DOI: 10.1145/3777367

Mohandes, S. R., Singh, A. K., Ibrahim, A., Ma, N., Kineber, A. F., & Shakor, P. (2026). Pioneering digital transformation: unveiling the blockchain and digital twin technologies' synergy. Journal of Engineering, Design and Technology, 1-25.

Mon, B. F., Hayajneh, M., Ali, N. A., Ullah, F., Ullah, H., & Alkobaisi, S. (2025). Digital Twins in the IIoT: Current Practices and Future Directions Toward Industry 5.0. *Computers, Materials & Continua*, *83*(3), 3675–3712. DOI: 10.32604/cmc.2025.061411

Mon, B. F., Wasfi, A., Hayajneh, M., Slim, A., & Abu Ali, N. (2023). Reinforcement learning in education: A literature review. *Informatics (MDPI)*, *10*(3), 74. Advance online publication. DOI: 10.3390/informatics10030074

Morales-Navarro, L., Kafai, Y. B., Nguyen, H., DesPortes, K., Vacca, R., Matuk, C., Silander, M., Amato, A., Woods, P., Castro, F. B. D., Shaw, M. S., Akgün, S., Greenhow, C., & Garcia, A. (2024). Learning about Data, Algorithms, and Algorithmic Justice on TikTok in Personally Meaningful Ways. *arXiv (Cornell University)*. /arxiv.2405.15437DOI: 10.22318/icls2024.704174

Movahed, A. B., Movahed, A. B., & Nozari, H. (2024). Opportunities and challenges of marketing 5.0. Smart and sustainable interactive marketing, 1-21.

Movahed, A. B., Aliahmadi, A., Parsanejad, M., & Nozari, H. (2023). A systematic review of collaboration in supply chain 4.0 with meta-synthesis method. *Supply Chain Analytics*, *4*, 100052. DOI: 10.1016/j.sca.2023.100052

Moya, B., Badías, A., Alfaro, I., Chinesta, F., & Cueto, E. (2020). Digital twins that learn and correct themselves. *International Journal for Numerical Methods in Engineering*, *123*(13), 3034–3044. DOI: 10.1002/nme.6535

Muhudin, A. A., Shafiullah, M., Al-Ramadan, B., Zami, M. S., Zamani, M. T., & Herzallah, L. (2026). Reframing BIM and Digital Twins for Intelligent Built Environments. *Smart Cities*, *9*(4), 71. DOI: 10.3390/smartcities9040071

Munir, H., Vogel, B., & Jacobsson, A. (2022). Artificial intelligence and machine learning approaches in digital education: A systematic revision. *Information (Basel)*, *13*(4), 203. DOI: 10.3390/info13040203

Muthuswamy, V. V., & Absamatov, A. (2025). *Determinants of students engagement and their role in boosting students' academic performance among higher education institutions*. Revista Electrónica de LEEME., DOI: 10.58262/LEEME.56.13

Nahavandi, S. (2019). Industry 5.0—A human-centric solution. *Sustainability (Basel)*, *11*(16), 4371. DOI: 10.3390/su11164371

Nahhas, S., Bamasag, O., Khemakhem, M., & Bajnaid, N. (2018). Added Values of Linked Data in Education: A Survey and Roadmap. *Computers*, *7*(3), 45–45. DOI: 10.3390/computers7030045

Nalayini, C. M., Arunkumar, S., & Madesh, S. (2025). Role of artificial intelligence in enhancing school digital twins. *Journal of Artificial Intelligence and Capsule Networks*, *7*(2), 209–231. DOI: 10.36548/jaicn.2025.2.008

Naresh, P., Sardar, T. H., Ramityal, B., & Almusharraf, A. TR, M., & Jain, V. (2026). A hybrid self-evolving edge-AI framework for scalable digital process twins in enterprise systems. Enterprise Information Systems, 2653241.

Nayak, M. M., Neupane, P., Pahurkar, P. P., & Shrimal, D. (2025). An AI-driven adaptive training platform with digital twin-based skill gap analysis and future readiness insights. *Journal of Collective Sciences and Sustainability*, *1*(2). Advance online publication. DOI: 10.64189/css.25410

Nguyen, A., Ngo, H. N., Hong, Y., Dang, B., & Nguyen, B.-P. T. (2023). Ethical principles for artificial intelligence in education. *Education and Information Technologies*, *28*(4), 4221–4241. DOI: 10.1007/s10639-022-11316-w PMID: 36254344

Noetel, M., Griffith, S., Delaney, O., Harris, N. R., Sanders, T., Parker, P., del Pozo Cruz, B., & Lonsdale, C. (2022). Multimedia design for learning: An overview of reviews with meta-meta-analysis. *Review of Educational Research*, *92*(3), 413–454. DOI: 10.3102/00346543211052329

Nozari, H. (2025). Integrating Neuromorphic Intelligence with Fuzzy Multi-Objective Models in Resilient Green Supply Chain Design. Process Integration and Optimization for Sustainability, 1-14.

Nozari, H. (2025b). Self-Evolving Neuromorphic Systems for Predictive Learning. AI-Augmented Creativity in Learning Analytics, 105.

Nozari, H. (2026). AI-Augmented Creative Assessment: From Static Tests to Dynamic Insight Generation. In AI-Augmented Creativity in Learning Analytics (pp. 25-42). IGI Global Scientific Publishing.

Nozari, H. (2026). Self-Evolving Neuromorphic Systems for Predictive Learning Interventions. In AI-Augmented Creativity in Learning Analytics (pp. 105-122). IGI Global Scientific Publishing.

Nozari, H. (2026a). Self-Evolving Neuromorphic Systems for Predictive Learning Interventions. In AI-Augmented Creativity in Learning Analytics (pp. 105-122). IGI Global Scientific Publishing.

Nozari, H. (2026c). AI-Augmented Creative Assessment: From Static Tests to Dynamic Insight Generation. In AI-Augmented Creativity in Learning Analytics (pp. 25-42). IGI Global Scientific Publishing.

Nozari, H., & Yordanova, Z. (2025). An intelligent digital twin approach for optimizing multi-channel supply chains in uncertain environments. Green Technologies and Sustainability, 100309.

Nozari, H., & Yordanova, Z. (2026). Agentic artificial intelligence-driven digital twin for real-time irrigation control with fuzzy sustainability objectives. An International Journal of Optimization and Control: Theories & Applications, 026040013.

Nozari, H., & Yordanova, Z. (2026). Digital twin–driven decision support for human capital management under uncertainty. Green Technologies and Sustainability, 100353.

Nozari, H., Fallah, M., Szmelter-Jarosz, A., & Krzemiński, M. (2021). Analysis of security criteria for IoT-based supply chain: a case study of FMCG industries. Central European Management Journal, 29(4).

Nozari, H. (2024). Green supply chain management based on artificial intelligence of everything. *Journal of Economics and Management*, *46*, 171–188. DOI: 10.22367/jem.2024.46.07

Nozari, H. (2025a). Optimizing transmedia storytelling strategies across platforms for Maximum audience engagement. *Entertainment Computing*, •••, 101061.

Nozari, H. (2026). Digital twin-based predictive maintenance in cold chain logistics. *Operations Research*, *60*(1), 481–499. DOI: 10.1051/ro/2025167

Nozari, H., & Edalatpanah, S. A. (2023). Smart systems risk management in IoT-based supply chain. In *Advances in reliability, failure and risk analysis* (pp. 251–268). Springer Nature Singapore. DOI: 10.1007/978-981-19-9909-3_11

Nozari, H., & Samadi, S. (2025). AIoE-Powered Neuromarketing for Decoding the Consumer Brain. In *Artificial Intelligence of Everything and Sustainable Development* (pp. 39–53). Springer Nature Singapore. DOI: 10.1007/978-981-96-7202-8_3

Nozari, H., Tavakkoli-Moghaddam, R., & Gharemani-Nahr, J. (2022). A neutrosophic fuzzy programming method to solve a multi-depot vehicle routing model under uncertainty during the covid-19 pandemic. *International Journal of Engineering*, *35*(2), 360–371.

Odabaşı, M., & Özkan, E. B. (2025). Simulation of Physiological Parameters for Homeostatic Maintenance: The Role of Digital Twin Technology. *DergiPark (Istanbul University)*. https://dergipark.org.tr/en/pub/abmyoder/issue/93995/1747252

OECD. (2023). Interoperability: unifying and maximising data reuse within digital education ecosystems. In *Digital education outlook*. Organization for Economic Cooperation and Development., DOI: 10.1787/12f8ebe3-

Oeij, P. R. A., Lenaerts, K., Dhondt, S., van Dijk, W., Schartinger, D., Sabrina, S., & Warhurst, C. (2024). A Conceptual Framework for Workforce Skills for Industry 5.0: Implications for Research, Policy and Practice. *Journal of Innovation Management*, *12*(1), 205–233. DOI: 10.24840/2183-0606_012.001_0010

Okita, S. Y. (2024). Digital twins in education. In Peters, M. A., & Heraud, R. (Eds.), *Encyclopedia of educational innovation*. Springer., DOI: 10.1007/978-981-13-2262-4_282-1

Okpala, C., Chikwendu, U., & Onyeka, N. C. (2025). Artificial intelligence-driven total productive maintenance: The future of maintenance in smart factories. *International Journal of Engineering Research and Development*, *21*(1), 68–74.

Olawade, D. B., David-Olawade, A. C., Aderinto, N., & Wada, O. Z. (2026). Ethical oversight of artificial intelligence in Nigerian healthcare: A qualitative analysis of ethics committee members' perspectives on integration and regulation. *International Journal of Medical Informatics*, *206*, 106140. DOI: 10.1016/j.ijmedinf.2025.106140 PMID: 41092592

Orwell, G. (1949). *Nineteen eighty-four*. Secker & Warburg.

Ouyang, F., & Jiao, P. (2021). Artificial intelligence in education: The three paradigms. *Computers and Education: Artificial Intelligence*, *2*, 100020. DOI: 10.1016/j.caeai.2021.100020

Ouyang, F., Wu, M., Zheng, L., Zhang, L., & Jiao, P. (2023). Integration of artificial intelligence performance prediction and learning analytics to improve student learning in online engineering course. *International Journal of Educational Technology in Higher Education*, *20*(1), 4. Advance online publication. DOI: 10.1186/s41239-022-00372-4 PMID: 36683653

Ouyang, Z. (2025). Self-regulated learning and engagement as serial mediators between AI-driven adaptive learning platform characteristics and educational quality: A psychological mechanism analysis. *Frontiers in Psychology*, *16*, 1646469. Advance online publication. DOI: 10.3389/fpsyg.2025.1646469 PMID: 41190123

Özer, M., Tanberkan, H., & Perc, M. (2025). Artificial Intelligence Threatens Critical Thinking in Education Systems. *Journal of Higher Education and Science*, *15*(2), 157–164. DOI: 10.5961/higheredusci.1747885

Panadero, E. (2017). A review of self-regulated learning: Six models and four directions for research. *Frontiers in Psychology*, *8*, 422. DOI: 10.3389/fpsyg.2017.00422 PMID: 28503157

Pandey, P. K., Mahajan, S., Pandey, P. K., Paul, J., & Iyer, S. (2025). Immersive learning trends using digital twins. *Digital Twins for Smart Cities and Villages*, 249-271. https://doi.org/DOI: 10.1016/B978-0-443-28884-5.00012-9

Papagiannidis, E., Mikalef, P., & Conboy, K. (2025). Responsible artificial intelligence governance: A review and research framework. *The Journal of Strategic Information Systems*, *34*(2), 101885. DOI: 10.1016/j.jsis.2024.101885

Parmar, H., Murari, U. K., & Singh, S. K. (2026, February). Smart Polymer-Integrated IoT Systems: A Mathematical Framework for Real-Time Sensing and Adaptive Material Behavior. *Macromolecular Symposia*, *415*(1), e70183. DOI: 10.1002/masy.70183

Pasquale, F. (2015). *The black box society: The secret algorithms that control money and information*. Harvard University Press. DOI: 10.4159/harvard.9780674736061

Pathak, R. K., & Upadhyay, P.Dr Rakesh Kumar PathakDr Prakash Upadhyay. (2024). Integration of digital twins technologies in education for experiential learning: Benefits and challenges. [IRJAEH]. *International Research Journal on Advanced Engineering Hub*, *2*(03), 442–449. DOI: 10.47392/IRJAEH.2024.0064

Perisic, A., Perisic, I., Lazic, M., & Perisic, B. (2025). Metamodeling approach to socio-technical systems' external context digital twins building: A higher education case study. *Applied Sciences (Basel, Switzerland)*, *15*(15), 8708. DOI: 10.3390/app15158708

Pester, A., Andres, F., Anantaram, C., & Mason, J. (2025). Generative AI and Digital Twins: Fostering Creativity in Learning Environments. In *Human-Computer Creativity: Generative AI in Education, Art, and Healthcare* (pp. 153–173). Springer Nature Switzerland. DOI: 10.1007/978-3-031-86551-0_9

Pham, T. A., Ioannou, P. G., & Likhitruangsilp, V. (2026). Designing a BIM-enhanced digital twin architecture for construction pollution management in building renovation projects. *International Journal of Construction Management*, •••, 1–26. DOI: 10.1080/15623599.2026.2651946

Pietrzykowski, M. (2023). Transdisciplinary Curricula as a Key Strategy for Education of Digital Innovators and Entrepreneurial Leaders in the Era of Digital Transformation. In *Bogucki Wydawnictwo Naukowe eBooks* (pp. 46–85). Bogucki Wydawnictwo Naukowe., DOI: 10.12657/9788379863761-4

Pinto, J. D., & Paquette, L. (2024). Deep Learning for Educational Data Science. *arXiv (Cornell University)*. /arxiv.2404.19675DOI: 10.1007/978-3-031-64487-0_6

Pitzalis, R. F., Giordano, A., Di Spigno, A., Cowell, A., Niculita, O., & Berselli, G. (2025). Application of augmented reality-based digital twin approaches: A case study to industrial equipment. *International Journal of Advanced Manufacturing Technology*, *138*(7), 3747–3763. DOI: 10.1007/s00170-025-15755-w

Pocobelli, D. P., Boehm, J., Bryan, P., Still, J., & Grau-Bové, J. (2018). Building information models for monitoring and simulation data in heritage buildings. *The International Archives of the Photogrammetry, Remote Sensing and Spatial Information Sciences*, *XLII-2*, 909–916. DOI: 10.5194/isprs-archives-XLII-2-909-2018

Poquet, O., Kitto, K., Jovanović, J., Dawson, S., Siemens, G., & Markauskaitė, L. (2021). Transitions through lifelong learning: Implications for learning analytics. *Computers and Education Artificial Intelligence*, *2*, 100039–100039. DOI: 10.1016/j.caeai.2021.100039

Prinsloo, P., & Slade, S. (2017). Ethics and learning analytics: Charting the uncharted. Handbook of Learning Analytics, 49–57. https://doi.org/DOI: 10.18608/hla17.004

Prinsloo, P., & Slade, S. (2017). An elephant in the learning analytics room: The obligation to act. *Proceedings of the Seventh International Learning Analytics & Knowledge Conference*, 46–55. https://doi.org/DOI: 10.1145/3027385.3027406

Psyridou, M., Prezja, F., Torppa, M., Lerkkanen, M., Poikkeus, A., & Vasalampi, K. (2024). Machine learning predicts upper secondary education dropout as early as the end of primary school. *Scientific Reports*, *14*(1), 12956–12956. DOI: 10.1038/s41598-024-63629-0 PMID: 38839872

Radianti, J., Majchrzak, T. A., Fromm, J., & Wohlgenannt, I. (2020). A systematic review of immersive virtual reality applications for higher education. *Education and Information Technologies*, *25*, 1–38. DOI: 10.1007/s10639-019-09928-1

Raftopoulos, G., Fazakis, N., Davrazos, G., & Kotsiantis, S. (2025). A Comprehensive Review and Benchmarking of Fairness-Aware Variants of Machine Learning Models. *Algorithms*, *18*(7), 435–435. DOI: 10.3390/a18070435

Rahman, A., Khan, M. A., Mahmud, F. U., Bishnu, K. K., Rahman, A., Mridha, M. F., & Hossen, M. J. (2026). A systematic literature review on the impact of generative AI in digital marketing: Advancements, opportunities, and challenges. *Computers, Materials & Continua*, *87*(3), 1–10. Advance online publication. DOI: 10.32604/cmc.2026.071029

Rahmani-Sane, G., Azad, S., Ameli, M. T., & Haghani, S. (2025). The applications of artificial intelligence and digital twin in power systems: An in-depth review. *IEEE Access : Practical Innovations, Open Solutions, 13*, 108573–108608. DOI: 10.1109/ACCESS.2025.3580340

Rajaram, A., & Almalki, F. A. (2026). Energy Efficient Decentralized Digital Twins with IoT and Blockchain for Self-Optimizing Urban Infrastructure and Sustainable Energy Management. *Sustainable Computing : Informatics and Systems, 50*, 101319. DOI: 10.1016/j.suscom.2026.101319

Raji, I. D., Smart, A., White, R. N., Mitchell, M., Gebru, T., Hutchinson, B., Smith-Loud, J., Theron, D., & Barnes, P. (2020). Closing the AI accountability gap: Defining an end-to-end framework for internal algorithmic auditing. *Proceedings of the 2020 Conference on Fairness, Accountability, and Transparency*, 33–44. https://doi.org/ DOI: 10.1145/3351095.3372873

Ramamurthy, K., Kulanthaivelu, S., & Jenish, S. A. (2026). Future directions and emerging trends of adaptive artificial intelligence in wireless sensor networks, Internet of Things, and Industrial Internet of Things. Adaptive AI in Sensor Informatics, 291-308.

Rebelo Marcolino, M., Reis Porto, T., Thompsen Primo, T., Targino, R., Ramos, V., Marques Queiroga, E., Munoz, R., & Cechinel, C. (2025). Student dropout prediction through machine learning optimization: Insights from Moodle log data. *Scientific Reports, 15*(1), 9840. DOI: 10.1038/s41598-025-93918-1

Redmond, W. D., & Macfadyen, L. P. (2020). A Framework to Leverage and Mature Learning Ecosystems. [iJET]. *International Journal of Emerging Technologies in Learning, 15*(5), 75–75. DOI: 10.3991/ijet.v15i05.11898

Regan, P. M., & Jesse, J. (2019). Ethical challenges of edtech, big data and personalized learning: Twenty-first century student sorting and tracking. *Ethics and Information Technology, 21*(3), 167–179. https://link.springer.com/article/10.1007/s10676-018-9492-2. DOI: 10.1007/s10676-018-9492-2

Ren, K., Xu, C., Xiong, C., Bin, J., Zhang, Z., Wang, T., He, C., Shao, Y., Fei, X., Jiang, Y., Chen, Y., & Huang, Y. (2026). Optimization of Thermal Flow Dynamics in Tobacco Leaf Curing via IoT-Integrated Deep Neural Network-Assisted CFD. *IEEE Internet of Things Journal, 13*(10), 21510–21525. DOI: 10.1109/JIOT.2026.3666820

Richter, F. R., Bays, P. M., Jeyarathnarajah, P., & Simons, J. S. (2019). Flexible updating of dynamic knowledge structures. *Scientific Reports, 9*(1), 2272–2272. DOI: 10.1038/s41598-019-39468-9 PMID: 30783199

Rivera, L. F., Jiménez, M., Tamura, G., Villegas, N. M., & Müller, H. A. (2022). Designing run-time evolution for dependable and resilient cyber-physical systems using digital twins. *Journal of Integrated Design & Process Science*, *25*(2), 48–79. DOI: 10.3233/JID210014

Rojek, I., Mikołajewski, D., Dostatni, E., Cybulski, J., & Kozielski, M. (2025). Personalization of ai-based digital twins to optimize adaptation in industrial design and manufacturing. *Applied Sciences (Basel, Switzerland)*, *15*(15), 8525. DOI: 10.3390/app15158525

Romero, P., Fitz, S., & Nakatsuma, T. (2023). Do GPT Language Models Suffer From Split Personality Disorder? The Advent Of Substrate-Free Psychometrics. *Research Square (Research Square)*. DOI: 10.21203/rs.3.rs-2717108/v1

Roullier, B., McQuade, F., Anjum, A., Bower, C., & Liu, L. (2024). Automated visual quality assessment for virtual and augmented reality based digital twins. *Journal of Cloud Computing (Heidelberg, Germany)*, *13*(1), 51. DOI: 10.1186/s13677-024-00616-w

Rouvroy, A., & Berns, T. (2013). Gouvernementalité algorithmique et perspectives d'émancipation. *Reseaux (London)*, *177*(1), 163–196.

Sadallah, M. (2019). Models and Tools for Usage-based e-Learning Documents Reengineering. *HAL (Le Centre Pour La Communication Scientifique Directe)*. https://theses.hal.science/tel-02911978

Sadiku, M. N. O., Musa, S. M., & Ajayi-Majebi, A. (2021). Artificial intelligence in education. *International Journal of Scientific Advances*, *2*(1), 5–11. DOI: 10.51542/ijscia.v2i1.2

Sajja, R., Sermet, Y., Cikmaz, M., Cwiertny, D., & Demir, I. (2024). Artificial intelligence-enabled intelligent assistant for personalized and adaptive learning in higher education. *Information (Basel)*, *15*(10), 596. Advance online publication. DOI: 10.3390/info15100596

Salendab, F. A., & Tago, K. L. (2026). Innovative approaches to revolutionize student-centered learning in the 21st century. In *Emerging Trends, Global Perspectives, and Systemic Transformation in AI* (pp. 33-62). IGI Global Scientific Publishing. https://doi.org/DOI: 10.4018/979-8-3373-5102-5.ch002

Salendab, F. A., Tago, K. L., Cogo, D. A., & Demafeliz, R. E. (2026). Transforming higher education: Theoretical foundations and innovative pedagogies for holistic student development. In *Higher Education Classrooms as Places for Inquiry: Stories and Methods from Practitioner Researchers* (pp. 207-236). IGI Global Scientific Publishing. https://doi.org/DOI: 10.4018/979-8-3373-0305-5.ch007

Samala, A. D., Rawas, S., Zainuddin, Z., Howard, N.-J., & Shilina, S. (2025). The role of non-fungible tokens in education: A comprehensive review and future directions. *Social Sciences & Humanities Open*, *12*, 101834. DOI: 10.1016/j.ssaho.2025.101834

Samuelsen, J., Chen, W., & Wasson, B. (2021). Enriching context descriptions for enhanced LA scalability: A case study. *Research and Practice in Technology Enhanced Learning*, *16*(1), 6. Advance online publication. DOI: 10.1186/s41039-021-00150-2

Santos, R., Piqueiro, H., Dias, R., & Rocha, C. D. (2024). Transitioning trends into action: A simulation-based Digital Twin architecture for enhanced strategic and operational decision-making. *Computers & Industrial Engineering*, *198*, 110616. DOI: 10.1016/j.cie.2024.110616

Schiff, D. (2021). Education for AI, not AI for education: The role of education and ethics in national AI policy strategies. *International Journal of Artificial Intelligence in Education*, *32*(3), 527–563. DOI: 10.1007/s40593-021-00270-2

Selwyn, N. (2016). *Education and technology: Key issues and debates* (2nd ed.). Bloomsbury Academic.

Selwyn, N. (2019). *Should robots replace teachers? AI and the future of education*. Polity Press.

Šereš, L., Pavlićević, V., Petrović, G., Horvat, D., & Ivanišević, R. (2022). Learning analytics: Prospects and challenges. *Strategic Management*, *27*(3), 48–55. DOI: 10.5937/StraMan2200020S

Shamsuddoha, M., Zimmerman, H., Nasir, T., & Sakib, M. N. (2026). Autonomous Supply Chains: Integrating Artificial Intelligence, Digital Twins, and Predictive Analytics for Intelligent Decision Systems. *Information (Basel)*, *17*(4), 371. DOI: 10.3390/info17040371

Sharma, A., & Ahmmed, M. Collaborative Intelligence in IoT Ecosystems. In Intelligent Mobile and IoT Ecosystems (pp. 170-192). Chapman and Hall/CRC.

Sharma, S., & Sharma, S. (2026). Robotic Systems and LLM Algorithms for Transforming Manufacturing Into Smart Autonomous Ecosystem. In Human-Robot Collaboration and Advanced Robotics in Modern Industry (pp. 231-262). IGI Global Scientific Publishing. DOI: 10.4018/979-8-2600-0298-8.ch007

She, M., Xiao, M., & Zhao, Y. (2023). Technological implication of the digital twin approach on the intelligent education system. International journal of humanoid robotics, 20(02n03), 2250005.

She, M., Xiao, M., & Zhao, Y. (2023). Technological implication of the digital twin approach on the intelligent education system. *International Journal of HR; Humanoid Robotics*, *20*(2), 2250005. Advance online publication. DOI: 10.1142/S0219843622500050

Shemshack, A., Kinshuk, , & Spector, J. M. (2021). A comprehensive analysis of personalized learning components. *Journal of Computers in Education*, *8*(4), 485–503. DOI: 10.1007/s40692-021-00188-7

Shen, A., Han, X., Cohn, T., Baldwin, T., & Frermann, L. (2022). Optimising Equal Opportunity Fairness in Model Training. *arXiv (Cornell University)*. /arxiv.2205.02393DOI: 10.18653/v1/2022.naacl-main.299

Shende, S. A., & Pandey, P. M. (2026). Multi-sensor IoT integrated framework for monitoring motion deviation, vibration and surface defect detection in extrusion-based additive manufacturing. *Progress in Additive Manufacturing*, •••, 1–19. DOI: 10.1007/s40964-026-01605-y

Shi, N., Li, Z., Li, Q., Zhang, J., Li, L., Sun, Q., Liu, S., & Wang, Z. (2026). Evolutionary Digital Twin for Oil and Gas Pipelines: A Cognitive Multi-Agent Framework with Continuous Feedback Learning. *Sensors (Basel)*, *26*(10), 3219. DOI: 10.3390/s26103219 PMID: 42198027

Shi, W., & Li, J. (2024). New Digital Divide Shaped by Algorithm? Evidence from Agent-Based Testing on Douyin's Health-Related Video Recommendation. *Communication Research*, *51*(7), 867–890. DOI: 10.1177/00936502241262056

Shoaib, M., Zhang, S., Ali, H., Ahmad, M. S., & Khan, M. A. (2026). Integrating circular economy while adopting digital twin for enhancing logistics efficiency: A hybrid Fuzzy Delphi-FUCOM based approach. *International Journal of Logistics*, *29*(3), 300–342. DOI: 10.1080/13675567.2025.2451750

Sholla, S., & Reshi, I. A. (2025). Ethical reasoning in technology: Using computational approaches to integrate ethics into AI systems. Journal of Information. *Communication and Ethics in Society*, *24*(1), 4–22. DOI: 10.1108/JICES-03-2024-0024

Slade, S., & Prinsloo, P. (2013). Learning analytics: Ethical issues and dilemmas. *The American Behavioral Scientist*, *57*(10), 1510–1529. DOI: 10.1177/0002764213479366

Smith, Brian. (2019). The Promise of Artificial Intelligence: Reckoning and Judgment. https://doi.org/DOI: 10.7551/mitpress/12385.001.0001

Smith, J. B., & Weiss, S. F. (1988). Hypertext. *Communications of the ACM*, *31*(7), 816–819. DOI: 10.1145/48511.48512

Smuha, N. A. (2021). From a “race to AI” to a “race to AI regulation”: Regulatory competition for artificial intelligence. *Law, Innovation and Technology*, *13*(1), 57–84. DOI: 10.1080/17579961.2021.1898300

Som, S., & Jamader, A. R. (2026). Metaverse Marketing Strategies Using IoT and 5G. In Digital Twins and Simulation Technology (pp. 55-73). Chapman and Hall/CRC.

Speicher, T., DeFranco, J., Stricker, C., Kumara, S., & Bilén, S. (2025). Digital twin technology for engineering education: An experiential learning case study. *Industry and Higher Education*. Advance online publication. DOI: 10.1177/09504222261443589

Splettstößer, A. K., Ellwein, C., & Wortmann, A. (2023). Self-adaptive digital twin reference architecture to improve process quality. *Procedia CIRP*, *119*, 867–872. DOI: 10.1016/j.procir.2023.03.131

Stephenson, N. (1992). *Snow crash*. Bantam Books.

Strielkowski, W. (2025). The role of micro-credentials in the future digitalized AI-driven education. *arXiv preprint arXiv:2511.07583*. https://doi.org//arXiv.2511.07583DOI: 10.48550

Strielkowski, W., Grebennikova, V., Lisovskiy, A., Rakhimova, G., & Vasileva, T. (2025). AI-driven adaptive learning for sustainable educational transformation. *Sustainable Development (Bradford)*, *33*(2), 1921–1947. DOI: 10.1002/sd.3221

Su, H., Liu, X., Yang, S., & Lu, X. (2023). Deep knowledge tracing with learning curves. *Frontiers in Psychology*, *14*, 1150329. Advance online publication. DOI: 10.3389/fpsyg.2023.1150329 PMID: 37063528

Sun, W., Xu, N., Wang, L., Zhang, H., & Zhang, Y. (2020). Dynamic digital twin and federated learning with incentives for air-ground networks. *IEEE Transactions on Network Science and Engineering*, *9*(1), 321–333. DOI: 10.1109/TNSE.2020.3048137

Syarifuddin, S., Kurra, T., Susanto, A., Saputra, H. D., Lumbantobing, M. A., Pancawati, R., Lieung, K. W., & Mara, A. A. P. T. (2025). Artificial Intelligence-Based Digital Twins Metaverse to Improve STEM Work Skills and Adaptive Expertise in Higher Education: A Conceptual Framework. *F1000 Research*, *14*, 1376–1376. DOI: 10.12688/f1000research.174205.1

Tadj, L. (2026). IoT-Enabled Model Predictive Control for Perishable Goods Production With Dynamic Spoilage Mitigation. *IEEE Access : Practical Innovations, Open Solutions*, *14*, 6768–6785. DOI: 10.1109/ACCESS.2026.3651980

Tang, L., Wen, M., Shan, Z., Li, L., Liu, Q., & Chen, Q. (2023). Digital twin-enabled efficient federated learning for collision warning in intelligent driving. *IEEE Transactions on Intelligent Transportation Systems*, *25*(3), 2573–2585. DOI: 10.1109/TITS.2023.3330938

Tan, S. C., Lee, A. V. Y., & Lee, M. (2022). A systematic review of artificial intelligence techniques for collaborative learning over the past two decades. *Computers and Education: Artificial Intelligence*, *3*, 100097. DOI: 10.1016/j.caeai.2022.100097

Tao, F., Qi, Q., Liu, A., & Kusiak, A. (2018). Data-driven smart manufacturing. *Journal of Manufacturing Systems*, *48*, 157–169. DOI: 10.1016/j.jmsy.2018.01.006

Tao, F., Sui, F., Liu, A., Qi, Q., Zhang, M., Song, B., Guo, Z., Lu, S. C.-Y., & Nee, A. Y. (2019). Digital twin-driven product design framework. *International Journal of Production Research*, *57*(12), 3935–3953. DOI: 10.1080/00207543.2018.1443229

Tao, F., Xiao, B., Qi, Q., Cheng, J., & Ji, P. (2022). Digital twin modeling. *Journal of Manufacturing Systems*, *64*, 372–389. DOI: 10.1016/j.jmsy.2022.06.015

Tao, F., Zhang, H., Liu, A., & Nee, A. Y. C. (2019). Digital twin in industry: State-of-the-art. *IEEE Transactions on Industrial Informatics*, *15*(4), 2405–2415. DOI: 10.1109/TII.2018.2873186

Tapalova, O., & Zhiyenbayeva, N. (2022). Artificial intelligence in education: AIEd for personalised learning pathways. *Electronic Journal of e-Learning*, *20*(5), 639–653. DOI: 10.34190/ejel.20.5.2597

Tavakkoli-Moghaddam, R., Ghahremani-Nahr, J., Samadi Parviznejad, P., Nozari, H., & Najafi, E. (2022). Application of internet of things in the food supply chain: A literature review. *Journal of Applied Research on Industrial Engineering*, *9*(4), 475–492.

Temple, L., Pereira, G. V., & Klausner, L. D. (2024). Unravelling the use of digital twins to assist decision-and policy-making in smart cities. *arXiv preprint arXiv:2405.20916*. https://doi.org//arXiv.2405.20916DOI: 10.18690/um.fov.4.2024.45

Thelen, A., Zhang, X., Fink, O., Lu, Y., Ghosh, S., Youn, B. D., Todd, M. D., Mahadevan, S., Hu, C., & Hu, Z. (2022). A comprehensive review of digital twin—part 1: Modeling and twinning enabling technologies. *Structural and Multidisciplinary Optimization*, *65*(12), 354. DOI: 10.1007/s00158-022-03425-4

Tlili, A., Burgos, D., Huang, R., Mishra, S., Sharma, R. C., & Bozkurt, A. (2023). Is metaverse in education a blessing or a curse? *Smart Learning Environments*, *10*(1). Advance online publication. DOI: 10.1186/s40561-022-00205-x

Tlili, A., Shehata, B., Adarkwah, M. A., Bozkurt, A., Hickey, D. T., Huang, R., & Agyemang, B. (2023). What if the devil is my guardian angel: ChatGPT as a case study of using chatbots in education. *Smart Learning Environments*, *10*(1), 15. Advance online publication. DOI: 10.1186/s40561-023-00237-x

Toofaninejad, E., Rezapour, S. M., & Kalantarion, M. (2024). Utilizing digital twins for the transformation of medical education. *Journal of Advances in Medical Education & Professionalism*, *12*(2), 132–133. DOI: 10.30476/JAMP.2023.100264.1883 PMID: 38660433

Trevisan, A. H., Dukovska-Popovska, I., Acerbi, F., Terzi, S., & Sassanelli, C. (2025). Teaching methods for building human capital for the twin transition: A skill-based approach. *Technology in Society*, *103172*. Advance online publication. DOI: 10.1016/j.techsoc.2025.103172

Tsai, Y.-S., Perrotta, C., & Gasevic, D. (2020). Empowering learners with personalised learning approaches? Agency, equity and transparency in the context of learning analytics. *Assessment & Evaluation in Higher Education*, *45*(4), 554–567. DOI: 10.1080/02602938.2019.1676396

Türkmen, G. (2025). The review of studies on explainable artificial intelligence in educational research. *Journal of Educational Computing Research*, *63*(1), 1–28. DOI: 10.1177/07356331241310915

Uhrmacher, A. M., Wilsdorf, P., & Kreikemeyer, J. N. (2024). Challenges and promises of self-adaptive simulation models. *Simulation*, *100*(12), 1281–1295. DOI: 10.1177/00375497241296878

UNESCO. (2021). *Recommendation on the ethics of artificial intelligence*. United Nations Educational, Scientific and Cultural Organization.

van Erp, T., Carvalho, N. G. P., Gerolamo, M. C., Gonçalves, R., Rytter, N. G. M., & Gladysz, B. (2024). Industry 5.0: A new strategy framework for sustainability management and beyond. *Journal of Cleaner Production*, *461*, 142271. DOI: 10.1016/j.jclepro.2024.142271

Veale, M., & Borgesius, F. Z. (2021). Demystifying the Draft EU Artificial Intelligence Act. *Computer Law Review International*, *22*(4), 97–112. DOI: 10.9785/cri-2021-220402

Verghis, A. M., Jose, B., Sheeja, P. R., Varghese, S., Mumthas, S., & Shaiju, K. S. (2025). Beyond personalization: Autonomy and agency in intelligent systems education. *Frontiers in Education*, *10*, 1610239. Advance online publication. DOI: 10.3389/feduc.2025.1610239

Vial, G. (2019). Understanding digital transformation: A review and a research agenda. *The Journal of Strategic Information Systems*, *28*(2), 118–144. DOI: 10.1016/j.jsis.2019.01.003

Vimal, S. P., Suryae, R. R., Rajasimhan, R., Periasamy, V. S., Rajagopal, M., & Ganesan, K. (2025, December). Cognitive Digital Twin Architecture Using Reinforcement-Optimized Deep Learning for Self-Adaptive Industrial Process Control. In *2025 First International Conference of Advances in Engineering and Computing Technologies for Sustainable Development (AECTSD)* (pp. 1-8). IEEE.

Vygotsky, L. S. (1978). *Mind in society: The development of higher psychological processes*. Harvard University Press.

Wachter, S., Mittelstadt, B., & Floridi, L. (2017). Why a right to explanation of automated decision-making does not exist in the General Data Protection Regulation. *International Data Privacy Law*, *7*(2), 76–99. DOI: 10.1093/idpl/ipx005

Wagner, S., Gonnermann, C., Wegmann, M., Listl, F., Reinhart, G., & Weyrich, M. (2024). From framework to industrial implementation: The digital twin in process planning. *Journal of Intelligent Manufacturing*, *35*(8), 3793–3813. DOI: 10.1007/s10845-023-02268-0

Walmsley, T. G., Patros, P., Yu, W., Young, B. R., Burroughs, S., Apperley, M., Carson, J. K., Udugama, I. A., Aeowjaroenlap, H., Atkins, M. J., & Walmsley, M. R. (2024). Adaptive digital twins for energy-intensive industries and their local communities. *Digital Chemical Engineering*, *10*, 100139. DOI: 10.1016/j.dche.2024.100139

Wang, H., Tlili, A., Huang, R., Cai, Z., Li, M., Cheng, Z., & Li, Y. (2023). Examining the applications of intelligent tutoring systems in real educational contexts: A systematic literature review from the social experiment perspective. *Education and Information Technologies*, *28*(7), 9113–9148. DOI: 10.1007/s10639-022-11555-x PMID: 36643383

Wang, K., Zhang, L., Jia, Z., Cheng, H., Lu, H., & Cui, J. (2024). A framework and method for equipment digital twin dynamic evolution based on IExATCN. *Journal of Intelligent Manufacturing*, *35*(4), 1571–1583. DOI: 10.1007/s10845-023-02125-0

Wang, M., Dede, C., Grotzer, T. A., & Chen, J. (2025). Understanding and managing the complexities in situated learning in immersive virtual environments. *Educational Technology Research and Development*, *73*(5), 3177–3200. DOI: 10.1007/s11423-025-10519-5

Wang, S., Wang, F., Zhu, Z., Wang, J., Tran, T., & Du, Z. (2024). Artificial intelligence in education: A systematic literature review. *Expert Systems with Applications*, *252*, 124167. DOI: 10.1016/j.eswa.2024.124167

Wang, T., Li, H. X., Wang, L., & Wang, X. V. (2026). Spatiotemporal dynamic modeling approach for distributed thermal processes under digital twin framework. *Advanced Engineering Informatics*, *71*, 104384. DOI: 10.1016/j.aei.2026.104384

Weerakkody, V., Osmani, M., Waller, P., Hindi, N., & Al-Esmail, R. (2016). Situating Continuing Professional Development in Life Long Learning in Qatar. *International Journal of Business and Management*, *11*(11), 81–81. DOI: 10.5539/ijbm.v11n11p81

Williamson, B. (2016). Digital education governance: Data visualization, predictive analytics, and "real-time" policy instruments. *Journal of Education Policy*, *31*(2), 123–141. DOI: 10.1080/02680939.2015.1035758

Williamson, B. (2017). *Big data in education: The digital future of learning, policy and practice*. SAGE Publications. DOI: 10.4135/9781529714920

Williamson, B., & Eynon, R. (2020). Historical threads, missing links, and future directions in AI in education. *Learning, Media and Technology*, *45*(3), 223–235. DOI: 10.1080/17439884.2020.1798995

Winner, L. (1980). Do artifacts have politics? *Daedalus*, *109*(1), 121–136.

Wu, H., Ji, P., Ma, H., & Xing, L. (2023). A comprehensive review of digital twin from the perspective of total process: Data, models, networks and applications. *Sensors (Basel)*, *23*(19), 8306. DOI: 10.3390/s23198306

Wu, X., & Qin, P. (2026). Adaptive Lighting and Thermal Comfort Control Strategies in Digital Twin Classroom via Deep Reinforcement Learning. *Electronics (Basel)*, *15*(4), 873. DOI: 10.3390/electronics15040873

Xu, Q., Ali, S., Yue, T., & Arratibel, M. (2022, November). Uncertainty-aware transfer learning to evolve digital twins for industrial elevators. In *Proceedings of the 30th ACM Joint European Software Engineering Conference and Symposium on the Foundations of Software Engineering* (pp. 1257-1268). DOI: 10.1145/3540250.3558957

Xu, X., Lu, Y., Vogel-Heuser, B., & Wang, L. (2021). Industry 4.0 and Industry 5.0 Inception, conception and perception. *Journal of Manufacturing Systems*, *61*, 530–535. DOI: 10.1016/j.jmsy.2021.10.006

Xu, X., Qiao, L., Cheng, N., Liu, H., & Zhao, W. (2025). Enhancing self-regulated learning and learning experience in generative AI environments: The critical role of metacognitive support. *British Journal of Educational Technology, 56*(5), 1842–1863. DOI: 10.1111/bjet.13599

Yağcı, M. (2022). Educational data mining: Prediction of students' academic performance using machine learning algorithms. *Smart Learning Environments, 9*(1), 11. Advance online publication. DOI: 10.1186/s40561-022-00192-z

Yamin, M. M., Imran, A. S., & Katt, B. (2023). Towards a digital twin framework for lifelong learning. *2023 IEEE Global Engineering Education Conference (EDUCON)*. DOI: 10.1109/EDUCON54358.2023.10099333

Yang, X., Yu, S., Wang, J., Chen, H., Huang, Y., Luo, Z., & Fu, L. (2024). Application of a digital twin for highway tunnels based on multi-sensor and information fusion. *Frontiers in Physics (Lausanne), 12*, 1335494. DOI: 10.3389/fphy.2024.1335494

Yan, H., Lin, F., & Kinshuk, K. (2025). Adaptive Practicing Design to Facilitate Self-Regulated Learning. *Canadian Journal of Learning and Technology, 50*(3), 1–22. DOI: 10.21432/cjlt28768

Yao, J. F., Yang, Y., Wang, X. C., & Zhang, X. P. (2023). Systematic review of digital twin technology and applications. *Visual Computing for Industry, Biomedicine, and Art, 6*(1), 10. DOI: 10.1186/s42492-023-00137-4

Ye, X., Gong, W., Yang, Y., Zou, L., Tu, Z., Huang, X., Li, Z., Ning, H., & Wu, L. (2026). Towards Agentic Urban Digital Twins (AUDiTs): Advancing new urban science through Human-AI co-learning agents. *Urban Informatics, 5*(1), 9. DOI: 10.1007/s44212-025-00099-3

Ye, Y. (2024, January). A higher education information management system based on digital twin technology and artificial intelligence algorithms. In *2024 Asia-Pacific Conference on Software Engineering, Social Network Analysis and Intelligent Computing (SSAIC)* (pp. 172-176). IEEE. DOI: 10.1109/SSAIC61213.2024.00039

Yitmen, I., Alizadehsalehi, S., Akıner, İ., & Akıner, M. E. (2021). An adapted model of cognitive digital twins for building lifecycle management. *Applied Sciences (Basel, Switzerland), 11*(9), 4276. DOI: 10.3390/app11094276

Yordanova, Z., & Nozari, H. (2026). Seamless Data Integration for Predictive Learning Environments. In AI-Augmented Creativity in Learning Analytics (pp. 293-318). IGI Global Scientific Publishing.

Yordanova, Z., & Nozari, H. (2026b). Seamless Data Integration for Predictive Learning Environments. In AI-Augmented Creativity in Learning Analytics (pp. 293-318). IGI Global Scientific Publishing.

Yordanova, Z., & Nozari, H. (2026). Enhancing Innovation and Resilience in Entrepreneurial Ecosystems Using Digital Twins and Fuzzy Optimization. *Digital*, *6*(1), 25. DOI: 10.3390/digital6010025

Yu, R., Lee, H., & Kizilcec, R. F. (2021). Should College Dropout Prediction Models Include Protected Attributes? *arXiv (Cornell University)*. /arxiv.2103.15237DOI: 10.1145/3430895.3460139

Yu, F., Lv, J., Han, H., Zhang, Y., & Zhang, J. (2025). Application of AI teaching assistant to college education of principles of chemical engineering. *Education for Chemical Engineers*, *53*, 138–148. DOI: 10.1016/j.ece.2025.08.004

Yun, Y., Dai, H., An, R., Zhang, Y., & Shang, X. (2024). Doubly constrained offline reinforcement learning for learning path recommendation. *Knowledge-Based Systems*, *284*, 111242. Advance online publication. DOI: 10.1016/j.knosys.2023.111242

Zaballos, A., Briones, A., Massa, A., Centelles, P., & Caballero, V. (2020). A smart campus' digital twin for sustainable comfort monitoring. *Sustainability (Basel)*, *12*(21), 9196. DOI: 10.3390/su12219196

Zarrabi, H., & Doost Mohammadian, M. R. (2024). Fusion of Digital Twin, Internet-of-Things and Artificial Intelligence for Urban Intelligence. Digital Twin Computing for Urban Intelligence, 77-92.

Zawacki-Richter, O., Marín, V. I., Bond, M., & Gouverneur, F. (2019). Systematic review of research on artificial intelligence applications in higher education. *International Journal of Educational Technology in Higher Education*, *16*(39), 39. https://link.springer.com/article/10.1186/s41239-019-0171-0. DOI: 10.1186/s41239-019-0171-0

Zayed, S. M., Attiya, G. M., El-Sayed, A., & Hemdan, E. E. D. (2023). A review study on digital twins with artificial intelligence and internet of things: Concepts, opportunities, challenges, tools and future scope. *Multimedia Tools and Applications*, *82*(30), 47081–47107. DOI: 10.1007/s11042-023-15611-7

Zhang, N., Bahsoon, R., & Theodoropoulos, G. (2020, October). Towards engineering cognitive digital twins with self-awareness. In 2020 IEEE international conference on systems, man, and cybernetics (SMC) (pp. 3891-3891). IEEE.

Zhang, H., Bai, T., & Shi, L. (2026). A theoretical method to adaptive design of complex engineering systems based on digital twin. *Digital Twin*, *3*(1), 2537841. DOI: 10.1080/27525783.2025.2537841

Zhang, J., Zhu, J., Tu, W., Wang, M., Yang, Y., Qian, F., & Xu, Y. (2024). The effectiveness of a digital twin learning system in assisting engineering education courses: A case of landscape architecture. *Applied Sciences (Basel, Switzerland)*, *14*(15), 6484. DOI: 10.3390/app14156484

Zhang, L., Guo, Y., Wang, S., Zheng, G., Qian, W., Huang, S., & Fang, W. (2026). A modeling and adaptive evolution method for simulation parameters of digital twin shop floor. *Robotics and Computer-integrated Manufacturing*, *97*, 103090. DOI: 10.1016/j.rcim.2025.103090

Zhang, L., Tang, C., Ye, Y., Yang, J., & Xu, F. (2026). Intelligent HBIM Framework for Group-Oriented Preventive Protection: A Case Study of the Suopo Ancient Watchtower Complex in Danba. *Buildings (Basel, Switzerland)*, *16*(5), 995. DOI: 10.3390/buildings16050995

Zhang, Y., Yun, Y., An, R., Cui, J., Dai, H., & Shang, X. (2021). Educational data mining techniques for student performance prediction: Method review and comparison analysis. *Frontiers in Psychology*, *12*, 698490. Advance online publication. DOI: 10.3389/fpsyg.2021.698490 PMID: 34950079

Zhao, N., Seitinger, S., Richer, R., & Paradiso, J. A. (2020). Real-time work environment optimization using multimodal media and body sensor network. *Smart Health (Amsterdam, Netherlands)*, *19*, 100164–100164. DOI: 10.1016/j.smhl.2020.100164

Zhao, T., Hu, F., Gou, H., Wang, J., & Bao, Y. (2026, February). Digital twins for static and dynamic responses of a continuous rigid frame bridge based on multi-task learning and optimization algorithm. In *Structures* (Vol. 84, p. 111006). Elsevier.

Zhong, Y., Li, C., Jiang, J., Fryer, L. K., & Shum, A. (2026). Can virtual reality promote cognitive, affective, and psychomotor learning? A synthesis of systematic reviews and meta-analytic evidence. *Journal of Educational Computing Research*, 07356331261434358. Advance online publication. DOI: 10.1177/07356331261434358

Zuboff, S. (2019). *The age of surveillance capitalism: The fight for a human future at the new frontier of power*. PublicAffairs.

About the Contributors

Zornitsa Yordanova is Associate Professor of Business Information Systems and Innovation at the University of National and World Economy (UNWE), Sofia, Bulgaria, and guest lecturer at WU Vienna, New Bulgarian University, and CITY College (University of York Europe Campus). Her research focuses on digital transformation, innovation management, open innovation, and process automation. She is PMP® certified and also consults multinational companies on digital transformation initiatives. https://orcid.org/0000-0002-6056-8445.

Hamed Nozari is a distinguished researcher at University of National and World Economy (UNWE), Sofia, Bulgaria, and innovator in industrial engineering, supply chain optimization, and artificial intelligence applications. Holding a Ph.D. in Industrial Engineering, he has made significant contributions to the fields of multi-objective decision-making, smart supply chains, and digital twin technologies. His research spans various interdisciplinary areas, including predictive maintenance in green supply chains, AI-driven marketing optimization, cybersecurity in smart economies, Digital twin, and autonomous AI for sustainable last-mile delivery. https://orcid.org/0000-0002-6500-6708.

***

Temur Abdullaev is associated with the Department of Educational Services at Mamun University, Khiva, Uzbekistan. He is involved in academic and administrative activities related to the organization, coordination, and enhancement of educational services within the higher education system. His professional interests include educational management, quality assurance in education, student support systems, and the effective delivery of academic programs. He is committed to supporting institutional development through efficient educational practices and learner-oriented service models. His work reflects a focus on improving academic operations and contributing to a supportive and well-structured learning environment for students and faculty alike.

Suresha B is an accomplished academician and an alumnus of IIM Ahmedabad. He holds M.Com, MBA, MA in Business Economics, PGDFM, M.Phil, and has received his Doctoral Degree in Management from Bharathiar University. He has completed the FDPM from IIM Ahmedabad. He has dedicated himself to extensive teaching and research in areas such as Investment Banking, Derivatives and Risk Management, ESG, Corporate Finance, Managerial Accounting, and Personal Taxation. He has been publishing research papers in top-tier journals and has received awards for his outstanding contributions to the field. He currently serves as Professor and Associate Head at the School of Business and Management, BBA program, at CHRIST (Deemed to be University), Bangalore. With over 24 years of teaching and research experience, he continues to inspire and guide students and actively mentors doctoral scholars and dissertation projects. He is a life member of the Indian Accounting Association and has served on the Board of Studies at CHRIST and other reputable universities. He has authored four books and published over sixty research papers in reputable nationally and internationally indexed refereed journals. His research interests include Market Efficiency, ESG, Sustainable Finance, AIML, digital literacy, Corporate Finance, Asset Pricing, and Tax Compliance.

Jaanavi Bakshi is a Master's student at BITS Pilani, Dubai Campus, currently pursuing an MBA with a focus on marketing, communications, and digital strategy. She has developed experience in content strategy, data-driven marketing, and community engagement through her work on cross-functional initiatives. Her interests lie in consumer behaviour, brand strategy, and the application of analytics to drive marketing effectiveness. She is particularly inclined toward research-driven approaches to understanding audience dynamics and building impactful communication strategies.

Deepak Gupta is a distinguished academician with over 20 years of teaching experience and expertise in Computer Science and Engineering. He holds a Ph.D. in Computer Engineering and has an extensive research portfolio, including many international journal papers, multiple conference proceedings, and several books. His research interests span machine learning, artificial intelligence, and data mining. Currently, Dr. Gupta serves as an Associate Professor and Head of Department of CSE (Emerging Branches) at ITM Gwalior, MP, India. He has also contributed significantly to the field through patents and copyrights and actively engages as a reviewer, conference chair and editor.

Nijumon K. John, a PhD graduate from Bharathiar University, Coimbatore, is an expert in capital markets, financial services, and entrepreneurship. His strong academic and professional background is evident through his extensive contributions. He has published numerous articles in reputed national and international journals, showcasing his research expertise. Additionally, Dr. John has authored three insightful books and co-invented two patents, emphasizing his innovative achievements. Since 2009, he has been an integral part of the School of Business and Management at Christ University, Bangalore. Presently, hc scrves as the Academic Coordinator for the BBA program at the Central Campus. Dr. Johns dedication to academic excellence and his profound understanding of financial and entrepreneurial domains make him a valuable asset to the institution and its students.

Feruza Jumaeva is a PhD holder and Lecturer in the Department of Social Sciences at Bukhara State Pedagogical Institute, Bukhara, Uzbekistan. Her academic work is connected with social sciences, higher education, and the development of student knowledge in contemporary society. As a lecturer, she contributes to teaching, curriculum delivery, academic mentoring, and the promotion of critical thinking among students. Her scholarly interests may include social development, education, cultural studies, and interdisciplinary approaches to understanding human behavior and social change. Through her academic role, Dr. Jumaeva supports the preparation of students for professional, civic, and research-oriented responsibilities. She is also involved in strengthening the learning environment through lectures, discussions, and academic guidance. Her professional profile reflects commitment to quality education, research engagement, and the advancement of social science knowledge within Uzbekistan's higher education system.

Filipe T. Moreira is a professor and researcher in the field of Education and Educational Technologies at the Polytechnic Institute of Porto, Portugal. His research interests focus on digital education, artificial intelligence in education, emerging technologies, and teacher training, with particular attention to ethical, pedagogical, and human-centred approaches to technology integration. He has participated in and coordinated national and international research projects and is the author of several scientific publications on digital transformation, innovation in education, and technology-enhanced learning.

Jamshid Pardaev is an associate professor working in the Department of Finance and Tourism at Termez University of Economics and Service, Termez, Uzbekistan.

Ankita Priti Roy is an Assistant Professor in the Department of Commerce at Kristu Jayanti (Deemed to be University), Bengaluru. She has completed her

Ph.D. in Marketing and holds an MBA in Marketing. With prior industry experience of two years at organizations such as ICICI Bank and Byju's (Think and Learn Pvt. Ltd.), she brings a blend of practical insights and academic rigor to her teaching and research. Her core areas of expertise include branding, consumer behaviour, and educational technology. Ms. Roy has actively contributed to the academic and research community through presentations at international conferences and publications in reputed journals and edited volumes. Her recent scholarly work includes contributions in Multi-Criteria Decision-Making (MCDM) and research focused on enhancing student engagement through personalization strategies on EdTech platforms. Her research interests further extend to emerging areas such as brand activism and the application of artificial intelligence in education, reflecting her commitment to exploring innovative, technology-driven approaches in contemporary marketing and commerce.

Fahad A. Salendab is a scholar and leader in the field of higher education, holding a Ph.D. in Educational Administration and a Master of Arts in English Language Teaching. As a Licensed Professional Teacher and Associate Professor, he has dedicated his career to advancing the quality of education through research, teaching, and leadership. A multi-awarded faculty member, Dr. Salendab is recognized for his outstanding contributions to education, research, and institutional development. He is a registered Writer, Author, and Editor of the National Book Development Board (NBDB) and serves as an editor for IGI Global Scientific Publishing, contributing to the dissemination of high-quality academic scholarship. He has published various books, book chapters, and research articles, reflecting his sustained engagement in scholarly writing and knowledge production. Several of his scholarly articles are also registered with the Intellectual Property Office of the Philippines (IPOPHL), highlighting his commitment to intellectual and academic innovation. His commitment to research is further demonstrated through his role as a Regular Member of the DOST–National Research Council of the Philippines, where he collaborates on initiatives addressing critical issues in education and development. He also serves as an editorial board member for various national and international research journals, supporting the advancement of scholarly publishing and peer-reviewed academic discourse. As an active participant in accreditation processes, Dr. Salendab ensures the continuous improvement of academic programs, demonstrating his strong commitment to quality assurance and institutional growth.

Ilxom Sayfiddinov is affiliated with the Department of Bank Accounting and Auditing at Tashkent State University of Economics, Tashkent, Uzbekistan. He is an academic professional engaged in teaching, research, and scholarly activities in the areas of banking, accounting, and auditing. His work supports the development of students' knowledge of financial reporting, banking operations, audit procedures, and the role of accounting systems in modern economic institutions. He is committed to promoting academic excellence through a balanced approach that combines theoretical understanding with practical relevance. His academic interests may include bank accounting, financial analysis, auditing standards, corporate governance, and financial management. Through his role at Tashkent State University of Economics, he contributes to creating a strong learning environment that encourages analytical thinking, ethical awareness, and professional competence among students. His professional profile reflects dedication to quality education, research engagement, and the broader advancement of accounting and auditing studies in Uzbekistan.

Arti Singh is an Associate Professor at Kristu Jayanti (Deemed-to-be University), Bengaluru, and also serves as Academic Coordinator at IGNOU. She holds a Ph.D. in Commerce with 18 years of teaching experience. Dr. Singh has published over 50 research papers in Scopus- and UGC-CARE–indexed journals, and has authored books on auditing, supply chain management, and marketing. She has received three funded research grants, including an ICSSR project and a nutrition study. Dr. Singh holds patents for an Employee Attendance Management Apparatus (2023) and a Portable Point-of-Sale Device (2024). Her honors include the Research Excellence Award (2024), National Faculty Award (2024), Utkrisht Teacher Award (2023), and Women of the Year in Finance (2022). She sits on the editorial board of Edwin Group, USA, and reviews for several international journals. Dr. Singh is active in academic communities in India and abroad and is regularly invited as a keynote speaker at international conferences.

Deepali Sinha is an Assistant Professor at the School of Law, Bennett University, serving since September 2023. She holds an LL.M. in Corporate and Commercial Laws and a B.A. LL.B. (Hons.) from Amity University, Noida, and is currently pursuing her Ph.D. at Chanakya National Law University, Patna. Her academic interests include Corporate Laws, Competition Law, and Medical Laws. She qualified the UGC-NET examination in June 2020 and serves as an editorial member of the Edwin Group of Journals. Her research contributions cover diverse themes such as prisoner rights, arbitration practices in India, medical ethics in commercial healthcare, and women's religious rights, published in reputed journals and edited volumes.

Index

A

B

C

D

E

H

I

K

www.ingramcontent.com/pod-product-compliance
Lightning Source LLC
LaVergne TN
LVHW062323300926
849161LV00007B/1555